SOUTH CENTRAL DREAMS

South Central Dreams

Finding Home and Building Community in South L.A.

Pierrette Hondagneu-Sotelo *and* Manuel Pastor

NEW YORK UNIVERSITY PRESS

New York

NEW YORK UNIVERSITY PRESS
New York
www.nyupress.org

References to Internet websites (URLs) were accurate at the time of writing. Neither the author nor New York University Press is responsible for URLs that may have expired or changed since the manuscript was prepared.

Library of Congress Cataloging-in-Publication Data
Names: Hondagneu-Sotelo, Pierrette, author. | Pastor, Manuel, 1956–   author.
Title: South central dreams : finding home and building community in south L.A. / Pierrette Hondagneu-Sotelo and Manuel Pastor.
Description: New York : NYU Press, 2021. | Series: Latina/o sociology | Includes bibliographical references and index.
Identifiers: LCCN 2020048478 | ISBN 9781479804023 (hardback) | ISBN 9781479807970 (paperback) | ISBN 9781479804047 (ebook) | ISBN 9781479804054 (ebook other)
Subjects: LCSH: Community development—California—Los Angeles. | Communities—California—Los Angeles. | Los Angeles (California)—Race relations. | Los Angeles (California)—Ethnic relations. | Minorities—California—Los Angeles.
Classification: LCC HN49.C6 H653 2021 | DDC 307.1/40979493—dc23
LC record available at https://lccn.loc.gov/2020048478

New York University Press books are printed on acid-free paper, and their binding materials are chosen for strength and durability. We strive to use environmentally responsible suppliers and materials to the greatest extent possible in publishing our books.

Manufactured in the United States of America

10 9 8 7 6 5 4 3 2 1

Also available as an ebook

ROOTS | *RAÍCES*

Strolling down 103rd, I walked past Jordan High
Where seeds are planted in the soil
Where Black babies are born to fly
What lies they told me of this land?
I can still hear '65
I feel the beat on '92 every time that I drive by
My family came from other lands
But my parents rebelled anyways
Moved to the U.S. of A
To the city they called L.A.
Gentrification and oppression
Hoods changing at rapid rates
But South Central? This land is sacred
Brown faces, Black space
I'm talking 42nd and Central down to the NG's
Grape and 103 to Florence and Normandie
They say it ain't safe after dark
We say it's home, don't get lost
Where my varrio is also my block
We're just tryna avoid the cops
Latino children speaking jazz, singing the blues, spitten these raps
Overcoming the trap so that maybe we can give back
Who's to tell this ghetto child how she or he identifies?
These intersections though? Are mine
This neighborhood taught me to thrive

By Melvin Earl Villaver, Jr., performing as Vin Villa
© 2016 by Melvin Earl Villaver, Jr., performing as Vin Villa
℗ 2016 by Riot Baby Music Publishing

CONTENTS

FIGURES AND TABLES

1

Making Sense, Making Home

PIERRETTE HONDAGNEU-SOTELO AND MANUEL PASTOR

South Los Angeles, traditionally considered the heart of Black Los Angeles, has undergone an astonishing demographic transformation over the last five decades. About 80 percent African American in 1970, the area is now about two-thirds Latino. The iconic neighborhood of Watts—the center of the 1965 rebellion against policing that eventually gave rise to momentum for a Black mayor and a new multiracial politics—is now 70 percent Latino. Historic South Central, an area along the Central Avenue corridor that birthed Los Angeles's most important Black cultural and religious centers of the twentieth century, and once hosted visiting luminaries such as Count Basie and W. E. B. Du Bois is now nearly 90 percent Latino.

In the earliest years of the demographic shift, much was written about the inevitable conflicts between new neighbors and longtime residents, with the focus on Black–Brown tensions feeding into a narrative that a permanent political alliance between communities of color was just a figment of progressive imagination.[1] Certainly, there were stories to justify the skepticism, including Latino families being assaulted or harassed by Black youth on the streets or at bus stops, and reports of anti-Black attitudes and actions on the part of Latinos. Many of the disagreements were exacerbated by the fact that the Latino influx, largely of immigrant families, occurred in an atmosphere in which economic deprivation, active gang warfare, and brutal policing hardly created the conditions for positive collaboration.

But both journalists and academics would do well to revisit the scene today. While visitors would not find a picture that is idyllic—tough economic and social challenges remain—they would encounter a quotidian reality where crime has sharply declined, where neighbors get along more often than not, where fusion culture often surprises and delights (consider the burgeoning phenomenon of Black taco trucks), and where the language of political organizers tends to consistently lift up the ways in which African Americans and Latinos face a common reality and common problems.[2] Indeed, one of the most important organizing groups in South L.A.—whose Black founder, Karen Bass, is now a congresswoman and whose successor, Marqueece Harris-Dawson is now a L.A. city councilman—is now headed by a Latino who is as likely to denounce anti-Black racism as he is to lift up the rights of immigrants.

How has this transition from a traditionally Black "inner-city" neighborhood to a new sort of Latino *barrio* unfolded? How did first-generation Latino immigrants and their second-generation children make a new home for themselves in South L.A., and what kinds of relations did they develop with African Americans? How did their experiences shift over time, and in the process, what kind of *Latinidad* has emerged? What impact did these changes have on Black identity in South Los Angeles, particularly in an era of change, including ongoing challenges to excessive policing and constant pressures for gentrification? And what are the consequences of all these developments for civic engagement, coalition building, and sociological theory?

Making Sense of South L.A.

We became interested in these issues for a number of different reasons. Intellectual curiosity was certainly one element: here was a case that seemed to challenge traditional assimilation theory. First, Latino immigrants are not assimilating to a white middle-class mainstream in South L.A.[3] Nor were they or their families, as segmented assimilation holds, downwardly assimilating into an African American "underclass" seemingly locked out of upward mobility. Second, we did not see firm evidence of ethnic succession in which an established group of residents departs and a new group simply takes over the space, erasing or reducing the local history to a set of symbolic markers displayed at ethnic celebrations. Instead, we seemed to be witnessing a sort of ethnic sedimentation in which the legacy of Black political resistance was fueling a new place-based identity for African Americans and Latinos alike.

Third, we were convinced that this particular case might have applications elsewhere. As we note in chapter 7, the two groups who are seeing their mutual exposure in metro areas rise over time are African Americans and Latinos. Yet, too often, demographic change is seen as a onetime shock, and the dynamics of transformations over time go unstudied. By revisiting a place where conflicts had been riven, we hoped to offer a study about Latino immigrant integration in historically African American neighborhoods that could inform other locations. We were specifically interested in how Latinos experienced quotidian interactions with African American neighbors and asked ourselves how that can bubble up to shape grassroots potential for alliance building and political action.

We were also intrigued by what the Latino immigrant experience could tell us about home and "homemaking." After all, the migrant experience is one of departing the place where one was born and seeking to survive, thrive, and perhaps find a new home elsewhere. Approximately 258 million foreign-born people are now attempting to do that around the globe, more than 60 percent of them in Asia and Europe.[4] Here in the United States, landing in a historically Black community is setting foot on what someone else considers to be their hard-fought territory, one historically defined not only by racially restrictive covenants and real estate practices but also by the assertion of hard-earned Black identity. In fact, we can think of both African Americans and Latinos as groups that have historically struggled to establish homes and communities in the United States.[5] And similarly, given the experiences of millions of African Americans in the Great Migration of 1915 to the 1970s, it is possible to see this earlier movement, in the words of Isabel Wilkerson, as "an unrecognized immigration within the United States."[6]

Home is an important theoretical concept, to be sure, but it is also a political vehicle. Indeed, what we discovered in looking at multiracial alliance building in South L.A. was how many organizers relied on facilitating a sense of "spatial identity"—a sense of South L.A. pride—that would intersect with "racial identity" and be the basis to bring communities together. Finally, home has another meaning: since the university where we work, the University of Southern California (USC), is perched on the edge of South L.A.—and because of our own connections with community organizers there—this is a sort of second home whose story seemed important to highlight.

To get a better look—to go beyond what we already knew from previous work there—we assembled a team of researchers that included two faculty leads, one postdoctoral scholar, several graduate students, and four professional researchers, with several on the overall team having grown up or then living in South Los Angeles. We used a mixed-methods approach, building up a detailed quantitative profile of South L.A. based on U.S. census data to chart the pace of demographic shifts and reveal the differences between neighborhoods; we conducted one hundred audio-taped, transcribed interviews with residents who identified as Latino, including both first-generation immigrants and a second generation of millennials who grew up in South L.A.; we gathered an additional twenty-five interviews with residents who identified as African Americans and who had experienced the demographics changes; we interviewed a racially diverse set of twenty-eight local leaders about the changes and needs they saw in the community; and we recorded typed observations and another set of fifty-three interviews with both African Americans and Latinos who gather in South L.A.'s precious few public parks and community gardens.[7]

One aspect of our data analysis that was unique involved the one hundred interviews with local Latino residents, partly because this was the truly untold story of South L.A. and partly because we were trying to emphasize generational change and intentionally designed the sampling strategy to capture that. These interviewees included average working-class renters and homeowners living in South L.A., the mechanics, housewives, hotel housekeepers, students, retired folks, and others who are not usually asked about their opinions, experiences, and perceptions of neighborhood change. As noted, these were complemented by observations by civic leaders based or working in South L.A.; still, we tried to stay close to the ground in our analysis, including in our analysis of interviews with Black residents describing their own experience with the demographic shifts. Immigrant integration occurs in specific neighborhoods and places. With our interview data, we sought to provide a close-up understanding of the textures of how various relationships changed over time in a specific place, South L.A.[8]

Since South L.A. is large—it spans some fifty square miles and includes just over eight hundred thousand residents—we decided to focus our interview sample on three neighborhoods: Watts, Historic South Central, and Vermont Square/Slauson. A closer view of these neighborhood places, including why they were chosen, is available at the end of our second chapter. In the following, we set the stage for the analysis of the interviews and these places by providing a context for the arrival of Latino immigrants in South L.A. in the 1980s and 1990s, foreshadowing some themes that will emerge later in this volume, and highlighting why homemaking is such a useful organizing concept for the data and our analysis.

Arriving and Evolving

Demographers now recognize that the 1980s and the 1990s were the big boom years for Mexican and Central American immigration to the United States. While Latino immigrants sought jobs and new lives in all fifty states, California and Los Angeles, in particular, continued as a magnetic gateway in this period, with more than one-fourth of all Mexican immigrants and well over a third of all Central American immigrants arriving in the United States settling into just Los Angeles County in the 1970s and 1980s.[9] Among our first-generation immigrant respondents, some had just crossed the U.S.–Mexico border, fleeing civil wars and economic devastation, and others moved to South L.A. after living in crowded, substandard apartments near downtown L.A. or Pico-Union, but whatever the causes, they all came searching for the same thing: a better life.

Since the turn of the last century, the settlement of Mexican immigrants in Los Angeles had been concentrated in the barrios of East L.A., while Central Americans arriving in the early 1980s flocked to the Pico-Union or Westlake area, located just west of Downtown and near MacArthur Park.[10] To be sure, Latino immigrants had always gone elsewhere in the L.A. region too, including to the San Fernando and San Gabriel Valleys, but East L.A. and Pico-Union served as the undisputed traditional entry point communities for, respectively, Mexican and Central American immigrants. But the volume of the immigrant influx in the 1980s and 1990s was more than these neighborhoods could absorb and new arrivals started going to other areas, leading a subsequent wave of immigrants to bypass traditional entry points altogether and head straight to places like the San Gabriel and San Fernando Valleys. Yet another locale was the mega-neighborhood of South L.A., where the stock of affordable rentals and potential for affordable ownership of modest, single-family stucco homes became a new magnet for both newly ar-rived Central Americans and Mexican immigrants and others who had been living in East L.A., in the Pico-Union/MacArthur Park neighbor-hoods, or near Downtown L.A. (see figure 1.1).

The 1980s and 1990s were tough times in South L.A. Factories and assembly plants that had provided jobs for decades shut down or moved operations elsewhere; gang wars, a crack-cocaine epidemic, and milita-rized policing were among the neighborhood problems leading many African Americans to exit even as Latino newcomers were arriving. As one Salvadoran woman now in her sixties recalled, neighborhood life back in the 1980s was a mixed bag: "*Mira, hay cosas que eran buenas.* . . . Look, there were things that were good, and bad things. At that time we were about the only Latinos on the block. . . . Everyone else was *Moreno* [Black]. But the majority of those who lived there were older people, and they were very nice. We never had any problems with any Black neighbors." Others among this first generation spoke with less equanim-ity, associating the neighborhood challenges with the demographic mix and bluntly and unselfconsciously articulating deeply rooted anti-Black prejudice; as one elderly woman said, "*La vida aquí esta mejor ahora.* . . . Life here is better now. There are fewer Black people."

Still, many of these first-generation Latina/o immigrant newcomers—even those with anti-Black sentiments—established a kind of next-door-neighbor civility (even if relations stayed somewhat superficial) with their older African American neighbors. But on the streets, at bus stops, at local storefront shops, and on public transit, the immigrant genera-tion often encountered hostility from youth gangs and a climate of vio-lence and racialized resentment. When asked to reflect on the 1980s and 1990s, a number of older Latino residents vividly recalled muggings, house burglaries, or having gold chains ripped right off their necks. One woman described the harrowing experience of being caught in the crossfire of a gang street fight orchestrated with machetes and bullets. Others recalled the chaos, daily fear, and the extraordinary precautions necessary when raising children while living next door to a crack house or in the center of contested gang turf.

Pushed inward by the language barrier, the work of daily survival, and the fear of street violence, most Latina/o newcomers in this first generation responded by "shutting in and shutting out." They built

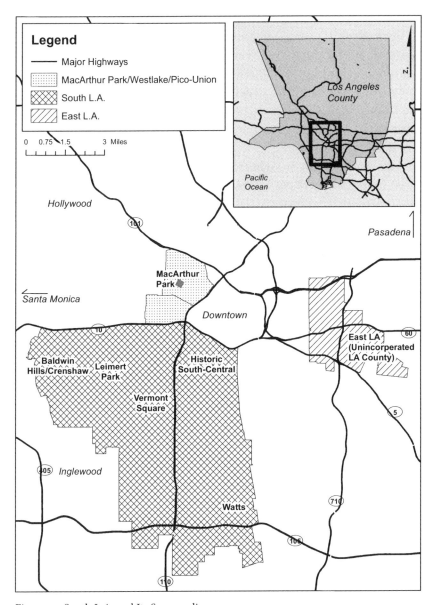

Figure 1.1. South L.A. and Its Surroundings

Source: Created by the University of Southern California (USC) Center for the Study of Immigrant Integration (CSII) project team with data from the *Los Angeles Times* mapping project, County of Los Angeles, Census TIGER/Line, and ESRI.

fences around their homes, put bars on their windows, and many kept to themselves, creating a bubble around their families. As one Mexican man, now a thirty-five-year-long resident of the historic Central Avenue neighborhood told us, "*No eramos personas de la calle.* . . . We weren't people of the street. We were people who went to work, the laundry mat, the market, and to work. Well, we would visit family [elsewhere] . . . but to go to the parks? You couldn't. People just didn't feel safe."

Anti-Black racism brought from Latin American countries was nurtured in the United States by our nation's own profound color line. Another factor helping foster social distance for the immigrant generation was a significant language barrier. When asked about her biggest challenge living in South L.A., one woman, a retired seamstress, said, "*El desafio, casi siempre.* . . . The challenge, almost always and to this day has been the language. That's been my challenge. For my kids, no, because they were little and they acquired the language quickly." In our interviews, we heard this over and over again. Consequently, for this first generation of Latino immigrants, interactions with African American neighbors and local civic associations usually remained limited. As a result, racially and linguistically segregated niches formed: during the 1980s and 1990s, Latino immigrant families embarked on their homemaking projects, creating isolated pockets of *Latinidad* in a context of a mostly Black-inscribed place. Even Latino immigrants who relied on Black institutions, such as a Black-owned community bank in South L.A., tended to have minimal interactions with African Americans because of a lack of fluency in English.[11]

But as we will see, there is another important aspect of these neighborhood racial dynamics that is often overlooked in research that focuses on first encounters: generational differences and change over time. First- and second-generation Latinos have radically different upbringings, and consequently, they think about race and the color line in different ways. While many people in the first generation migrated to South L.A. with anti-Black racist ideologies—which were often hardened in the tough street climate of the 1980s and 1990s and sustained by their own monolingual limitations—the second-generation Latinas/os who were raised in South L.A. expressed different perspectives and had a different set of experiences than their parents.

As youth, some of these younger Latinos reported facing hostility and threats from African Africans in the schools or on the street, but even among those who had, a majority of the second generation now express deep affinity and respect for African Americans. Many of them feel strongly identified with African American people, places, and culture. For example, Aurelia Campo grew up in Watts.[12] Although she recognized the difficulties in her community—and these were amplified when she went off to college—Aurelia took pride in growing up here:[13]

> Even though there was race problems that we did have, growing up in South L.A. made me a better person. It made me a more well-rounded person. It allowed me to see other people not only based on their status, but on truly who they are. So it kind of adds to your personality a little bit more.

Reflecting on his own upbringing, twenty-nine-year-old Edwin Coto said, "You know, you grow up in the aura of Blackness . . . listening to Vicente Fernandez, but also George Clinton and Al Green." This deep affinity was virtually nonexistent among their parents' generation.

Indeed, the Latina/o second generation in South L.A. grew up with Black friends and even first loves. They attended the same schools, played on sports teams together, and followed similar styles and music. Like the children of Mexican and Central American immigrants elsewhere in the United States, they generally spoke English fluently. And that meant that in their South L.A. neighborhoods and schools, they communicated with their African American peers and neighbors in a way that their parents simply could not. One young woman reflected, "We grew up together. You know, they fed us collard greens; we fed them beans. You know, we grew up in each other's homes, and we grew up together. So to us, it's a similarity. They're our people. We struggle, we consider them our people."

For this generation of Latinos raised in South L.A., their sense of *Latinidad* was inflected by Blackness and informed by understandings of racism, with home defined more by the familiar streets of the neighborhood than by the divided lines of ethnicity or the call of war-torn and economically stressed "home" (or sending) countries. Indeed, one striking aspect of our findings is the way in which second-generation Latinos raised in South L.A. see themselves as very different from Latinos from

Figure 1.2. #WeAreSouthLA
Photo Credit: Lucy Castro.

East L.A., whom they perceive as nationalistic and backward-thinking in their racism toward African Americans. When several hashtags, #ILoveSouthLA and #WeAreSouthLA, emerged in the early 2010s, replete with evocations of daily life and images of African American and Latino faces, it may have seemed odd to those who think of the area as simply one of economic and social turmoil, but it was very much reflective of an emerging hybrid identity in which Black and Brown youth found common ground and pride in a common home (see figure 1.2).

Identities and Integration

In this book, we tell the story of how Latino immigrants and their families made new homes in a particular place and context: South L.A. It was a place and a time in which African Americans were being displaced by processes of deindustrialization, hyper-incarceration, and urban distress—and yet Latino immigrants and their families found home in a neighborhood where Black people and their cultural institutions remained and remain nonetheless very present and often vibrant. As noted earlier, this is not the well-worn sensationalistic saga of Black/ Brown conflict, with one group triumphing over another, nor is it a fable of seamless harmony. Instead, it is the story of Latino immigration at its highpoint in the 1980s and 1990s, spreading from the traditional Latino immigrant neighborhoods of destination, such as East L.A., and finding refuge in African American neighborhoods with affordable housing.

This transition was neither free of tension, nor monolithic, but through daily struggle, Latino families embarked on the process of setting roots and establishing new homes. Home involves the materiality of residential dwelling and neighborhood amenities but following the work of others, we focus on immigrant homemaking as processes rooted in a special attachment to place. As many sociologists such as Harvey Molotch have noted, forming an identity or connection to a place is to become submerged in "living, breathing assemblages that have a specific historicity and distinctive forcefulness."[14] For Latino newcomers, this process involved developing a sense of security, familiarity, autonomy, and future-making, and a special attachment to place.[15]

What makes our contribution novel (although not unique as this topic is now receiving increasing attention in the literature) is that we examine how immigrant homemaking unfolds in an American context where race is particularly salient. One of the unexpected outcomes is a new racial identity formation among the second-generation Latinos raised in these neighborhoods, one based on affinity and experiences with African American people, culture, and traditions. They experienced a relational racialization which scholars Daniel HoSang and Natalia Molina define as one "formed in relation not only to whiteness but also to other devalued and marginalized groups."[16] Another outcome— perhaps to be expected—is the deep love and pride of place that Latino residents feel for the place of South L.A., partly because of the ways in which living and growing up there tested and developed resilience. We examine both the material and relational aspects of this homemaking process later.

While we are cautious about generalizing from our particular study to other locales also experiencing Black–Brown demographic shifts—such as Oakland or Orlando—we think our approach may be useful for guiding future research in these places for three reasons. First, many studies of Black/Latino relations focus on either competition in the economic realm (i.e., jobs, wages, other resources) or collaborative efforts in shared cultural expression or coalition politics. These are important dynamics, to be sure, but our study shifts the focus to neighborhood life and how daily exchanges, encounters, and challenges transform people and the places they live.

Second, our study highlights change over time and generations. Latinos are not monolithic, and we show critical divergences of experiences and perceptions between first-generation Latino immigrants and their second-generation children. While we sociologists like to assertively lay claim to discovering social patterns, we also acknowledge the diversity of experience within those categories, and this generational dimension is important. But most of all, this work suggests the need to both understand history and revisit sites of study to capture the dynamics of change to see how and why tensions are transformed over time.

Third, we believe that our work signals a new kind of immigrant integration that deserves further study, one where neither assimilation to whiteness nor transnational connectivity to countries of origin captures the dominant dynamics. Our findings are in agreement with the analysis by historian Abigail Rosas of how Latinos and Africans have worked together through community investment projects in South Central L.A.[17] And although the place and context are different, the outcomes we see are also similar to what sociologist Jennifer A. Jones found in North Carolina, where Latino immigrants find inclusion and interracial alliances with African Americans, leading to what she calls a "minority linked fate."[18]

Through our empirical research and analysis, we advance a paradigm of immigrant integration as a process of homemaking, and we do so by highlighting how processes of racial identities and place identities are connected. Our focus on generational differences continues a long tradition in immigration studies and allows us to underscore the fluidity of these dynamics. This transformation swings not toward whiteness and not toward transnational connections but rather toward a place-based identity that feeds into a sense of common struggle and potentially coalitional politics from the bottom up. And while observers of immigration scholarship will recognize our focus on generations as part and parcel of research on immigrants, our approach is very different than assimilationist researchers' penchant for comparing outcomes among the native-born with the immigrant-born or children of immigrants.[19] Rather than investigating outcomes, we are focused on processes and the potential of an emergent, new type of immigrant integration and Latino identity.

Understanding Immigrant Integration

So how does this story—and our take on it—challenge traditional theories of immigrant integration? While there is no grand theory dominating the field, in American sociology, three theoretical paradigms of immigrant integration prevail: assimilation, transnationalism, and exclusion. Each one has its merit, but none of them provide a fully productive framework for understanding the Latino immigrant experience in South Los Angeles. In a short review here, we explain why that is and why we find it more useful to see immigrant integration as a homemaking process that, in the United States, occurs in a society deeply stratified by race.

Assimilation theory, based on the experiences of European immigrants in Chicago between the 1880s and 1920s, endures as the dominant frame in both contemporary U.S. scholarship and the popular imagination. The basic idea is that as immigrants shed their cultural values, language, and old ways of life, they will experience inclusion, acceptance, and upward social mobility. They will then leave the inner city, departing for better neighborhoods in the suburbs, enacting what sociologists have called "spatial assimilation" and participating in a "common cultural life."[20] One hundred years later, these ideas still prevail in American sociology, although sociologists have nuanced this framework with various modifications, such as "segmented assimilation" and "bumpy line assimilation," showing that these processes are not necessarily monolithic.[21]

In their book *Remaking the American Mainstream*, sociologists Richard Alba and Victor Nee offer a reformulated "new assimilation theory," drawing attention to the role of institutional changes and civil rights policies and challenging the idea of a singularly static, Anglo-American "mainstream."[22] They emphasize that assimilation is not a linear process of ethnic obliteration and instead underscore the many contributions and influences that immigrants have made to redefining American culture and society.[23] And totally reversing the direction of change, Tomas

Jiménez extends this idea by introducing the concept of "relational assimilation," highlighting how "established individuals" (people with three or more generations in the United States) are adapting and assimilating to social, cultural, and economic shifts prompted by the latest influx of immigrants.[24]

Many scholars in contemporary sociology continue to productively use some variation of the assimilation framework.[25] Jody Agius Vallejo adds Latino-specific context to variations in assimilation theories in her volume, *Barrios to Burbs*, documenting the various ways that Mexican Americans move into the middle class.[26] Yet even as she focuses on mobility, she also notes an ongoing connection that implicitly counters simplistic versions of assimilation, stressing how those who have made that move up put energy into giving back to those who are on their way. Another critical take on assimilation is offered by scholar Catharine Ramírez. She draws our attention to the "paradox of assimilation," the ways in which some groups "are transformed into insiders, while others are rendered outsiders on the inside."[27] In particular, she emphasizes how the dynamics of racialization and citizenship mean that some groups will only be assimilated as subordinated, abject subjects.

For our study of Latino immigrants who came to live in African-American neighborhoods, an assimilationist frame, even when complicated and nuanced, has limited utility. After all, assimilation to a generalized white mainstream does not accurately capture what has occurred. For one thing, Latino immigrant families in South Los Angeles live far away from anything resembling white, mainstream neighborhoods. Their closest contact has been with Black Americans and other Latinos, including Latinos with national origins different than their own, and it is in this local context that they have adapted to life in South L.A. Those who managed to save enough money to sink roots into homeownership often did not move to white suburbs to do so, as spatial assimilation would hold. In fact, many of our first-generation interviewees said they came to South L.A. precisely because this was the place where they could afford to buy a house. Finally, the sting of racism is deeply felt (or, better put, deeply conceptualized) by a second generation who have experienced subpar schools, over-policing, and labor-market discrimination and are likely to attribute that to the ways in which white supremacy and anti-Blackness have resulted in public disinvestment, criminalization, and inadequate opportunity.

So while our volume is more adjacent to the complexity in Vallejo's work and Ramírez's work, we think the concept of home is a key differentiator. Part of the reason is that South L.A. has a history of disinvestment, but it is also a place of achievement: African Americans were able to expand beyond Central Avenue decades ago, and Latinos were able to finally buy homes here, in more recent generations. As for second-generation Latinos, generally presumed to want to move "up" and "out," as assimilation theory would predict, many of them, even after completing college, have chosen to return to or remain in South L.A., a place that they love and a place where they feel at home. When we interviewed in this area, Watt's native Lydia Quintanilla had taught at the local school for the past eleven years, along with working for the City of Los Angeles, for "young people of color to have more opportunities," unlike herself, who was pushed out to Long Beach for high school. She intentionally chose to live, work, and raise her children in the community and looked forward to purchasing a home in the area. Instead of leaving, many of those who grew up in South L.A. remain committed to fostering deeper roots and to social justice and civic engagement work in a place that remains in need of improvement. South L.A., in short, has become not a stepping-stone to the suburbs but a neighborhood of both choice and struggle.

If assimilation does not capture the South L.A. story, what about the transnational framework that emerged in the 1980s and 1990s as an alternative approach to understanding international migration and immigrant integration?[28] This perspective begins with the observation that new forms of transportation and communication have eased movements across nation-state borders, intensifying "social circuits," associations, practices, and institutions that span across borders. Initially innovated by anthropologists working on migration between the Caribbean and the United States and Michoacan and California, sociologists developed classic monographs on transnational migrant communities, religious associations spanning borders, and transnational civic and political associations.[29] While immigrant integration and transnationalism were initially seen as antithetical in some of the earlier scholarship, today, scholars recognize how one may fuel the other.[30]

The transnationalist turn yielded innovative and often multisited research, but it does not help us explain what we uncovered in our study of Latino South L.A. In the 1980s, Mexican hometown associations emerged as vibrant transnational civic organizations, promoting ethnic solidarity and political empowerment and often serving as agents of philanthropy and hometown development projects.[31] These organizations were fostered, in part, by changing political spheres in Mexico, as the ruling political party in Mexico at that time, the Partido Revolucionario Institucional, sought legitimacy and support from the Mexican residents working and living in the United States. But for various reasons, including problematic management of development projects, security threats, and immigrant acquisition of U.S. citizenship, participation in these transnational hometown associations has declined.[32]

While figure 1.3 shows some of the enduring transnational ties, the vibrant transnational activity highlighted in the literature seemed lacking among our South L.A. interviewees. For instance, we asked all our first-generation respondents if they participated in transnational hometown associations or regularly returned to partake in social events or interactions in their country of origin: the answer was a resounding no. While nearly all of them *did* send money home to relatives and they relied on cell phones and social media to stay in touch, these actions are generally considered very low sorts of baseline levels of transnational activity. Those who could afford the cost of travel and who met the legal status requirements for border crossing did return occasionally for family events such as a wedding or a funeral. But this too was rare, partly because of expense and partly because of those legal requirements. One reason is this: nearly a third of all Latino adults (and nearly 45 percent of Latino foreign-born adults) in South L.A. are undocumented as compared to an 18 percent figure for Latino adults in the rest of Los Angeles County.[33]

We are not the only ones to note a trend of declining transnational circulation and increasing permanent settlement among Mexican and Central American immigrants in Los Angeles. For example, a study of ninety Mexican immigrants interviewed in Los Angeles in 2008 by prominent Mexican researchers found that only seven of ninety interview respondents described their stay in Los Angeles as a temporary phase before returning to Mexico.[34] Similarly, most of our respondents

Figure 1.3. Mural in Historic South Central
Photo Credit: Walter Thompson-Hernández, USC CSII project team.

said they did not plan to return to live in their country of origin, partly because of concerns about security in Mexico and Central America given the violence perpetrated by narco-cartels, gangs, and military police and partly because of second-generation rootedness in South L.A. With a damper put on their dreams of return, most of our interviewees—both the first and second generation—have made their peace with living in the United States, in general, and South L.A., in particular. They are, in short, making homes, and it is those processes that are structuring their lives and that of their children.

A third paradigm that has emerged in immigration studies stresses the forces working against immigrant integration and for immigration exclusion, such as increasingly fortified borders, amplified detention and deportation regimes, and heightened racialized nativism and nationalism. Scholars from sociology, history, anthropology, and ethnic studies have drawn attention to the ways in which racial exclusion and discrimination, detention and deportation regimes, and illegalities created by immigration regimes create conditions for non-integration, including liminal legalities, legal violence, spaces of nonexistence, incarceration, and even death.[35] A related branch of scholarship, mostly in legal studies, examines the criminalization of immigrants as a key mechanism of deportation, particularly through the use of 287(g) programs that encourage cooperation between immigration authorities and local law enforcement.[36]

While a focus on exclusion and liminality has produced urgently needed critical scholarship, we must acknowledge that these processes are unevenly applied to immigrant communities living in different places. The current era of deportation and detention terror became quite evident with the rhetoric of the Trump presidency, but the practice began with the border militarization programs of the 1990s and continued into the middle years of the Obama administration. But this has not been a universally applied campaign: interior enforcement has been more brutal in some states (e.g., Arizona) than in others (e.g., California), and climates of fear and repression have been harsher in rural areas than in cities.[37]

Part of the variation is explained by the fact that some metropolitan regions have developed a strong infrastructure of immigrant rights groups and service organizations.[38] In this arena, Los Angeles is an undisputed leader. The 1980s and especially the 1990s were watershed years for multiracial coalition building and alliances for social justice in Los Angeles, with community-based organizations, labor unions, religious advocates, civil rights groups, and allies forging a progressive agenda in favor of immigrant civil rights.[39] By the 1990s, even a conservative white Republican mayor supported the campaign to raise the wages of immigrant janitors in Los Angeles, and today, the City sponsors an office of immigrant affairs to support immigrant integration and well-being. Moreover, Los Angeles has the highest concentration of Mexicans living out of Mexico, and today, nearly half of the county's population is Latino.

In part because of the immigrant-serving infrastructure and social movement organizing and in part because of the numbers, undocumented immigrants do not seem to feel as threatened in Los Angeles. While federal immigration policies and vociferous, xenophobic, racialized nationalism espoused by top elected officials have created an atmosphere of terror nationwide, the impacts in places such as California and Los Angeles, in particular, have been less severe. In the neighborhoods of South L.A., our Latino interviewees generally did not discuss a fear of detention and deportation but rather suggested that their most pressing concerns were about affordable housing, education, jobs, and other elements of quotidian existence, something that helped drive policy commonalities with African American neighbors. At the same time, part of the reason why detention did not surface as highly as in other locales is because the objects of policing in South L.A. are disproportionately Black male bodies, allowing for many immigrants to fall under the carceral screen. We are not saying that deportation is not a threat—but in understanding the immigrant experience in South L.A., we need an analytical frame that acknowledges exclusion but better squares with the realities on the ground and perceptions and experiences narrated by Latino residents.

What's Home Got to Do with It?

If assimilation theory, transnational dynamics, and the new research on exclusion do not fully capture the daily experiences expressed by our interviewees' life trajectories, how might we supplement our understanding to better articulate what seems to be emerging in this new terrain? An emerging body of research produced by immigration scholars, most of them working outside the United States, has shifted attention to what Italian sociologist Paolo Boccagni has termed the "migration–home nexus."[40] This way of thinking is a departure away from a focus on global circulation and movement and toward reflective inquiry of what home means in the age of global migration.

Home is at the core of everyday life, but it is also so basic—we all have a "home"—that it is often taken for granted rather than interrogated as a concept. However, a number of researchers around the world are now asking how migrants, in this era of hyper-mobility, establish a sense of place and rootedness, the rights of belonging, and feelings and practices of home.[41] In the book *Migration and the Search for Home*, Italian sociologist Paolo Boccagni defines home as "a special kind of relationship with place," one that involves both materiality and the realm of relationships, memories, and symbols. Most fundamentally, home provides a sense of security, familiarity (both in terms of emotional intimacy and comfort), and control (see figure 1.4).[42]

Figure 1.4. Bungalow in the Vermont Square Neighborhood
Photo Credit: Walter Thompson-Hernández, USC CSII project team.

This issue of security is key, and in some contexts, transnationalism may facilitate access to social protections and well-being.[43] In other cases, transnational ties may provide a sense of existential moorings. An ambitious study of diverse Latino immigrants in Miami conducted by sociologists Maria Aranda, Sallie Hughes, and Elena Sabogal hinges on Anthony Gidden's concept of "ontological security."[44] Latino immigrants in Miami gain a sense of safety and confidence that their reality is what it appears to be "by embedding themselves in relationships with emotionally significant people and places that are territorially positioned in the country of origin and in Miami, which constitute two poles of translocal space." By doing so, they establish a kind of "translocal social citizenship."[45]

But for the reasons we have detailed earlier, this was not the case in South L.A. We conducted the bulk of our interviews in a time (2014–15) when the fortification of the U.S.–Mexico border, deportation and detention regimes, and intensified crime and violence in Mexico and Central American created a situation in which transnational practice, for the majority of our first-generation respondents, was generally confined to phone calls and sending money home to families. Even respondents who had been active in Mexican hometown associations in the 1990s reported that they were now less involved and committed to these activities.

This suggests an important insight: we need to consider not only how immigrants adapt to their new locales but also how homemaking practices transform the new locale. As Adriano Cancellieri observes, immigrant homemaking is a process through which immigrants "re-territorialize themselves by breathing new life" into their new dwellings.[46] "They imbue domestic spaces with their own memory and meaning," changing the materiality of the place, and, by doing so, move toward feelings of belonging and practices of emplacement (see Figure 1.5). This may be quite uneven: as Alarcón, Escala, and Odgers remind us, there is no single modality of immigrant integration, and based on this premise, these researchers advocate that we pay close attention to observing tensions among economic, sociocultural, and political integration.[47] Unevenness in immigrant integration in South L.A. is certainly the case: we see Latino immigrants in South Los Angeles establishing economic and sociocultural integration through work and homemaking but very much lagging in the civic and political sphere.

The utility of this immigrant homemaking approach is that we can better examine how neighborhoods and nations become "home." Scholars working in new Latino urbanism have emphasized immigrant ethnic agency and the transformation of the new locales but with a focus more generally on urban environments and neighborhoods. One of the very best examples of this scholarship comes from urban planner James Rojas, who has shown how East L.A.'s unique identity is defined not by the built environment but by the "enacted environment," that is, the ways Mexican immigrant and Mexican American residents inhabit homes, front yards, driveways, and streets.[48] And in another context, examining Chinese immigrants in Vancouver, sociologists Lauster and Zhao draw attention to the work of Chinese immigrant homemaking, looking at both the physical and emotional efforts required at different stages of settling in, settling down, and, often, "settling for" circumstances that may be less than those that were initially anticipated.[49]

Figure 1.5. Salo's Mini Market Mural, Historic South Central
Photo Credit: Walter Thompson-Hernández, USC CSII project team.

It is this framework of "homemaking" that guides our analysis. Our adoption of this perspective was more inductive than deductive, more learning that other approaches did not fully explain the data than hitting the field with all our theories neatly lined up. While we have adopted it as a main prism for interpreting our data, there is a wrinkle that this case study adds: Mexicans and Central Americans have made new homes in long-standing African American neighborhoods undergoing dramatic changes, forcing us to consider what it means to make home in a place where the sense of loss and erasure by an oppressed, racialized group is a key part of the story.

Brown Meets Black

Truly understanding that dimension of establishing Latino homes in Black space is challenging, partly because research on relations between African Americans and Latinos has traditionally been easily divided into two camps, with one emphasizing conflict and competition over jobs, wages, and resources and the other stressing cooperation sparked by shared oppression in the U.S. racial system. But as many commentators have pointed out, simplistic a priori notions of either conflict or consensus are not sufficient; we need research examining the dynamic, nuanced, and place-specific character of Black–Latino relations.

In this context, it is helpful to return to the old idea, first proposed by Gordon Allport, a psychologist writing in the era of legal Jim Crow segregation, that contact between people of different racial groups would bring about understanding and acceptance if four conditions held: common goals, support from social institutions, equal status, and intergroup cooperation.[50] The idea that friendship across racial groups would diminish racial prejudice was later further developed in a series of publications by social psychologist Thomas Pettigrew.[51] In this view, living in racially nonhomogeneous neighborhoods (like South L.A.) would increase the likelihood of face-to-face interactions with members of other racial groups and diminish racial prejudice.

A contrasting view is offered by researchers who have suggested that processes of neighborhood racial-ethnic transition can lead to perceptions of "threat" or "invasion." They emphasize racial threat as an outcome, suggesting that as segregation declines and as newcomer groups approach parity, the initial group responds with hostility and exacerbated racial discord. Most of this literature is based on white Americans' reactions to new African American neighbors, which erupted in full-throated expressions of racial hostility and white flight in the 1960s and 1970s.[52] Echoing this view, João Costa Vargas reports in his compelling ethnography, *Catching Hell in the City of Angels*, that Latinos were perceived as unwelcome entrants and not well liked by African Americans in South L.A. in the period he covers, the mid-1990s.[53]

A similar view is offered by sociologist Cid Martinez in his book *The Neighborhood Has Its Own Rules: Latinos and African Americans in South Los Angeles*.[54] His study of extra-legal mechanisms of violence prevention (which he calls "alternative governance") documents strategies of avoidance used by both Latinos and African Americans. However, these mechanisms are not shared, and so the space is divided rather than subject to either new forms of bonding or ethnic succession. As Martinez sees it, "the Latinoization of South L.A. has created a new type of urban space. The ghetto itself is now divided into two parallel worlds—one black and the other Latino."[55]

Divided Worlds?

This sense of separate spheres resonates with what we were told by some first-generation Latino immigrants, but even among these Latino residents, our study reveals their experiences and recollections of magnified moments of intimacy and support from African American individuals. For example, Karla Sonora reports that her single mom found solace provided by key individuals and the community's Black church networks. Despite not knowing English, Karla's mom developed a friendship with their African American neighbor, dropping each other's kids off at school when needed. "They were so supportive of each other and helped each other and they didn't even understand each other," she recalled, "but they both sort of were like—you're a mom, and you get it. You know?" These experiences later provoke reflection, connection, and new narratives that belie the separate worldviews. And the divided spheres view certainly does not describe the contemporary world of the second generation, suggesting that what Cid Martinez may be offering in his tension-ridden rendering is a snapshot periodization rather than a characterization of the transformation over time.[56]

Perhaps a better approach involves a more nuanced view of contact theory in which we include an understanding of how racial histories play a part in structuring the outcomes, how perspectives on home and neighborhood context may change over time, and how Black and Brown identities can be mutually constituted. First, it is important to recognize that racial meanings and racism circulate transnationally. For example, contact with U.S. anti-Black racial discourses often precedes migration and, in turn, return migrants and transnational connections help circulate these meanings, hierarchies, and prejudices learned in the United States to other places.[57] So it is not just contact but context and consciousness that determine outcomes.

Second, there is an important temporal dimension in race relations. Part of it is just having a longer stretch of interaction in which contact can become a connection. But there is also the issue of eras. In this sense, Costa Vargas's emphasis on scarcity and conflict may have fit South L.A. in the 1990s, but it does not describe the contemporary reality we witnessed in the mid-2010s when we were most actively in the field. One key difference is the crime level and the way that drove fear and separation: in 1994, the number of reported homicides in the City of Los Angeles was 845, with a population of over 3.6 million, but it has declined substantially, and by 2014, when we embarked on this study, the count was 260, with a population of just over 3.9 million.[58]

Finally, there is also another possible dynamic that surfaced in our data: the creation of a new shared identity. Indeed, a burst of movement organizing in response to challenging conditions has helped to contribute to the notion of Black–Brown unity as a sort of political and movement project, one often tied up in place, including evocations of South L.A. as a sort of sacred ground.[59] Fueling this is the fact that the second generation of Latinos raised in South L.A. is more or less inflected by Blackness, culturally (in terms of preferences for music and the like), socially (with friends, neighborhoods, peers), and politically. For example, while they could make no claim to the depth, severity, and persistence of the racism experienced by African Americans, the second-generation respondents often had a common narrative about the shared fates of "Black and Brown" communities and they voiced complaints about ways in which their common neighborhood had been marginalized.

Echoing this perspective, John Marquez, writing about African American political influences on Latinos in Houston, develops the concept of "foundational blackness" to refer to how "oppositional culture derived from African American history and responsiveness to expendability, have been a basis for how Latinos/as have developed their own methods of survival and resistance over time."[60] This concept, most relevant to the political sphere, resonates with our study in South L.A., particularly as it manifests itself in the persons of the Latino second generation who grew up with African American peers and who have now returned to work for justice and opportunity in schools and community organizations.

One contrast with what Marquez found in Houston, however, is that our second-generation Latino interviewees did not see themselves as disposable or expendable. Rather, their embrace of the Black experience was more of the celebration of struggle, and so they expressed optimistic outlooks for the future of South L.A., a vision likely also informed by the relative success of community organizing over the last several decades that we review in chapter 6. And similar to work by Jennifer Jones on Latino–African American relations in the South in which she finds evidence of shared "minority linked fate," second-generation

Latinos in South L.A. often saw their futures as one shared with African Americans.[61]

The world saw a glimpse of this shared struggles viewpoint in the 2018 March for Our Lives event in Washington, D.C., that was originally organized by youth who had lived through the horrible shooting tragedy at a high school in Parkland, Florida. Recognizing that this was a national platform—and pressed by criticism that gun violence was not a new problem for many low-income communities of color—the Parkland youth opened their stage to others, including young people from South L.A. Representing was a young Latina named Edna Chavez, who began her speech by announcing that she was from "South Los Angeles—*el sur de Los Angeles.*" In decrying violence, she announced that during her adolescence it was "normal to see flowers honoring the lives of Black and Brown youth that have lost their lives to a bullet." She then noted that instead of schools "making Black and Brown students feel safe, they continue to profile and criminalize us."[62]

Understanding Black and Brown community linkage and identity construction through shared space is not entirely new. In her book *Spaces of Conflict, Sounds of Solidarity*, Gaye Theresa Johnson examines both conflict and alliances between Mexican Americans and African Americans in post–World War II Los Angeles.[63] She argues that while both groups have been pitted against one another and "manipulated by the white power structure to compete with each other for jobs, housing, prestige, and political power," Black and Brown shared struggles and cultural expressions have led to alliances and shared "spatial entitlement." According to Johnson, "[s]patial entitlement entails occupying, inhabiting, and transforming physical spaces, but also imagining, envisioning, and enacting discursive spaces that 'make room' for new affiliations and identifications. . . . Blacks and Mexicans in Los Angeles turned oppressive racial segregation into creative and celebratory congregation. They transformed ordinary residential and commercial sites into creative centers of mutuality, solidarity, and collectivity."[64]

This sense of mutual homemaking in shared space is also captured in a volume edited by scholars Josh Kun and Laura Pulido that highlights contemporary interethnic coalitions and shared cultural production and enjoyment in Los Angeles.[65] But while mutual homemaking is an important theme in both their work and ours, it is important to realize that this is occurring on land that was hard-won and carefully cultivated by African Americans who challenged racial restrictions to move to many parts of South L.A. As a result, there is also a deep sense of loss and sorrow on the part of Black Angelenos as they have seen "their" home change. In the words of one local civil rights activist, "[w]e got what we wanted, but we lost what we had."[66]

This is a real phenomenon, one exacerbated by current forces that are promoting gentrification in South L.A., a topic to which we return late in the book. The impact of the Latinization of South L.A. on African Americans and their own identity is an important topic—and to set the context, we included a range of interviews that included twenty-five Black residents, a large number of Black men at public parks and in the community gardens in Watts, and nearly thirty longtime civic leaders, many of whom are African American. But while we do offer a sense of the Black reaction to the Latino arrival (and to the current pressures of gentrification), to be clear, our book is not primarily about the Black experience in South Los Angeles. This is an important topic, one addressed in books edited by University of California, Los Angeles scholars Darnell Hunt and Ana-Christina Ramón, in books by the historian Josh Sides, in the ethnography conducted in South L.A. in the mid-1990s by João Costa Vargas, and in an article by two researchers associated with this project.[67] We are instead trying to fill what we saw as a gap in the research on the evolution of Latino experiences and identities in Black space.

Expansion, Not Erasure

To analyze the process of identity construction, it is useful to turn to the work of Wendy Cheng, a researcher who examines how the daily social interactions that unfold in a San Gabriel Valley suburb provide a platform for negotiating racial hierarchies.[68] Building on Omi and Winant's influential work on racial formation, Pulido's concept of "regional racial hierarchies," and continuing in the tradition of Leland Saito and others who have examined racially heterogeneous suburban areas as sites of dynamic interracial social interaction, coexistence, and contestation, Cheng develops a theory of place-based racial sedimentation.[69] This

means that even as one racial group becomes more numerically dominant, it is possible to see the influences of others who have come before
them.

Using this geologic metaphor, Cheng suggests that "in any landscape
only the uppermost layer may be visible, but nonetheless the cumula-
tive processes that formed all the layers below still shape the uppermost
layer and may cause shifts and ruptures at any time." Regions and specific places are defined by social relations, not just physical boundaries, and these quotidian interactions accumulate.[70] As Cheng puts it,
"people's accounts of their daily lives—the decisions they make, the
people they regularly interact with, and even their seemingly mundane
interactions—cumulatively add up to a not necessarily fully articulated,
yet fully formed, regional racial consciousness."[71]

Of course, this is impacted by preexisting views. With the vast majority of immigrants to the United States now hailing from Asia and
Latin America, inquiries have centered not only on how Asian and Latin
American newcomers are changing the U.S. racial composition but also
on how the racial terms, understandings, and categories they bring with
them shape U.S. race relations.[72] Building on Peggy Levitt's concept of
"social remittances," which refers to the values, practices, and ideas that
circulate with migrants across national borders, a number of researchers
have focused on transnational "racial remittances," the racial prejudices,
practices, and discourses that circulate across national borders with
immigrants.[73]

This body of research shows how immigrants are influenced by U.S.
racial categories even before they migrate, which they may learn through
U.S. military and government contact, images, and ideals disseminated
in U.S. media or from transnational migrants.[74] For example, sociologist
Sylvia Zamora shows how Mexican migrants who return to their communities of origin transmit particular images of African Americans, as
"boisterous, aggressive, and prone to violence."[75]

These images and racial schemas do not remain static. Even when
Mexican immigrants come to the United States with anti-Black prejudices, these racial attitudes may change over time in the United States.[76]
In particular, Zamora cites the power of children to influence their
parents' views. As she observes, "[a]lthough immigrants are known to
pass on their racial attitudes to their children, the reverse is also true.

U.S.-born children who form meaningful relationships with Black teachers and peers bring these experiences into the household, exposing immigrant parents to new ways of relating to black Americans that can potentially foster a sense of commonality."[77]

Indeed, many second-generation respondents in this study mentioned the prevalence of anti-Black racism among the older generation, partly growing out of negative encounters but also out of deep-seated racial attitudes, and how they (their children) were trying to dispel those beliefs. Aurelia Campa from Watts noticed a change in her mom. She said, "I think because she sees the way we interact, and because we kind of tend to talk to her and like. . . . 'Maybe if a Black person did this to you when we were younger, it doesn't mean every single Black person are like that.' So we try to open her mind a little bit more." And when the children of Mexican immigrants fall in love with African Americans and have children, a new multiracial "Blaxican" identity furthers the project of transformation.[78]

Echoing Wendy Cheng's exhortation to closely examine the power of interactions and place, Zamora also reminds us how these racial discourses remain subject to change depending on what happens in the new locales. "Bad encounters," she notes, "especially early in the migration process, can confirm racial attitudes carried over from Mexico. . . . Yet negative attitudes are also being challenged by everyday life occurrences, such as raising children who make friends with black youth, or friendly greetings among neighbors."[79] This focus on youth and the younger generation of children of immigrants having more exposure to different racial groups and being more comfortable with diversity than their parents is also a central theme in research conducted by Van C. Tran.[80]

As we will see, this is very much echoed in our own work. And one key outcome of the interaction is not just a reduction in prejudice against another group, in this case African Americans, but also the assertive adoption by younger Latinos of the themes of struggle against racism and inequity that have characterized Black politics in America. When one listens to younger civic leaders and activists in South L.A., the talk is not Brown versus Black but rather of Black and Brown together, with Black usually highlighted in the first spot, given the foundational role of the Black movement for civil and human rights. In

Figure 1.6. Twenty Years in South L.A.
Photo Credit: UNIDAD Coalition.

short, something very different than "divided worlds" or "group conflict" is going on, and understanding the South L.A. experience is useful
for theorizing quotidian experience in urban America, understanding
emergent identities of *Latinidad*, and building alliances for efforts to
change that experience.

Perhaps the best emerging framework that fits this phenomenon is the
"relational formations of race" approach advocated by Molina and colleagues.[81] Highlighting new research and rethinking, the editors of this
volume highlight work that shifts away from a Black–white binary, that
sees race as socially constructed and that takes seriously the ways in which
"marginalized" populations actually help constitute each other's identities
and so generate political collaboration against oppressive structures. As
Natalia Molina provocatively puts in her own intervention in the book, "to
be Mexican in Los Angeles meant to be just one part of a multiethnoracial
setting that in no small part shaped how people understood the social,
cultural, racial, and political meaning of 'Mexican' in Los Angeles."[82] To be
Latino in South L.A. is exactly that with more contact, more interconnec-
tion, and more variation across generations and geography.

Decentering whiteness in understanding racial formation is a welcome and necessary evolution that not only challenges yet one more remnant of white supremacy but also allows considerably more space for new and deeper analysis. While this shifting and decentered terrain is the racial landscape that we explore in this volume, we are also well aware that the United States operates within a system that privileges whiteness and often pits Latinos and African Americans against each other. As Vanessa Ribas puts it, "[t]he position of whiteness at the core of this system means that subordinated groups' relations with one another are refracted through their relations with whites and whiteness."[83] This broader racial structure has instrumentally shaped South L.A. from the outside—white people may not be present in person (at least until the recent wave of gentrification), but whiteness and white power over economic and political resources definitely are. At the same time, most of our focus in this volume is on South L.A. from the inside—how its residents have built resilience in the face of racism and economic deprivation, developed relationships on their own terms, and forged solidarities for mutual self-determination (see figure 1.6).

Concepts, Methods, and Road Map

Given this discussion of the literature and the theory, what are the key concepts we use to guide our analysis? To understand the Latino transformation of historically Black South L.A., we rely on four key concepts:

- *Spatial transformation:* the shifts in South L.A. challenge the traditional spatial assimilation view in which an immigrant group establishes a sort of platform neighborhood in a low-income area and then moves on. We find it more useful below to consider how an immigrant group and their children "stick" and how they then choose to transform the place.
- *Racial-ethnic sedimentation:* the traditional model is based on a notion of ethnic succession, that is, the process by which a new ethnic group essentially replaces a previous ethnic group in a neighborhood, often with implications for political power as well. We suggest that what best explains the transformation in South L.A. is the idea of sedimentation— one group building on another and incorporating rather than excising the past.

- *Place-based racial identity:* race matters, but in this study, we emphasize the significance of place and daily experiences in shaping racial identity. We note that this is quite consistent with the theories on the relational formations of race.
- *Homemaking:* this is an active process of creating a sense of security, familiarity, autonomy, and future-making activities attached to place.

While these guiding concepts help orient the reader to the large amount of data that is to come, it is also important to stress four potentially unique features of the empirical research that also deeply informed the work: (1) it was rooted and, in fact, prompted not just by scholarly debates but also by public community engagement; (2) from the get-go, we were fully committed to a mixed-methods approach; (3) to ensure accuracy, the research team included members who were not the usual "outsiders" but rather had a community history that deepened our understanding and helped build trust with interviewees; and (4) we utilized recursive community feedback on preliminary findings, presenting along the way to make sure we were getting the story as it was perceived by those living it.

On the first of these features, we actually began the research because local community leaders and organizers approached us with questions about social and demographic change in South L.A. They wanted to know more about Latino residents, their experiences in the neighborhoods and with their African American neighbors, and the key issues that mattered to them, hoping that such information might help reformulate new directions for local community organizing. We took up the challenge, starting by immersing ourselves in readings of both historical texts and up-to-date scholarly social science literature on immigrant integration, race, and urban studies. As a research team, we sat around the seminar table discussing these issues, debating the relevance of assimilation theory and the current threats of gentrification. The project was thus formulated in dialogue with academic theory, but it was fundamentally rooted in a public sociology of close community engagement.

On the second aspect of our work, to get an understanding of the contemporary Latino experience in South L.A., we designed a mixed-methods project. Before discussing methods, let us offer a word on nomenclature. We are aware that terms like *Hispanic* and *Latino* have been, from their origins, a social construct used for political ends.[84] We also acknowledge that others are using the term *Latinx* or *Latine* to move away from gendered binaries that are being challenged throughout our nation. These challenges have great merit, and we have utilized some of this emerging language in some of the reports associated with the research center that housed this project, USC's Center for the Study of Immigrant Integration (CSII), which has since merged with a related effort and been renamed the USC Equity Research Institute (ERI). That said, interviewees in this project used Latino almost exclusively and sometimes Hispanic, a more common term in some parts of our nation. Language and terminology are in constant flux across space and time—and this book reflects the period in which we conducted the research.

In any case, on the quantitative side, we assembled a multiyear database that covered the historic neighborhoods that define South L.A.; we describe the exact contours of those designations in the next chapter. We relied mostly (but not exclusively) on data collected by the U.S. Census Bureau, including historical data from the Decennial Census for each decade going back to 1970 and summary data from the American Community Survey (ACS). Our work also relied on microdata—that is, individual answers to the Census and ACS—that allowed us to provide breakdowns by detailed demographic characteristics, such as race and ethnicity, nativity, and legal status (with the latter generated by a method described in chapter 2).

On the qualitative side, five members of the team conducted in-depth interviews with one hundred Latino community residents, with the sample focused on residents of three iconic South L.A. neighborhoods: Watts, Historic South Central, and the Vermont Square area (we explain why we chose these areas in our detailed demographic profile in chapter 2). We also interviewed twenty-eight civic leaders—elected officials, government staff, and nongovernmental organization leaders—who were Black, Latino, Asian American, and white. While our focus is on understanding the Latino residents of South L.A., we wanted to include some perspective from the African American community, so we conducted interviews with twenty-five Black residents, mostly from Watts for reasons we explain later. And because of our stress on how quotidian life impacts a sense of home and place identity, we included interviews and ethnographic field visits with African Americans and

Latinos, mostly men, at public parks and urban community gardens in the three study neighborhoods.

Third, to carry all this out, we assembled a group with particular connections to the local community. Manuel Pastor, who headed up the quantitative component, is trained as an economist and has worked for decades with progressive community organizations, particularly in South L.A., on issues of urban equity, race, and immigration. Pierrette Hondagneu-Sotelo, who directed the qualitative component, brought several decades of interviewing and ethnographic research experience in California Latino immigrant communities. Dr. Veronica Montes was a postdoctoral fellow at USC and brought a particular ability to connect to the first generation, having herself been a Mexican immigrant who had been undocumented when she arrived in the 1980s. Key staff at USC's CSII, including Pamela Stephens, Alejandro Sanchez-Lopez, Vanessa Carter, and Rhonda Ortiz, provided well-honed technical support, expertly coordinated project management, and participated in the field interviews. Walter Thompson Hernández, then a research assistant who later became an author and *New York Times* global reporter, conducted the bulk of the interviews with the second generation.[85]

Hondagneu-Sotelo and Montes did most of the interviewing of the older cohort of "first-generation" Latino residents, and together, they designed the interview guide and trained a younger group of interviewers, who conducted most of the interviews with the younger Latino residents. This team included Jessica Medina, Kristie (Hernández) Valdez-Guillen, and Walter Thompson-Hernández, all of whom were born and raised in or near the South L.A. study neighborhoods. The twenty-five interviews with African American residents in Watts were conducted by Janice Burns-Miller, an Afro-Latina planner and researcher who has long-standing community ties. The interview study of public parks and urban community gardens was led by Hondagneu-Sotelo, assisted by three USC students, Antar Tichavakunda, Jose Miguel Ruiz, and Adrián Trinidad, two of whom were raised in or near South L.A. and who remain deeply involved in local community issues.[86]

Finally, we fulfilled the *compromiso* or social commitment of our study, through dialogue with South L.A. itself. The early quantitative data was presented to Latino leaders at Los Angeles Trade Technical (one of the local public community colleges). As the qualitative pieces filled out, we presented that data at community-oriented events, such as one organized by Charles Drew University of Medicine and Science, a historically Black medical school located in South L.A. (which is actually where we able to recruit the researcher who carried out the interviews with Black residents). We also presented our initial findings at a public forum at USC, inviting both academic experts and community leaders to comment. In the fall of 2016, we produced a popular report on the research which was widely distributed to residents, local leaders, and community organizers. This may have also been the first academic report we know that was also accompanied by its own rap video, produced by a young South L.A. resident who was a friend of one of the members of the research team and taken with the themes of the report.[87]

The fact that we stress our attention to *compromiso* suggests a key feature of this work: we are not disinterested researchers divorced from the subject of our study. Indeed, part of what motivated this work was a request by community organizers and leaders that someone tell the tale of the transformation of South Los Angeles in a way that would go beyond the usual media focus on Black–Brown conflict. We ourselves saw the need: in our own interactions with the community, we not only saw tension, but we also experienced dissonance between the nearly exclusive academic and reportorial stress on division and the daily accommodations and political realignments happening on the ground. There was a story there to be told.

Some might question our closeness to the community and the organizations that requested the research. But while claims to objectivity and rigorous social science research are traditionally made by positivistic declarations in favor of distance and disinterest, we take a different stance. In our view, closeness to community enhanced and deepened the research—it helped generate new contacts and helped us establish trust with interviewees. At the same time, our determination to get this story right also meant that we needed to tell it like it is—even when we recorded and observed data that were not always flattering.

So how exactly do we tell this story? Chapter 2 provides a brief history of South L.A., underscoring that it has always been a place of change. Before it became the heart of Black Los Angeles, African Americans were largely shut out of most of what is now South L.A. due to racially restrictive real estate practices, with a tipping point coming in the wake of the 1965 Watts Rebellion. We historicize the entry of Latino immigrants in the 1980s and 1990s and offer a detailed statistical profile of South L.A. between 1980 and 2016. This serves as a backdrop for the qualitative work of the next four chapters.

Chapter 3 relies on forty interviews with first-generation Latino immigrant residents to provide a subject-centered analysis of home-making processes in these traditionally African American neighborhoods, showing how this has changed over time. Chapter 4 draws on sixty interviews with 1.5- and second-generation Latinos who grew up in South L.A. Here, we show the deep impact of Black culture on Latino identity. And chapter 5, drawing on interviews with African American and Latino men who gather at public parks and urban community, highlights how men in these neighborhoods find sanctuary and solace in nature, conviviality, and sociability and yet often do so while remaining in distinct locales.

Chapter 6 focuses on the evolution of civic life in South L.A. Drawing on interviews with twenty-eight civic leaders as well as with Black residents who directly experienced the demographic change, this chapter charts the emergence of South L.A. as a key site for building Black–Brown coalitions and shared political projects. Even as it does look forward, it also highlights a deep sense of Black loss that complicates current organizing and is exacerbated by gentrification pressures that are steadily growing over time. Chapter 7 discusses the implications of this research for rethinking theory, considers how the research can be extended to cover other locales of Black–Brown encounters, and closes with a discussion of the future of South L.A.

A final word before moving on. This book has two primary authors listed on the cover, but, apart from the introduction and conclusion, the other individual chapters list other names as well. We adopted this approach because the two primary authors, Pastor and Hondagneu-Sotelo, fundamentally shaped the ideas behind this book, determined the organization of its contents, and were the primary authors on all the chapters as well as leaders in framing, editing, and assembling of the manuscript. At the same time, the authors listed for each chapter played a key role in extensive data collection and analysis, as well as writing in the respective chapters that include their names. Without their knowledge and skill—and without the broader team that contributed other parts of the research, data processing, editing, and organization—we would not have completed this ambitious project. And while honoring their work in this way may seem like an unconventional and novel method of attribution, the whole point of this volume is that South L.A. represents an unconventional and novel case of identity formation. *Y con eso, empezamos.*

2

Always Changing, Always Contested

MANUEL PASTOR AND PAMELA STEPHENS

The most recent transformation in South Los Angeles—from over-whelmingly African American to predominately Latino—may have captured public attention but change in South L.A. is not new. From the European American farmers who took over *rancho* lands in Watts in the late nineteenth century to the Mexicans and Japanese attracted there later by railroad work and cheap housing to the white industrial workers purchasing modest homes between Central Avenue and Watts in the interwar period to the wave of African American migrants flee-ing the Jim Crow South in the early and mid-twentieth century to the Latin American immigrants escaping political turmoil and economic crisis in their home countries in the 1980s, people have historically come to every part of South L.A. looking to make a new home and forge a brighter future. Once ranches and farmlands, then white suburbs, and now Black and Latino spaces, South L.A. has been a location that is con-stantly being remade.

In this chapter, we provide the historical and quantitative context for understanding this most recent remaking of South LA as a Latino (as well as a Black) home. To do that, we start with a brief history of South L.A.; our focus is on the highlights necessary to understand the con-temporary period and interested readers will want to explore the more detailed histories and resources we cite. What emerges is the portrait of a place that has sat at the intersection of such key dynamics as race rela-tions, deindustrialization, and policing in Los Angeles, all of which have given rise to two of the most costly civil disturbances in U.S. history as well as to a new and vibrant level of community organizing that is part of the story we explore later in this book.

We then turn to a profile of the area's changing demography, not only noting the growth of the Latino community but also noting certain key characteristics such as share foreign-born, the national origin of the immigrant populations, the nature of their legal status, and the rather striking growth in the Latino youth population (alongside an equally startling decrease in the Black youth population). We stress how relatively high rates of homeownership suggest a sinking of roots even as economic progress seems to be stymied by the working poverty affecting much of the Latino population. While this data profile builds on earlier efforts, what is unique here is the emphasis on the immigrant and Latino part of the South L.A. story.[1]

While the data profile we offer is extensive, there are many features of economic and social life we leave out—for example, access to parks and nature, the rate of immigrant naturalization and extent of Latino political power, and the rising housing costs and gentrification pressures impacting the area. It is not that we think these issues are unimportant but rather that we have space constraints. And not to worry: we introduce those data points later when we turn our attention in chapter 5 to public parks and gardens and in chapter 6 when we explore civic life in South L.A., including the state of (better put, lack of) Latino representation, the nature of coalition building in Black–Brown space, and how residents are organizing to secure a claim to home in South L.A. before that home gets priced away from them.

The goal of this chapter is straightforward: we are trying to set a better historical and empirical base for understanding the qualitative data from our in-depth interviews and observations in the rest of the book. Indeed, we conclude the chapter by arguing that to truly understand the reality of South L.A.—indeed, to understand reality anywhere—one needs to go beyond tables and numbers to hear and then lift up the stories of the residents as they seek to find their way and make their home in a changing neighborhood. It is exactly this mixed-methods approach that we thought best—but we begin here with the part of the mix that relied on historical and quantitative analysis.

Decades of Change

Los Angeles's complex and often tortured multiracial character began with the Spanish conquest of Native American lands—a genocidal erasure of indigenous cultures and people in the area that was further

accelerated when California became a U.S. state.[2] However, it is important to note that that the forty-four founders of the city—known as "El
Pueblo de Nuestra Señora la Reina de los Ángeles del Río Porciúncula"—
included people of mixed African, Spanish, and indigenous descent,
fostering a myth of multicultural harmony in the region. Indeed, two
of California's subsequent Mexican governors had African ancestry,
including Pio Pico, after whom the region's famous Pico Boulevard is
named. Yet, as geographer Paul Robinson notes, this Black heritage was
later suppressed in a celebration of the "Spanish" influence on Southern
California.[3]

With the conclusion of the Mexican–American War in 1848, Mexico
lost approximately one-half of its territory in the north, and Los Angeles
became part of the United States. After the war, most *Californios*—those
of Mexican heritage living in the territory—lost title to or possession of
their large ranchos to the U.S. government; as Hondagneu-Sotelo notes,
"[r]ancho land holdings were reappropriated, stolen, subdivided and ultimately sold in the 1880s real estate boom."[4] Land was "annexed bit by
bit" by Anglo-American farmers who transformed it into farms yielding
sugar beets, celery, and beans in South L.A.[5] They were later joined by
other farmers, including Japanese families who operated "truck farms"
(smaller agricultural holdings producing vegetables and fruits for local
and other markets) in nearby Compton, Torrance, and Inglewood. Residents of Watts went so far as to boast about their country living.[6]

The bucolic image of the South L.A. environs might surprise those
less familiar with the area's history, but it is important to recall that Los
Angeles was itself a small town in a largely rural setting for most of the
mid- to late nineteenth century.[7] San Francisco in the north was the center of California commerce and finance; for example, in 1880, the population of San Francisco was more than twenty times that of Los Angeles.
But an era of Southern California boosterism soon took hold, and real
estate fever set in as the century turned; by 1920, Los Angeles's population equaled that of its northern rival, with the rest of L.A. County adding another 60 percent to the population of the burgeoning metropolis.[8]

The population explosion laid the groundwork for Los Angeles's
Black community and for what would later become known as South
Central. Leaving behind the racial violence of the Jim Crow South in
search of better jobs and better homes, African Americans came to Los

Angeles and joined the small number of other Black Angelenos already here.[9] The attractiveness of Los Angeles was certified by none other than the famous sociologist and co-founder of the National Association for the Advancement of Colored People (NAACP), W. E. B. Du Bois: in 1913, he observed that Los Angeles's Black population was "without doubt the most beautifully housed group of colored people in the United States."[10] This was in no small part because of the relative economic and housing freedom that was afforded to African Americans throughout the city, although not long after Du Bois's reflections, things started to change for the worse.[11]

Still, there was some basis for Du Bois's optimism: while racially restricted housing covenants limited exactly what properties could be purchased, by 1910, 40 percent of African Americans in Los Angeles were homeowners—compared to only 2.4 percent of African Americans in New York City and 8 percent in Chicago.[12] However, the employment side of the equation was not so appealing: most African American women worked in domestic service while the men frequently worked as railroad porters, barbers, janitors, chauffeurs, and waiters.[13] Nonetheless, some observers have described this era as something of a "golden era" for African Americans, perhaps because the number of African Americans in Los Angeles was small enough to not constitute a threat to whites, whose racial attacks were more focused on Mexicans, Chinese Americans, and Japanese Americans.[14]

In the 1920s, African Americans built strong communities just south of downtown Los Angeles, mostly because segregation maintained by both racial covenants and intimidation limited their potential geographic spread.[15] As a result, Central Avenue emerged as "the primary artery of black life, and the intersection with 12th Street remained the center of things."[16] In a way that echoes today's contemporary Black–Brown reality in South L.A., the area was actually mixed: Black residents joined Mexicans, Filipinos, Italians, and others who packed into Central Avenue in an array of housing that ranged from well-tended bungalows to dilapidated shacks.

Black-owned businesses and buildings—that were to become famous as markers of Black cultural life in Los Angeles—sprung up in the Central Avenue district, including the Lincoln Theater in 1926 and the Somerville Hotel. The latter was built in 1928 for the NAACP convention;

renamed the Dunbar Hotel in 1930, it became the West Coast entertainment mecca and sleeping spot for Black performers and elites who were racially barred from other hotels. Also in this era, Black architect Paul Williams, later to become famous for posh homes in fancy neighborhoods as well as for landmark buildings and parts of the Beverly Hills Hotel, designed buildings in the corridor, including the Second Baptist Church, a new Elks Hall, and the 28th Street YMCA.[17] Harlem transplant John Kinloch wrote of Central Avenue in 1944:[18]

> Paris is lovely
> It is beautiful
> It is lush and
> Wonderful
> I would gladly
> Trade it
> All
> For a corner
> At
> 41st Street & Central Ave

Even as South Central was being formed as a new center of Black culture and influence, change was lurking. The pastures and farmlands of the broader South L.A. area were being filled in by manufacturing and industry, with housing tracts co-located alongside, as Los Angeles sought to craft a new sort of "industrial suburb"—close to employment, far from the city center, and ready to house a largely white working class. Compton, South Gate, and Huntington Park, among other municipalities that adjoined the city of Los Angeles, utilized racially restrictive covenants and racially discriminatory real estate practices to keep the new suburbs nearly all white.[19] The pattern was also seen in the parts of South L.A. that were in the City of Los Angeles proper. For example, Watts, once a separate city but annexed by Los Angeles in 1926, included African Americans and Japanese Americans but "[a]s of 1920, most Watts settlers were of European descent—Germans, Scots, Greeks, Italians, and Jews."[20]

The ability to both house needed workers *and* segregate them by race was strained when manufacturing skyrocketed during World War

II due to government contracting. Thousands of Black migrants from the South, especially from Texas and Louisiana, came to Los Angeles seeking jobs in wartime munitions plants, which later transitioned to automobile, tire, and steel jobs that were often near South L.A.[21] The incorporation of Black workers was a new development; prior to the war, discrimination in manufacturing against Black jobseekers was rampant.[22] While the public sector, especially jobs provided segregated services to the African American community provided some reprieve, many workers were pushed into domestic service jobs that employed "over half of Los Angeles' black population as late as the 1930s."[23]

Wartime necessities broke down the traditional racism in employment and housing, and this eventually provided a basis for economic stability for many African American households. As Josh Sides notes, "[a]t its peak in the 1950s and early 1960s, the manufacturing sector provided the economic foundation for a black middle class in South LA. At its high-water mark in 1960, 24 percent of employed African American men and 18 percent of employed Black women in Los Angeles worked as manufacturing operatives."[24] But the glide path there was not so smooth. During the period of rapid in-migration to meet wartime needs, the limited housing stock made available for Black residents became apparent. As Sides explains, "[d]uring WWII, fifty thousand new residents packed into the prewar boundaries of Central Avenue, ten thousand new residents moved to Watts, and seventy thousand crowded into Bronzeville/Little Tokyo."[25] Mayor of Los Angeles at the time, Fletcher Bowron tried to meet demand during and after the war by promoting public housing. But while some units did get built, including the Jordan Downs complex in Watts, public housing was portrayed as largely serving minorities and was challenged after the war by the so-called Committee Against Socialist Housing.[26] In a hotly contested election in 1953, Bowron lost his seat as mayor, and housing production once again reverted mostly to the private market.

Bowron's loss came just five years after the 1948 Supreme Court decision *Shelley v. Kraemer*, which ended racial covenants and partially opened up the housing market to African Americans.[27] But as legal constraints were lifted, others appeared, including white-on-Black violence aimed at deterring residential integration and real estate steering often reinforced by professional associations of realtors and local governments. Despite this, in the 1950s, the Black middle class began to move out to other neighborhoods, including Compton and West Adams, an area south of Downtown and one filled with large mansions and other desirable housing stock. Robinson reports that as African Americans spread out across South L.A., class heterogeneity became the norm after the late 1950s.[28] Meanwhile, school populations shifted: "The three large South Central city high schools, Jefferson, Fremont, and Jordan, which had been multiethnic, became almost exclusively black in the two decades after WWII" (see figure 2.1).[29]

While increased residential mobility was a welcome change, the growing Black population continued to face issues of discrimination and exclusion. One such flashpoint was California Proposition 14 (1964), a ballot measure that sought to override a 1963 fair housing law passed by the California legislature; as such, it was designed to reinstitute legal discrimination by race in housing.[30] While it was eventually struck down in court, the fact that whites voted for it by a two-to-one margin was not lost on African Americans. Tensions about long-lasting economic and social inequities boiled over in 1965 in the form of the Watts Rebellion. Prompted by what many believed was the unlawful arrest of an African American motorist in Watts, the widespread uprising also reflected simmering problems such as poverty, racism, and police brutality.[31] When the dust settled days later, thirty-four people were dead, roughly one thousand were injured, and there had been nearly $40 million (or nearly $320 million in today's dollars) worth of property damage.[32] But this was not the only effect: the rebellion prompted a wave of white flight that, in turn, allowed for a farther geographic spread of the Black population.

By the 1970s, African Americans were moving as far west as Baldwin Hills, partly because the Fair Housing Act of 1968 had further opened up doors.[33] Baldwin Hills, Windsor Hills, View Park, and Ladera Heights were becoming middle- and upper-class neighborhoods, and the heart of Black Los Angeles had seemingly shifted to Leimert Park.[34] Conversely, places east of Central Avenue were associated with Black poverty.[35] Class heterogeneity had become class segregation, but there was an emerging strong geographic base—the area we now call South L.A. was roughly 80 percent African American in 1970—providing a potential launching pad for the sustained Black progress that Du Bois had originally envisioned.

Figure 2.1. Jordan High School, Watts
Photo Credit: Walter Thompson-Hernández, University of Southern California (USC) Center for the Study of Immigrant Integration (CSII) project team.

All this could have led to a sort of Black renaissance in Los Angeles. Sweetening the prospective deal: in 1973, voters elected Tom Bradley, a South L.A. resident and the first-elected Black mayor of a largely white major U.S. city.[36] While his election was historic, Paul Robinson argues that he was more representative of the Black elite and made little progress for everyday Black Angelenos.[37] Part of the reason for that was that the economic foundation of South L.A. was crumbling under the pressures of deindustrialization, a process that gained full national and regional steam in the 1970s. As usual, pressures for African Americans were felt even earlier: "After climbing steadily for two decades, the proportion of the black male workforce employed as operatives in manufacturing firms began to fall in the 1960s, and the absolute employment of black men in manufacturing dropped in the early 1970s."[38]

As the 1970s gave way to the 1980s, other forces began to ravage South L.A. and instead of being the base for a Black renaissance, the area became what one civic leader we interviewed called the "capital of Black misery." The crack-cocaine epidemic burst onto the national scene, causing drug dependency, increases in crime and gang violence, rising tensions between law enforcement and residents, and ultimately a hyper-criminalized environment—and South L.A. was ground zero for this epidemic.[39] Fear led to bars and fences that could be not only spun as providing a sense of safety but also constituted a form of containment of the local population in public housing in Watts (see figure 2.2). While there was a growing Latino presence in South L.A. in this period, Black people faced the brunt of crime and homicide rates during this era.[40] South L.A. gangs soon became a "favorite topic of news stories, television programming, and Hollywood movies, both entertaining and frightening people all over the nation and around the world."[41] The consequences were directly felt by many young people, particularly young men, who were, to borrow from Kendrick Lamar's "Good Kid," caught between the red and the blue, between the competing gangs that sought to lure them to their ranks and the blue uniforms and red sirens of police who wanted to drag them into the criminal justice system.

Indeed, police were often as threatening to residents as the gangs, a fact made clear in 1988 when eighty-eight Los Angeles Police Department (LAPD) officers raided two apartment buildings on 39th Street and Dalton Avenue, just west of Memorial Coliseum. Intended as a show of force, the police smashed furniture and sprayed graffiti. According to reporting by the *Los Angeles Times*,[42]

[d]ozens of residents from the apartments and surrounding neighborhood were rounded up. Many were humiliated or beaten, but none was charged with a crime. The raid netted fewer than six ounces of marijuana and less than an ounce of cocaine. The property damage was so great that the Red Cross offered assistance to 10 adults and 12 minors who were left homeless.

Police–community relations were further poisoned by the videotaped beating of Black motorist Rodney King in March 1991—and exploded into a second wave of civil unrest in April 1992, when a jury acquitted the officers accused of beating King. Further complicating the picture was that while South L.A. was the cultural heart of Black Los Angeles, culture did not always extend to ownership, particularly of local businesses.

Figure 2.2. Public Housing, Watts
Photo Credit: Walter Thompson-Hernández, USC CSII project team.

Even before the 1992 unrest, racialized tensions between Korean American shop owners and African Americans were exacerbated by the 1991 murder of fifteen-year-old Latasha Harlins by a Korean shopkeeper.

Together, these various phenomena—the slippage of employment, the rise of gang and other violence, the risks and realities of over-policing, and the relative lack of Black ownership opportunities—led to a new migration: the out-flight of middle-class and working-class African Americans from South L.A. who had provided a stabilizing presence but were now eager to provide a safer environment for their children.[43] Between 1980 and 2007, 130,000 African Americans moved from neighborhoods such as South L.A. in L.A. County to the exurbs, seeking safer neighborhoods.[44] By the 1990s, African Americans were moving to "the northern reaches of the county in Palmdale and Lancaster, and east into Riverside County."[45] The African American population in Fontana, Rialto, Victorville, and Moreno Valley (all in the Inland Empire) grew sixfold between 1980 and 2000.[46] This diaspora resulted in increased economic bifurcation within South L.A.'s Black community—part of a broader trend in the region's overall economic restructuring.[47]

As Robinson notes, this Black outmigration in the 1980s and 1990s made room for in-migration, and Latinos filled the gap.[48] While the presence of Latinos in South L.A. was not an entirely new phenomenon, Mexicans in Southern California had long been concentrated in Boyle Heights, East Los Angeles, and parts of the San Gabriel and San Fernando Valleys.[49] With the economic crises in Mexico and the wars in Central America that gained ground in the 1980s, migrant outflows stepped up and traditional entry points filled up. As a result, immigrants often moved directly to (or soon hopscotched to) South L.A.—and figure 2.3 shows the respective shifts in the immigrant and U.S.-born population in South L.A. over this period, particularly the surge in the 1980s.

Part of the reason why South L.A. became a Mexican immigrant destination of choice was another demographic change: while many still think of Mexican migrants as lone male sojourners, throughout the 1980s, 1990s, and to the current day, immigration to Los Angeles, in particular, and California, in general, began to include more women and migration became more family-based.[50] Part of this was due to shifting labor demand: while agriculture continued its pull, services and assembly in urban and suburban areas were open to a more female workforce. Moreover, as restrictive immigration policies and border enforcement intensified in the 1990s, temporary stays became more challenging, back-and-forth visits became less the norm, and so grew the numbers of women, children, and permanently settled families.

The built environment of South L.A. was often appealing to these Mexican (and later Central American) newcomers: There was an abundance of single-family homes and low-slung apartment buildings with affordable rents and purchase prices. Moreover, there was relatively easy proximity to job centers such as Downtown L.A. and the Alameda Corridor. And the departure of many small business owners from South L.A. in the wake of the 1992 civil unrest opened up new opportunities for immigrant entrepreneurs; as Zappia notes, "Latin American immigrants moved into South Los Angeles neighborhoods, setting up businesses, churches, and clinics."[51]

Meanwhile, thousands of Central Americans—including indigenous Mayans—were uprooted by war, violence, and economic crisis and came to Los Angeles during the 1980s. The initial stop for many

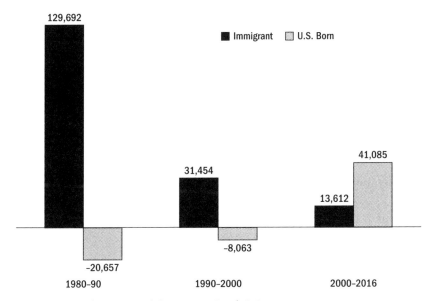

Figure 2.3. Population Growth by Nativity, South L.A., 1980–2016
Source: U.S. Census Bureau, Geolytics Inc.

was Westlake, a neighborhood around MacArthur Park and abutting Pico-Union. These migrants established important self-help and advocacy organizations—like the Central American Resource Center and others—but by the mid-1980s, this area became a very poor, dangerous neighborhood, plagued by crowded, substandard housing, gang violence, drive-by shootings, and crack cocaine.[52] As with the Mexican migrants, Central American families looking to get out saw the promising streetscapes and housing fabric of South L.A. In 1990, approximately 20 percent of Latinos in what was then called South Central were from Central America, far short of the 44 percent of Latinos in Westlake and even shy of the 23 percent for the city as a whole—but as we explore later, the share of Central Americans in South L.A. increased considerably over the following decades.[53]

Much of this demographic change seemed to fly under the media radar until the 1992 civil unrest. While the media cast the civil unrest as a primarily African American affair, Latinos actually constituted slightly more than half of those arrested and were "the single largest ethnic group in the damaged neighborhoods."[54] Indeed, in South L.A., where most of the damage occurred, Latinos were already more than 45 percent of the population. Yet as Los Angeles's Latino political leaders (mostly based in the Eastside) scrambled to understand what happened, they came face-to-face with a striking fact: Despite the dramatic demographic changes, there were virtually no Latino-based civic organizations in South L.A. that could contribute to a discussion of the rebuilding process.

The general lack of Latino civic infrastructure persists but what has emerged—partly from the devastation of 1992 and the rethinking it provoked—are new forms of interethnic community advocacy and mobilization. Formed before the civil unrest, a group called the Community Coalition (initially led by now-congresswoman Karen Bass) developed a distinctly Black–Brown model of neighborhood community engagement, with an initial focus on abatement of liquor stores as environmental nuisances.[55] After the unrest came the formation of Action for Grassroots Empowerment and Neighborhood Development Alternatives—now called Strategic Concepts in Organizing and Policy Education—which worked to bring together Black and Latino residents, developing and winning campaigns for workforce development.[56]

While many Latinos shied away from the public square—worries about legal status probably impacted some immigrants while language and other challenges were also extant—others became engaged in the more general revival of organizing, particularly among immigrants and workers, in contemporary Los Angeles. But one key feature of Latino organizing and engagement in South L.A. has been its focus on interconnected communities, particularly the intersections between Black and Latino youth who have grown up together. One astute historian of Black Los Angeles notes that "[s]uccessive waves of Latin American, Asian, and European immigrants ensured that the black freedom struggle would develop in a strikingly multiracial context."[57] But it might be equally said that the Black freedom struggle in South L.A. also set the context for the ways in which Latinos in the area would understand the realities and challenges of racism, poverty, and neglect of their neighborhoods. As one Latino leader reflected on his early days in organizing at Community Coalition, he said:

> [I] spent the first year there learning the organizing model and [was] really being attracted to this Black/Brown unity piece, which I thought was really essential . . . [it was] a very great model in terms of organizing peo-

ple around their shared experience with systems of oppression . . . there was something very unique to what the Community Coalition was asserting in those spaces. Which was, one, people can speak for themselves and should be allowed to develop solutions to these policy problems. And then, two, the campaigns are only a means towards a bigger end, which is building a mass space movement by people who are most impacted by all of these systems of oppression.

He went on to share how the power built in South L.A. was unique to that of other areas in Los Angeles. In his perspective, "Black folks in South Central had more of a tradition of setting up nonprofits to try to solve social problems" as opposed to adopting models or franchising operations created by white-led organizations. This sense that those most impacted by systems of oppression should drive the agenda meant that Latino leaders committed to social change should both follow the lead of and work to meet the needs of their Black neighbors.

This broad issue of Black–Brown relationships and the context they set for civic engagement is a topic we explore in subsequent chapters, particularly chapters 4 and 6. For now, this brief history reminds us that South L.A. has always been a place in transition, a locale where people go with hopes of a better life. It has also been a place where the racial, economic, and social dramas of Southern California and the nation have played out—racially restrictive covenants and practices, dramatic riots and rebellions, drug epidemics and excess policing, dramatic job losses and population displacement, and a simultaneous stew of interethnic tensions and forward-looking coalition building. When commemorating the twenty-fifth anniversary of the 1992 civil unrest, a broad swath of local organizations came together under the slogan "South LA is the Future."[58] It is a newer slogan, but it is clear that South L.A. has signaled what is to come—both good and bad—for a long time.

Defining South L.A.

In the preceding historical overview, we offered no specific definition of South L.A., something that may have been appropriate since South L.A. was actually evolving and changing in form and boundaries over the decades discussed. Indeed, even the name has evolved: long termed

"South Central," the area (or at least the portions of it in the Los Angeles City jurisdiction) was officially rechristened as "South L.A." by a 2003 city council resolution. The change was designed to eliminate the "stigma" associated with "South Central" and so promote business investment. It was also logical given the geographic fact that much of South L.A. now lies far from its Central Avenue origins.[59] Of course, as many pointed out at the time, changing the name did not change the level of economic distress or public disinvestment—and many older residents and now some younger residents who want to reclaim an older history tend to prefer "South Central." But South L.A. is also quite common—and our point here is that while fuzziness to highlight the contestation over the borders and very meaning (and even name) of a place is a proper approach for a historical account, offering a data view of both the demographic change and the contemporary reality requires that we stabilize the boundaries of our geography.

To do this, we define South L.A. by the same boundaries as those in the *Los Angeles Times* neighborhood mapping project.[60] Figure 2.4 illustrates that South L.A. is a set of twenty-eight smaller neighborhoods, comprising more than fifty square miles—and, as such, includes a variety of conditions and experiences. For example, View Park–Windsor Hills on the western edge of South L.A. is more affluent than, say, Athens; Hyde Park, also on the west side, is far more African American than Florence. Note also that South L.A. is defined by both us and others to include areas that are not part of the City of Los Angeles but are rather part of the unincorporated areas of L.A. County (e.g., both the aforementioned Florence and Athens neighborhoods).

It is a broad and diverse landscape, and to provide focus for our resident interview work that is the subject of the next two chapters, we dove deep into three broad areas, which then became the focal points for interviewee recruitment. These include (1) Central Avenue—which includes three *Los Angeles Times*–defined neighborhoods, Historic South-Central, South Park, and Central-Alameda; (2) Vermont Square—which also includes Vermont-Slauson; and (3) Watts. These three neighborhoods are outlined in figure 2.4 for the reader. While they have their differences, they all reflect different aspects of the demographic landscape of South L.A.

For example, the commercial density of Central Avenue, with pedestrians flowing into the *panaderías*, *quincenaria* shops, and markets, is

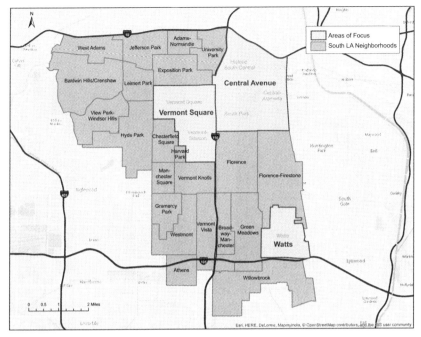

Figure 2.4. Map of South L.A. Neighborhoods
Source: Created by USC CSII project team with data from *Los Angeles Times* Mapping Project,
Census TIGER/Line, and ESRI.

the most Latino and became majority Latino first. Of the three, Vermont
Square, with pristinely well-kept homes on cozy streets alongside the
big avenues and boulevards, has the greatest share of Central Americans
in its Latino population. And while the share of Latinos in Watts mir-
rors that of South L.A. as a whole, its Latino population has grown the
fastest of the three neighborhoods we consider (see figure 2.5).[61] Watts
is also iconic and its residents are uniquely proud of their home; parts
of Watts have an almost a rural feel that contrasts with vast avenues like
Manchester Boulevard and the slew of mechanics shops, Food for Less
stores, check-cashing venues, and fast-food restaurants that populate
the streetscapes. The neighborhood is also home to the famous Watts
Towers—built by an Italian immigrant—as well as scars left from the
Watts Rebellion and other telltale signs of this onetime home of Black
Power in Los Angeles.

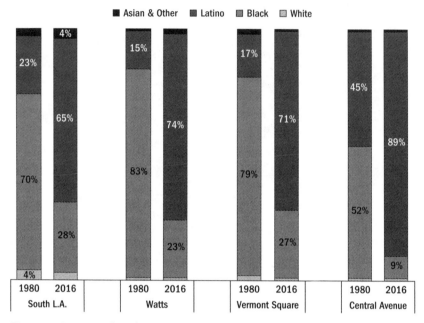

Figure 2.5. Demographic Change in South L.A. Overall and by Neighborhood, 1980–2016

Source: U.S. Census Bureau, Geolytics Inc.

Those historical details are among the qualitative differences that led us, along with the data examination, to choose these areas. For example, the Central Avenue area is rich in cultural heritage, but it has the weakest remaining Black political infrastructure; it is home to one of the area's oldest and most prominent Black churches, Second Baptist (the church where the Rev. Dr. Martin Luther King, Jr. preached when he came to L.A.), but it is now an institution that finds itself with commuter parishioners and detached Latino neighbors.[62] As noted, Watts has a very distinct identity—as one resident put it, "I think of Watts as by itself. It's not South L.A., it's just Watts"—as well as a very established Black-led political and social service infrastructure that was forged in struggle but has sometimes been slow to adjust to the new demographics. The Vermont Square area has, for reasons we explore later, been ground zero for the more interethnic organizing efforts of groups like the Community Coalition. For a glimpse of these places, see figures 2.6, 2.7, and 2.8.

Figure 2.6. Slauson Swap Meet, Vermont Square Neighborhood
Photo Credit: Walter Thompson-Hernández, USC CSII project team.

Figure 2.7. Pee Wee's Liquor Market, Vermont Square Neighborhood
Photo Credit: Walter Thompson-Hernández, USC CSII project team.

Figure 2.8. Blue/A Line Train, Watts
Photo Credit: Walter Thompson-Hernández, USC CSII project team.

In what follows, we make occasional references to these three neighborhoods to tease out some nuances in the mega-neighborhood that is South L.A. and to provide better context for the neighborhood-based interviews discussed in chapters 3 and 4. In doing both that and offering an overall picture of South L.A., we draw from a variety of data sources. The crux of this quantitative analysis focuses on changes in demographics, so we rely heavily the U.S. Census Bureau—including historical data from the decennial census for earlier decades and summary data from the 2012–2016 American Community Survey (ACS) for the current period. We also analyzed ACS microdata, using a pooled 2012–16 version available from the Integrated Public Use Microdata Series.[63] This allowed us to provide neighborhood and sub-neighborhood data broken down by more detailed demographic characteristics like nativity.[64] With a bit of work, we were even able to estimate legal status, helping provide a sense of the experience of the undocumented population.[65]

Demographic Change over Time

The most striking trend in recent decades in South L.A. has been the overall growth of the Latino population. About 80 percent African American in 1970, this was "Black space" not only in its cultural importance to Black Southern Californians but also in its very demographic composition. By 2010, however, South L.A. was 64 percent Latino, and by 2016, it was about two-thirds Latino.[66] As we see later, it still remains a sort of iconic location for Black Angelenos but increasingly, it is self-defined by its residents as "Black and Brown" space.

The demographic transformation has been geographically uneven. As seen in figures 2.9 and 2.10, Latinos have been moving into South L.A. from the north and east, where there are other established Latino communities (e.g., Pico-Union, East L.A., etc.). Neighborhoods that had a sizable Latino population—like the Central Avenue neighborhood, which was already 45 percent Latino in 1980—are now overwhelming Latino. But even some neighborhoods with relatively small Latino populations a few decades ago—like Vermont Square/Vermont-Slauson and Watts—are now majority Latino. As noted early, among our three areas of study, the share of the Latino population in Watts grew the most, increasing from 15 percent in 1980 to 70 percent in 2010, and 74 percent in the 2012–2016 period (recall figure 2.5).

The demographic shifts in South L.A. are partly a function of countywide trends. Between 1980 and 2016, L.A. County's Latino population more than doubled while its Black population declined by 15 percent (and its already-small, non-Hispanic white population fell by about a third).[67] While the boom of manufacturing jobs in Los Angeles brought a large Black population into South L.A. and helped to establish a healthy Black middle and working class, nearly 150,000 Black residents left the South L.A. area over the 1980s and 1990s, as deindustrialization and disinvestment, coupled with rising crime and over-policing, helped push residents away (see figure 2.11). As a result, the countywide Black population became more dispersed. In 1980, nearly half (47 percent) of African Americans in L.A. County lived in South L.A. whereas in 2016, about 28 percent of the county's Black population did.

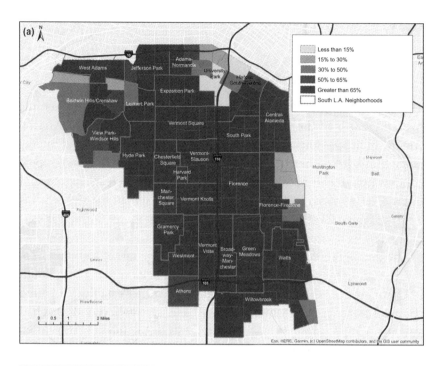

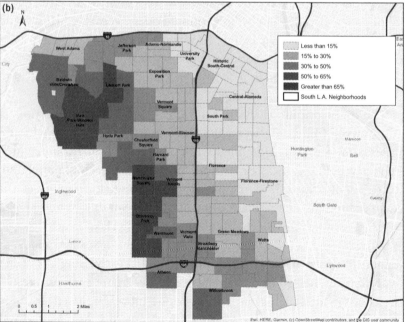

Figure 2.9. Map of Percentage Non-Hispanic African American by Census Tract,
(a) 1970 and (b) 2012–16

Source: Created by USC CSII project team with data from U.S. Census Bureau, Geolytics Inc,
Census TIGER/Line, and ESRI.

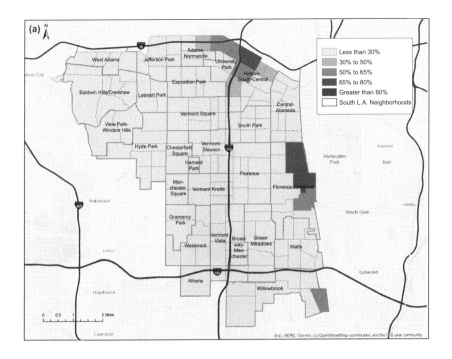

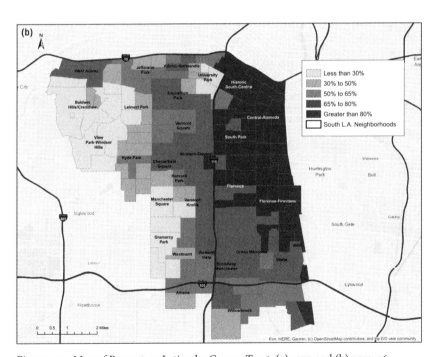

Figure 2.10. Map of Percentage Latino by Census Tract, (a) 1970 and (b) 2012–16
Source: Created by USC CSII project team with data from U.S. Census Bureau, Geolytics Inc,
Census TIGER/Line, and ESRI.

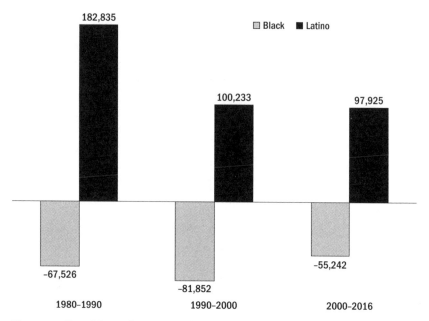

Figure 2.11. Decadal Population Growth by Race/Ethnicity, South L.A., 1980–2016
Source: U.S. Census Bureau, Geolytics Inc.

Despite the dispersal, it is important to realize the asymmetry of Black and Latino experiences. While Latinos now make up the majority of the population in South L.A., the Latino community is not concentrated in South L.A. in the same way as is the African American community: about 11 percent of the county's Latinos live in South L.A., up from 7 percent in 1980 but still well below the 28 percent share of L.A. County African Americans who live in South L.A. As such, South L.A. still serves as an important political and economic anchoring space for the region's Black population but is less of a prominent geographic feature in the Latino "imaginary" of Los Angeles than, say, Boyle Heights or even new suburban locations like the San Fernando Valley.[68]

Another sort of asymmetry is at play, as well: in general, Black residents in Los Angeles are more likely to run into Latinos in their daily life than vice versa. Exposure indices—which measure the likelihood of encountering a person of another group in a neighborhood based on the concentration of those groups—are quite different for African Americans and Latinos: the exposure of African Americans to Latinos has been on a steady rise in Los Angeles (quadrupling between 1970 and 2000) while the exposure of Latinos to African Americans barely moved over that period.[69] Essentially, many Latinos have been moving into Black neighborhoods, but few African Americans have been moving into areas with high concentrations of Latinos. This means that African Americans, particularly civic leaders, have to think about services for and alliances with Latinos while Latino residents and leaders in traditionally Latino areas, such as East Los Angeles, often have the relative luxury of not having to think about Black–Latino relations.

As the Black population declined in South L.A. and with international migration on the rise—in the 1970s and 1980s, roughly a quarter of the new immigrants to the United States settled in Los Angeles County—the area's immigrant population grew. The share of the population in South L.A. that is foreign-born doubled from 18 percent in 1980 to 35 percent in the 2012–2016 period. In absolute terms, the number of immigrants in the neighborhood increased 161 percent, exceeding the countywide rate of 109 percent. The increase was particularly acute in two of our focus neighborhoods: while the Central Avenue area saw just over a doubling of its immigrant population between 1980 and 2016 (because much of that change occurred in the 1970s), Watts's immigrant population grew 439 percent and Vermont Square's grew 291 percent over that period. In recent decades, the foreign-born population has stabilized, a phenomenon typical of all of Los Angeles; overall, South L.A.'s immigrant population increased by a scant 5 percent between 2000 and 2016.[70] The slowing growth suggests a key fact: Latino residents are now firmly entrenched.

Figure 2.12 shows the nativity of South L.A. residents and, for those who are foreign-born, how long they have lived in the United States. As can be seen, over the past two decades, the proportion of recent arrivals—immigrants who have been in the United States less than ten years—has declined while the share of those living in the country twenty-one and more years has increased substantially (from less than 1 percent of the total population in 1980 to nearly a fifth by 2016). A related data point: Just over half of Latinos in South L.A. in 2016 were born in the United States. Among Latino immigrants in South L.A., well over half (57 percent) have been in the country for at least twenty years.

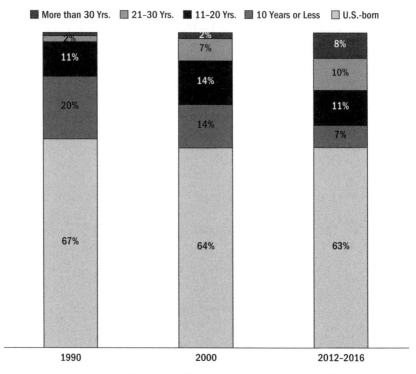

Figure 2.12. Population by Nativity and Years in the United States, South L.A., 1990, 2000, and 2012–16

Source: U.S. Census Bureau, Geolytics Inc.

South L.A.'s Latino population is more diverse than that of the county. For example, between 1990 and 2016, the number of Latinos identifying with Central American heritage (both immigrants and their children) in South L.A. increased by about 80 percent, compared to an increase of about 50 percent countywide while the increase in those identifying with Mexican lineage increased by about the same amount (approximately 40 percent) in both South L.A. and the county over the same period. Figure 2.13 compares the diversity in South L.A.'s Latino population with that of the county over the past quarter century. As can be seen, in 1990, about three-quarters of the county's Latinos were of Mexican origin, a figure that was the same in 2016. On the other hand, in South L.A., Central Americans not only made up a larger share of Latinos in 1990, but that share grew over the past two decades. So only

70 percent of South L.A. Latinos are of Mexican descent, while Central Americans now make up more than a quarter (27 percent) of the area's Latino population.

We noted earlier that when civil wars and other political violence ravaged Guatemala and El Salvador in the late 1970s and 1980s, large numbers of Central Americans fled to Los Angeles, initially settling in neighborhoods like Westlake and Pico-Union. As the county's Central American population became more established and those areas became increasingly overcrowded, residents started moving into South L.A. Figure 2.14 illustrates how that played out geographically: when we examine growth trends for Central Americans in our three areas of focus, Vermont Square—located due south of Pico-Union—has a higher concentration of Central Americans than Watts and Central Avenue. About 80 percent of Latinos in Watts and Central Avenue are Mexican, while in Vermont Square only half are Mexican and a full 45 percent are Central American.

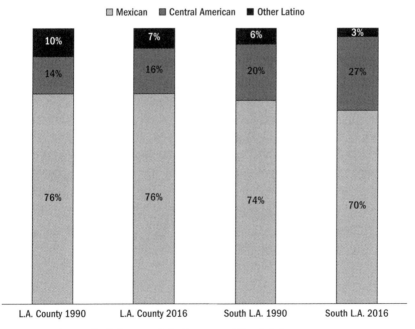

Figure 2.13. Latinos by Subgroup, L.A. County and South L.A.
Source: U.S. Census Bureau, Geolytics Inc.

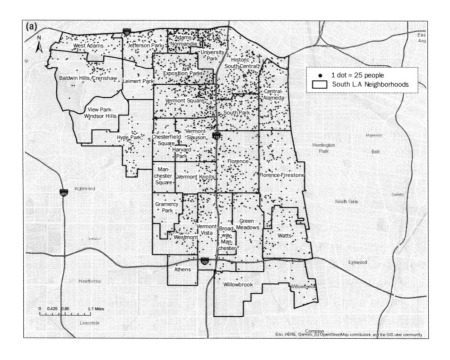

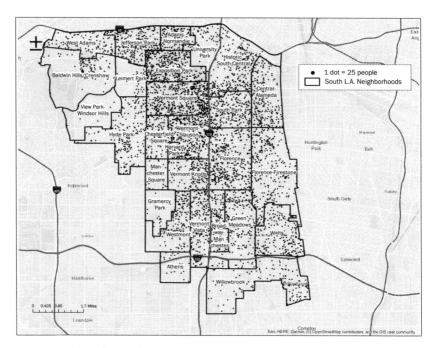

Figure 2.14. Map of Central Americans in South L.A., (a) 1990 and (b) 2012–2016
Source: Created by USC CSII project team with data from U.S. Census Bureau, Geolytics Inc.,
Census TIGER/Line, and ESRI.

Perhaps the most dramatic shift has been in the youth population: between 1980 and 2016, the Black population under the age of eighteen in South L.A. actually fell by two-thirds while the Latino youth population grew by 170 percent (see figure 2.15). Equally dramatic is the impact on schools as illustrated in figure 2.16: while every one of the eight major public high schools in South L.A. were majority Black in 1981—with six being more than 90 percent Black in their student body composition—by 2016, only two of these high schools were majority Black, and four of the eight were more than 80 percent Latino. It is little wonder that the schools emerged as both an early site of conflict and contestation and then, later on, as part of the soil for forming a more common identity between Black and Brown youth of South L.A. (a topic we explore in chapter 4).

Contestation in the schools has been about more than demographic change, *per se*, but such change has complicated the terrain. Damien M. Schnyder has written of the broader structural forces disrupting the education of Black students in Los Angeles, including policies like those that

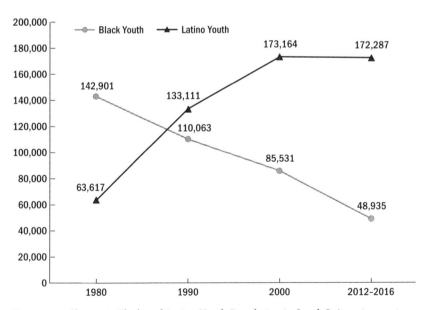

Figure 2.15. Change in Black and Latino Youth Population in South L.A., 1980–2016
Source: U.S. Census Bureau, Geolytics Inc.

Figure 2.16. Demographic Composition of Schools in South L.A., (a) 1981 and (b) 2016

Source: California Department of Education, Enrollment by School.

Note: AAPI = Asian American/Pacific Islander.

criminalize truancy and leave teenagers owing hundreds of dollars in tickets—the beginning of the school-to-prison pipeline.[71] As we note in chapter 6, the growing Latino population has led schools to redirect services and even the default language for communication to fit the majority; this has led some Black parents to feel disengaged with the education system, something local community organizers have sought to address. This is a challenge in other arenas of daily life as well. A Latino employee at Fred Roberts park, for example, bemoaned the fact that there are few African American kids in the programmed activities and asked, "Where are the activities for the Black kids? It seems like all are for Latinos." Meanwhile, with poor educational outcomes common, the charter movement has had an appeal to some residents; in 2008, a report called "The State of South LA" noted that "[s]ixteen of the 51 charter elementary schools in LA County are in South LA" and that they enrolled more Black students than Latino students, helping explain one part of the pattern shown in figure 2.16.[72]

Putting Down Roots

As the Latino community has grown and become more established in South L.A., it has also put down roots in the neighborhood—mainly through buying homes, building families, and raising the children that helped to shift the school population. While homeownership rates are lower in South L.A. than the county, rates for Latinos have increased over the past few decades. Figure 2.17 shows homeownership rates in South L.A. for Latino and Black households from 1980 to the present, comparing against the county. In 1980, when Latinos were just under a quarter of South L.A.'s population, their homeownership rate was 22 percent. By 2016, that rate was 32 percent, with surprisingly little difference between the homeownership rates for U.S.-born and immigrant Latinos (see figure 2.17).[73]

The most significant increase in homeownership for Latinos occurred in the 1990s, following the surge in the Latino population in South L.A. Black homeownership remained relatively constant over the past few decades until the foreclosure crisis and the 2008 economic downturn severely clipped Black homeownership. While Black and Latino homeownership in South L.A. is a topic that merits an entire book, it is important to note that the interviews of Latino immigrant residents

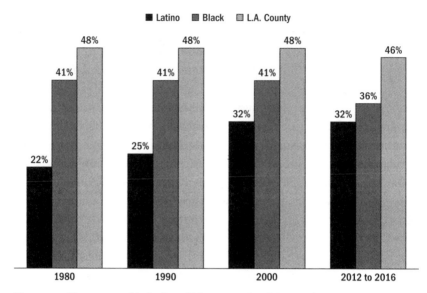

Figure 2.17. Homeownership by Race/Ethnicity in South L.A. and L.A. County, 1980–2016
Source: U.S. Census Bureau, Geolytics Inc.

who came to South L.A. in the 1980s and 1990s suggest that they were attracted precisely because this was the only area in L.A. where they could afford to buy a house. This speaks to the systematic devaluation, stigma, and capital divestment accruing in historically African American neighborhoods; as geographers Bledsoe and Wright note, anti-Blackness often paves the way for spatial realignments such as gentrification, urban renewal projects, community displacement, and mass incarceration—and in this case, for Latino working-class immigrants to buy affordable homes.[74]

As can be seen, many African Americans still own homes in South L.A., but the significant decline in Black homeownership in the last period depicted in figure 2.17 was partly because the region's Latinos and African Americans had high incidences of predatory lending and so had higher foreclosure rates than their white counterparts.[75] This is a nationwide trend, and in 2019, Black homeownership fell to the lowest point since 1968.[76] Historian Keeanga-Yamahtta Taylor argues that it is not redlining or exclusion that account for this loss but, rather, systematic predatory inclusion and financial exploitation of African Americans by lending institutions that explain this trend.[77]

The fact that Latino homeownership remained stable over this period is interesting, and we do not have direct evidence to explain why, although perhaps immigrant households may have been gathering multiple families together to sustain payments during the crisis while younger Black homeowners may have had more financial strains and less access to this strategy even as older Black homeowners have been more tempted by recent gentrification pressures to sell and move away. One Black resident shared her views on this trend as follows:

> I think we're pushing ourselves out . . . we lived on a street that was all Black, all Black homeowners. And you know, when the parent died the children sold the house and moved on . . . if your momma leaves you something, you're gonna try to hold on to that. . . . [T]hat's a legacy your mom and dad worked for so why would you give it to someone else?

The difference in the homeownership patterns can be complicated with a look at length of ownership: basically, Black homeowners are more long-settled in South L.A. than in the county while Latino homeowners in South L.A. are more recent arrivals to the real estate market than their co-ethnic counterparts countywide. Figure 2.18 shows that, for example, 38 percent of Latino homeowners have been in their homes for less than ten years and another 33 percent have been homeowners in South L.A. for between ten and nineteen years. Flipping to the African American pattern, 44 percent of Black homeowners in South L.A. have been in their homes for thirty years or more, much higher than for the county as a whole. In general, African American homeowners are aging in place: to further illustrate this point, the median age for Black homeowners in South L.A. (sixty-four years old) is higher than that of Latino homeowners (fifty years old), an ethnic age gap in homeownership that is twice that of the rest of the county.

Aside from being younger, Latino households in South L.A. have different structures: they are more likely to be multigenerational and, of course, far more likely to be mixed status (i.e., to include household

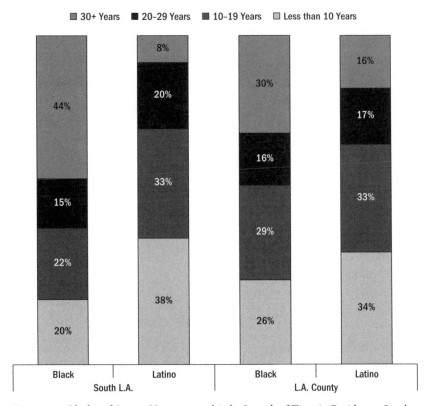

Figure 2.18. Black and Latino Homeownership by Length of Time in Residence, South L.A. and L.A. County, 2012–16
Source: CSII analysis of 2012–2016 pooled IPUMS data.

members that are undocumented or noncitizen immigrants, as well as U.S. citizens). More than three-quarters of Latino households have more than one generation living together—14 percent having three or more generations.[78] Comparatively, only 40 percent of South L.A.'s Black households are multigenerational, with about 6 percent having three or more generations, living together under the same roof. Latino households are also mixed in another sense: The overwhelming majority (94 percent) of Latino youth in South L.A. are U.S.-born, and of these, nearly 80 percent are second generation—they are native-born, with at least one immigrant parent. Furthermore, slightly more than

half of all Latino youth in South L.A. live with at least one undocumented parent, and the vast majority (91 percent) of those youth are
U.S.-born.[79]

The pattern hints at an important feature in South L.A.: the lack of
legal status is a key feature of the Latino community. While about 18
percent of all Latino adults in the rest of Los Angeles County are undocumented, one-third of Latino adults (and about 45 percent of foreign-
born Latino adults) in South L.A. are in that immigration limbo.[80] This
creates many issues with regard to economic advancement, but the
question here is why South L.A. has become host to such a significant
unauthorized population. One factor might be simple network effects,
particularly for Central American immigrants. But another factor may
be the nature of policing in this part of Los Angeles.

Much writing on immigrant integration has, in recent years, been
about deportation and its consequences.[81] Given the generalized uptick in deportations during our time in the field in 2014–15 (this was
the period when the Obama administration was breaking historical
records for removals), we were anticipating this to surface as a major
concern and were struck by the relative lack of verbalized deportation
fears from our Latino respondents.[82] Why so little focus by residents
on this issue? We return to this issue in chapter 6, but it is important to note that there is a long-standing order followed by the LAPD
that prohibits officers from stopping residents to query about their
immigration status.[83] But in addition, there is also a long-standing
pattern of policing being targeted at Black people, and that may lead
to a sense of Latinos being under the policing radar, particularly in
South L.A.[84]

Indeed, a law enforcement official interviewed as part of this project reported that his meetings with African American community
members were often filled with complaints of mistreatment of young
Black males; by contrast, meetings with Latino community members
tended to include complaints about slow response times and desires
for a stronger police presence. Of course, younger Latino respondents
also reported feeling harassed by the police, and frustration about over-
policing was a point of unity with younger Black residents. In any case,
we do not have enough data to suggest what all the reasons are that a

high share of undocumented is not matched by a high level of fear of deportation and think that this merits further research and study.

Settling versus Succeeding

While Latinos in South L.A. may be long-settled, they are not integrating by other measures—particularly measures associated with economic progress. For one, Latinos in South L.A. have lower rates of English-language acquisition than their counterparts countywide: only 43 percent of Latino immigrants speak English at least "well" compared to 52 percent in the county. The rates of such English ability for Latino immigrants also varies by local geography: 43 percent of Latino immigrants speak English at least "well" in Vermont Square, but the figure declines to 41 percent in Watts and 37 percent in our most heavily Latino sub-neighborhood, Central Avenue. Of course, lower English-language acquisition does not discount the rootedness of the Latino population, but it has implications for engaging with English-speaking neighbors, for political participation, and for economic progress.

Moreover, South L.A. is one of the most low-income areas of Los Angeles County. In 2012–16, the overall poverty rate for South L.A. was 33 percent, nearly double that of the county (18 percent). Figure 2.19 shows not only that median incomes for South L.A.'s Latino and Black households have been low and stagnant and well below the county median over the past few decades but also that the median Latino household income is higher than that of Black counterparts. At the same time, Latino households are larger than Black households: the average household size for Latinos in South L.A. is 4.1 people, whereas it is 2.1 for African Americans, with Watts having the largest household sizes for both groups of our three focus neighborhoods. Partly because of these household size differences, poverty rates for Latinos in South L.A.—which are partly a function of family size—are slightly higher than for their Black neighbors: in 2012–16, 34 percent of Latinos were in poverty compared to 31 percent of African Americans.

But while Latinos and African Americans in South L.A. both face challenges to economic success, these challenges are often manifested in different forms, especially because of a difference in participation (or not) in the labor force. For African Americans, unemployment is a major barrier.

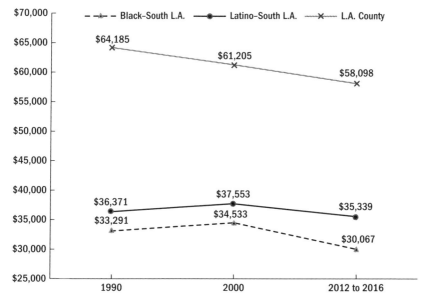

Figure 2.19. Black and Latino Median Household Income (2016 $), South L.A., 1990–2016
Source: U.S. Census Bureau, Geolytics Inc.

As figure 2.20 illustrates, between 2012 and 2016, the unemployment rate for Latinos in South L.A. was 9.6 percent, quite close to the county average of about 9 percent, and has actually been on the decline since 1990. For African Americans in South L.A., that rate was nearly 19 percent, and this is the result of a steady climb over the past three decades. Since high unemployment rates can discourage people from entering or reentering the workforce, another difference can be seen in labor force participation rates: between 2012 and 2016, the rate for African Americans was 52 percent compared to 66 percent for Latinos.[85] There is also significant variation in labor force participation rates by gender—while Black men and women in South L.A. have similar rates (53 percent and 51 percent, respectively), the rate for Latino men (77 percent) is substantially higher than that for Latina women (54 percent).

In any case, what the data suggest is that for Latinos, working poverty is a more salient issue than unemployment. Defining those in working poverty as full-time workers between the ages of twenty-five and sixty-

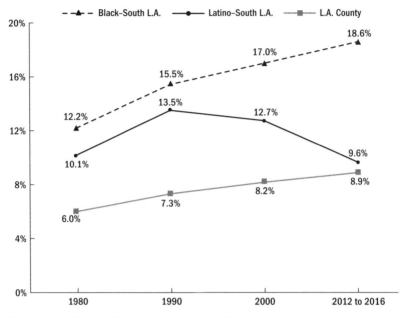

Figure 2.20. Black and Latino Unemployment Rates, South L.A., 1980–2016
Source: U.S. Census Bureau, Geolytics Inc.
Note: A person is unemployed if they are in the labor force and currently looking for work. The unemployment rate is the share of unemployed persons out of the total labor force (the sum of those currently employed and those unemployed).

four living at or below 150 percent of the federal poverty level, figure 2.21 shows that 32 percent of Latino full-time workers in South L.A. are in working poverty, almost triple the rate for African Americans. Differences in earnings help explain this: the median wage for a Black year-round full-time worker from South L.A. is $19 an hour versus $11 an hour for a similar Latino worker from South L.A. One could think this was a function of age: the median African American full-time worker in South L.A. is six years older than a Latino full-time worker, and wages do rise with experience. But this does not explain away the wage differences: figure 2.22 shows that the median wage for Latinos hovers around $11 an hour across all age groups, while it steadily increases for African Americans with age.

Educational attainment explains part of the challenge. Of working-age Latino immigrants (i.e., people aged twenty-five to sixty-four), 66

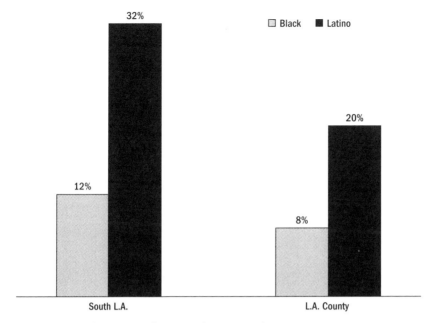

Figure 2.21. Working Poverty by Race/Ethnicity, South L.A., 2012–16
Source: CSII analysis of 2012–2016 pooled IPUMS data.
Note: Working poverty is defined here as the share of full-time workers between the ages of twenty-five and sixty-four living at or below 150 percent of the federal poverty level. A full-time worker works at least fifty weeks in a year for at least thirty-five hours a week.

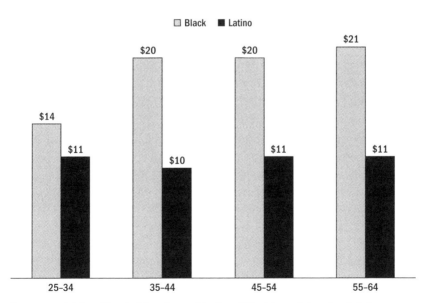

Figure 2.22. Median Hourly Wage (2016 $) by Race/Ethnicity and Age, South L.A., 2012–16
Source: CSII analysis of 2012–2016 pooled IPUMS data.
Note: Wages are reported for full-time workers between the ages of twenty-five and sixty-four. A full-time worker works at least fifty weeks in a year for at least thirty-five hours a week.

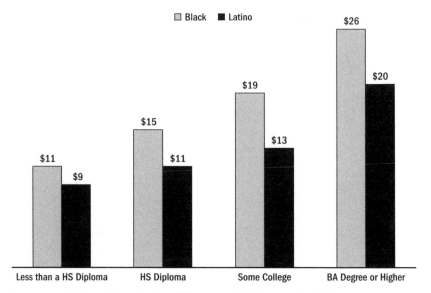

Figure 2.23. Median Wages by Race/Ethnicity and Education, South L.A., 2012–16
Source: CSII analysis of 2012–16 pooled IPUMS data.
Note: Wages are reported for full-time workers between the ages of twenty-five and sixty-four.
A full-time worker works at least fifty weeks in a year for at least thirty-five hours a week.

percent have less than a high school diploma, compared to just 24 percent of U.S.-born Latinos, and only 14 percent of African Americans in that same age bracket (see figure 2.23). The combination of uncertain legal status and low education make economic progress difficult—and the fact that Latinos, particularly immigrants, may stay in the labor market even when wages are low and conditions are poor, adds to a narrative of economic competition between groups, a factor that can stress relations between groups (as we will see in the complaints we report in chapter 6 from African American residents about Latinos taking jobs, particularly the service jobs that can serve as entry-level positions for Black youth).

Beyond the Numbers

Always a mecca for new migrants, South L.A. has seen a dramatic shift over the decades from a largely white area (albeit always racially mixed in parts) to a largely African American and now a largely Latino mega-neighborhood. This last shift has been particularly dramatic, but it has also been uneven: the east side of South L.A. (which was actually the heart of "South Central") has shifted the fastest and the most, while the west side has been better able to retain Black residents. As a result, understanding the current panorama of identity and homemaking in South L.A. means that we need to understand neighborhood details as well as group-level breakdowns by ancestry, time of arrival, and other factors.

This chapter has tried to do that in a quantitative fashion, highlighting the influx of immigrants (especially Central Americans), the dramatic shifts in the youth population, and the higher-than-average share of undocumented individuals and mixed-status families. We have also stressed how Latinos have been sinking roots in South L.A.: having children, forming families, and moving strongly toward higher rates of homeownership. There are also key challenges: Latinos are disproportionately represented in the working poor, suggesting both persistent issues with education and pay but also leading to some degree of friction with a local African American population far more likely to be experiencing joblessness. And the data suggest a broad range of phenomena—immigrants with limited English abilities, rapidly changing high school populations, and other factors—that can make it difficult to glimpse common ground between Black and Brown in a new and constantly changing home.

Finding such commonalities can also be challenging because the data also reveal what one can also detect in interviews and in writings by commentators like Erin Aubrey Kaplan: a sense of loss and "erasure" by Black Angelenos as South L.A. has gone through this demographic transition. While we explore this more in chapter 6, this is not a phenomenon limited to South L.A.; in another community that has experienced a dramatic transformation from being historically African American to predominantly Latino, East Palo Alto, Tomás Jiménez writes about how Black respondents report a "diminished visibility of black identity . . . resulting, in part, from the presence of a large and poor Latino population that had become the material and symbolic focal point of the city."[86]

As for Latinos, an older generation of immigrants arrived in a period of relatively high crime, a fact that also led them to shy away from many of their Black neighbors as they sought to seal themselves and their children from the persistent gang and police violence already impacting the Black community. While this economic and social distress could have a point of commonality—both groups needed economic stability and neighborhood stability—it was also fodder for division, particularly given the anti-Black attitudes many immigrants brought with them. Yet a generation into the change, we find a large share of young people in South L.A. working to define home together and build the sort of Black–Brown political unity that can, they hope, address both joblessness *and* working poverty, incarceration *and* deportation, long-term disinvestment *and* emerging pressures of gentrification.

Of course, little of this nuance on generational divides and community commonality shows up directly in the numbers collected by the Census—and to understand what is really happening on the ground requires going to the ground. As a result, part of this research project involved the deployment of a group of qualitative researchers to capture the lived experience of Latinos in South L.A., conducting one hundred formal interviews with Latino residents and supplementing those with a smaller number of interviews with civic leaders and African American residents as well as an extensive round of observations and interviews in public parks and urban gardens. Although we occasionally return to the quantitative data to illustrate a point, the rest of the book largely draws on those interviews. And it is to those stories and those voices that we now turn.

3

Echando Raíces, Settling In

PIERRETTE HONDAGNEU-SOTELO AND VERONICA MONTES

When immigrants move to a new place, how do they make themselves "at home"? How do they come to feel as though they belong, that they are attached to a new place? This is not something that simply happens on its own, and it is not always (or in our case) primarily a matter of integration into whiteness or some generic Americanness, with a mandatory shedding of linguistic and cultural substance to approximate metrics similar to the U.S.-born white mainstream.

Rather, homemaking—coming to feel that you belong and are attached to a new place—is an active practice involving transformations of the self and the landscapes that immigrants are newly occupying. We think the lens of homemaking is powerful in explaining this process, partly because it offers an agency-centered perspective that forces us to see immigrants as subjects shaping their own destiny. And because this is about not just encounter but transformation, it is important to understand the context in which this process of homemaking occurs.

As sociologists Angela S. Garcia and Leah Schmalzbauer note, "engaging the complexities of the physical and demographic characteristics of places" is critical to understanding immigrant integration.[1] In the United States, the homemaking process always involves race and new racial negotiations. And in the neighborhoods we examine, immigrant homemaking involves a process of relational racialization whereby Latino immigrants gradually overcame their anti-Black prejudices and learned to see the humanity of their African American neighbors.[2]

As legions of feminist scholars have shown, domestic homemaking and social reproduction involve work. And the process of immigrants making new homes similarly requires constant effort.[3] Drawing principally from the theoretical work of Italian sociologist Paolo Boccagni, but also from the work produced by anthropologists, geographers, and sociologists working in Italy, England, the Netherlands, Canada, and the United States, this chapter looks at how Latino immigrants made new homes for themselves in historically African American areas of South Los Angeles.[4]

We are specifically looking at the "first generation" of arrivals, Mexicans and Central Americans that came to South L.A. in the 1980s and 1990s; in the following chapter, we look at the second generation, the children of these newcomers who were either born or grew up in South L.A. Time, as well as place, plays an important role in shaping both of their stories. For example, when Latino immigrants began entering the historically Black urban areas of South L.A. in the 1980s and 1990s, those communities were reeling from the aftermath of deindustrialization, with rampant poverty, joblessness, a crack-cocaine crisis, and violence from both street gangs and police. Wariness was the norm.

Yet it is also important to acknowledge that Latino immigrants entered this urban context not as blank slates, but after being raised in Latin American nations embedded with strong ideologies of European supremacy, colorism, and anti-Black and anti-indigenous racism. Anti-blackness cultivated in their countries of origin by national narratives and media stereotypes, as well as by prejudices conveyed by migrants returning from the United States, and buttressed by U.S. color lines, shaped Latino immigrants' initial and mostly negative views of new neighbors.[5] Additionally, linguistic barriers between English-speaking African American residents and monolingual Spanish-speaking Mexican and Central Americans also widened social distance. "*Nos saludamos no más.* . . . We just greet one another," many people said, describing their cordial but superficial relations with African American neighbors.

Digging deeper into the narratives of how Latino immigrants made new lives for themselves in South L.A., however, we heard an interesting set of complexities. On the negative side, we heard testimonials of traumatizing assaults and theft at the hands of African Americans, usually young men. And sometimes in the same breath, we heard heartfelt declarations of gratitude to elderly African Americans for having offered critical support and guidance, especially in the realm of Black parental mentorship. Age and gender inflected these racialized stories, with Latino immigrants most often recalling Black male youth as threatening assailants and evoking Black adults and elderly folks as hospitable neighbors.

While newcomer Latino immigrants responded with both the negative and positive perceptions of African American reception—which we call perceptions of Black threat and Black embrace—over time, they experienced daily institutionalized interactions with Black people.[6] Their experiences and personal trajectories varied, but Latino interviewees ultimately articulated feelings of empathy, solidarity, respect, and gratitude toward Black neighbors. And, importantly, as we show in this chapter, Latino immigrants gradually formed new outlooks and relationships with their African American neighbors.

Of course, the context changed over time as well. The Latino families who arrived in the 1980s almost all said something like "We were the only Latino family on the block," or "My daughter was the only *Hispana* in her classroom. The rest were Black." Over the years, this changed, and even in the same family, an older sibling might have attended a school where the student body was nearly 100 percent African American, but by the time a younger sibling passed through the same school, she found herself in an increasingly Latino school milieu (as was evident by the school transformation data shared in chapter 2). As the African American population diminished due to joblessness, incarceration, and outmigration, more Mexican and Central Americans settled in South L.A.

Consequently, the second wave of Latino immigrants, who arrived in 2000 or afterward, had a different set of experiences. Unlike the Latino immigrants who arrived between the 1970s and the late 1990s, these new immigrants encountered South L.A. neighborhoods where the number of Latino residents outweighed African Americans and where Latino culture, at least in terms of storefronts and street life, had a strong presence. Scholars have typically framed these neighborhood transitions as ethnic succession, with the new group replacing the old one. Yet this frame does not fully fit the story here because even as the actual number of African American residents decreased, African American people and culture remain prominent in South L.A. The long-standing presence of Black cultural institutions continues to have a presence and an impact on shaping Latino life.

Every place and context where home is made is unique, just as every immigrant group has its own particular social characteristics, and within any group, we can find a myriad of individual idiosyncrasies and preferences. Throughout this analysis, we seek to emphasize the broad patterns defining first-generation Latino immigrant experiences while respecting individual inflections of difference, including the divergent experiences for those who made their homes in our three focus neighborhoods: Watts, Historic South Central, and Vermont Square. We organize our analysis along four distinctive arenas of this homemaking process: establishing security, achieving familiarity, securing control/autonomy, and experiencing a sense of future-making.[7]

A methodological consideration before moving on: how representative is this sample of the underlying Latino population in the three focus neighborhoods? As we detail in the appendix, the answer is comforting: the gender and employment mix of our interview sample is consistent with the underlying population. The age distribution is different but in ways that were part of a sample design in which we were trying to pull strongly from Latinos who arrived in the first wave and those who grew up as a second generation in South L.A. We do find that our sample is somewhat overeducated compared to the population, an issue that impacts the second generation more than the first generation discussed here, and we raise that issue when we focus on that latter generation in the following chapter.

Becoming Secure

Arriving at the home of Señora Zandrita Castro, a retired garment worker and seamstress, homemaker, and now an active grandmother, the first author found herself standing on the sidewalk, where a substantial iron fence and locked gate blocked her from knocking on the door or ringing a doorbell. Across the street and behind a similar fence, three Chihuahuas unleashed a yapping chorus of rage, disturbed by her presence and by a man walking by with a pit bull. This was not unusual. As we went around South L.A. to conduct interviews in people's homes, this would be a familiar occurrence: standing on the sidewalk wondering how to get past the iron fence and a double-locked gate. In this instance, Señora Castro's tawny-skinned eleven-year-old granddaughter eventually came out to open the gate.

Zandrita Castro and her husband Saul had come to Los Angeles from El Salvador in the 1970s. They initially lived in a cramped apartment downtown, where she worked as a *costurera* (in garment assembly) and he as a mechanic, and in 1984, after saving money by renting a room to relatives, they were able to purchase a three-bedroom, 1,100-square-foot house near Western Avenue for their growing family. Owning their own family home was a dream come true, but as soon as they moved in, the nightmare began: living across the street from a crack house. "*Teniamos miedo de salir.* . . . We were afraid to go out," she said. Crack-cocaine customers drove by and parked in front at all hours of the night, running in and out to get merchandise from the drug dealer. "*Se parqueaban los carros.* . . . They parked cars right here on the street, and they wouldn't let people pass by. And one had to put up with it, because if not, they would shoot you." She clarified, so as to leave no doubt: these were Black people and they scared her:

> *No, no tenia amistades.* . . . No, I didn't have friends, because as I said, there were only Black people living here. And just one Mexican woman over there. But no, I didn't go out. I was scared. Even in the living room . . . when they looked in I thought they might come in through the window.

The interview occurred in her cozy backyard patio, outfitted with comfortable chairs, a hammock, and shade structure. Things were now calmer in the neighborhood, but she vividly described surviving a litany of assaults and theft: having a gold chain yanked right off her neck while she was walking back from the market, home burglaries, and the threat of assault. She implicated Black people in all these offenses. Moreover, she claimed African American teachers had treated her children unfairly, that Black mothers at the school had shunned her because of her lupus butterfly marks on her face, and she blamed a Black hospital technician for her loss of a late-term baby. As we spoke about the past, she portrayed African American people as hostile and dangerous threats to her well-being. Unlike what is now common in many white liberal American sectors of society, she did not use the language of color-blind racism to soften her narrative.[8]

In her home, she had felt the need to shut off from a world filled with risk. We conversed on the patio, near a backyard cinder-block wall and just below the patio roof where her husband had erected a tall impassable metal shield. No one, not even a small child, could crawl through that remaining sliver of space. When asked, "Did the house already have fences and bars on the windows when you moved in?" she said:

No, mi esposo las puso. . . . No, my husband put them on. And even so, when we went to celebrate our silver anniversary they [burglars] got in through the front door. Because out in front there were some young men smoking marijuana, and I don't know, when my son left, they entered and they robbed us of everything. Everything. The money that we had saved for my silver wedding anniversary, the rings, all of the gold, all of the money. My husband had brought a little money from El Salvador. That was gone too.

The small property is now fenced and fortified on all sides, and she reported that a pit bull lives next door. "*Ya después. . . .* Later my husband put in an alarm system," she added, "and there's more precaution. So now, *gracias a Dios,* we're now better." With the fences, locks, gates, an alarm system, the neighbor's guard dog, and the impermeable metal shield in the back, she now feels safe in her home.

While she spoke bluntly about her experiences and perceptions of Black threat, toward the end of our conversation, when probed about how her relations with African American neighbors have changed over the years, her face lit up when she revealed this: she has an African American son-in-law. At first, this had been difficult to accept. When she first learned of her daughter's love for him, she said, "I cried for three days." Today, she absolutely adores this man, and together with her husband, daughter, and grandchild, they form a three-generation household. "*El me quiere mucho. . . .* He loves me a lot and I love him a lot. He's a really good person." The son-in-law has even learned enough Spanish to politely greet her friends, and she said, "He even calls me 'mom.' He's always very attentive to me . . ." But what has filled her life with meaning and given her the deepest sense of love, security, and protection is her granddaughter, who counts both Salvadoran and Black heritage:

> *Porque esa niña es. . . .* Because that girl is someone, and it's because of her that I am alive. Look, that girl is so affectionate with me. She sleeps with me. . . . And if I am sick, *mamí,* she brings me my image of Jesus' heart, and she puts it on my breast, or beneath my pillow. "*Mamí, mamí . . .* this is so you'll take care, *mamí.*" Whenever I am sick, she's there.

As figure 3.1 shows, fences and locks remain, as do many of her unreflective, knee-jerk, prejudiced ways of speaking about Black people, but an

Figure 3.1. Heavy metal fences and gates surround many residential dwellings in South L.A., Vermont Square neighborhood.
Photo Credit: Walter Thompson-Hernández, University of South California (USC) Center for the Study of Immigrant Integration (CSII) project team.

African American son-in-law and granddaughter are now in the house and in her heart. In this instance, we see the paradox of an older Latina woman clinging to racist anti-Black narratives and memories, but fully embracing and appreciating the daily practice of intimate private life together with the Black people she loves.

Home as Haven

Home has been described as a haven or a nest, a special place where people can feel secure enough for relaxation, intimacy, and social and physical restoration. Security is essential, and Boccagni reminds us, home requires "a sense of personal protection and integrity which is attached to a place of one's own, where outsiders should not have free access."[9] Other migration scholars have elaborated on other critical features such as ontological security, food security, and the ways in which transnational circuits may enhance socioeconomic security, and feminist scholars remind us of the threats of gendered, domestic violence that may lurk inside homes and families. These are important aspects of immigrant home security, but in this section, we are primarily concerned with the nitty-gritty of the physical and material security of homes and the people in a context of neighborhood violence. Making new homes in South Los Angeles required Latino immigrants to expend continual efforts and creativity to safeguard against threats and vulnerabilities. Fences and gates are part of the story.

In East Los Angeles, one also sees many front yards enclosed with fences, but there the fences define and invite social interaction. As the urban planner James Rojas compellingly argues, the fences of East L.A. define the front yard as "a place for personal expression and for creating tradition Mexican housing forms," in effect, moving the threshold from the front door to the sidewalk, and simultaneously extending the footprint of the house to the yard.[10] Residents use the yards for fixing cars, socializing, or just hanging out on the driveway or porch. The fences, he says, allow the homes to become "an extroverted form that sets the stage for the enacted environment."[11] Fences may be shaped by cultural legacy too, he suggests, as these replicate some of the interior, personalized outdoor spaces found in Mexican and Spanish homes with courtyards.[12]

The fences of East L.A. may open homes to the street, but in South L.A., the fences and gates shut homes and residents off from others. When Latino immigrants came to South L.A. during the postindustrialization crisis and chaos of the 1980s and 1990s, as gang violence, crack cocaine, poverty and joblessness reigned, the material security of homes became very important. Their strategy of survival and homemaking was to "shut in and shut out." As the previous example suggests, there are temporal, gendered, and spatial aspects to this. This section shows how achieving material security was a fundamental step in Latino homemaking in South Los Angeles. This was not a onetime thing event but required ongoing maintenance.

The fortification of these modest-sized homes came about in this context of the 1980s and 1990s. Fences, gates, multiple double-bolt locks and chains, and, in some instances, porch cages—elaborate iron contraptions wrapping around a porch, were installed so that a home could be closed off from intruders. Many people in the first wave of Mexican and Central Americans who came to South L.A. in the 1980s and 1990s still recalled meticulous details and, even decades later, expressed a kind of trauma about incidents of street violence or home robbery they had witnessed or experienced. Being trapped in the crossfire between rival gangs armed in the street with machetes and guns. Being held up at a bus stop by an assailant holding a broken bottle to the throat, while innocent bystanders just stood around, not coming forward to help. Seeing a youth shot to death right in front of the house. Latino newcomers were not prepared for these scenarios, and an aura of trauma lingered in some of their narratives. Even a woman who had lived through militarized civil war in El Salvador said, "*Nunca en mi vida*. . . . Never in my life had I seen anything like this in my country."

The Warmth of Other Neighbors

Other respondents narrated a different story, one which involved finding a welcoming Black embrace and hospitable neighbors. A few blocks away from the Castro home lives another Central American family who also bought a house here in the same era, the 1980s. Zoila and Ricardo Carrillo moved here from the Lincoln Heights neighborhood on the Eastside, because this was the only L.A. neighborhood where they could afford to buy a house. They quickly put up fences and gates, but Señora Carrillo described these as one of many sorts of home improvements, and she spoke with more equanimity about her perception of Black threat:

> *Mira*. . . . Look, there were good things and bad things. At the time we bought our house we were practically the only Latino family on the block. And two houses down lived a Mexican man and an *Americana*, that's it. Everyone else was Black. But the majority who lived here were older people, and they were very nice. We never had any problem with a Black neighbor.

Although she had received significant help from African American teachers and mentors for her children, "magnified moments" of Black embrace for which she was grateful, she too agreed that back then, she and her family "were afraid to go out."[13] Like the Castro family, they drove to another part of town for church services or to visit parks. And in some ways, she said, the arrival of more Latinos added new problems to the neighborhood, such as loud parties, graffiti, and *cholo* gangs. Like several other respondents, she maintained that back then, her elderly African American neighbors had welcomed them, while African American youth on the street represented a threat to her family's safety. While she felt gratitude to the Black teachers and mentors who had helped her children, her major complaint about African American neighbors from that era of the 1980s and 1990s was that they had let their houses and yards go untended:

> *La comunidad* . . . The community started to change when Latinos arrived, and sometimes there were problems, more noise. The only thing is that when Blacks lived here, the yards were neglected. They would park on the lawn. Now that doesn't happen and the properties have been fixed up. They've been re-stuccoed, windows replaced, new cement—it's changed the look.

When they purchased their house, it was, as she put it, "*bastante arruinadita* . . . very run down.*" But "my husband fixed it up. We changed the wood. We fixed it up little by little until we made it pretty." While the homes of African Americans in the neighborhood were run down, she said, Latinos got in there and fixed their houses up. When asked to explain why, she said, "Perhaps because there's more money, I don't know. Or maybe the Latino works and likes to fix things. And as these were older [African American] people who lived here, that's possibly why they didn't fix things up." But even as there are racial tinges to her characterization, she also did not reduce the phenomenon to a Black/Latino binary, but rather, she reflected with empathy on similarities and limitations of her current life-course stage. In this regard, she now saw herself implicated too: "And now that we too are older we realize that it's no longer the same as when we were younger and first got our house, and we lifted up the cement. Now that we're older, we don't have the same strength."[14]

While she did not cite African Americans as a source of danger, she and her husband had also felt a level of fear and uncertainty. "*Bueno.* . . . Well, I think basically you feel insecurity because it's another kind of people, another race. Perhaps unconsciously you always feel fear. Be-

Figure 3.2. Many homes such as this one in Watts feature well-tended gardens with fruit trees and roses, and it is also common to see heavy bars barricading the windows. Photo Credit: Pierrette Hondagneu-Sotelo, USC CSII project team.

cause when we first arrived, the first thing we did was put up a fence. Why? I don't know, but one does it." Home maintenance and home security are related, as seen in figure 3.2. Living in a well-maintained house where the faucets don't leak and the paint isn't peeling gives a sense of security, well-being, and protection. Unlike building a fence, however, home maintenance requires more or less continual effort and resources, and homeowners are more likely to expend resources on this than renters. As we noted in chapter 2, increases in homeownership have been a key feature of the Latino experience—and literally of the experience of homemaking—over the past few decades in South L.A.[15]

Safety and Policing

One might think that Latino families who moved to South Los Angeles would just call the police when victimized by a home burglary or street assault. But Latino respondents could not rely on the police, who they perceived as slow, ineffective, and unreliable. While a few of the older respondents complained about over-policing—a more common complaint from their sons and daughters who are the subject of chapter 4—these first-generation immigrants were more commonly concerned about under-policing. They did not say they wanted to see more police, but they experienced a lack of supportive police protection and perceived that the police were not here to protect them. In this context, Mexican, Guatemalan, and Salvadoran immigrants living in South Los Angeles took things into their own hands and resorted to self-defense. Sometimes, they armed themselves with rifles and machetes to protect their families and their belongings.

Julio Ortega, an energetic Guatemalan jeweler who always dressed in a dapper fashion, and his Mexican wife, Demitria, now ill and retired from various service jobs, had bought two houses for their family in Watts. The first one they lost to the bank when he was unemployed and missed payments, but he rationalized the loss by saying that he never liked that house anyway. That site was very dangerous, situated next to one of the three local housing projects. The current house sat on a quiet street with good neighbors, both African American and Latino families, and the Ortega home had been lovingly outfitted with matching furniture sets and graduation photos inside, and, outside, a decorative fence, statuary, and tropical fruit trees. One night at 2 a.m., Julio Ortega heard one of the dogs barking. He discovered two men breaking into his garage to steal a gas-powered lawnmower and weed-eater, so he ran out in his underwear armed with a machete. "*Eran dos morenos. . . .* They were two Black men. They were ready to lift it into their truck, but I took the machines away from them. I don't know where this courage and anger came from," he said. "*Pero nunca me he dejado de nadie. . . .* But I've never let myself be taken by anyone."

Women were prepared with armed responses too. Mirta Palomares, a stocky, jovial, yet quietly self-assured sixty-one-year-old Mexican woman and retired forklift driver, had moved from East L.A. to Watts when she and her husband found an affordable house here. Three generations lived in the home, and Mirta loved living in Watts. She kept a plot at the Stanford Avalon Community Garden, boarded her horse in Compton, enjoyed seeing the grandchildren run around the house and yard, and cheerfully fixed her own plumbing, proudly showing a photo in which she held a wrench with a grandchild strapped to her back. She walked "*a gusto*" (at ease) in the streets, by the railroad tracks, and to the *marketas*. But recently, she said, an intruder entered her home and she had handled it on her own, with a rifle:

> *Ahora es cuando he tenido problemas.* . . . Now is when I had problems, as the other day an individual got into our house. And I had never been scared before this, and it was just a few days ago. I had gone out to throw away the trash, and I heard the dogs barking, so I fed them. I went back inside, but I didn't check towards the right. I started undressing to bathe, when I hear my daughter say, "*Mami*, do you want to go out for a smoke?" Once we were on the porch, we realized someone had entered. . . . I felt like something got stuck in my throat—really, I'm not sure what I felt, but yes, I felt a little scared. . . . I don't know how, but I finally found my voice. It was like I was in a dream. I couldn't yell, but finally I found my voice and I started yelling thousands of cuss words. But the first thing I did, I said to my daughter, "Bring my rifle."

She found the stranger just sitting inside her house. As soon as she screamed and held up the rifle, he fled. Was this a hot prowl burglary or simply a confused, unhinged intruder? "I don't know what he wanted to steal," she admitted, but after he was gone, she did call the police. "They responded quickly, but they did nothing. They said they would go around the block to see what they could see." This was nothing new. "It's rare to find police who work," she said. "We once had a very good police here, only unfortunately, she made some mistakes, and now she's been in jail for three years [for drug use]. But when she was here, no one stole anything here." For now, Mirta Palomares would be keeping her rifle.

Watts resident Julio Ortega had gone a step farther. Besides just calling the police, he had contacted his local city council representative about conditions on Avalon, a boulevard located around the block from him in Watts, where open prostitution and drug deals occurred at a bus stop in front of a liquor store. "You go there at the bus stop, and you can't stand there because of the *malandro* hustlers that are there." He continued:

> If you call the police, the police do nothing. I went with [others to speak with] Councilman Buscaino, and he did nothing. Now with whom can I

go, who can we complain to about this? We already went with the principals. What we want to do now is get a group together to speak with [Mayor] Garcetti. Because in reality, they don't do anything here. It's the only problem we have.

Señor Ortega will try again with city authorities, but his efforts thus far seem to have fallen on deaf ears. And his experience may help explain why even Latino residents who do get involved in civic engagement wind up being dissuaded and discouraged, a topic we explore in chapter 6. He said, "*Se nota cuando alguien te escucha. . . .* You can tell when someone listens. Once they hear you, they will act. But this was one year ago. There's not been any change. There's been no change, but yes, I pay my taxes."

Avoiding Problems

Latino newcomers used other security strategies for personal and physical safety on the street. Some avoided public transportation. Everyone tried to stay observant on the street. One couple said they kept single dollar bills ready for panhandlers, most or all of whom were Black in their neighborhood. Knowing how to distinguish different micro-zones of the neighborhoods in South L.A. was probably the most-cited safety strategy. Everyone agreed that things were no longer as dangerous and violent as two decades ago. One man said, "*Ha estado tranquilo. . . .* It's been calm. You hear gun shots over here, once in a while over there, but it's no longer like it once was, when you heard a lot of gunfire." In the Historic South Central neighborhood, Pablo Segura declared that unlike years ago, it was now possible to be out on the street until 10 p.m., safe and without threats of assault.

People also used narrative rationalizations to keep themselves feeling safe and secure in areas of violence and vulnerability. They blamed the media for sensationalizing and exaggerating violence in South L.A., and they reminded themselves (and our interview team) that violence occurs elsewhere too, in poor *colonias* in Mexico and even in the poshest, upper-class neighborhoods of Southern California. For example, years ago, Rodrigo Torres had been assaulted in his home by two African American men with pistols, his wife had her gold chain ripped off her neck while walking to the *marketa*, and his father, now deceased, had been held up at gunpoint. Yet he thought life here was safe enough, in part because of his frame of reference:

> *Sabes una cosa?* . . . You know something? I never thought about these things in racial terms. I come from a poor barrio, *a colonia* in Juarez. So [here] I did not see myself in a *barrio* full of criminals.

He also underscored that some of the most brutal murders in Los Angeles had happened not in South L.A., but in upscale Westside suburban areas. "*Yo siempre pongo un ejemplo* . . . I always give an example. The OJ matter was not in South Central, and the Melendez brothers who murdered their parents were in Pacific Palisades. So, what then? Are people supposed to leave Pacific Palisades? No. Clearly not."

When asked if he had ever thought of leaving, he answered decisively. "*No, porque todo es cuestión económica.* No, because it's all an economic question. . . . And I feel the news media exaggerates many things and creates panic where there is no need . . . the majority of people live without being assaulted." He continued:

> *Lo que pasa es que la gente dice.* . . . What happens is people say, "Oh, going to South Central is about all fear, no?" That's the first thing they say. But really, there are good areas and bad areas, so you cannot say all of South Central is abysmal—because it has its good sides too.

What's Different Now

All our interviewees agreed that safety and security had improved during the last fifteen or twenty years. Official crime reports also substantiate these perceptions; for example, as noted in chapter 1, the number of homicides in the City of Los Angeles dropped from 845 in 1994 to 260 in 2014.[16] This means Latino immigrants who came to South L.A. around 2000 or afterward found safer, calmer city streets. Some of them had still experienced assault or theft, but the frequency of these instances diminished. The neighborhoods they moved into also now included more Latino residents and fewer African American neighbors, leading to a different sense of cultural comfort as well.

Demographically, post-2000 Latino immigrant newcomers were different from earlier cohorts of Latino immigrant arrivals. This second wave tended to include more people who were undocumented or in mixed-status families. And because of the challenge of living with illegality, they suffered more economic precarity. Some of them had job trajectories derailed by the economic recession of 2007. The majority of this second wave came to South L.A. to rent apartments, not for home-ownership, and homeownership did not seem to be on their horizon.

Moreover, unlike the earlier wave, who had arrived directly from the border or from nearby Latino neighborhoods in downtown, Pico-Union, and the Eastside, the later wave came from a myriad of places, including out-of-state locales, or more distant suburban or exurban places where they had experienced racial hostility from predominantly white populations. Having experienced a white racial threat elsewhere made South L.A., with its mix of African Americans and Latinos, more appealing. Finally, in this later wave of Latino arrivals, we see women out in the public sphere more than in the earlier phase. For all these reasons, the domestic "shut in and shut out" security strategy was less common for this later arriving cohort of Latino immigrant newcomers to South L.A.

Black Embrace and the First Generation

So how did the first-generation Latino immigrants begin to break out of their own earlier Latino ethnic bubbles? While a few people reported little to no contact with African Americans, others reported finding a welcoming Black embrace, enacted through routine institutionalized interactions with African American neighbors and coworkers. For example, Maria Larios, an animated and very involved mother in her late thirties, came to South L.A. after having lived in two other neighborhoods: mixed race but predominantly white Van Nuys in the San Fernando Valley and the Mexican American mecca, East L.A. She claimed that in neither of those places had she found the compassion, conviviality, and emotional support that she had found in South L.A., in a Black church, where now she counts the congregation members among her dearest friends.

Maria Larios and her husband, a carpenter, were both jobless during the Great Recession, which hit the construction sector particularly hard.

They needed assistance to feed the family, and a Latina friend told her about a Black church that gave food donations. She began going there for free food, but then she began volunteering so that she could then access more food and spend less time waiting in line. This instrumental action led to conviviality and solidarity, as she eventually became a member of a beloved, tightly knit African American group of friends. She explained it this way:

> *Cuando el perdió* . . . When he lost his [construction] job, we were at zero. What do we do? Where do we go for food? That was the very first time I had ever spoken with a *moreno* [a Black person], directly like that, talking about things—my English is now more fluid. And we started going there for food, to a Black church. We went to ask for food, and we were in line waiting . . . and that day they needed volunteers. If you work inside as a volunteer, they give you a little more food . . .

This predominantly Black Christian church included a few other Latinos too, like the Latino deacon, who, she said, is married to an African American woman. For two years now, she has been attending services at this church, volunteering, and simultaneously enjoying conviviality and ongoing emotionally supportive relations with African American friends.

Fatima Serrano, also in her thirties, similarly came to South L.A. around the same time, 2010. She had lived with her husband and two sons in the California desert cities of Indio and Hemet, and while she liked the peace and quiet out in the country, job opportunities were slim. And on top of that, she and her family suffered arbitrary racist harassment from the police in those desert areas. By contrast, she said, she immediately felt "at home" in South L.A., which she experienced as free of police hostility.[17] Food, too, was her entry point to connecting with Black people, in this instance, first at an Afro-Belizean restaurant where she worked as a waitress. At the restaurant, she got to know Afro-Belizean police officers, and when her truck routinely broke down on the freeway, they regularly offered help. After her marriage to her Mexican husband fell part, she partnered with her new companion, an Afro-Belizean hip-hop artist. Whether for safety, access to jobs, or educational resources, we found that Latinos in South L.A. did not report reliance on transnational sources of support. Rather, they sought out help locally, and sometimes this fostered and strengthened new connections with African Americans.[18]

Gaining Familiarity

The prior section examined security at home, and the safety of physical bodies—security from arbitrary police harassment matched by worries about police neglect, home burglaries, physical assaults, and robberies on the street, as well as relief from hunger and the security provided by moments of Black embrace. But knowing how to stay safe also meant understanding the micro-geography of South L.A. Based on previous interactions, interviewees knew which streets and scenes to pursue or avoid. The production of "familiarity" informed these mappings—and in the immigrant homemaking process, there is a symbiotic relation between security and familiarity.

So how do people go from being routed by structural forces to a locale to actually feeling rooted in a new place? This aspect of home-making involves routine and time. "Rootedness implies being at home in an unselfconscious way," says the geographer Yi Fu Tuan, and he suggests this develops after a "long habitation at one locality."[19] It involves acquiring both routines and knowledge of place. Sociologists Kusenbach and Paulsen, commenting on the significance of quotidian domestic routines, observe that familiarity "emerges through the repetition of home-based routines such as sleeping, relaxing, cooking and eating, grooming, cleaning and so on, which comprise daily life."[20] And they suggest also, the ways in which these processes induce emotional attachments, as "[r]epetition and routine generate memory and anticipation."[21] And Boccagni reminds us that familiarity also requires developing a "cognitive . . . orientation in space, stability, routine, continuity and even permanence."[22] And, most important, this takes time.

Knowing Place

Familiarity with a place develops over time, and it includes cognitive knowledge of both the dwelling and the nearby neighborhood. This means getting familiar with both positive and negative aspects of place.[23]

We can easily see how this dovetails with practices of security. As noted earlier, in South L.A. respondents cited a continuum of micro-zones of safety and danger in the neighborhood. They traverse freely at some of these places, while other areas require that they walk with caution or avoid altogether. Similarly, we can think of the domicile as a place where one may negotiate how to escape domestic violence, sexual assault, or even an ill-tempered sibling while figuring out where the restorative spots and activities are located. All of that requires routine familiarity, gained over time.

Learning how to avoid dangerous spots in the neighborhood and negotiating safe routes of transit is an important part of the familiarity process in South L.A. Watts resident Julio Ortega, the Guatemalan jeweler who had defended his property with a machete in the middle of the night, complained about ongoing problems with a spot around the block. On Avalon, there were calm areas in front of Pentecostal churches, residences, and burger joints, but at a nearby bus stop, there was open prostitution and drug dealing. Now that he is familiar with the scene, he has figured out how to avoid face-to-face conflict or harassment there. He said, "*Si me dieron ganas. . . .* If I felt like going for a coffee and a donut, I go in the car, that's how I go there. On foot, you cannot, because there are people there and just seeing them makes you fearful." He has developed a safety strategy, but it has required realizing regular, familiar patterns of neighborhood life (and, in this case, having access to a car).

Parents teach these routes to kids. As adults get familiar with the local neighborhood, they issue directives to their children and teens. Avoid Martin Luther King Park. Walk here, not there. Do not go out alone past 8 p.m. Macrino Gutierrez, a forty-five-year-old father of three, emphasized these sorts of lessons to his teens. "*Les decia a mis hijas. . . .* I would tell my daughters, when you are walking in the street, don't just look, but observe. Always observe. . . . Observe your surroundings. Do not just go along walking and looking, but you must observe the actions of those around you." These are strong directives, but after a while, people learn to live according to these informal rules, which grow out of daily routines and experiences of place. The rules of place—where one may go, how, and when—eventually become naturalized. Familiarity helps breed a sense of safety.

Figure 3.3. Latino family members feel love and connection with one another and with their homes and the neighborhoods of South L.A.
Photo Credit: Walter Thompson-Hernández, USC CSII project team.

Getting rooted and familiar with a place also means learning about welcoming and restorative spots and developing routines there. This is the positive, affective aspect of familiarity. By experiencing predictable routines, one starts to feel there is stable ground, producing a sense of ontological security.[24] The accumulation of these routines, domestic and scaled out into the larger neighborhood, leads to emotional texture and predictability of home and to the accumulation of memories rooted in the new home, both the domestic sphere and the extra-domestic neighborhood. This, too, deepens emotional attachments to place (see figure 3.3).

Familiarity also involves forming attachments to recognizable, welcoming places that resonate with homeland pasts. As Teresa Mares notes, food plays an important role in satiating immigrant longing for home.[25] This unfolds not only in the kitchen but also at food establishments and other services that help build an urban home environment. In South L.A., this now includes a thick commercial infrastructure of *carnicerias, panaderias, peluquerias* (butcher shops, bakeries, hair salons), and restaurants serving tacos, pupusas, and semitas. At all these places, and sometimes at Korean-owned liquor stores too, one can easily conduct all commercial transactions in Spanish. Taco trucks, ambulatory popsicle vendors shouting, "*Paletas!*" and Latino vendors selling produce out of trucks add to the ambiance. And it is not just the food but also the visual transformations of the buildings, with bright paint and signs in Spanish, the aroma of *carnitas*, and the interactions that lend a new legibility and familiarity.

This has grown over the last several decades, as has the Latino landscape of worship, including more Catholic churches and Latino Pentecostal storefront churches. Whereas the earlier-arriving Latino immigrants who came to South L.A. in the early 1980s often had to drive out for Mass or to buy tortillas, that is no longer the case. The nearby familiarity of these commercial and religious amenities and the entire enacted environment made people feel at home. As Señora Bertila Lunares confirmed, "I tell you, everything is close at hand here. If I don't have a gallon of milk, I run to the corner market and it doesn't close until 10 p.m. Here, at the other corner, if I'm hungry, they sell tacos." Giggling, she said, "It's here every day."

Making Place

Familiarity with the streets, and even casual familiarity with neighbors, also develops over time and creates this sense of rootedness. Julietta Martinez, a homeowner resident of Watts, said she felt comfortable here because of all the time and knowledge she had of the place now, which she found peaceful: "*Eso, los años que tenemos. . . .* That, all the years we have living here. The fact that we have lived quietly [*tranquilos*]. We haven't had problems with anyone. We know all the streets—not all the people on all the streets, but here on our block, we know all the people. They know us. We talk a lot with them, '*hola*,' '*hola*.' So we are tranquil. When people ask us why we live in Watts, we tell them that we live well." She had been assaulted on the corner once when they first moved here, but that was long ago. As she reasoned, "*Años atrás . . .* Years ago it was different here, but today everyone lives at ease in Watts."

As families hold parties, rites of passage, and collective neighborhood celebrations, they develop strong emotional attachments and positive memories. A forty-year-old Mexican immigrant mother in the historic Central Avenue neighborhood said:

> *Navidad es bien.* . . . Christmas is good, how shall I say, a good fiesta in this place. I have not gone elsewhere, so I cannot tell you what they do in East Los Angeles or things like that, but from what I can see, in our community, they are very devoted, strong believers. So in December, so these traditions aren't lost . . . some people always organize the dances, celebrations . . . *Las Posadas.* These are traditions people are trying to hold on to. And even my children like these.

Another Mexican mother in Watts echoed these sentiments and added that African American children are welcome at their celebrations. "*Pero como en las Posadas.* . . . Well, like in the Posadas [in the neighborhood]. If Black children come, or the little girls to the piñatas, they are welcome. We never say no. To eat, to grab some candy, to hit the piñata—all of it." Familiarity here is about inscribing and enacting Latino homeland traditions in the new place. And as underscored here, it also involves sharing and conviviality with African American neighbors.

The Martinezes, who had raised five children in Watts, now have several adult children who own houses nearby, and with the grandchildren coming over, they are echoing earlier child-rearing experiences and memories in the same house. But they also talked about their relationships with neighbors as part of this process. Neighborliness helped them build familiarity and a sense of security. When a neighbor's home alarm goes off, another neighbor comes to report, and together they go check it out. "*Entonces, esa es la cosa.* . . . So that's the thing, to live and *convivir* with people is really, really nice, and it's good for everyone." And Señora Martinez also admitted that now that she has learned some English, it is far easier for her to communicate with African American neighbors: "*Pues tal vez* . . . Well, maybe there were some difficulties at the beginning, but little by little, they became friendlier with us, because we have some English. That helps them. When you arrive here knowing some English, that makes it easier to relate to them [African Americans]."

Seeking Autonomy

Expressing autonomy, control, and freedom is a key aspect of home, and Latino immigrant residents of South L.A. conveyed strong satisfactions with this dimension of life here. Latino homeowners spoke enthusiastically about this, resonating with a strong cultural norm of homeownership in the United States and in the Western world more generally.[26] How much do the goal and pride of homeownership resonate with Mexican and Central American cultural norms? In Mexico, history, struggle, and national identity are bound up with access to *la tierra*, land, and with self-determination and independence from tyrants. The legacy and the imaginary of a *ranchito*, free from the hacienda lord, is a vivid one that still resonates in Mexico, even though that country is now primarily urban.

Many of the residents who moved to South L.A. were driven by their desires to buy a home and realize a new liberty, a dwelling with more elbow room, free from restrictions and arbitrariness of landlords. Buying a home was also about planning for the future, investing in property for security, stability, prosperity, and leaving something for their children. Nevertheless, even Latino renters spoke about South L.A. as providing sites for homes less encumbered by the restrictions and regulations than they had experienced elsewhere in Los Angeles.

In South L.A., the enforcement of city zoning and housing standards is lax, a problem typical of many low-income communities of color. But while this has its downsides, there are also some interesting possibilities. In neighborhoods like Watts, where there are lower population density and proximate unincorporated areas with relatively lax enforcement of zoning, people who wanted to use their house and yard spaces as they wished could feel freer to add backrooms to their house, turn up the music, or keep three dogs and maybe a few chickens. In this section, we examine how residents expressed control and autonomy in the realm of play, looking particularly at *fiestas* and family celebrations, and in the realm of work, as a number of Latino immigrants used their homes as sites of informal-sector income generation.

Privacy as Privilege

Expressions of control and autonomy at home are bound up with home privacy, a privilege that either goes unrecognized or is regularly denounced in this era of privatization of public goods and spaces. Critics of privatization make many important points, but they forget the flipside, which is this: privacy, for the individual and the family, can be a cherished relief when the broader economic and social system seems stacked against you and/or when economic circumstances have forced an unwanted "doubling up." Latino immigrants, both renters and homeowners, relished their newfound privacy and autonomy in their South L.A. homes.

Respondents spoke with frustration about the challenges they had previously faced while sharing crowded apartments or living in garages, dwellings that are not uncommon for Latino immigrants. For example, Maria Larios, a relative newcomer to South L.A., had previously lived in Van Nuys, Denver, East L.A., and El Paso, almost always in living quarters where her young family doubled up with relatives. She offered no romanticized rendition of collective sharing in these circumstances. Instead, she talked about relatives who imposed rules, constant surveillance, and many directives. "Living with family is always the same," she maintained. "[They say,] 'Your kid is crying. Don't touch that food in the refrigerator. Your child broke this.'" She had tired of those arrangements, and even worse were the logistics of eight or more people sharing a bathroom. Naturally, people wanted to avoid these problems. Maria Larios was now much happier renting an apartment in South L.A. with her partner and two sons.

Longtime homeowners in Watts, Julietta and Fernando Martinez recalled how much they had disliked being renters. They came to Watts with the goal of homeownership, which was about escaping the tyranny of landlords:

> *No queriamos* . . . We didn't want to continue renting. We wanted to have something, a house that was paid off, one where we didn't have to wait and report to the landlord, "*Señor*, the door is broken. Can you replace it?" One where the landlord arrives to say, "I'm going to need this place empty next month. And I'm giving 30 days to get out of here." So the two

of us worked, and discussing matters, we figured out a way we could do it and we got animated.

Space constraints do not allow for a discussion of home-buying strategies here, but it is worth noting that the Martinez family was able to buy their house by co-signing and co-living with Julietta's sister and brother-in-law. After purchasing their home, they shared homeownership and rented out rooms to two other families. So initially, four different families lived in four bedrooms. For them, buying a house and eventually having only their immediate nuclear family living there was a hard-won achievement.[27]

Family Fiestas

Celebrating *fiestas* to commemorate baptisms, birthdays, anniversaries, and rites of passage, such as the *quinceanieras* (sweet fifteens), are an important part of home life for many Latino families. An extensive array of *familia*, relatives from near and far, as well as friends, are typically invited. These can be quite elaborate, with an array of painstakingly prepared dishes, drinks, music, and sometimes, rented tables and chairs on the patio or driveway, and maybe even a hired DJ. Naturally, people like to enjoy their *fiestas* without outside interference or complaints. Respondents said this was one of the best things about home life in South L.A.: you can party, and you can play your music loud and late.

Julietta Martinez and her husband do not throw frequent parties, but with five young adult children, there are now numerous causes for celebration. In an animated cadence, she said, "*Y el día que tienes una fiesta.* . . . And the day you have a party, you have the music going until midnight, one, two, until three in the morning and no one says anything." She liked having parties without neighbors or the police trying to shut things down. And she reasonably conceded, "Sometimes it's their turn." Indeed, she was proud that "[n]o one says anything either. We understand that once in a while it's normal to make noise, that you have to enjoy yourself." Commenting on Black home-based wakes, she returned the favor of tolerance: "When they hold a funeral, there they are, one, two or three days, all day and all night. And we respect what happens. What else are we going do?"

Another woman was also enthusiastic about the freedom to hold parties in South L.A. "My daughters' *quinceanieras* went until 3, 3:30 or 4 in the morning. And the neighbors don't meddle because we invite them too. Here, when we've had our *fiestas*, the police have never come. They have never bothered us." Her husband concurred: "Here there's more freedom. One is freer, to do whatever. One is free to do what one wishes." And Josefa Paredes similarly relished these occasions: "If we're having a party, and there's a DJ, only until 12 a.m." Yet she conceded that sometimes, "[t]hey stay longer, and for example, the kids stay and sometimes among themselves, they make a racket [*es el escandalo*]. They stay outside, and they're laughing, '*ja ja ja*' but the neighbors put up with it. No one complains because they are making noise. That's the good thing about being here."

Home-Based Work

Latino residents in South L.A. creatively used their homes to generate income, enjoying the freedom to incorporate these activities either inside the dwelling, in a garage workshop or storage space, or on the driveway facing the sidewalk. In some respect, these activities harken back to the early twentieth century, when predominantly white residents in nearby South Gate, many of them migrants from the Midwest and rural areas, took to home-based animal tending, gardening, or car repairs to make money.[28]

In South L.A. today, Latino homeowners are engaged in a number of home-based work projects. Not everyone, of course, but here are a number of activities that some of our respondents did: informal mechanics performed on the driveway or garage, an elaborate jewelry workshop in the garage, vending of all sorts—including preparing tamales at home to sell on the street and informal swap meets selling used clothing and other items on the sidewalks in front of the house, babysitting other people's children, and home-based seamstress work of elaborate wedding dresses and *quinceañera* dresses, with industrial sewing machines set up in the living room. These are some of the ways in which people are using their dwellings and yards to fulfill economic needs.

Most of the customers and clients for these services were other Latinos but not entirely. One resident of Watts said that his Latino neighbor, who does informal mechanics on his driveway, often has African American customers. "*Ellos mismos . . .* They also benefit from that," he said, "because they don't have to go to any big mechanics shop to see about their car. They can just go around the corner, where there is someone who knows how to do these jobs, and sometimes they charge less." A Salvadoran woman who sets up an elaborate sidewalk swap meet, using her garage to store a huge amount of meticulously folded clothing, bedding, and other items told us that African American women are included among her buyers. Twice, our interview team saw Latino men leading ponies, one walking down the sidewalk adjacent to Ted Watkins Park in Watts and the other bathing his pony with a garden hose in front of his house near Central Avenue. We did not interview them, but imagined these men keeping small ponies in backyards so that they can earn money offering pony rides at birthday parties or park gatherings. Again, all these activities speak to the ability to mold home and yard life to accommodate economic necessity and to do so relatively free of restrictions and regulations.

Some people supplemented formal sector salary with these activities, while others pieced together various sources of home-based income. Arturo Medina had been laid off from his job as a sheet-metal worker, but he now relied on apartment rental income and a small business renting party chairs, tables, tents, and tarps, which he stored in his garage. He also does a little mechanics work in the driveway. "*Me mantengo trabajando. . . .* I support myself by working," he said. "It's now been since 2005 since I've had a steady job, with a salary, but I keep working. I have different sources of income." A Guatemalan woman, Isadora Anderson, who had raised her son while being a single mother, had managed to build two rental units onto her house, and she also owned another rental property in the neighborhood. She would soon be retiring from her job as an elder caregiver in Pacific Palisades, but she would be comfortable in her retirement, she said, with these sources of property-based income, two of which were built into her home.

Vivir Bien

A final illustration of the ways in which Latinos in South L.A. enjoy a degree of freedom and control at home is provided by Sra. Rosalinda

Guevara. She is an energetic sixty-ish Salvadoran, and after she and her Mexican husband lost their first Watts home in a short sale, they purchased another one just a few blocks away, at a very good price, $150,000 in 2001. At the time of the interview, they guessed that the three-bedroom house, with detached garage and ample yard, was now worth nearly three times as much (and it is likely worth more today given gentrification pressures we discuss in chapters 6 and 7). Since moving in fourteen years prior, they had made many improvements. They now owed less than $100,000 on the house, but since Rosalinda retired from her jobs in hotels and garment assembly, she needed to make some money. She did that out of the home, but she also focused on creating a special home environment.

First, there was the vibrant garden, with the assortment of plants that a mixed marriage of a *Salvadoreña* and a *Mexicano* would have—*nopales* and *chiles* for him, *chipilín* and *guayaba* for her, each plotted in "his" and "her" garden patches. More meticulously tended ornamentals and edibles adorned the yard, including avocado and citrus trees, ferns, tomatoes, and roses. As we toured the garden, several times she proudly mentioned how she had all by herself laid down the St. Augustine grass, which now wraps all the way around the house, installing little squares one bit at time until the runners took off. She also tends a little coop of chickens, feeding them grain every morning and showering them with vitamins and salad in the afternoon. In return for all this continual labor, she got seven eggs a day and a bounty of fresh fruits and vegetables.

But it was not just about the food, she said. It was the whole lifestyle of living well, *vivir bien*, which for her, hinged on homeownership:

> *Era mi ideal tener mi casa.* . . . It was my ideal to have my home, a place to live, to feel comfortable, a place to arrive and say, "Now I'm going to plant this, now I'm going to do that, now I'm going to cut that." Right? It's part of living well. It's not about having a lot of money—but rather, it's about working and living well. So that no one is telling you, "Now you have to do this, now you must do that."

She disliked living in apartments. "*Para vivir en apartamento.* . . . Living in an apartment is uncomfortable," she said. She grew up in a house in El

Salvador, and later during the civil war, when she and her first husband departed the country for Costa Rica, they had bought property there. Her two adult children still live in those houses.

Rosalinda and her current husband also used their Watts home to generate income. They set up a small trailer in the backyard, where a young couple and their baby, newly arrived from Tijuana, lived. Indoors, a small apartment had been crafted for a longstanding boarder and friend (they had rented to him in their last house, too). These renters provided income but she also described them as *como la familia*, or "like family." "Every Saturday and Sunday," she said, "I cook for everyone. And sometimes he cooks. Everyone together. And we come out here to eat." By taking in boarders, she is repeating a long tradition of immigrant women supplementing the household economy, and in the process, she is widening the home to community conviviality.

Another source of income came from her ongoing business of selling used clothing on her driveway. Daily, she unlocked and swung open the sturdy iron gate, and under a big canopy shade tent on the driveway, she sold dresses, pants, and other items here on the northern edge of Watts. Her garage, where we sat for the interview, was packed to the ceiling with the merchandise neatly folded and stockpiled in big plastic storage bags. But this was not without risk. One day she decided to close up shop early, around 3:30 p.m., and just minutes later, gunshots rang out and a young African American teenager, her next-door neighbor, was shot in front of her driveway. He managed to crawl to his front porch, where he died. The detectives later told her that, if she'd been out there, she too would have been killed. Since then, she and her husband do not linger on the sidewalk after 5 p.m.

Her home is a Shangri-La, a place where she can live well, earn money, eat home-grown tropical fruits and eggs, and affectionately coo to her teal-plumed rooster, "*Dónde estás, baby? . . .* Where are you baby? Come here, baby." But living here requires some extra precautions. And big iron gates and locks. "*Como en todas partes. . . .* Like everywhere," she reasoned, "there are risks, right? Not just in the South [of Los Angeles], not just here. In the north, and everywhere, there are risks."

Mi Ranchito

Scholars have discussed the significance of immigrant residents having the control and freedom to transform home décor and domestic material items in the home and researchers working in urban planning and landscape studies have emphasized how changing exterior housescapes reflect transnational, immigrant, and ethnic community influences and agency.[29] As Amos Rapoport notes, "it involves personalization, owned objects, and taking possession."[30]

But illustrations such as the example from Watts described earlier suggest nothing less than the *rancho-ification* of home in the inner city. This typically means a close connection with a plot of land, plants, and sometimes with some animals too. Not everyone engages in it, and significantly, it is not necessarily a nostalgia or reproduction of the homeland. For example, Rosalinda Guevara grew up in the city. She only learned about gardening and tending chickens in Watts, in part from her Mexican husband and their membership, for a time, to the community garden in Watts. To have a rancho is also an attitude, a kind of subjectivity. It is about feeling like you control a particular outdoor space of land where you can do what you wish and where your energies there will help sustain you.

For obvious reasons, it is mostly older folks, both men and women, who are engaged in the project of rancho-ification. Adults who are raising children and working at home and sometimes at multiple jobs are just too busy. It is also closely tied to homeownership, but it also takes root in more public, community places, as we will see in chapter 5, which covers the Stanford Avalon Community Garden in Watts. At the community gardens, an important project of placemaking and homemaking is created by Mexican and Central American men. And nearby, African American men are engaged in a similar project.

Exercising control over a home also involves fulfilling responsibilities. Homeowners feel especially beholden to place, in part because of duties and obligations of home maintenance, which are more or less endless. These are experienced as both burdensome and comforting. South L.A. homeowner Andres Durantes shared that after buying a house, he finally felt at ease. About his house, he said,

El hecho de que compras una casa. . . . The fact that you buy a house in a particular neighborhood or place, well you feel—at least speaking for myself and I think for others too who may have been here longer— you feel at ease. You then feel that sense of comfort, that feeling that this is my *barrio*, or this is my neighbor. And it's up to me to protect it. It's my turn to take care of it. It's my turn to clean. It's my turn to ensure that it looks good, because you feel that sentiment that now, this is mine.

Making a Future

Home is the place of dreams, hopes, and plans. It's a place to launch the children into the future. For homeowners, it's a place to build future equity and hope for prosperity. Those plans may or may not come true, but home is where these hope-making endeavors root. "Making home," as Sara Ahmed and colleagues state, "is about creating both pasts and futures through inhabiting the grounds of the present."[31]

For Latino immigrant families, it's about sacrificing so the kids can have a better future. Sociologist Robert C. Smith has called this the "immigrant bargain."[32] Second-generation youth must step up and try harder, *con ganas* (wholeheartedly, with vigor), because their parents have made sacrifices for them. Some youth may be reminded of this daily. But where does this unfold? Home. And as we will see in this section, raising children opens Latino immigrants in South L.A. to contact with their children's school, neighborhood friends, teachers, and possibly African American boyfriends and girlfriends, some of whom may become spouses and members of the family.

Of course, not everyone is raising children here. What does future-making mean for those who are childless or who have their children living in their country of origin or elsewhere? Not having children here means that in general, there is less contact with African Americans. As we see in the next section, one of the critical spheres of positive interactions that Latino immigrants reported was receiving child-rearing advice, support, and guidance from African Americans.

Black Parental Mentorship

Schools, libraries and interactions with neighbors and clerks provided the setting for encounters where African Americans offered educational support and guidance to Latino parents. One Salvadoran mother, Señora Carrillo, fondly recalled the African American senior citizens who volunteered to read to children at the local library. "*Ibamos tres veces* . . . we would go three times a week," she recalled. "Elderly grandparents, *morenos,* came to read to the children . . . as I didn't know the language, I couldn't teach the children, but they read to them in English. It was really lovely." This same Salvadoran mother said that every fall, she quarreled with the elementary school principal and the bilingual coordinator, insisting that they keep her daughters out of segregated bilingual classes, thereby ensuring her daughters would be immersed in English-only classes *and* learning side by side with Black children. We can think of this as an immigrant integration strategy that relied on closeness with and a unique appreciation of African American students, teachers, and volunteers.

African American neighbors also provided Latina immigrant parents, especially single mothers, with parental mentorship on acceptable forms of child discipline. As Mary Waters found in her study of West Indian immigrants, immigrant parents accustomed to spanking and hitting their children as a form of punishment and discipline are shocked when they learn that these practices are not fully accepted in the United States.[33] In South L.A., African American next-door neighbors helped translate the new rules to Latino immigrant parents, and sometimes, they also served as surrogate parents or grandparents too.

Salvadoreña Andrea Rosas was now elderly, a grandmother many times over, but she had been a single mother raising four children in the turmoil of the 1980s' Central Avenue neighborhood. When asked how she had managed, she fondly recalled an elderly African American man who had lived next door. "*Don Samuel,*" as she respectfully called him, had helped her by spending hours counseling her, giving advice on how to discipline children here and alerting her to the fact that here it was not permissible to beat your children. With self-deprecating laughter, and clutching her hands over her face, she recalled the despair with which she had greeted this news, chuckling, "*Ay por qué.* . . . Oh, why,

I wondered, had I even come to this country then?" Don Samuel, she concluded, had served as a key mentor to both she and her children. She plaintively declared: "*El era* . . . He was like a father to them. He was Black. He was elderly. How he loved my children." As a struggling single mother trying to make ends meet by selling at swap meets, she also fondly remembered an older African American woman who had worked at the local post office. The postal clerk always gave Andrea's children Christmas gifts, and she warned Andrea not to send her children to Jefferson High School at a time when there was a lot of violence and racial strife there. In these instances, elderly Black folks provided critical advice and orientation to this struggling single mother, serving as her cultural compass on key child-rearing decisions.

Another single mother, Guatemalan Isadora Anderson (née Sanchez), recalled the challenges she faced when her preadolescent son went through a rebellious phase, defying her authority, seeking out friendships with kids on the street who were involved with petty vandalism, and throwing rocks at buses. When she spanked him, he called the police on her and an officer had then advised her: "*Señora* . . . I do the same thing . . . but give it to him on his butt, because if he goes to school with bruises and marks, then we have to get involved." At ages thirteen and fourteen, her son became increasingly defiant, and at that point, an African American police officer stepped in and became a father figure to the boy. "*Me dijo la policía* . . . The police officer told me, 'I'm going to take charge of this matter, because he needs the strong hand of a man, the strength of a father.'" The police officer began coming around regularly, arriving in uniform, and telling her son to obey his mother and to do his household chores and his homework. She reported that her son initially resisted, but eventually, the police officer and the boy formed a friendship.

Single mothers also formed parenting bonds across racial lines. Latina single mothers who were working jobs, paying the bills, and raising children in the inner-city found that they shared similar struggles with African American single mothers, and sometimes their shared struggles transcended language barriers. While it was mostly women who reported these close shared parenting experiences, Julio Ortega described a relationship of mutual support when he took in an African American man who needed a place to stay. It started as just one or two nights, but the man, Jack Jones, became a boarder and eventually helped with child care when Julio drove his wife to her evening job at LAX airport.

"*El era* . . . He was as a little older than me," he said. "He helped me with the rent and with the food bill, and he also cared for my kids." "*Yo le di hogar* . . . I gave him a place to stay. He was from Louisiana. And me with my half English, he understood me. You can ask my wife. You can ask my son. He loved him a lot. We got along well." According to Julio, this contact was transformative for him: "*Y me empezó* . . . and he started telling me about South Central, about the gangs, about Black African Americans, OK? And then he would visit me here, and he always visited, but he died, the gentleman died. But from then on, with the neighbors, with Blacks, I get along well."

A more recent Latina newcomer to South L.A. was thirty-eight-year-old Maria Larios. At the African American Christian church, she now counted Wanda, Larry, Deb, and Sheila among her closest friends, and with them, she had thrown herself into volunteer work and simultaneously found a daily dose of multidimensional support. As a group, they went out to give sandwiches to the homeless people who sleep under freeway overpasses. Close up, "*con drogadictos* . . . with drug addicts, drunks and those that are on the street," Maria had learned understanding and empathy for the plight of the homeless, addicted people sleeping on the street.

This direct experience and advice from her new friends at the church were now helping her navigate a crisis with her eighteen-year-old drug-addicted daughter. Some of her new friends had experienced similar difficulties with their children, and one couple who was employed at the juvenile detention center had directed her to sobriety programs that would help her daughter, now that she was no longer a minor. "*Gracias a Dios*. . . . Thanks to God, I enrolled in that program, and those are things that would not have happened if I was not here [the Black church]." She reflected, "*A lo mejor* . . . it may be that a Latino doesn't help you the same way that a church or a Black person or a Christian does."

Indeed, as a strategy for having a better future, she told us that she has now advised her daughter to get a Black boyfriend. And she told her son that he should get a Black girlfriend too. For her, the Black embrace is one of regular, daily, institutional interactions and friendship and solidarity. The Black population has diminished in South L.A., but in a small

Christian church, she has found a niche for friendship, support, and a road to her future.

Futures Gone Awry

Not everyone finds a golden future in South L.A. Jesus Portillo had moved to Watts with his family during the 1980s, a decade of dangerous schools and streets. During that time, his nephew was kidnapped from middle school in Watts and held in an abandoned house for a week, part of a *cholo* gang recruitment strategy. Armed with a pistol, the boy's father took things into his own hands and rescued his son. Today, that boy, Jesus Portillo's nephew, is a college graduate, thanks to earning a generous scholarship.

Jesus's son was not so fortunate. He made many friends in school, including gang members. Jesus had tried desperately to get his son transferred to another school, pleading with the school administrators, but he failed. "*Hay que machetearla*," he had advised his kids, meaning "You have to whack away at your studies," like a machete, but they never studied or got good grades. "*El no era ganga, pero se juntaba a veces con ellos. . . .* He wasn't in a gang," Jesus said, "but he would get together with them sometimes . . . and the truth is, they killed him." The future didn't turn out as Jesus Portillo had planned, and neither Black threat nor Black embrace were part of his story. In spite of his sorrow and loss, he remains upbeat and is an active civic leader at the Stanford Avalon Community Garden. His daughter lives nearby, but she, too, is a disappointment, a "*vaga*," basically a slacker. Jesus now dreams of returning to his home state of Guerrero, Mexico, to cultivate land, but he has no real plan to make that happen.

Voices of ambivalence popped up among the first generation but only among some men—usually men who were property-less, undocumented, and missing family. For them, the homemaking project remained undone. Macrino Gutiérrez, a forty-five-year-old father of five, said that here, he only feels at home in nature, when he goes camping. As a resident of South L.A., he misses the daily post-workday camaraderie he had enjoyed with extended family and friends in Tijuana. Job insecurity and illegality hung like a cloud over this life here.

A twenty-five-year resident of Watts, Don Macario said, "*Estoy a gusto. . . .* I'm at ease here because I work steadily and I live tranquilly," but he, too, was undocumented, without family, and in fact, his job situation was not steady employment but a series of informal gigs carting vegetables from gardens to markets in his truck. He lived in a rented room, had no close family here, and he had been formally asked to leave the Stanford Avalon Community Garden, possibly due to excessive drinking. These voices of ambivalence and dissolution were a minority among our interviewees. More commonly, respondents declared an ardent love for South L.A., a deep sense of attachment to the people and the place, and a resilient faith in what good things the future might bring for them, their families, and the place they now called home.

Homemaking and Belonging in a Multiracial Community

Most Latino immigrants living in South L.A., from the early arrivals of the 1980s and the 1990s to the more recent newcomers of the millennium agree that they feel attached and "at home" in South L.A. Homemaking here has been a major achievement of their lives, one accomplished with heartache and headaches, family joy, and collaborations with others. Feelings of belonging and place attachment developed over time and were most strongly expressed by women, by homeowners, and by people who had raised children to adulthood here. Most of the first-generation Mexican and Central American immigrants who fit this profile said they feel rooted and attached to this place and to their home and family here.

> *De aquí no me voy.* . . . I am not leaving here . . . for more than half of my life, I've now lived here. I feel that it's my country. And then, well, my children are here. Me, with my children? It's everything. (Zandrita Castro)

> *Sí, me siento bien!* Yes, I feel good here! I couldn't live anywhere else. . . . It's my city. It's my house. I think we're going to die right here. (Zoila Carrillo)

> *Bueno, no soy de aquí.* . . . Well, I'm not from here, right, I've now made myself here. That is to say, this is mine, because I have spent more time here than in Guatemala. I now feel more from here in the north, than from there. (Julio Cesar Ortega)

Tengo mi familia. . . . I have my family, I have grandchildren, and now my father is buried here. . . . This city, these jobs gave me the power to support my family . . . this represents for me, a stage of stability, to own the first house. My nest. It's mine, although this is relative because I just refinanced. . . . But more than the land, it's as I say, my family. (Rodrigo Torres)

As for Black–Brown relations, the first wave of Latino immigrants generally had limited contact with African Americans, but when they did, they reported magnified moments of either positive intimacy (especially in the realm of child-rearing help) or of trauma (assaults, robbery). These were often fleeting and ephemeral encounters but, nevertheless, memorable and often life-changing interactions. And in both the earlier and later waves of Latino immigrants, there were some families who became more porous and open to nonfamilial outsiders, Black or Latino, and others who built not only fortified iron fences but also metaphorical fences that kept out all nonfamilial persons, Black or Latino, living in a family bubble. This was not a norm but rather one more indicator of how an important part of homemaking is feeling and enacting control over what you do at home and how you raise your children.

The later-arriving Latino immigrants, those who came around 2000 or later, arrived in South L.A. at a time when the African American population had diminished and the Latino population had increased. They found themselves living not only among more Latino neighbors but also amid thick Latino commercial infrastructure, with Spanish-language transactions available nearly everywhere. Crime, street violence, the crack epidemic, and racialized animosity had diminished after 2000, and while both Latinos and African Americans are still victimized by petty crimes and sometimes, assault, battery, and homicide, in general, a calmer street culture prevails.

Perhaps because of that—as well as simply the passage of time and the accumulation of encounters between neighbors—Latino contact with African American neighbors are today not confined to only fleeting magnified moments but now also involve more regular, sustained institutional contact. Sometimes this unfolds in schools, workplaces, or surprisingly—given what we know about religious segregation—

churches. And as we have seen, close relations form in the private sphere, such as among friends and family, and these are also enduring institutional encounters.

Indeed, the African American community has played a foundational role in Latino immigrant homemaking. Latino immigrant anti-Black prejudice remains, mostly expressed among the older first-generation immigrants, but even here it has been disrupted and modified by their homemaking encounters—and sometimes by their shared homemaking projects—with African Americans in South L.A. As we will see in the next chapter, the second-generation Latino youth and now young adults who were raised in South L.A. have had a different set of experiences than their parents. They think and act differently than their parents, and sometimes, they actively try to dislodge their parents' anti-Black prejudices.

4

Being Brown, Knowing Black

PIERRETTE HONDAGNEU-SOTELO AND
WALTER THOMPSON-HERNÁNDEZ

I grew up in South Central, so yes, I speak English, but I roll
my eyes. I have a neck roll, but I'm Brown.

How does the experience of growing up with Latino immigrant parents
in a Black inner-city neighborhood affect second-generation Latinos?
What we suggest here is that the tug between Latino immigrant parents
and culture in the home, and African American people and culture in
the schools and streets, and importantly, an awareness of how both are
seen by the larger society helps produce a unique Latino identity. And
while it would be inappropriate to ignore intergroup tensions, by and
large, second-generation Latinos appreciate living in a Black and Brown
neighborhood in South L.A.: this is their home, and they remain fiercely
proud of this place and how both Latino and Black cultures have formed
their unique identity.

Other scholars have taken up the question of Latino identity formation in the context of Black–Brown encounters, often with somewhat
different conclusions. Those working within the paradigm of segmented
assimilation have suggested that the ghetto and closeness to poor African Americans causes downward mobility for Latino youth, one that
is set in motion by the cultural transmission of disaffected attitudes,
oppositional cultural practices, and a reactive ethnicity.[1] A divergent
perspective, based on a study of a small number of second-generation
adolescents who affiliate with high-achieving African American students
cites Latino youth who link into a Black culture of educational mobility
during adolescence and momentarily identify as "Black Mexicans."[2]

Meanwhile, a study of Latino millennials in Chicago finds that they
identify as an "ethnorace," different from yet in solidarity with African

Americans.[3] By contrast, a study of second-generation Latino young men in inner-city Los Angeles neighborhoods concludes that while such youth adopt Black cultural forms, such as dress and music, "second generation Latinos did not identify with inner-city Blacks."[4] What this range of research on Latino youth and their relations with African Americans suggests is the need for specificity, for understanding how a particular place, a particular time, and even a particular civic culture can inform different patterns of ethnic and cultural identification.

We return to this topic of variation by place, time, and broader civic culture in chapters 6 and 7. In this chapter, we ask, "How did being raised in South L.A.'s Black neighborhoods shape the current narratives of identity and home for young Latino adults?" Perhaps unsurprisingly (particularly given the diversity of research described earlier), our sixty subjects do not speak in a monolithic voice, and we take note of these variations. Even within the same family, siblings can have a radically different set of experiences and viewpoints, as temporal demographic shifts in the neighborhood mean siblings experienced different school contexts. Yet in the search for patterns, three broad findings emerge from our analysis of the Latino second-generation in South Los Angeles.

First, this Latino second-generation has been deeply influenced by African American people and culture. Unlike their immigrant parents, they were socially formed by their everyday interactions with the neighborhoods, people, and culture of South L.A. As John D. Marquez concluded in a study of Houston neighborhoods undergoing similar transformations, Black people and cultures of resistance are "foundational" to Latinos raised in Black neighborhoods.[5] An inseparable part of being Latino raised in South L.A. is being raised with Black cultural influences and interactions. None of the second-generation Latinos we interviewed called themselves "Black Mexicans" or "Black Latinos" (although that was the chosen identity of one of the interviewers who grew up in the area and that added to our learnings), but they did identify with Black cultural influences that have shaped them, and they proudly saw themselves as different and distant from Chicanos in East L.A. The framework of ethnic "sedimentation" suggests "the coexistence of complex and multiple histories and identities in a given moment," and this captures the long-lasting influence of African American histories, interactions, and culture in the lives of these second-generation La-tinos. Public schools, as we will see in this chapter, serve as key sites where this occurs.[6]

Second, as they grew up in South L.A., the second-generation Lati-nos experienced both overt hostility and strong support from African Americans. Their experiences offer an opportunity for us to reconsider contact theory when intergroup contact involves both negative and positive encounters. Many of the young adults we interviewed reported that as children and adolescents, they had endured street assaults and racial bullying and, in high school, some witnessed or participated in "race riots," physical fights between Latinos and African Americans. But the very same respondents were as likely to recall deep friendships with Black youth or to express gratitude for a special African American mentor or teacher. One young woman said that for her and her sis-ter, African Americans were like "extended family," and following this analogy, we can see cross-racial family fights interspersed with family bonds. Social segregation and the color line between African Ameri-cans and Latinos in South L.A. remain, but for this generation, in par-ticular, it has been blurred.

Third, these Latino second-generation respondents talk unabash-edly about their love for South L.A. (including more than a little pride at being part of the neighborhoods that gave rise to West Coast hip-hop and gangsta rap). They feel a special place-based racial identity and see South L.A. as home, a place of roots and belonging with problems and future promise. The interviewees from Watts emphasized a singu-lar pride of place, seeing Watts as distinctive in promoting resilience, toughness, and small-town familiarity. For the second-generation Lati-nos, a sense of shared struggle and survival now meshes with aspirations for homeownership, and to give back and lift up the community; this, as we will see in chapter 6, is reinforced by a civic culture now stressing Black–Brown solidarity as the most effective way to challenge the struc-tural inequalities that impact the lives of South L.A. residents.

Before we jump into the interviews that give rise to these three themes, it is useful to consider just how representative these interviews were. As reviewed in the appendix, we are actually remarkably close to the underlying population in terms of gender and work experience, with an age distribution that differs by design. The one quirk of this sample is that it is highly educated: only about 44 percent of U.S.-born Latino adults in the three focus neighborhoods have been to college in some form while that figure is 70 percent for our U.S.-born Latino interviewees.

This was a product of our recruitment strategy, as we relied on three research assistants, Latino college graduates in their twenties, who were raised in or near South L.A. While they used innovative snowball samples, they also recruited their friends and acquaintances, who naturally tended to have similar educational profiles. While this presents some issues regarding representativeness, this overrepresentation of college graduates does offer a particular insight into Latino young adults who achieved educational and occupational mobility and yet remain committed to South Los Angeles. In addition, these are uniquely reflective respondents. They narrated not only their experiences of growing up in South Los Angeles, but they offered critical analyses of social, historical, political, and cultural dynamics.

The data also show that some of the respondents grew up in single-mother households, but most were raised in two-parent, intact families, and many of them reported that their parents had moved to South L.A. to buy a house (in keeping with the pattern noted from the first-generation interviews in chapter 3). They grew up in low-income families but often with a good deal of stability. A typical pattern was living with their nuclear family, with relatives newly arrived from Mexico or Central American who might "come and go," staying for a year or more until they got on their feet. Now in their twenties and thirties, many of the respondents still lived with their parents, although some had established their own households and had children of their own. At the time of our interviews, a handful had become homeowners too. Finally, it is important to note that since we drew our sample in Watts, Historic Central Avenue, and Vermont Square/Slauson neighborhoods of South L.A., we do not include the voices of young Latinos who moved away or who are currently incarcerated, in the military, or away at college.

In terms of social class, the respondents grew up in a range of modest circumstances, from solid working-class homeowner families to the working poor. Among the poor, many articulated what sociologist Emir Estrada has termed "economic empathy" for their parents.[7] For example, several college students who were living with their families were helping to pay the household bills. One twenty-three-year-old woman described, "We were very poor—poor to the max, to the point that we had eight to ten people living in one household. . . . My mom, she works more than 40 hours a week and every two weeks she gets paid $500. Me seeing that, the struggle, I took the initiative to get a job, you know, and now I'm helping her just pay one bill."

In the following, we examine the childhood, adolescent, and young adult trajectories of these interviewees through the lens of immigrant homemaking. As with the first generation, we analyze their experiences through the dimensions of security, familiarity, control and autonomy, and future-making. We find various parallels to the first-generation experience of new arrivals but with a distinct bent toward including the African American community as part of what, for this group, constitutes home across all the various dimensions.

Becoming Secure

A sense of safety and security is an essential part of home. As youngsters in the 1980s and 1990s, the second-generation Latinos faced a series of danger zones in their South L.A. neighborhoods. For them, it was not about protecting home but about protecting themselves on the streets and in school. Indeed, many of the respondents related firsthand experience with violence in the streets or the schools, yet they described these incidents in a matter-of-fact way. Unlike the Latino immigrant generation, the second-generation underscored that they were not traumatized by these events. Violence was "normalized," and they described enduring violence perpetuated not only by African Americans but also by Latinos, gang members, and the police. Importantly, the accumulation of diverse experiences with African American friends, pupils, and teachers outweighed any propensity to categorize all African Americans as the perpetuators of danger and agents of violence.

For example, thirty-one-year-old Carla Hernández grew up with her parents and brothers in Watts, on a street bordering the territory of two rival gangs of the era, the Crips and the Bloods. "They would meet up at my house, right in front of my house and shoot at each other," she said matter-of-factly. "So I learned how to dodge bullets. There is still a bullet hole in the house." A bullet once scraped her six-year-old brother's cheek while he walked home from school, and a bullet hole is still visible in the house. Like other girls and women, Carla also faced direct sexual harassment and the threat of assault on the street. Once while walking to school, a man had tried to pull her into a motel, but she escaped. "Encounters with death were fairly normalized for me," she reflected. "Like I remember a drive-by shooting. Kids were around the pool [at the park]. One of the kids got shot and fell into the pool, and the pool turned red." She reflected that "now people call it trauma. But at the time, it was like that is just how life is here."

Yet, like many of the second-generation respondents, Carla also recalled the cultural richness and a kind of positive excitement in growing up in Watts. She described fond memories of supportive African American neighbors, such as the family who looked after their house when her family departed for Mexico every summer. In school, she learned about the history of Black struggles for civil rights, and consequently, African American struggles for racial and social justice had motivated her studies. As an adolescent, she felt, she said, "this level of pride and excitement of growing up in a community with such a rich history and so I immersed myself in school to learn more about that and my friends."

Childhood was both bucolic and dangerous. A now twenty-eight-year-old man who grew up in the Vermont Square neighborhood recalled happy memories but in the same breath, he described the ordinariness of shootings. "Growing up here in the early '90s, it was cool because at that point it was a lot of kids like our age," he said. "We used to play football, Blacks and Hispanics, but I guess that was the good stuff. You had to be careful. Back then it was lot of shootings, drive-bys. Actually I don't know what year it was, but I remember a couple of bullets flew into our house." The young man pictured in figure 4.1 offered similar sentiments while the young people depicted in figures 4.2 to 4.4 offer a range of observations explored later in this chapter.

Black–Brown Tensions

Not all of our respondents dodged bullets at home or on the street, but young people growing up here needed to stay alert to their immediate surroundings, and some narrated how threats accelerated as they grew up. For thirty-three-year-old Aurelia Campa, who grew up in

Figure 4.1. "I'm still proud of it, you know? I appreciate where I grew up from, you know? It was a struggle, but like I learned from it. That's all I got."
Photo Credit: Walter Thompson-Hernández, USC CSII project team.

Figure 4.2. "I think for South L.A., the best thing you can do is what they did with me. Open people's eyes. Open their eyes and start seeing into the future and seeing how their decisions affect everything that can happen."
Photo Credit: Walter Thompson-Hernández, USC CSII project team.

Figure 4.3. "The older population, the older Latinos, the older African Americans, they don't really get along. . . . You might as well get along 'cause at the end of the day, we're still living in the same communities, we have the same struggles."
Photo Credit: Walter Thompson-Hernández, USC CSII project team.

Figure 4.4. "I can still walk in my neighborhood, and I hope my kids realize that there's a lot to be done to improving the condition of how we live, but I hope they grow up knowing to do their part."
Photo Credit: Walter Thompson-Hernández, USC CSII project team.

Watts, violence reached a crescendo with the high school "race riots." She explained the trajectory this way:

> While I was growing up, majority of the population was African American. . . . We were the minority so we got picked on a lot, especially in elementary because there were more Blacks and they felt they owned the neighborhood. . . . Middle school is when it started changing. There started to be more Latinos in the neighborhood, but we still had the race riots. Like I remember running out of the middle school because it was Blacks against Mexicans, and so people would try to run home before they would start fights.

In the 1990s and early 2000s, fights between African American and Latino youth broke out in a number of Los Angeles high schools, including Jefferson and Locke. A systematic study of high school race riots by sociologist Martin Sánchez-Jankowski concludes that this type of conflict emerges when a large number of newcomer students alter the racial-ethnic demographics of a study body, particularly in schools in poor neighborhoods—and as the data presented in chapter 2 on school composition show, rapid change was clearly the case in Los Angeles in the period in which this second generation was coming of age.[8]

In these situations, established groups feel their existence is under threat and, under particular structural conditions, may respond with violent attacks against these perceived intruders. No particular group is more prone to be a victimizer, and Sánchez-Jankowski's case studies reveals that African Americans were more often "victims than victimizers" in the case of change in Boston in the 1980s, "whereas in Los Angeles and Oakland they were more victimizers than victims."[9] His study also reveals that race riots usually emerge in poor, low-income neighborhoods where school administrators tend to be ineffective in curtailing these interracial fights. In those situations, students are placed on "lockdown" and prevented from leaving the campus while armed police are called in to quell the fighting.

Of interest for our analysis is how Latino second-generation youth reacted and how these events shaped their outlooks on race and South L.A. While these youth grew up in a context in which they faced bullying and gang attacks from both Latino and African American perpetuators, as well as seemingly arbitrary police harassment, the "race riots" and interracial fighting were uniquely racially charged events in their upbringing.

First, for the males, there was no way they could avoid physical conflict. To not fight back when attacked would signal they were easy targets. Twenty-six-year-old Carlos Rodriguez shared that "if you are weak, you'll get picked on." But a surprising finding emerged—fighting back not only offered a modicum of protection but sometimes helped them broker new friendships with African American students as well. One thirty-six-year-old Latino male raised in Watts shared this:

> My first day at Markham was the first interracial fight I ever had in my life and it was because I was lost during lunchtime. I was trying to navigate a campus that I was new to. I ended up somewhere behind where the bungalows are. I turned the corner, there were three Black guys standing there and the next thing I knew, I was in the middle of a fight.

While he lost the fight, he claims he was "still able to get one or two of the guys good enough where no one ever bothered me at Markham." The following day at homeroom class, students had already heard about the confrontation, and "one of the Black guys that I befriended there actually got me to know other kids in the school." Proving himself by fighting back helped him garner respect and build friendships, including with African American students. Still, he talked about safety strategies at school and moments "when the bell would ring and everyone would just make a run for it, because you knew something was going to happen."

Another male interviewee, Carlos Cordoba, was born in Watts in 1995 and experienced a more generalized climate of violence at that same middle school. Elementary school had been peaceful and "innocent," but he confessed that once he got to Markham Middle School, "I was actually scared going to that school." Fighting was required. "I wouldn't say it left me traumatized," he said, "but it gave me the impression that survival should be primary to you." At the school, he encountered other types of non-racialized organized fights too, such as "the freshman hunt," where seventh and eighth graders beat up sixth graders. He treated middle school as a training ground for fighting. "When I got to high school, I was ready to fight," he said. "African Americans and Latinos? They would just be in their groups."

Gangs and Violence

Only one of our interviewees talked openly about his gang affiliation, and the magnetic appeal and addictive draw that violence came to represent for him.[10] Carlos Rodriguez grew up in various neighborhoods of South L.A., moving from one rental to the next with his mother and three brothers, and now works as a tattoo artist and piercer. "I grew up fighting naturally, Black people, Hispanics," he said. "And I've done that since high school. I've seen a lot of friends like, disappear, because of gangs, you know? I tried hard to stay out of it, but it's hard." Strong bonds between friends and striving for "notoriety" and "money and girls" had propelled his gang life, but this had not curtailed friendships with African Americans. "I fought with a lot of Black people, but I also had friends that I used to sleep over at their house. I had a friend that our family and his family were super cool, and his grandma loved us like crazy! And we loved her." He bragged about the racial diversity of his friends, now drawn from his immersion in the punk music and skater scenes, and while he condemned the "stupidity" and "ignorance" of fighting, he was still caught up in it.

Twenty-nine-year-old Horacio Luna, with tattoos that covered his face, also talked about fighting, and he admitted to instigating his own racially motivated attacks on African Americans. He grew up, he said, "[h]aving to kind of look after yourself, watch your back a little bit because anything can happen, you know, among colors or whatever. And it wasn't just colors, it might have been other, your own people, you know what I mean, who get out of hand." After an accidental explosion that resulted in his disfigurement, he became a victimizer of African Americans, initiating fights and acts of petty sabotage. "See, I had my accident that happened, and it was due to a Black. But it wasn't his fault . . . but I was holding a grudge. . . . You know, we were all playing . . . My whole right side of my body was different due to a fuckin' game. So I held a grudge. . . . I started fighting. I started snatching shit. I started popping their tires from their low-rider cars."

Girls faced fewer threats and less compulsion to fight in the school "race riots" or in street fights, but they also had to navigate these dangers. As a teenager, Yvette Ramirez had bused out to Roosevelt High School in Boyle Heights, a quintessential (and historically significant) Chicano/Mexican school in East L.A., but interestingly, she never felt accepted in that Chicano milieu (a fact that squares with our notion of a distinctive sort of Latino identity emerging in the context of Black–Brown South L.A.). For that reason, she opted to transfer back to her neighborhood and attend Fremont High School, but just then racial-ethnic violence broke out:

> Immediately when I got there, there were the Brown and Black riots in the schools. We used to be on lockdown, and there was more heat [police], so that eventually kind of bled into the African Americans gangs and the Latino gangs that had never had beefs before that, and now they started beefing, right? And it was like, Wow. Just when I think I'm back home, now there's this pressure. The climate changed. It became really hostile.

She had returned to South L.A. schools to be accepted but instead encountered the opposite. "That was really tough and it hurts because this is home. I was away from home for so long, and I come back, and it's like, man—it was tough." She also described being threatened and beaten by the police, a topic which we visit later.

Getting Calmer

Compared to the 1990s and even the early 2000s, all our interviewees agreed that there was less violence and calmer in the neighborhoods now. Their testimonials cover a range of settings in the neighborhoods, but in all these sites, they concurred on the decline of conflict and crime:

> It's changed a lot. There's not as much violence. . . . When I tutor, I have to go into the projects, so I'm able to see. It's not as scary as it once was. Like, I'm able to walk in the projects and not feel like I'm gonna get jumped. The people there are a lot friendlier. You don't see as much gangs . . . (Jose Orozco, Watts)

I've noticed definitely a decrease in people being robbed in the street, not as many shootings. I've definitely noticed that it's a lot more peaceful than when I was growing up. (Sarah Gonzalez, Historic South Central)

Back then, everybody would be like, "Fuck the wetbacks" or, "Fuck you, Black people." . . . There was a lot of hate. Now it's just like everybody's either wanting to smoke weed with each other or just trying to get a drink or trying to pick up on girls or go to shows. It's more chill. (Carlos Rodriguez, now living in Watts)

A critical voice of dissent on whether time had brought improvements was seventh-grade teacher Cecilia Rodriguez. She mourned the loss of a stronger, stable African American community that had anchored her childhood in the Vermont Square neighborhood. But the objective reality indicated by crime data—and one felt by the respondents, like the one pictured in figure 4.2—was that the level of violence had diminished dramatically. And with more security came a growing sense of home.

Gaining Familiarity

As we have argued, another dimension of homemaking is familiarity. Second-generation Latinos described two types of familiarity that were necessary for them to survive and thrive in South Los Angeles: closeness to African Americans, and the ability to distinguish between safe and dangerous zones, which often led to staying in what one interviewee called a protective family "bubble," going only between home and school. Gendered patterns prevailed, with girls held in tighter bubbles than the boys. Sociologists from Nancy Lopez to Robert C. Smith have found similar patterns in New York City, with Latino immigrant parents allowing sons to enjoy spatial freedom to roam the streets while holding daughters on strict home "lockdowns."[11] The term *lockdown* suggests a carceral, coercive, and punitive dimension, but our respondents reserved that term for police lockdowns of the schools. The demarcated zones of familiarity varied, as did who might be included in the protected area, so we use the term *bubble*.

Navigating a Black Space

Lydia Quintanilla now works as a teacher in Watts, but she initially came to Watts as a ten-year-old girl newly arrived from Mexico, part of the 1.5 generation of immigrant youth raised in the United States. As a non-English-speaking child, she sensed that her ability to thrive in this new society would depend on her closeness and reliance on Black friends and teachers. She explained: "Why would I hang out with the Latino kids? I needed to learn English, and the Black kids knew English, so I needed to play with them." She discovered some African American kids did not welcome her, so she naturally gravitated to those who did, and they became her peer group. "In middle school, like 7th and 8th grade, most of my teachers were African American and most of the kids were African American as well. So it just seemed the norm for me."

In her high school years, things changed. Her mother worked in Long Beach, and they decided that since those schools were better and safer, she would use her mother's work address to enroll there. She lost contact with many of her African American friends. A family–school bubble enveloped her, and with no teens on her block and scarce commercial opportunities in Watts, she no longer spent time in the local neighborhood. "Watts was the place where we slept," she said. "On weekends, it was like, stay home, do whatever you need to do and then if we needed to go to the grocery store, things of that nature, our errands were never in Watts. We were always gearing toward like Lynwood, or Southgate or Huntington Park, which were more Latino neighborhoods. I don't remember ever growing up and going to the post office, which is down the street, because we did it in Long Beach before we came back."

As a teen, Lydia Quintanilla recognized danger spots in Watts, but she identified police harassment, not Black people, as the key danger to avoid. As a girl and a neighborhood local living on a relatively calm street where "everyone knew who you were," she did not fear gangs or experience cross-racial fights in the schools. But staying in her bubble zone protected her from the police:

> I never felt unsafe. I just chose not to leave my area of the block be-
> cause I didn't know what kind of trouble I could get, plus I was actually
> more intimidated by the cops than I was by the people in the neighbor-

hood. Going home from school, you would see them harass people. You would hear about kids getting hit up by cops. You kept hearing stories about cops. So it was more just to limit my exposure from that than the people in the neighborhood, because after a while, everyone knew who you were. So you really didn't have anything to really fear. . . . You would hear gunshots from other parts of Watts, but not from ours.

Cecilia Rodriguez, now also a teacher who has returned to serve the community where she grew up, related similar experiences growing up in the Vermont Square neighborhood with strong African American support:

We were among the first Latino families to move into the area. There were other Latinos sprinkled around, but most of the community was African Americans, but they were families, and they were—they were individuals who were poor, but had an incredible culture, were very amicable with their neighbors. I remember the lady who was behind us, she kept a garden in her back yard and she would see me playing in my backyard and sometimes she would give me vegetables.

Her Guatemalan father and Salvadoran mother moved the family from Lincoln Heights, a traditional Mexican immigrant gateway neighborhood on the Eastside so that they could buy a house. Cecilia explained that her parents "were not used to seeing African Americans, so to a certain extent, they were wary of the unknown." But Cecilia herself now spoke in a wistful tone, not only expressing gratitude for her childhood immersed in a rich African American culture but also regretting the disappearance of supportive African American neighbors and culture:

In the picture from my first grade, I'm the only non–African American in that picture, along with the teacher. Everyone else was African American. The funny thing is I never felt that color difference when I was in school. To me, I was just like my friends. . . . Throughout school, you could feel that African American culture. As years, progressed, you started to see more Latino students, and some of that culture started to dwindle a little bit. I didn't see it leave the school as much as my [younger] sister. My sister went to the same school and didn't see that presence of that [African American] culture when she was there.

Being in a "Bubble"

As a child, Cecilia played, studied, and shared birthday party celebrations with Black children and was immersed in an African American culture. But as she grew older, the demographics of the neighborhood changed, the local schools deteriorated, and she bused out to attend predominantly white schools in the San Fernando Valley, enduring hours in transit daily. Busing out for high school, and even middle school, was a common experience for many of our second-generation respondents, as we discuss later, but what is important to note here is that her parents did not allow Cecilia to socially gather with white suburban school friends, who would go to the movies or the mall on weekends. In her case, the bubble excluded white suburban friends. "The distance was used as an excuse of why I couldn't go ahead and hang out in those types of places," she said. "I would go to special things like their birthdays, but when it came to more casual things, I wouldn't join them." She explained her parents' stance, and the imposition of "the bubble" this way:

> I'm coming from a Latino family where my parents didn't see that as something that you would do as a teen or as young child in high school. They saw it as more as those are things you do with your family. . . . They were overprotective. We had heard a lot of things that had happened to other people, and because we are like in this unknown place . . . they did go ahead and try to create, like, a bubble in the house, where in the house you are living and breathing the culture that you are, and once you walk out of that house, you kind of just, you still live by that culture.

Many other respondents, mostly females but including males, described a similar "home to school" bubble. Thirty-four-year-old Jackie Sanchez, who grew up in Watts, said, "It was just you go to school, and then you walk home, and then that's it." Jose Oro, also in his mid-thirties, lives in Vermont Square and related a similar experience, saying, "It was a lot of just straight to school, and straight home kind of thing." Henry Quintanilla, a thirty-five-year-old who grew up in Watts, said that he and his brother were either at school or at home playing video games or reading the discarded *Encyclopedia Brittanica*s his father brought home from his Westside landscaping jobs.

Did they resent this confinement to home? For most of them, the answer is no. Fernando Menendez, a thirty-six-year-old from Vermont Square, expressed gratitude for his restrictive Mexican immigrant parents. "Thank God my parents were pretty strict," he said. "They did not allow me to do any of that stuff, those activities in the street." Significantly younger Sarah Gonzalez, a twenty-three-year-old woman raised in the historic Central Avenue neighborhood, claimed that she was not bothered by these restrictions in the least. "Honestly, in high school I hardly went out because I think my mom just, I don't why, she felt like I was safer at home," she said. "I didn't go out much, and I didn't have a problem with that. I was always okay being at home." Like others, she reminded us that their families lacked money and the neighborhood offered few places for youth. Public parks in the neighborhood were unsafe. "There wasn't any cool places to go to. . . . And not only that, the resources! We hardly had any money, like spending money. So where would I go without money?" Home, in short, was safe, familiar, and, indeed, family.

Micro-Geographies

For Latino youth coming of age in South L.A. during the 1990s and the early 2000s, familiarity with the neighborhood required negotiating the bubble and an intense mapping of the micro-zones of safety and danger. During this time, South L.A. was broken up into distinct gang territories controlled by Bloods, Crips, Florencia, and more. Even if youth were not gang-affiliated, simply walking into another gang neighborhood could provoke trouble. Horacio Luna said that he and his friends dealt with this by walking only on "the big streets" so as to avoid confrontations with smaller groups of gang-affiliated men in alleyways or quieter streets.

There were many places considered off-limits, and steering clear of these become "second nature" and "commonsense" habits. Public parks and the projects were routinely avoided. As Jackie Sanchez, who grew up among three large public housing projects in Watts said, "We never went into the projects because it was just like a whole different world . . . like no way you would go in there." Parks, the projects, liquor stores, and some bus stops were seen as sites of drug deals, gang gatherings, and danger and so places to skip in one's daily movements.

Indeed, simply walking from school to home or home to bus stop involved intricate mappings and timing. "You had to pick like which route you go to school. Like, do you take 103rd or do you take 105th, you know? And there was some people who either had to cut through the projects or not." Jackie Sanchez said, "Some kids had to arm and defend themselves," and she recalled a friend who was expelled from school for doing so, even though he never used it. "Sadly, he used to carry a blade because he and his sister had no choice," she said.

"Being known" to others was another safety strategy. Jackie Sanchez reflected that perhaps "part of the reason it felt so comfortable to us was that like we had been living there for such a long time that people just knew who we were. . . . We didn't think we were like targets because it was like, we've been here. We know so and so." And in the Central Avenue neighborhood, Sarah Gonzalez reported, "I definitely tried to avoid associations with gang members and people I knew that were involved in drugs. . . . Fighting—I tried to stay away from that."

While the first-generation Latino immigrants discussed in the previous chapter generally complained about under-policing, the second-generation Latino youth growing up in South Los Angeles were more likely to complain of over-policing. Even youth who lived in the bubble were poignantly aware of seemingly arbitrary police harassment. Twenty-seven-year-old Karla Sonora from Vermont Square claimed that while the police had never bothered her or other brothers, "I definitely saw them messing with other people, especially our neighbors, who were like drug dealers. There was always some drama over there." The fact that the local drug dealers were seen as part of the neighborhood and policing them was seen as harassment is interesting and speaks again to normalization of the challenges in that era in South L.A. In any case, what is clear here as well is that strategic mapping of micro-zones was used to help youth stay safe from police harassment and brutality.

For Latino youth who ventured out beyond the home–school bubble and the careful mappings of micro-zones, police brutality was indeed a possible threat. Yvette Ramirez, the daughter of Salvadoran and Mexican parents, had routinely ignored her parents' rules and restrictions, venturing out into other neighborhoods as a skateboarder. It wasn't gangs or African American youth but police who represented her biggest threat. "Cops were beating our asses back then," she declared. "They didn't care if you were a guy or a girl, and I was a skater. . . . There was a couple of times when they roughed me up pretty bad, and they busted my board once." She wished now that she had access to cell phone cameras and social media. "I would come home bruised with bruised ribs, and like, a black eye, and I would say, 'The cops just beat me up.' Nobody was going to believe it because it wasn't on video." And Carlos Rodriguez, still affiliated with gang life, said that he felt the police harassed him for walking, riding his bicycle, or just "wearing the wrong shit." He did not hide his contempt for the police: "Cops are looking for something, just to get provoked and just shoot. I'm hostile towards cops."

Seeking Autonomy

Children and adolescents may not enjoy the same degree of autonomy and control over their lives as adults do, but they still exercise everyday agency as they develop into young adults. As sociologists Jennifer Bickham Mendez and Leah Schmalzbauer remind us, "Latino youth are not merely emergent participants in society, but political and social actors in the here and now," and they advocate taking a perspective that acknowledges "intersecting social locations of youth and the specificity of place."[12] In this section, we use those declarations as points of departure for an examination of Latino youth's experiences with schools, mentors, and peers in two very different locales: South L.A. schools and the suburban schools to which many of them bused out during high school. Our focus is on understanding their agentic practices and encounters and the ways in which these social encounters shaped their identities. And as we will see, they also articulated agency and autonomy by seeking to temper their parents' most strident manifestations of anti-Black racism.

School as a Safe Space

Adolescence is a critical period of social formation. Overall, the respondents are proud of how South L.A. helped them develop, and they expressed a special gratitude for what they learned from local schools, teachers, and mentors. Given that our sample overrepresents educational high achievers, it is not surprising that they acknowledged their teachers. But a surprising finding was this: we found that even second-generation Latinos who lived through high school race riots, who were expelled, or had otherwise poor school achievement also described gratitude for particular teachers in the local schools. They recognized schools were underfunded and under-resourced, but they credited committed teachers and innovative programs for helping them become the people they are today. And in this vein, they expressed gratitude for key African American teachers and mentors.

For the most part, the second-generation respondents articulated strong pro-school attitudes and motivations to get the best education possible. While the modal education of their Mexican and Central American immigrant parents was modest and included limited English-language skills, their immigrant parents encouraged them to pursue education, even though they had little knowledge to offer about the routes to scholastic achievement. Typically, the Latino second generation embraced the immigrant bargain, studying and striving to atone for their parents' sacrifices.[13] For example, twenty-three-year-old Kathy Mendoza said that her mother, who struggled to support the family on minimum-wage jobs, always urged her "to strive . . . to have a better future." She reflected that "what motivated me, maybe the most, was seeing my mom struggle, and I wanna give her that happiness, yeah, of me giving her that Bachelor's degree."

But just getting to the starting line for college was a challenge filled with roadblocks and obstacles. Key teachers and mentors, they said, guided them along the way. One example is Sarah Gonzalez, who is today a University of California, Los Angeles (UCLA) graduate. The daughter of a struggling single mother, she attended elementary, middle school, and high school in South L.A. "I had great teachers there, many of who I still remember today," she said. "They made a big impact on my life and I feel there's a lot of things that I learned from them that have helped me now through the years." As a high achiever, she was tracked into honors and Advanced Placement (AP) classes, and she reverently held up the local teachers and administrators, not only for what they taught her but also for their community leadership and advocacy.

"Growing up, in my eyes, those were the biggest advocates for change, for improvements in our community."

Some of our interviewees called out a strong gratitude for life-transforming African American mentors. Yvette Ramirez is now a mother of three children and employed in a neighborhood educational access program, but she had once been an "at-risk teenager." She thanked two influential Black women for putting her on the right path. First, an eighth-grade physical education teacher took a special interest by telling her, "I'm going to check up on your classes, and if you do well, I'm going to take you for a really nice lunch." She excelled, and her teacher rewarded her with lunch at the Chart House, an upscale seafood restaurant with an ocean view. She still remembers what she wore for the special occasion, shorts and high tops, her very best clothes. Most important, she still remembers what that teacher told her on that day: "You have potential." At age sixteen, due to family conflicts, she left home, and her friend's African American mother took her in and served as a life-transforming "other mother." This woman taught her many important life lessons, and Yvette credited both these women for transforming her life. "It was both of them," she said. "It was two beautiful wonderful African American women that have been very influential for me. And I think a big part of who I am is because of them."

Most surprisingly, and in contrast to the generalized teacher bashing and blaming in the media, even second-generation Latinos who did not graduate from college expressed gratitude to local teachers and schools. A young man who now works as a tattoo artist and piercer said that while his elementary and middle school experiences were "horrible," high school introduced him to "teachers that kind of cared." One unique teacher took him and a few other students surfing, and there, in the Pacific Ocean, taught lessons in "the craziest ways." Fernando Hernández, who was expelled from high school in Watts, still felt positively about his high school experiences, saying, "I'm happy that I went to these schools because it made me who I am today."

Busing to High School

Before a school building boom in the 2000s, the local schools in South L.A., like many in the Los Angeles Unified School District, were often overcrowded.[14] Combining that with a generalized climate of violence, the high school "race riots" of 1990s, and a shortage of AP and honors class selections, it is unsurprising that many of our respondents opted to bus out to high schools across town, typically in more suburban neighborhoods such as Santa Monica or the San Fernando Valley. Sometimes local teachers, but also parents and peers, informed this decision. The outcome offered them access to a broader curriculum of AP and honors courses and usually smaller classes, but an unanticipated consequence is that they also received an education in how others viewed them and South L.A.

Attending high school across town was an eye-opener, provoking a critical moment of identity formation that solidified their love and pride for South L.A. Interpersonal interactions with teachers and students at suburban schools forced these second-generation Latinos to confront social stigma, and through these encounters, they, in turn, inverted their self-image to embrace their place-based identities. But to call this a reactive ethnicity is not quite hitting the mark, as that often is taken to imply an oppositional identity. A sociological concept offered by Charles Horton Cooley—"the looking-glass self"—may be more useful for understanding this process of identity formation, one that unfolded alongside the general turmoil that is adolescence.[15]

Being made to feel inferior in these new educational settings tore them up emotionally and existentially and ultimately pushed them toward stronger feelings of belonging and attachment with South L.A. As teenagers bused across town, they quickly learned that the world feared them and their neighborhood. They were made to feel contaminated, inferior, and stigmatized, and as youngsters, some of them internalized this self-hatred. "There was a lot of hatred towards the community we were living in," said Karla Sonora, who attended high school in a white suburban area. "You know, the ghetto," she explained, "only ghetto people live there. . . . I had a bad feeling of what it meant to be from South Central."

Students like Karla not only grappled with self-hatred but also relished feeling tough and resilient. As a high school student, she admitted that "it kind of felt good sometimes that people were like, 'Oh, she's tough, she's from like the ghetto.'" Youth such as Karla embraced toughness as a coat of protective armor against the slings of racial insults but not as an oppositional or reactive ethnicity. She noted,

I was just like some nerdy kid. I was born here, and like I saw the struggle, and like I want to be better. . . . I did want to get out of South L.A. because I wanted to show that you know, that I could do more. It was almost like my identity was defined in like not trying to be from South L.A. anymore—that was me growing up, you know, trying to figure that out.

Working through these contradictions was not easy, but she is proud of how this shaped who she is today, confidently proclaiming, "It makes me who I am. And there's no need to be feeling ashamed about it. But it's hard when you're a kid and you're hearing you should feel ashamed about it, and you're like, 'Oh crap, okay.'" Love, pride, and South L.A. attachment was a hard-won process.

Sometimes this process began in middle school and continued through college. Thirty-one-year-old Cecilia Rodriguez from Vermont Square started busing out to the San Fernando Valley in middle school, and she recalled an Asian American boy falling asleep on the bus and missing his Koreatown stop. He awoke in terrified hysteria as the bus reached her stop, and while her father was going to offer him a ride, the boy simply sprinted away in fear once he discovered he was "in the hood." According to Cecilia, even as seventh and eighth graders, "[a]ll of the students that were South L.A., we knew where we're coming from. We knew what everyone else thought."

The process continued when she attended an Ivy League college. Her first two years she struggled while sitting in business classes with the children of elites who discussed people like her parents as nothing but a disposable-like "machinery component." As she noted,

[t]hat's when I realized that I was actually proud of being from South L.A. Getting through that psychology, I realized how difficult it is for a person like myself from South L.A. to actually get into a university and succeed. . . . Instead of stigmatizing the fact that I'm from South L.A., I should be proud of it because I beat the odds and I have proven the statistics wrong.

Grit, determination, and resilience got her through it. Today, she feels nothing but love and affection for, and deep connection with, the neighborhood where she grew up. In fact, she reflected that "[t]he term South Central still has some type of endearment. It still has its history, and it still holds a lot of roots in the community."

Not all the students bused out to suburban schools. Yvette Ramirez bused out to a predominantly Chicano/Mexican high school in East L.A. and had the unusual experience of being rejected by peers of the same racial-ethnic origin. "Even though we're brown," she said, "the fact that you're not from there and you speak differently immediately makes you an outcast." She remarked with wry irony that while her second-grade teacher had ridiculed her Spanish accent in South L.A., at Roosevelt high school, the students ridiculed her African American speech style and mannerisms. "That was the most racism I had encountered in school," she concluded. Feeling stigmatized and rejected, she transferred back to school in South L.A.

Going from South L.A. schools to other educational settings provoked a number of identity challenges, including social policing of racial boundaries and tests of authenticity. After she attended a primarily white, suburban middle school, one woman noted that "[f]riends from elementary school saw me and was [sic] like hey . . . you sound like a white girl now." Yet she added, "I had this other accent, you know, and I still do, it comes out sometimes . . . and it definitely is influenced by the Black culture." Carla Hernández, another young woman from Watts, recalled that in college, she "resonated" more with the African American students than with the Latinos, but she was stunned to find that they did not see her as one of them. "I got reality handed to me that they were like, you belong in that box," she said. This conflicted with her identity, nurtured in South L.A.'s African American neighborhoods. "Growing up, it was largely Black, but I was excited, like I learned about the culture and I adapted in my own ways or I appropriated by braiding my hair or learning how to cook Gumbo."

Dealing with the Racism of Your Elders

Second-generation Latinos raised in South L.A. not only acknowledge African American influences in themselves, but they also recoil at their immigrant parents' anti-Black prejudices. Rather than being a wedge in the family, however, the second generation simultaneously struggle to understand their parents and to resocialize them on racism. This, too, is another way in which the second generation exerts control and autonomy in their Black and Brown home (see figure 4.3).

While not everyone said their parents held anti-Black views, the majority of respondents identified anti-Black racism as a characteristic associated with their parents and the older generation. As Fernando Hernández, who grew up in Watts and did not finish high school, declared, "Some of my neighbors can't stand African Americans." But he quickly qualified that this was the older folks, and he suggested that contacts with Black violence had poisoned their views:

> Those are elderly people who grew up in a different generation and in a different era. They might have had an act of violence against them . . . it might have been a group of African Americans that mugged them. I don't know, but because of that, they let that dictate their whole relationship, their whole point of view on African Americans.

Growing up, Fernando said his own parents tried to keep him away from African American friends. He ignored his parents' admonitions and stayed close with Black friends:

> I identify more with African Americans, but don't get me wrong—I know I'm full-blooded Hispanic. I know my origins. I know where my family is from, where my roots come from. But I'm not going to turn my back on the people that I grew up with, or some of my best friends, people that really have been there with me, had my back. Whether it be fighting or I might be down and out, they gonna come help me, right?

He still tries to change his parents' attitudes by talking to them, bringing his friends around, and showcasing his best friend's responsibility to family and work. Of this friend, he said, "He didn't graduate high school, like me. Yeah he hangs out . . . smokes weed, drinks beer like me, but he's a genuine, good person." Does this strategy work? Fernando felt his parents were making progress. "I talk to them all the time like that, and I honestly think that that does make a difference."

Second-generation respondents who called out their parents' anti-Black racism also put it in context of the immigrant experience that typically included modest English-language skills, working in occupational niches that did not overlap with African Americans, and isolation. These conditions created situations of minimal contact. They also recognized that African American assaults on their parents had left racial bruises. Karla Sonora did not excuse her mother's racism but expressed empathy for the harassment and mistreatment her mother suffered as a monolingual newcomer. She described one particularly brutal encounter that solidified her mother's anti-Black fears and anxieties:

> My mom you know, is from Mexico and like doesn't speak a lot of English, but enough to get by. I definitely saw her so many times be disrespected by like Black people in my community. She was assaulted once like for trying to move out—this car was like parked in front of her. . . . She honked at them . . . it was these two Black women, and they like took the keys out of the car and were like beating her and like my nephew got out of the car, grabbed the keys and put it in the ignition. My mom was able to get away.

In her job helping people at a local drug prevention clinic, Karla now encounters Latino clients who hold similar views. "Now that [she's] older," she realized that this is a community-wide problem "and that we need to talk about this . . . it's still so real." As for her mother, she is proud of the mutually supportive relationship she developed with an African American neighbor:

> It was so cute—she didn't speak any Spanish. She was a Black woman and like my mom, you know, didn't speak English, but they like communicated some way. Like she would drop us off at school and my mom would drop her kids off at school sometimes. And like they were really close and still are. . . . I do feel like there is starting to be like a better understanding of like how common the Black and Brown experience is but I think it [racial tension] is still there.

Thirty-three-year-old Aurelia Campa from Watts shared similar struggles with her mother too. "I'm more open-minded than my mother is because she's old school Latina, and she already has certain stereotypes and she won't let go because she doesn't really interact with Blacks," she said. Laughing, she concluded that her mother was "not as bad as she once was." What prompted the change? "Her children!" she exclaimed.

Making a Future

The second-generation Latinos that we interviewed expressed love, hope, and pride for South L.A. They were proud of their social formation in the South L.A. setting, and they felt a strong sense of belonging and rootedness to this place. Some of them had lived their entire lives here, while others deliberately returned to these neighborhoods after college. None of them minimize the acute problems that still plague South L.A., but they overwhelmingly express a strong social commitment to place and to building a better future here. It is a perspective, as we will see in chapter 6, that both inflects the area's civic culture and is reinforced by a particular style of community organizing that has become a main vehicle for neighborhood empowerment,

The outlooks of these second-generation Latino residents of South L.A. resonate with the familiar immigrant narrative of hope, but in addition, refract through a special attachment to the place and people of South L.A. This is the only home they have ever known, and they experience South L.A. as a Black and Brown home, a place where they feel as though they belong. There was no discernible sense of Latino triumphalism, nor did they articulate an antagonistic "us versus them" mentality against African Americans.

Unlike the conclusions reached by Maria Rendón, who finds that neighborhoods with deep histories of racially charged violence tend to "strain race relations and 'brighten' rather than 'blur' ethnic and racial boundaries and identities between the Mexican second-generation and Blacks," second-generation Latinos in South L.A. expressed a place-based racial-ethnic identity.[16] They are proud to be survivors who grew up in challenging circumstances, including high crime neighborhoods, school disadvantages, racial violence, and low-income families, but they also believe that their everyday challenges and interactions in these neighborhoods have made them stronger, more resilient, and more tolerant of racial difference than Latinos raised in non-Black environments.

These second-generation Latino residents of South L.A. are redefining the American dream. For them, the goal is not spatial assimilation and moving up and out to the suburbs. They see their futures here in South L.A. Second-generation interviewees spanned in age from eighteen to forty, and some of them aspire to buy a house and raise their kids in the same neighborhoods where they were raised. Many of them also want to invest their own talent and efforts into the project of community uplift. Typically, this involves not only moving back to the neighborhood but also working in South L.A. jobs oriented to social justice and public service, as teachers, counselors, or community organizers.

Community Uplift and Giving Back

A documented pattern among upwardly mobile young adults raised in poor Latino immigrant families is "giving back" by offering financial and social support to poorer co-ethnics, usually parents and relatives.[17] We found this pattern manifested at a larger community and neighborhood level. Among our respondents, a number of college graduates had returned to South L.A. to "give back" not just to family members but also to the communities that launched them. As they did so, they were simultaneously anchoring their own private futures in these neighborhoods while working to improve the community.

Henry and Lydia Quintanilla are now married with two young children, and they rent a duplex in Watts, which is owned by a relative. The couple shares strikingly similar backgrounds, as they were both raised in Watts by Mexican immigrant parents who became homeowners, and they both graduated from the highly competitive University of California at Berkeley. They only met and fell in love after they returned to Watts, she to work as a teacher and he as an administrator of public programs for the City of Los Angeles. They cherish Watts. Common experiences in the neighborhood, shared identities, and exposure to elite educations compelled them to return and practice helping, social justice professions. They are now raising their own children here too.

After eleven years of working as a teacher in Watts, Lydia Quintanilla adamantly declared that she was doing this work to remedy the poor local schools that had pushed her out to attend high school in Long Beach. Articulating some of the "missionary zeal" that sociologist Glenda M. Flores finds among Chicana/Latina teachers, she underlined a place-based specificity to her mission:[18]

> I was very intentional about working in the community that my parents own a home in, and my perspectives as a professional was if I was not allowed to attend this high school because it was not a good high school, or it wasn't a good option for Latino kids like me, then I want to be a Latina teacher that can make it better for those kids. They can see a bridge for them to have a better future. So I'm proud of it. I'm proud of having grown up there. I'm proud of working there.

And while she sought to help all her students, she also recognized that Latino and African American youth faced different challenges. For "African American youth growing up in Watts, it's a much more dire situation," she explained. "It's a more difficult reality. There's just so many factors that keep them from being successful. It's just the cycle of violence, the repetition cycle of poverty, lack of resources, the drug abuse, the broken families." Yet at the same time, she brimmed with optimism. "It's exciting because there's transformation happening, transformation at the level of schools," she said. "There's hope that something good can happen."

Her husband Henry had also returned to Watts after college, also motivated to remedy the wrongs he had experienced in the local schools. "I remember growing up in high school and listening to the way the administrators spoke about my classmates. I remember one administrator just blatantly not caring who was around." He now dedicates his public service work to helping be part of the solution, and he criticized his peers with a more individualistic orientation to social mobility. As he noted,

> [h]ow many of them are coming back to improve the community? None. Because it's kind of the mentality, "I got mine and now I'm going to go elsewhere." Me and a few other people who have graduated from college have come back and still live here, but we try to impact people that are around us, We are still attached to the neighborhood, and we don't want to leave it.

While this is powerful evidence of the attachment we have noted, it also suggests a possible bias we have noted in our interviews: because our sampling technique relied on drawing from the neighborhoods, we are focused on individuals who are still in or came back to the South L.A. locales in which they were formed.

While that is a methodological challenge, it also brings a useful longitudinal perspective. For example, now that they are in their late thirties, the Quintanillas have noted changes among African American and Latino youth, whom they see becoming more diverse, with multiple, blurred subcultures, and compared to their own youth, they see social media and new transportation links connecting South L.A. youth to other parts of the city too. Henry marveled, "Now you see Black guys who are skaters, whereas growing up, Black guys really wouldn't be doing that kind of thing. They weren't open to it. Now you have Black guys that are into rock . . . and Black and Latino kids who are hipsters. Whaaat?!"

While they celebrate positive changes in the neighborhood, they worry that rising home prices and gentrification may price them out of homeownership, and they see plenty to be done still in the realm of job development, commercial infrastructure, and Latino civic participation, sentiments expressed by the resident seen in figure 4.4. They recognize problems remain, but for the time being, they are happy to be building their futures here, and they expressed gratitude to Watts. "I've benefited from growing up in Watts and South Central because you're able to relate to different people," Henry said. "I work for the City, and I work with people who are Black, and I can draw upon my experiences growing up in Watts to relate to them, and make more friendships, and foster those friendships." Meanwhile, his wife, Lydia, aspires for her two children to enjoy the same rich cultural experiences and sense of belonging that she had:

> I'm very proud of growing up there. I'm proud of my professional work here as I think about settling down and purchasing a home and things of that nature. I can't tell you that I want to live here, forever. But I can tell you that I want my kids to be proud of growing up in this area too, of having roots in this area as well.

Place-Based Identity and African American Affinity

Latinos raised in the neighborhoods of South L.A. unambiguously identified as *Latino*, *Hispanic*, or *Chicano*, as the sons and daughters of

Mexican and Central American immigrant parents, but many of them pushed back against the imposition of a uniform Chicano, or East L.A. template of identity, which they criticized for perpetuating anti-Black racism or ethnic narrowness.[19] They contrasted this with their own broader, more inclusive versions of *Latinidad*, rooted in their families and neighborhoods of South L.A., acknowledging not only a history of struggle but also African American influences and solidarities and a myriad of Latin American cultures.

Like the Quintanillas, Cecilia Rodriguez is another educational high achiever who returned to work and live in the same neighborhood where she grew up, in Vermont Square. After earning a degree in business from an Ivy League university, she felt unfulfilled in a business career, so she studied for a master's degree in education. She now works as a seventh-grade math teacher at the local middle school, and on the side, she runs a small tutoring and tax preparation business for neighborhood customers. The daughter of a Salvadoran mother and a Guatemalan father, she identified strongly as Central American and part of what she loved about her neighborhood in South L.A. was the openness and blending of multiple Central and South American cultures and people.

The Vermont Square/Slauson neighborhood, as we saw in chapter 2, is characterized by a high proportion of Central Americans, many of them immigrants and refugees who left crowded, nearby Westlake neighborhoods in the 1980s and 1990s. Many Belizeans settled here too. Part of what Cecilia loved about her neighborhood was this mélange of *Latinidad* and the diverse array of Spanish accents heard on the street and in shops. She drew a sharp distinction between her sister and herself and their cousins, who were raised in East L.A. and Lincoln Heights. Her cousins, she claimed, had become "Mexicanized," and she was proud that her neighborhood had allowed her and her sister to retain both strong Central American identities and affiliations and solidarity with African Americans. She noted that her sister felt deeply insulted and offended by the cousins' nationalism and anti-Black racism. Speaking as a booster for South L.A., Cecilia claimed:

> I would never move to East L.A. There's no way you're gonna take me out of South L.A. to move to East L.A. It goes back to those ethnocentric tensions that exist within Latino pockets. I think of East L.A. as being

very Mexican . . . you don't wanna go to East L.A. because you would lose some of that identity. And I think that being a Latina in South L.A. has allowed me to keep that because there's so many different types of Central American and Mexican and South American individuals mixed together.

Cecilia stridently criticized her cousins' anti-Black racism too:

> My cousins who grew up in Lincoln Heights or in East L.A., they will make comments, ignorant comments, that have to do with race when they refer to African Americans, and my sister and I react very differently. To us, it's like you're talking about our extended family. They [African Americans] were the ones that were around there, that saw me walk home, that were extending a helping hand to my parents when they needed it. So to me, I see it differently.

Other respondents similarly denounced what they identified as East L.A. versions of anti-Black racism and violence. Based on their shared experiences in the neighborhoods of South L.A., their testimonials echoed these sentiments as they expressed more affinity with African Americans than they did with co-ethnic Latinos from the Eastside:

> I don't relate to Latinos in East L.A. . . . . It's completely different and I think that you know that it is because you grew up around Black culture. And not just Black culture that you see on TV, but actually Black culture and waking up in the morning and your neighbors are Black and your friends are Black. (Eugenio Ramirez, Vermont Square)

> You might be a Latino in East L.A. and you might grow up with a hatred for African Americans. . . . I know for a fact that there is whole housing projects in East L.A. who if an African American moves in, they will actually come to your door and ask you to move out because they don't like Black people living there. (Fernando Hernández, Watts)

> I work in the Staples Center. . . . So you have people from the Eastside that actually do need to work on their relationships with African Americans. Because, "Let's hang out." "Who's going?" . . . Yeah, but he's Black . . . that kind of sucks. Right here in the Southside . . . it's easy to get to know

people and make friendships, no matter the ethnicity. (Pedro Sanchez, Vermont Square)

The interviewees also identified with the popular culture, slang, and styles of South L.A., which are heavily influenced by African American culture. Because of their upbringing, this went beyond the typical white suburban youth fetishizing of "ghetto cool" styles. They felt "more mixed in" with African Americans, and many of them underscored that their Latino identities are inflected with African American cultural traditions and practices. One young woman, Analisa Espinoza from Vermont Square, put it this way:

> I feel like in South L.A. you get more of the flava . . . you're more in tune with your African American community. Like East L.A., they're probably more Americanized, but they're still probably more Mexican American and Latino or Salvadoran. . . . Here you're more mixed in.

While second-generation Latinos in South L.A. embodied elements of Black popular culture, styles, slang, and musical preferences, they were adamant that they also practiced elements of Latino cultural heritage. Twenty-nine-year-old Edwin Coto remarked, "When I got to college, I noticed the differences. I would always, you know, I have my earrings, I got my do-rags." Yet he proudly claimed both Latino and African American cultural influences. And Kathy Mendoza, who lived at home with her mother and studied criminology at a local state college, made it clear that while she embraced the critical messages of Black artists such as rapper Tupac Shakur, she distanced herself from any kind of reactive ethnic identity. "In my little Nissan Versa, I still bump Tupac," she said, "but that doesn't mean I'm gonna have his gangsta mentality. No. I just listen to what he had said. He's a force."

Neighborhood Love and Pride

What do second-generation Latino residents love about South L.A.? First, they remain fundamentally proud of the local people and the culture that shaped their upbringing here. They see South Angelenos as more open-minded and less judgmental than other people, and they credit that racial tolerance and all the challenges they encountered while growing up for shaping who they are today.

"I know I'm very proud of being a Latina here in South L.A. I always say it with *orgullo* [pride]. Even when someone asks me, 'Where did you grow up?' I'm always quick to say 'Watts.'" That is the voice of Aurelia Campa. She grew up in Watts, went away to attend a state college, but withdrew before graduating and returned home. She now lives at home and works as a special education assistant in local schools. She recognized the stigma of the place, especially during her college years, as "most people know it because of the violence, because of the gangs, of the poverty." She did not deny those problems, but she saw her social formation in Watts as having made her "a better person."

A mother of three children, Yvette Ramirez, expressed similar views. She was now raising her kids here and hoped they would adopt this type of outlook. Contact and conviviality with African American neighbors and critical mentorship helped her grow. She recalled block parties from her childhood, when African American neighborhoods revered her mom's "rice water" (*horchata*) while her family sampled southern-style barbeque. "Maybe I was lucky," she reflected, "and that's probably one of the reason why I wanted to stay here. Because I want my kids to know that—that it doesn't matter where you're from. We don't judge anybody." The project of lifting up South L.A. continues, she said, and she sees her children as part of the next step. "I hope my kids realize that there's a lot to be done to improving the condition of how we live, but I hope they grow up knowing to do their part."

And a twenty-five-year-old UCLA graduate, Sarah Gonzalez, now working at a local nonprofit, expressed pride that many South Angelenos were already working toward better futures here:

> I've met great people that do a lot of great work, that are very motivated, that are doing great things with themselves, within their lives, that [are] very committed to making a positive difference in their own way. So I'm proud of that. I'm proud to find out that there's a lot of great people that live or have lived in South L.A.

Food is a marker of culture and home, and second-generation Latinos relish these simple pleasures and comforts of their South L.A. home. For

Yvette Ramirez, a busy working woman raising three children, it was not only the familiarity and accessibility of Latino foods but also African American dishes that made life better in South L.A.:

> What I love is probably the convenience. What I'm most proud of is that on a Sunday morning, when I'm tired because I haven't stopped, and I know that Sunday is going to be just as turbulent as the other days, as far as my schedule, that I can wake up the sound of the tamale man, "Tamales!" We get too busy working around the house, and around the kids' schedule and I can just go down to Vernon and Figueroa and pick up some bomb ass tacos or homemade tortillas and be able to feed my kids. There's still that taste. And if I want some good ass fried chicken, I can also find some.

Others contrasted this with other more upscale neighborhoods lacking these cultural amenities. "The *taqueros* on the streets, the people selling corn on the cob. It's just part of South L.A.," reflected Sarah Gonzalez. Food clearly anchors a sense of belonging.

The second generation love the food and the feel of their local neighborhoods, but the young people who grew up in Watts expressed a special identification and affinity for Watts. Many of them claimed it was unique and distinct from the rest of South L.A. (and yes, Watts is at the southeastern border of South L.A.). While the 1965 Watts Rebellion catapulted Watts onto the national stage, the area has a long and storied history, and young Latinos who grew up there contrasted the sense of local community with an imagined greater anonymity of South L.A.

> I feel like South Central is a complete different monster. . . . And like, I lived in Watts. . . . So that's where I'm from. (Marco Rivera, twenty-nine years old)

> Watts is much smaller, and I feel like South L.A. is a little bit more dangerous, personally. It's more populated over there, too. I don't know how to describe Watts I really don't. It's just, to me, normal [laughter]. 'Cause I've lived here my whole life. (Emiliana Orozco, twenty-eight years old)

> There is more unity [in Watts] . . . the block where I live, like, we're a lot tighter. We help each other out a lot." (Aurelia Campa, thirty-three years old)

Part of me will always be from Watts. . . . I never shy away from working in Watts and speaking positives about Watts. (Lydia Quintanilla, thirty-five years old)

At Home in South L.A.

Scholars have used terms such as "foundational Blackness" and a "relational consciousness of race" to describe the racial identities we found among the Latino second generation raised in South L.A.[20] Our contribution to this debate emphasizes the ways in which these racial identities have been shaped by place and by a range of experiences with African American people in multiple venues. This included fights and friendships, grudges and gratitude. Unlike what happened with their immigrant parents, one altercation with an African American person did not sear anti-Black prejudice into their racial imaginations and mappings of the world. This suggests a melding of contact theory and relational racialization as an appropriate framework for understanding how proximity and regular encounters produced these racial outlooks.[21]

While young Latinos raised in other cities have experienced themselves as expendable or rejected by society, our respondents express an agentic disposition and positive confidence about their future.[22] They feel they belong. In this respect, they echo Maria Rendón's "resolute optimists," yet they remain clear-eyed and critical about structural barriers they have overcome and those that remain (e.g., racism, poorly supported schools, a lack of commercial investment, to name a few).[23] Notably, they did not attribute their relative success to only kin but also to place. Consequently, they want to repay not only the "immigrant bargain" of succeeding to compensate for immigrant parental sacrifice, but they want to give back to the communities that shaped them.[24] Their American dream is not the house in the suburb but the multiracial home of South L.A.

South L.A. is home, a place of love where they feel a sense of security, familiarity, autonomy, and hope. They remain acutely aware and proud of how they have overcome territorial stigmatization and all kinds of challenges. Urban theorists and historians have noted the important role

Figure 4.5. I Love Watts Mural
Photo Credit: Walter Thompson-Hernández, USC CSII project team.

played by Latino immigrants in revitalizing American cities in recent decades, sometimes crediting the role of transnational homeland practices and connections, but young Latinos in South L.A. remain resolute in their appreciation and solidarity with African Americans in South L.A.[25] They recognize the diminishing number of African Americans in South L.A., but their hope for the future is to pass on to their children an appreciation for Black culture. South L.A. is central to who they are and who they seek to become.

Love and pride of place and appreciation for both African American and Latino culture prevailed among our respondents. Fernando Hernández had not graduated from high school in Watts, but he loved Watts and the person it had made him (see figure 4.5). What made them different in Watts? "We're tougher," he said. "We've had to persevere our whole lives, whether it's getting bullied or whatever. . . . If you make it through, you come out stronger. You really do. There is an acronym for Watts and it's We are All Taught To Survive." He noted,

This is home to me . . . I may not have the job I want, or the income I want, you know, but . . . I am content with where I am right now . . . just as an all-around life, the people I am surrounded with, I am happy. I wouldn't change a thing. I love it here.

This was not atypical of the deep admiration many of our younger respondents shared for South L.A., a place into which their parents had arrived but a place where they and their parents had been able to set roots, find friends, and make lives. Yet another aspect of homemaking and crafting meaning in a new locale involves connecting to public spaces, such as parks and gardens, and it is to that aspect of the experience in South L.A. that we now turn.

5

Sharing Ground, Carving Space

PIERRETTE HONDAGNEU-SOTELO, JOSE MIGUEL RUIZ, ANTAR TICHAVAKUNDA, AND ADRIÁN TRINIDAD

Homemaking is more than what happens in the domestic hearth—it extends outward into micro-geographies, ties with neighbors, and a sense of both pride in the past and hope in the future. The local neighborhood has often served as an important site of home and belonging for immigrant and ethnic communities. To deepen our understanding of these connections, geographers Alison Blunt and Olivia Sheringham urge us to pay attention to "the interconnectedness of domestic and urban realms," and they introduce the term "domestic urbanism" for considering parts of the city as home.[1] Similarly exhorting us to see multiple scales of home, sociologists Paolo Boccagni and Jan Willem Duyvendak draw attention to who can make legitimate claims on public space in multifaceted diverse societies.[2] And taking note of the "subjectivities of place," sociologists Angela Garcia and Leah Schmalzbauer remind us of the ways immigrants' sense of belonging may be shaped by plant nature.[3]

Taken together, these are important points of departure for scaling out to see homemaking in the city. Homelike activities and relationships may unfold in many places in the city (i.e., churches, clubs), and in this chapter, we focus on public parks and community gardens. And one critical form of homemaking has to do with attachment to the activities and relationships that unfold in the precious few shared green spaces in South Los Angeles.

For African American and Latino residents, especially for boys and men, the public parks of South Los Angeles serve as critical sites of belonging, sovereignty, and personal restoration. These are common grounds, places where one can go for free to relax alone while meditatively staring as a cloud moves overhead or to take the kids, gather with others to play basketball or soccer, or join in a drum circle. At the gardens, coaxing food from seeds takes deliberate, long-sustained efforts, but that, too, can be relaxing and can bring about another state of mind. Other important unwinding activities happen at the parks and gardens too. Inebriation. Sharing barbeque. Playing dominoes or cards. These sites are not without tension and problems, of course, but they are critical places for social restoration, healing, and coexistence with others.[4] For many men in South L.A., the public parks and urban community gardens are a home away from home.

This chapter reports on a kind of homemaking and coexistence that African American and Latino men find in the parks and community gardens of South L.A. Our data are based on observations and interviews that we conducted with fifty-three people at four sites: Martin Luther King, Jr. Park, located near Vermont/Slauson neighborhood; Fred Roberts Park, on the edge of historic South Central Avenue; and two large community gardens in Watts, the Stanford Avalon Community Garden and the Greater Watts Community Garden (see figure 5.1).[5] Our primary focus is on the men who congregate at the parks and gardens. Drawing from intersectionality insights, we acknowledge that while men in South L.A. enjoy masculine privileges in public space, they remain marginalized by processes of racial oppression, hyper-employment or underemployment, and regimes of criminalization and immigrant illegality. At the public parks and community gardens, they are finding "home away from home."

We begin by reviewing the background of park development in Los Angeles, particularly the scarcity of such space in places like South L.A. We then explain the focus of our study on parks and gardens, briefly discussing the methods and further explaining the focus on men's experience. We then highlight how parks and gardens help African American and Latino men find sanctuary, demonstrate responsibility, enjoy conviviality, and experience a sense of being "at home." In line with the focus of this book, we also note that while Latinos and African Americans often experience parks and gardens in their separate racial-ethnic groups, there is a spirit of togetherness, civility, and commonality that reflects the general tone (seen in chapter 6) of South L.A. as shared Black–Brown space.

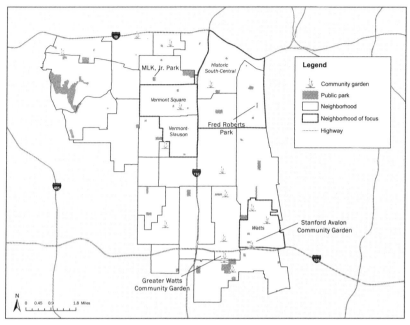

Figure 5.1. Public Parks and Community Gardens, South L.A.
Source: Created by University of Southern California (USC) Center for the Study of Immigrant Integration (CSII) project team with data from Cultivate L.A. (4/1/17 version) for community gardens, L.A. County for parks, Census TIGER/Line, and ESRI.

Studying the Parks

Los Angeles has plenty of beautiful open park space—but it is generally located far away from the neighborhoods where it is needed most.[6] Griffith Park, with over four thousand acres of natural wilderness areas, hiking trails, shady picnic tables, and recreational facilities, including fields, a merry-go-round, and pony rides and capped off by the cinematic Griffith Observatory, is truly spectacular. But it remains far from the low-income urban neighborhoods where most African American and Latino residents live. The Santa Monica Mountains National Recreation Area, with over five hundred miles of hiking trails, is situated even farther away in the mountains behind Malibu, requiring a very long, congested freeway trek up the dreaded 405 Freeway from South L.A., and Latinos who have visited report feeling excluded and unwelcome.[7]

And, of course, Los Angeles has miles of beautiful public beaches, but these are also distant from South L.A.

Los Angeles developed as a city with small, private "homestead" gardens in backyards, and developers and city officials failed to add grand public parks, such as San Francisco's Golden Gate Park or New York City's Central Park. In part for this reason, and due to residential segregation, many urban planners, sociologists, and geographers find evidence of racial and social class inequalities reflected in the public parks of Los Angeles. When it comes to L.A. parks, it can be said, as geographer Jason Byrne has suggested, that "green is white."[8] Public parks are seemingly open to "the public," but not everyone enjoys access, as fewer well-maintained parks are located in the neighborhoods where poor and working-class Latino and African American residents live. Regimes of power and inequality have produced a scarcity of public green spaces in the African American and Latino neighborhoods of Los Angeles.

Parks and Gardens in South L.A.

Public parks and community gardens do exist in South L.A., and in recent years, these have flourished because community activists, city officials, and nonprofit organizations have vigorously advocated for their expansion and improvement. After decades of neglect, new public investments by the City and County of Los Angeles have allowed South L.A. residents to reclaim the public parks. One can observe new recreational and exercise facilities, renovated recreational centers and landscaping, programming for children and youth, and new mini-parks.[9]

A Summer Night Lights program began in 2007 and by 2019 expanded to thirty-two L.A. parks and recreation centers, providing sports, arts, and other evening programming for youth, and this led to significant drops in violent crime.[10] Mayor Antonio Villaraigosa's 2012 program to add fifty parks and L.A. County's Comprehensive Parks and Recreation Needs Assessment study completed in 2016, and efforts by public agencies, sometimes assisted by nonprofits and supported with private funding, constitute significant attempts aimed at building new parks and improving the infrastructure of older parks, especially those located in poor communities where people of color live.

It is not just governmental action. Organizations such as Los Angeles Neighborhood Land Trust, Los Angeles Community Gardening Coalition, Community Services Unlimited, the Los Angeles Food Policy Council, Rivers and Mountains Conservancy, and T.R.U.S.T. South L.A. are some of the groups working on these issues in South L.A. Activist individuals have also brought about change. Until 2015, it was illegal to grow carrots or cabbage in the parkway space between the sidewalk and the curb, but legalization of this practice, by L.A. city council vote, occurred only after African American designer and resident Ron Finley (aka "gansta gardener") challenged citations he received from the Bureau of Street Services for growing vegetables in front of his home in South L.A. His challenge received widespread media and public support.[11]

Urban community gardens have also met with great enthusiasm and new support.[12] Today, there are forty-nine public parks and sixteen urban community gardens serving diverse communities in South Los Angeles, as seen in figure 5.1 (shown earlier). This is a welcome but somewhat new development. Ten and twenty years earlier, L.A. parks and gardens were fewer and alarmingly neglected. Before Stanford Avalon Community Garden opened in 2006, the land had been nine acres holding Los Angeles Department of Water and Power utility lines, essentially a "dead space" scattered with garbage, needles, and abandoned sofas. Fred Roberts Park had been established in 1957, but since the city made no significant renovations for decades, it became very rundown until it reopened after new infrastructural improvements in 2012. Indeed, a nineteen-year-old park-goer who grew up in the neighborhood described the Fred Roberts Park of his childhood as "just dirt" and "always tough."

Martin Luther King (MLK) Park was also in disarray and threatened with closure by the city until Community Coalition began working with neighbors in 2008 to improve the park and organized residents to march for city reinvestment in the park. They also mitigated the negative impact of a nearby liquor store by working directly with the owner, Mr. Park. Many of our interviewees testified to the dramatic transformations in infrastructure, programming, and safety at MLK Park. One young man said, "It was full of gangs [before]. It's clean now. . . . Back in the day, you couldn't come to this park," and a caregiver whom we met at MLK Park while she was pushing a senior citizen in a wheelchair concurred that "this park has come a long way." Meanwhile, new mini-parks emerged in South L.A. neighborhoods too, prompting, as one journalist remarked, "delight" and "surprise" among residents and providing much-needed shade and green space in what can be an otherwise oppressively hot, asphalted city streetscape.[13]

In general, L.A. is spending more money on improving existing parks and adding new park space.[14] The improvements are real, yet many people remain on guard about their own security. In this chapter, we focus not on evaluating people's satisfaction with recent transformations but, rather, on discerning what these places mean to them and how they make a "home away from home" at these sites. In particular, we ask, "How do Latino and African American men create home-like places for themselves in the public gardens and community gardens of South L.A., how do they narrate what this does for them, and to what extent do these activities promote community cohesion and cross-racial relationship building?"

Why Men?

First, we must explain our focus on men. Current research on public parks emphasizes class and racial inequalities, but a focus on gender exclusions seems to have fallen by the wayside. Four decades ago, second-wave feminists, primarily working in geography and urban planning, made important interventions on this issue. Geographer Linda McDowell noted that "there are strong pressures exerted on women to physically restrict themselves to the domestic aspects of cities and urban life."[15] In an article titled "Women in Urban Parks," Galen Cranz declared that "[t]he role of women in public spaces is still as problematic as it was in the nineteenth century."[16] These declarations still resonate in the first decades of the twenty-first century.[17]

Our research confirmed that many women and girls stay away from the public parks and community gardens in South L.A. Early observations conducted by a diverse team of University of Southern California (USC) undergraduates, graduate students, and postdoctoral fellows showed us that women and girls rarely go to the parks alone or with female friends. Indeed, as we describe in the portion of the appendix in which describe our overall research process, we began the research with a team conducting observations in several green sites, and it quickly became apparent that sending young female USC students to South L.A. parks alone was ill advised.

At our research roundtables, the young Latina students said they were regularly greeted with catcalls and sexual harassment by men at the parks (by contrast, at the community gardens in Watts, they were made to feel welcomed by an older set of African American and Latino men). Their experience as researchers was not unique: concern for safety prevents many women from using the public parks in the same way men do. Violent crime is down in South L.A., as it is everywhere in the United States, and nearly everyone agreed that streets and parks in South L.A. were safer than they used to be. Still, without our prompting or solicitation, our interviewees said these places should be approached cautiously. This fear factor both guided who used the parks and who could conduct ethnographic work in them and that was a limiting factor.

Indeed, even many of the *men* we interviewed testified that their local parks had been totally off-limits to them just a few years ago. For many of them, coming to the park with children or younger siblings in tow was a relatively new development.[18] Daniel, a forty-five-year-old father of three, recalled that growing up as an adolescent around the local parks, "You had to be aware of your surroundings. There was a lot of muggings, a lot of gangbangers. . . . It was rough and I've seen it change now." And Frederick called MLK Park "a sometime-y park," clarifying that "[t]his is where damn near everybody throws their little hood functions and get-togethers and all. It's safe sometimes. . . . You just gotta get an understanding with everyone."

MLK Park was in fact widely described as a "Crip-controlled park," and we observed drug sales, mild and intense levels of intoxication, and open prostitution regularly occurring there. But these parks are spaces of coexistence, not only for African Americans and Latinos but also for homeless people, gang members, and sex workers who share the space with soccer and basketball players and parents pushing kids on swings. We sought to interview anyone who we could respectfully approach to speak with us, and this included gang-affiliated men and sometimes a few people who were drinking or had just smoked marijuana.[19]

Gangs are still around, but gang violence has subsided, and today one is less likely to come across gang fights in the parks. Trepidation and fear remain, a trauma hangover from decades of public violence. Growing up in South L.A., youth were explicitly instructed by their parents to avoid the parks, and this is especially true for women and girls. For example, thirty-one-year-old Cecilia Rodriguez raised near Vermont Square and now a teacher who lives and works in that neighborhood, recalled that her parents had forbidden her to walk through MLK Park on the way to the school bus stop. When asked to explain why this was the case, she said:

> There was a lot of crime. There was a lot of drug dealing going on there, and my parents knew it, so you just stayed away from it. That was one of the places. To date, they don't like it when I walk south on Western to King. If I'm walking north, it's fine, but if I'm walking south to King, they still don't like it, even though I'm 31 years old now. And it has to do a lot with their perception of safety.

Another young man recalled the parks of his childhood as "crazy" with "people getting it on in the bushes" and "shooting up." This has changed, but in interviews conducted with first-generation Latino immigrant community residents, a number of women told us they still steer clear of the public parks in their local neighborhoods. They do not think these are safe or desirable green spaces, so they prefer to drive to parks in more affluent neighborhoods, such as Kenneth Hahn Park, located farther west near Culver City and Baldwin Hills, where they go to jog or power walk or take their children and grandchildren to the playground.

Indeed, gardens and parks reflect society and its broader mix of sexual harassment, misogyny, and unfair domestic burdens, all of which restrict women's activity at parks and community gardens. When women and girls do go to the parks we studied, we observed that it is typically in the company of children and family. In other words, it becomes an extension of domestic duties—supervising young children on playgrounds, watching kids at soccer or baseball practice, or doing food preparation and enjoying a family picnic. Some of the South L.A. parks feature recently installed exercise equipment, and you might see a mother and daughter or two friends using the equipment. But the indoor Zumba classes that have proliferated in storefronts and recreation centers around South L.A. seem to be more popular alternatives for women's exercise than the outdoor park equipment. Although we interviewed women at the parks and gardens, for the previously mentioned reasons, we decided to focus our analysis on men's experiences.

Not only are the public parks sites of conviviality and relaxation primarily for men and boys, but the big, expansive community gardens in Watts where we did our research—Stanford Avalon Community Garden and the Greater Watts Community Garden—are also predominantly male. At these sites, there are some women who are very dedicated, talented gardeners, but they are fewer in number, and often, but not always, they are cultivating with a spouse. Men over age fifty-five predominate in these gardens. When we asked the male gardeners why there are not more women tilling the soil, they said the women are tied up with looking after kids and cooking and cleaning or that the women are lazy and do not want to do the work. It *does* take substantial time and hard labor to cultivate here. Some of the garden plots span 1,500 square feet, and growing food in that expanse of soil takes lots of muscle, dedication, and time.

Turning some research lemons into knowledge lemonade, we decided to pursue an intersectional analysis of men and marginalized masculinities. As we see it, both African American and Latino men in South L.A. are simultaneously empowered by masculine privilege in family/work/public spaces and yet marginalized by processes of racial subordination, class, and regimes of criminalization, incarceration, and immigrant illegality. Taking these conditions into account, we focus on how the men use South L.A. parks and gardens to create a sense of place and belonging, and we examine the extent to which Latino and African American men are collaborating, sharing, and engaging with one another.

The Sites of Study

Long ago in the nineteenth century, when he designed Central Park, Frederick Law Olmsted envisioned parks as urban pastoral sites where people of different social classes would mingle. Today, that romantic image prevails when people think of community gardens too, often in multicultural contexts.[20] In reality, both parks and community are contested spaces. Community gardens are sites of struggle for food justice, cultural autonomy, and against land displacement.[21] Moreover, as Loukaitou-Sideris notes, contemporary parks have been seen as "a battleground where different social groups fight over territorial turf."[22] Parks and gardens are neither Edenic utopias nor war zones, but in neighborhoods with scarce stretches of plant nature, public parks and gardens take on outsized significance.

Because context and contestation matter, each green space we studied presents its own social world—and each has a particular history. MLK Park is located on Western Avenue, just outside the Vermont Square neighborhood. Its 2.4 acres are divided among spaces of coexistence for multiple activities: adult and youth soccer, basketball and baseball, a Sunday afternoon drum circle, a small playground, temporary, makeshift homeless encampments, a recreational center, and a beautiful library on one corner, situated directly across the street from a liquor store. Once the site of organized dog fights and violent gang battles, it had been deliberately avoided by many local residents, and the City had planned to close it. Community Coalition successfully organized for the revitalization of MLK Park, and today, it is a vibrant and well-used park for both local residents and for people who once lived in the area. Still, drug sales, open prostitution, and intoxicated people passed out by the restrooms are still regular sights at this park. In this regard, it remains a shared space of coexistence. Park-goers have offered a range of reviews on the recreational facilities at this park.[23]

The Fred Roberts Park in the historic South Central Avenue neighborhood is smaller, about three-quarters of an acre, and while families, children, and some African Americans use the park, the park users here are primarily Latino, reflecting the current local neighborhood demographic. The park opened in 1957, but with the lack of public investment in South Central during the late twentieth century, the city made no renovations or improvements here for over fifty years, until between 2009 and 2012; many of the men we interviewed noted that the park, until recently, had been "a dump" and "just a lot of dirt."[24] A recreation center with programming for children, including Tae Kwon Do lessons, now draws parents who bring their children, and basketball courts attract youth who come here for pickup games. A fenced and newly renovated soccer field conveniently has a hole in the fence, allowing soccer players to play after hours. Just as at MLK Park, park-goers here praised recent transformations and upgrades at this park, but they also expressed wariness about coming here at night, and the park users were mostly men.

The community gardens in Watts were born of racialized political struggle. One of the garden sites we selected is distinctively African American and the other is Mexican and Central American. The Greater Watts Community Garden formed in the post–civil rights era when the Black Power movement in Watts and South Central L.A. gave rise to new political, artistic, and cultural organizations centered on Black autonomy and sovereignty. The Black Panther Party is the most well known of these, but also important were the Watts Writers Workshop and Community Services Unlimited. Some of the community gardeners here were involved in these organizations, including one who worked on the 1973 documentary *Wattstax* (who unfortunately did not wish to participate in one of our interviews).[25] Today, most of the gardeners here are older, retired African American men, and some of them arrive very early in the morning to tend their substantial plots, and throughout the day, they join friends for conversation and dominoes and hang out under shade structures. There are approximately forty plots here, and we were told that five women are cultivating here, four of them with a spouse. Except for one white woman who tended a plot with her Black husband, everyone here was African American. Many of them have family roots in the South, especially Texas, Louisiana, and Oklahoma but also Mississippi, Georgia, and Alabama. Gardening here is an expression of survival, conviviality, and connection with Southern homeland roots.

The Stanford Avalon Community Garden is located under the power lines only a few blocks away, and it, too, was born of political struggle. It is the offshoot of the South Central Farm, forty acres of land situated in a very industrial zone of South L.A. that had been cultivated by more than three hundred Mexican and Central American families until it was bulldozed in 2006 (the struggle of the South Central Farm is discussed further in chapter 6).[26] In the aftermath, organizers and cultivators appealed to the City and established the nine-acre Stanford Avalon Community Garden (SACG) in Watts, which includes 209 plots. This is a large area, and a freeway (the 105 Century Freeway) runs right through it, as does the four-lane Imperial Highway and a currently unused railroad track. Each plot is rented out for a monthly fee of $20, and the fee covers the water bill, and it is collected by a nonprofit organization, the

Los Angeles Community Gardening Council. During our time at SACG, we learned of two Black gardeners cultivating there, and although there are several women, the majority of growers here were Latino immigrant men, many of them retirement age. They refer to themselves as *campesinos*, peasant farmers.

Finding Home in Common Ground

A walk in the park or growing collard greens—what could be simpler? We contend, however, that for men in South Los Angeles, inhabiting public green spaces is an achievement. Their daily practices at the parks and community gardens and their conviviality and engagement with plant nature are assertions of the right to belong in a certain place. For the African American and Latino men that we interviewed in South L.A., the public parks and community gardens are extensions of home, places where they enact what Blunt and Sheringham call "domestic urbanism," the city as home.[27]

In a study of nearby parks in Compton and South Central, sociologist Randol Contreras found African American and Latino men responding with "spatial anguish," which he defines as "shame that comes from living in a stigmatized space."[28] While our interviewees voiced concern over neighborhood problems, such as gatherings of drug addicts or homeless people at a park, they overwhelmingly expressed love, pride, and attachment to the local parks and community gardens. They experienced these sites as positive, homelike places. In the following subsections, we present our ethnographic and interview data organized by the five themes that emerged in our analysis of what the men find at the parks and gardens in South L.A.: (1) solace and sanctuary in urban nature, (2) experiences of themselves as responsible family men, (3) male sovereignty and sociability, (4) belonging and feeling "at home," and (5) an emergent civic culture.

Sanctuary and Solace in Nature

The Latino and African American men who gather in the parks and community gardens of South Los Angeles find solace in nature. The community gardens in Watts attract mostly older, retired men, some of whom are now physically disabled and sickly. Some have suffered alcoholism, illness, family separations, and dissolutions. Others are now caring for sickly spouses, and most of them put in long years of dedication to their jobs. At the public parks, a more diverse and younger set of Latino and African American men gather to play basketball or soccer and to enjoy conversation, barbeque, and drum circle. Some of them go to the parks so that their children can do sports or use the swings at the playground. While there are similarities, the parks invite more itinerant sociability than the gardens. At the gardens, the men come several times a week, if not daily, returning to the same spot to spend a mixture of time working the soil alone and socializing with familiar friends.

The men say that coming to the parks and community gardens restores them. In Spanish and in English, among young and old, they testified to the therapeutic draw of these green spaces. At MLK Park, Lorenzo said, "I don't know what it is, but it's like when I'm here, I just forget about my stresses. It just goes away." We heard some version of this at all the sites. "*Aqui me relajo*. . . . This is where I relax," and "*Es una terapia* . . . It's a therapy." Twenty-four-year-old Frederick said he came to MLK Park for "[c]hilling with friends, and wanting to get away from all of the problems." Even though he called the park "gang famous," it still drew him enough to take the metro all the way up from Watts about twice a week. He was struggling with life after incarceration, hoping to get his GED and continue with higher education. He came here, he said, "Just to think, get away and stare at a cloud or something. As a grown-up, it's more about thinking and just getting away from all of the problems." Another young man, Darnell, said being at the park returned him to the carefree times of childhood. "You free right here. Kind of remind you of childhood, so you get to drifting off . . . you let go of whatever going on in your mind. You sit here, and it's like meditation." An older park-goer said, "The park to me is like a sanctuary—it's like going to church. You know what I mean, a piece of sanctuary, quietness and just watching people be happy. That's what the park means to me."[29]

At the Fred Roberts Park in the historic South Central Avenue neighborhood, Latino immigrant men of diverse ages also seek peace and relaxation. Twenty-nine-year-old Cesar, a DREAMer (provisionally authorized) college student who was born in Mexico but grew up in the vicinity, said he never came to the park as a child and stayed away as a young adolescent because of fear of assaults from gang members. Now that conditions had improved, he, like others, "come here just to relax and drift away from the stress." Sometimes he brings a book.

At the same park, we also interviewed Tiburcio, a forty-eight-year-old street vendor from Puebla, Mexico, who sells food at the park. He is illiterate, undocumented, and separated from his family. On days when not selling popsicles and *chicharrones* at the park, he sells flowers near the freeway onramps. For him, the park invites daydreaming and dreaminess, even when he is selling popsicles. He shared, "*Hay veces. . . .* There are times when I come here and I laugh when I see the children playing. I forget my problems that I've had all day." He continued, generously sharing his fantasies: "*A veces me digo. . . .* Sometimes I say to myself, how nice you would look right here with your wife, maybe eating an ice-cream while the children play," he said. But he quickly added that this scenario was unlikely, as "*dos glorias no se puede tener . . .* one cannot have two glories," by which he meant having work and family in the same place. For Tiburcio, the park is a site that allows him to imagine the impossible and to recharge his energy to continue forward as an undocumented informal-sector worker struggling to survive in the United States while his family is in Mexico.

Parks are often appreciated as settings for sports, but these also serve as sites of reflection. Big life decisions occur in silence at these green spaces. One of the most acutely realized moments of this research project occurred when Antar Tichavakunda approached a young man whom we will call Isaac, sitting alone on the grass, wearing pink socks and no shoes in the middle of MLK Park. Isaac had spent the night in the park and revealed that he had just escaped assault from a rival gang. With a long-standing warrant out for his arrest, he was sitting alone in the dew and contemplating turning himself in to the authorities. As an Afro-Belizean, he worried not only about prison but also about deportation. He shared the following:

> I'm here at the park [laughs]. I'm here for clarification for that clear mind of thought. And I'm trying to prepare myself to go into jail for eight years. Hopefully they don't fuckin' kick me out of the country, you know? I'm praying, you know what I mean?

Figure 5.2. Planting a Garden
Photo Credit: Pierrette Hondagneu-Sotelo, USC CSII project team.

At the end of the conversation, he and Antar prayed together for his future. We do not know what happened to him, but instances such as this show how the parks can provide a momentary refuge in times of crisis.

At the community gardens in Watts, the men spend many hours alone, amending and tilling the soil, sowing seeds, pulling weeds, and watering by hose (see figure 5.2). This takes consistent dedication. Some of the men are there daily, while others come several days a week. Tomas, a middle-aged father of three daughters, could only find time away from his busy work and family schedules to come tend his plot about twice a week. Growing and eating his own vegetables had helped him lose fifty pounds, he said, promoting physical health. But he also emphasized what this place meant for his emotional well-being:

> *Yo creo que la conexión con la tierra.* . . . I think the connection with the soil is really important. . . . Nature, the trees and plants, gives us oxygen and allow our minds to think with clarity. So, I might be stressed out and

about to make decisions, but once you go to the plants, you clear your mind, your thoughts and your feelings.

He continued, opining that lack of closeness with nature is what causes so many problems in the world: "That's why I think so much violence exists in some people. Why? Because they don't have a natural *desahogo* [outlet]. I'm happy here. I like what I'm doing. That's why I'm here."

A few blocks away, at the Greater Watts Community Garden (GWCG), African American men are cultivating similar experiences. Jason, a spry sixty-three-year-old with a sinewy build and a hyper-kinetic energy, served as the volunteer president for one side of GWCG, which is divided by a street. He arrived at the garden early each morning, around 6:30 a.m., to tend to his substantial array of both edible and ornamental plants. Of his experiences here, he said:

> I like the freedom, the sanctuary type of thing, you know what I mean? That freedom of mind. It's like yoga, but it's more physical, right? Yoga is more mental, but this is physical so it gets me that sanctuary, that freedom of mind and that free thought, you know? So, you are not obligated to your responsibilities. . . . More than anything, that and giving away. Giving anything away.

At GWCG, the African American gardeners grew copious quantities of food, and yet they proudly told us, "We don't sell anything here." We were initially skeptical of the claim that they grew food only for their own consumption and to give to others, in part because of the large scale of produce, but then we, too, became recipients of food and plant gifts. The gardeners here saw collective sharing as part of their cultural tradition. As Julia, one of the few women gardeners at GWCG told us, gifting food was a fundamental part of her childhood in East Texas. "My job was to take something, a jar of peaches to Miss So-and-So, by way of sharing. We had animals too and every now and then they would kill a pig . . . my job would be to take bacon to So-and-So. There was a sense of sharing in the community and I grew up with that." And Jason similarly recalled his childhood in rural Sacramento, saying "My mother was a Samaritan. . . . If there was someone without a dinner, or was hungry, or came through, she fed everyone from her garden and also her kitchen."

African American gardeners here continue this tradition, giving food away to hungry people, and in the process, they create community and invoke a sense of spiritual peace. They are also continuing a long tradition of agriculture as a site of Black resistance, as the sociologist Monica M. White has shown.[30] One Sunday morning, we observed an older gentleman who we shall call Mac, wearing twill coveralls over his nice street clothes as he loaded multiple bags of collard greens, beets, and beans into his wife's late-model luxury car. She was dressed in her Sunday finest and on her way to church to distribute the food to families in her congregation. As another farmer put it,

> [e]verybody is pretty joyous at what they see. A lot of people really. You don't see this every day. . . . When they come here [for free produce], they are excited. They're really stimulated and it's hard to say no to them. I give them whatever I have to the last. It doesn't matter to me because I can grow more, right? I just want them to come back and tell me how good it was. (Jason, at GWCG)

One can observe other elements of spirituality and Zen-like calm practiced at the community gardens. Over the course of a year at SACG, Pierrette had interviewed and conversed several times with José, a married father of eight and a construction worker in his forties, who tends a diversely planted vegetable plot. He has been working in L.A. factories and construction since migrating from Mexico at age fourteen, and now his construction jobs often necessitate a fatiguing two-hour freeway drive each way daily, to and from home. When interviewed, he said the garden was not only a place to grow vegetables and herbs for his family but also a place where he feels "*en casa*" or "at home," a place where he relaxes in solitude and can express his "*amor por la tierra* . . . love of the land."

Several months later, on a Sunday afternoon as Pierrette approached, José was sitting alone in silence. Here is what she later recorded in field notes:

> I strolled to the very end, and then I saw J.R., sitting alone below his shade structure, constructed of plastic tarp draped over plastic tube pipes. From a distance, he seemed to be in quiet prayer, with his eyes downcast.

I wasn't sure I should interrupt him, but I called out "*Buenas tardes*," and he responded, "*Hola, pase no más.*" ["Good afternoon" and "Hi, come on in."] . . . He was spending his Sunday afternoon in Zen-like solitude, intently de-thorning beautiful fresh paddles of *nopales* that he had just harvested. I wish I had had a video camera to capture this, because there was a skill and simplicity to this repetitive, careful work, and a very calming vibe. We both sat on chairs under his shade structure, and our conversation rambled to topics like the weather and if we will have a big wet winter, our families, and work . . . (Field notes, SACG, 13 September 2015)

Cultivating alone in silence, close-up with plant nature, and de-spining nopales as gifts for relatives, these can be seen as both spiritual practices and practices of self-care that occur in relative solitude for these men. Hard work and hardship have defined their lives as Latino immigrant workers and African American men in Southern California. With plant nature in the parks and gardens, time slows down, and these men create places for solace, sanctuary, and self-care.

Responsible Family Men

While white middle-class men may see traditional, hegemonic bread-winner responsibilities as a yoke from which to flee, for poor and working-class African American, Chicano, and Mexican immigrant men, fulfilling these traditional responsibilities and positioning oneself as "a family man" can be an elusive and hard-won achievement.[31] At public parks and community gardens, Latino and African American men can experience themselves as responsible family men. Going to the park with children or raising vegetables for family consumption and income generation allows these men to express an ethic of care and to perform visible contributions to their families. This is an important claim for poor and marginalized men of color who frequently contend with negative cultural stereotypes of Black and Brown men as uncaring, irresponsible fathers.

Parks serve as public sites to enact fatherhood. Family leisure is expensive in cities like Los Angeles, and the parks provide free places to take the kids for play, sports, and leisure. Lorenzo, interviewed while sitting with his wife and his five-year-old daughter on a red blanket, watching a soccer game, and enjoying music from the adjacent African American drum circle, said it was important to bring children to explore and experience "adventure" at the park. He recognized the dangers of parks in South Los Angeles, but he added "since the police have taken over" he now felt sufficiently safe to relax and bring his child. While this father remained concerned about what he called "the unsavory groups" at MLK Park, he and his wife said that the presence of undercover police here added a sense of comfort. Marshall, with three young children in tow, said, "All my kids is small, so this park has a small section and a mid section . . . I just let them do them, and I just sit here and be a dad."

Interestingly, Terrence put his fathering practice at the park in terms of racial politics: "I feel like man, you gotta do this for your own race, for your own self. You ain't gotta have no money to go to the park. Park is free. The time you spend with your kids is precious." When interviewed, he himself had not been to the park for the past six months, yet he raised a critique of African American fathers, opining that "[t]here are not a lot of Black men that are out here that take kids out there. They're too busy doing other things, as far as gangbanging, shooting somebody, robbing." And he contrasted this with Latino fathers, saying, "If you see somebody with their sons, I mean you might see a lot of Latinos, because they have a lot of them. And they work." In this instance, Terrence, who was himself African American, drew on familiar negative stereotypes of Black fathers and racial hierarchies to narratively position himself as a "good" father.[32]

There was also racial discourse involving positive interactions across racial and linguistic boundaries. An African American couple were interviewed together as they watched their six-year-old son play t-ball, while their teenaged daughter looked on slightly bored. The thirty-ish African American mother in this couple, Janice, voiced appreciation and gratitude for the Latino immigrant men who were helping coach her son, and she suggested that their efforts were exactly the kind of shared commitment that enhanced MLK Park. Here, language was no barrier, and she spoke appreciatively of what she saw as the collective ethic of care for children in the community:

I like to see the Blacks and Latinos in the park. We shouldn't have to go way out to some other park to do this [youth sports]. We should be able to do this here. . . . We're all family people. We are all dedicated to all of the kids—it's not just one of the kids. I mean, it's men out here—they don't even speak English, but they help all of these kids. They don't have to do that, you know.

These dynamics resemble similar processes witnessed by sociologist A. James McKeever in youth sports at a San Fernando Valley park.[33] In that context, Latino, African American, and Armenian American youth benefitted from a multiracial, intergenerational mentoring system led by African American and Latino male coaches and park employees.

Another variant of fatherly care that we detected occurred on Sunday afternoons near the drum circle at MLK Park. Members of a motorcycle club, a mature group of muscular African American men in their fifties and sixties, gathered under shady picnic tables with refreshments to enjoy the live music. We interviewed two of them, and they explained that in their youth they had been involved in "negativity," but they now saw themselves as responsible elders. Clad in black leather vests bearing the name of their biker club, they came to the park on Sunday, they said, to "chill and spread positivity." They positioned themselves as fatherly "old heads," gathering at the park to enjoy the afternoon's music scene and to serve as positive role models for younger men.[34] And this, too, took on a cross-racial cast. One of them said, "Look around you, man. This right here is a Latino park. You see Blacks, Jamaicans, Haitians, doing what they do. . . . It's a Sunday and we all come together."

This tone was echoed by a young, bearded, bespectacled, and slightly obese man named Ramiro, who was bringing his little brother to the library at MLK Park. "People kind of keep to their own. But then you have this," he said, motioning to his ten-year-old brother playing with an African American boy. "It's all love. He just came over and asked to play. It's cool, you know?" His comments, and those of others, reminds us of how the parks offer opportunities for shared activities between Latino and African American park-goers. And children often facilitate shared activities across racial boundaries.

At SACG and GWCG, children remain noticeably absent. Children and grandchildren may occasionally visit or help with garden labor but not often. The men do not want kids, or really anyone for that matter, trampling their radishes or small seedlings. Instead, the Latino immigrant men fulfill family duties by growing food for their families, by earning income through the sale of produce, and by connecting to ancestral practices they were taught on by their fathers, mothers, and grandparents on ranchos in Mexico and Central America.

As sixty-four-year-old Jorge said, "*Sí, como se cultiva*. . . . Yes, how to cultivate, how to harvest, yes they [parents and grandparents] taught us so that we could do the same." And we heard similar refrains from the African American gardeners at GWCG. They spoke of the farms and backyard gardens that their grandparents and parents had maintained in the South or in rural California. "I'm using what I learned," Jason said, "hand to hand from my mother." Henry proudly recalled that in Mississippi, "[his] father grew enough food for the neighborhood." For both groups of men, re-creating a kind of rural geographic habitus in the middle of inner-city Watts simultaneously anchors them to the earth and to their families of the present and the past.[35]

Income generation occurs at SACG, too. A number of the men sell the produce they grow, although this practice was then, at the time of our research, technically illegal.[36] On weekends, we saw Latino residents from near and far walking through a wide dirt access road that links the garden plots, inquiring about purchasing herbs, tomatoes, and greens. Some of the cultivators sold small clusters of produce for $2 or $5 a bunch, handing these over the chain-link fence, while others harvested crops which they transported to *marketas* in East L.A., the San Fernando Valley, or elsewhere. The men said that they are not supporting themselves with this income; rather, proceeds help cover their cultivation costs, which include monthly $20 plot rental fee, plus fertilizer, soil amendment, tools, and sometimes renting a rototiller, or to supplement their earned income or social security. For example, seventy-seven-year-old Ricardo is still working in a college cafeteria, where he has worked over twenty-five years, but at SACG, he cultivates crops, selling part of his harvest. He discussed *papalo*, a pre-Columbian wild-growing culinary herb also known as "butterfly leaf" in Nahuatl that grew wild in the hills back where he grew up in Mexico; here in Los Angeles, he discovered he could grow it and sell it in expanding ethnic markets, stating, "*Papalo*, I knew what that was, but not as a business. Here, I figured out it can be a business, and many people use it."

Our research offers no evaluation or judgment of how well the men we interviewed act or do not act as "responsible family men." Rather, our research underscores how the parks and gardens provide a platform for the men to experience and narrate themselves as responsible family men, as socially valuable elders, fathers, and older brothers. While family, church, or club contexts may offer similar possibilities, the parks and gardens serve as public sites where these men can experience themselves and assert themselves as strong family men. In a world that frequently marginalizes working-class men of color, this is no small thing.

The men do this against tough odds. Simultaneously holding multiple jobs is the only way many Latino immigrant men can make a living in L.A., and long hours may incur family absence. One young man related this about this father:

> My dad is a huge soccer fan and he's really into sports, but 'cause he came from Mexico at a young age, all he did was work . . . he actually told me I'm sorry, that once he got here, the main thing was working. . . . He had to work and stuff, so he couldn't really go and play at the park. He couldn't really practice soccer and basketball [with us].

Certainly, many African American and Latino men's family lives have been disrupted not only by overwork but also unemployment, incarceration, deportations and detentions, addiction, and violence.[37] In this context, coming to the parks and gardens offers a chance at redeeming loss for an alternative family narrative. Engagement with nature is a way to heal and make life bearable despite these circumstances.

Male Sovereignty and Conviviality

Parks and gardens are public places where Latino and African American men can hang out and enjoy male camaraderie and a sense of male sovereignty. Often, but not always they are spending time together with men similar to themselves in age, language, leisure interests, and racial-ethnic group. More privileged men may access this same kind of homosocial conviviality in other venues (fraternal organizations, the gym or the golf course, the pub, etc.), but in South L.A., the public parks and community gardens are one vehicle to serve this purpose. In this context, men's sovereignty and sociability are achievements.

Just as African Americans seeking leisure in public parks may encounter surveillance and control, Latino immigrant men may find the right to public outdoor spaces in the city to be contested.[38] As David Trouille's ethnographic research on men who gather to play soccer in the public parks of affluent Los Angeles Westside neighborhoods near the University of California, Los Angeles has shown, Latino men are not welcomed in many public places, and boundaries may be enforced even when liberal dispositions lead affluent white residents to express and mobilize their opposition in subtle ways.[39] Other times, boundaries and exclusions are enforced with racialized violence. In 2016, for example, the news media reported that five Latino men playing soccer at an L.A. County public park were assaulted with knives by white men screaming, "Heil Hitler," and other racial threats.[40]

Different activities organize men's camaraderie at the parks and gardens. At the gardens in Watts, once their cultivation work is over, the men enjoy chatting, cooking, and sometimes eating and drinking together. At both SACG and GWCG, most of the men have built small shade structures, or *casitas*, at the back of their plots, and some have innovated benches or chairs out of overturned plastic containers and the sort. They joke around with their buddies, sometimes playing cards or dominoes. For the older retired men, this is particularly important. One man, now retired for nearly a decade, explained, "*Platicamos asi no más. . . .* We sit and just talk, we just talk about our own matters." See figure 5.3 for a glimpse of this and figure 5.4 for a broader view of a community garden.

There are more or less consistent clusters of friends, and some of them create a very homey-like environment for themselves at the gardens. Wade, who came to GWCG "pretty much on a daily basis," explained that in retirement, the garden gave him a sense of purpose and a reliable community:

> When you ain't got a job to go to, this is the path to pass your time. You can help yourself, you can help people . . . you come here every day and you don't make any money. Don't sell anything. It's mostly you see people, ask yourself if they might need these vegetables, and maybe you got it.

Figure 5.3. Three Gardeners
Photo Credit: Pierrette Hondagneu-Sotelo, USC CSII project team.

Not everyone gravitates to socializing. At both gardens, some of the men prefer their alone time among the plants. Henry had been at GWCG for about six years, but he mostly kept to himself, explaining, "I don't really BS with the guys that much." He would typically spend about eight hours at the garden, but he preferred dedicating his time there to working in his plot and relaxing in nature. A tall, fit retiree who was an army veteran, he had studied sociology in college and once had a career selling local residential real estate, and he clarified that alone time at the garden was important to him:

> I don't really have that much time to talk because it's lost time. I mean, you come here and you take the time to come over here and get something done. I'm just kind of focused, and it's relaxing. I like to sit in my little space over there and watch the birds and the hummingbirds and the bees and kind of pay attention to that. It's, you know, very relaxing to me.

At GWCG, there are about forty people growing food, but only five are women, and except for one woman, these women are gardening with husbands or male partners. When we asked Jason to explain why more women weren't here, he said, "Well, to be honest with you, they have this thing about not letting women have a garden [plot]." He said he himself was open but that "I've had more women, but after about a year or two, they kind of fade out. Right. They don't even come back." When asked, "Why do you think that is?" he said, "I think it's more than they can handle." We do not know whether this refers to not being able to handle the hard physical labor or not fitting into the male homosocial sphere. Maybe both.

At the public parks, it is primarily soccer and basketball, but also "hanging out," that bring Latino men together. The latter may include an informal and relatively inexpensive "happy hour" for working men. At Fred Roberts Park, when the workday is over, Latino men driving pickup trucks from their jobs gather in the parking lot to see their friends while enjoying a few beers. Outdoors, and in the liminal space between work and home, a temporal multisensory world takes hold. Marijuana smoke wafts around the parking lot and picnic benches. Ranchera music blares from radios and boom boxes. Liquor stores, widely identified as neighborhood blight and local nuisances, are located across the street from

Figure 5.4. Community Garden
Photo Credit: Pierrette Hondagneu-Sotelo, USC CSII project team.

nearly all the public parks we observed in South L.A., providing afford-able access to wine and beer. The gardens and parks become sites of male conviviality, relaxation, and camaraderie, with inebriation and music contributing to a laid-back atmosphere.

At MLK Park, a long-standing drum circle provides live music at a collective men's gathering on Sunday afternoons. The drum circle started years ago at the Ted Watkins Park in Watts, and for reasons that remain unclear to us, it had migrated to MLK Park. Now men of diverse racial-ethnic backgrounds, but primarily African American men, came from near and far to play Afro-Cuban-style congo drums and cowbells here on Sunday afternoons. Other groups, such as the men in the biker club, sat at nearby picnic tables, enjoying the music. The drum circle included a full set of trap drums and electric key-boards, and, often, one or two women might dance (but we never saw women playing music).

Damion, a forty-seven-year-old African American construction worker who had been raised in Watts, came to drum here every Sun-day. When discussing security issues at the park, he asked one of our interviewers, Antar, who is young, tall, African American, and athletic, if he would dare to test the group, but he quickly and emphatically an-swered his own question. "You wouldn't! I told you, we got a Sergeant of Arms and everything. And you know who the number two is?" he asked, pointing proudly to his own stocky former football player chest. Continuing the theme of group sovereignty, he added that "[y]ou can't mess with this drum circle. It ain't even a question right here. It's a force of energy. You don't mess with the circle."

Damion described the drum circle with pride and shared that "a white guy from New York, real cool," had come to the drum circle to take video that is now posted on YouTube.[41] He described violence here as a thing of the past and talked about shared coexistence at MLK Park. "Now it's controllable, though. We share the park with the soccer players and stuff like that. So everybody gets along as far as this park." But when Antar motioned to a familiar character nearby (described in field notes as "strung out with saliva dripping from his lips, clad in worn, stained sweats"), Damion casually laughed and asked if Antar had been there on Father's Day when a man threw a woman in a trashcan. This exchange helps explain why sites such as these remain risky for women; women, unless they are accompanied by others or are members of the homeless or addict population and therefore have no choice, are not hanging out at MLK Park by themselves.

In her study of Chilean political refugees who gathered for years at *la cancha*, a local soccer field in London, sociologist Carolina Ramírez points to the importance of a marginalized group feeling a sense of cohesion and attachment to green space.[42] When the soccer site became more inclusive and diverse, with players from elsewhere in South America and also white British soccer players, the Chilean refugees' sense of belonging was unsettled. This is exactly what the men at the big community gardens in Watts do not want, and many of the men at the parks may feel similarly too. Some of the young guys hope to meet up with girls at the park, but twenty-one-year-old José, who came to the park twice a week to play soccer with his buddies said he prefers to be away from girls at the park. "We'd probably clown someone if they brought a girl here," he said. It is possible to condemn this stance as sexist exclusionary behavior on the part of the men *and* to see this as an expression of male sovereignty among men who do not normally experience a sense of control or group belonging in other public spaces.

Belonging and Feeling "at Home"

At both the community gardens and the public parks, Latino and African American men say they feel at home. The "homey" affect is particularly strong at the gardens, where the men form attachments to place, plants, and people. Part of feeling at home at the urban community gardens is feeling they have earned sweat-equity rights to the land, developing a routine and building relationships with people over time. At SACG, many of the men came from the bulldozed South Central Farm. They recounted how when they first came to see the terrain in Watts, they found abandoned lots in disarray. As one man explained,

> [w]e had to clean it up. Each one of us had to clean up his place. We cleaned all of this. And well, we dug, we took out all the weeds, we pulled out all the high grasses and we dug the soil to sow. Each person cleaned his plot.

Figure 5.5. A Homelike Gathering Place at the Greater Watts Community Garden.
Photo Credit: Pierrette Hondagneu-Sotelo, USC CSII project team.

The men spoke proudly of the improvements they have made to the soil and the locale—like those seen in figures 5.5 and 5.6—and it gives them a righteous sense of belonging to this place and to this city.

The community gardens in particular, more so than the parks, reproduce the routines of familiarity and family that commonly happen at home. One retiree at SACG described his daily routine at the garden as an extension of what he begins at home every morning: "*Me siento muy a gusto*. . . . I feel really good here. I relax a lot here. I get up, I bathe, I change, I go and maybe get something at the market and then I come here." Another older Latino man shared this: "*Me siento muy comodo*. . . . I feel really comfortable. I feel really happy with all the vegetation that there is right now. I feel really proud to be here sitting down and looking at my things here. When it's time to cut, I feel good. Yes, I'm happy to be here." He even added, "Yes, I feel good, as if I lived here."

For some of the men who are retired and live without family members, the garden fills a big void. When we asked sixty-three-year-old Jason, who lived alone and served as president of one side of GWCG, to describe a typical day, he said:

I would get here probably—don't laugh—around 6:30 a.m. in the summer months. During the winter months, later because you know, the sun rises later. . . . From 6:30 to about nine or ten, I would generally maintain my plot pulling weeds or whatever. Then around later hours, I would water. Then I just kind of hang out and assist others.

He grows food, starting seedlings from seeds in a little hothouse that he has built on-site, and he also tends a collector's array of ponytail palms and staghorn ferns, the latter carefully showcased on driftwood he collected back when he drove bulldozers in canyons to build dams. He typically stays at the garden until 4:30 p.m., but he clarified, "[I]f there's a bunch of people out here, then I stay longer." During the afternoon and evenings, he spends time "[j]ust talking. Sitting down. Maybe some wine or something. And then basically what happens is a lot of times during that time, we get a lot of people come in and wanting things. Especially on the weekends."

Jason also spends time caring for others, helping the older garden-ers, who are now in their seventies and eighties, and need assistance

Figure 5.6. A Shaded Casita at the Stanford Avalon Community Garden, Outfitted with Plastic Chairs and Chicken and Rooster Figurines as Décor.
Photo Credit: Pierrette Hondagneu-Sotelo, USC CSII project team.

Figure 5.7. A Festive Gathering Featuring Carne Asada and Live Ranchera Music at the Stanford Avalon Community Garden.
Photo Credit: Pierrette Hondagneu-Sotelo, USC CSII project team.

with physical work. Fit and in his early sixties, he referred to himself as "the baby boy" in the group. The president of the other side of the garden was not in good shape. "Albert, he has a bad back. He got hit by a car and it must have kicked him 10 feet in the air. He's lucky to be walking now. And I know he is physically not able," he said. "So I assist him." He added, "I think this is a better pass time than doing nothing. And it's helping others, you know what I mean? So yeah, I feel great when I'm here. Excellent. It's actually hard for me not to be here." Figures 5.7 and 5.8 show their camaraderie and care of the gardens.

Ricardo, at age seventy-seven and still employed five days a week in a college cafeteria, declared, "*Esto es mi vida.* . . . This is my life. I feel more at home here than my real home." And Arturo, a seventy-year-old re-tiree, suggested that the community garden is what keeps him alive. "*La verdad* . . . Truthfully, if it wasn't for this, I'd go back to Mexico." When he visits Mexico, he misses his plants and friends at the garden. These are gendered, outdoor homes away from home, and a series of homelike, domestic practices anchor social life here. Indeed, the older, retired men described a domestic shared culture of care, arriving early in the morning to work, and then sharing cooking and meals.

At the public parks, the rootedness, routine and pull of particular place was not as strong, but even so, the Latino men we interviewed also said they felt they belonged, as though it was a home away from home. Some of them saw the parks as crucial elements of their upbringings. Nineteen-year-old Rogelio stated:

> Just growing up here, it's just the park that I knew since I was little. Hanging out here all the time, seeing what goes on here kind of made me and shaped me who I am today. And I realize that more recently, more now than ever especially now that I come back. If it wasn't for coming here, I wouldn't be this certain way or I wouldn't have done the things I have done, certain things so like I feel like, this park is like, yeah I would say it's like another home I guess. I have a really strong connection with this park.

Figure 5.8. One of the more rudimentary-built casitas. The white cabinet holds gardening tools.
Photo Credit: Pierrette Hondagneu-Sotelo, USC CSII project team.

And forty-five-year-old Donaldo echoed similar sentiments, echoing a sense of rootedness that comes from routine:

> If I were to move out of the location, I would someday come back to this park again. For some reason, I know it. I grew up with it. . . . There was a point in time when I came here every day. Every day. Even when I was going to school, I'd get off from school and wait for my brothers to get off from work to come out here and play basketball. It was every day.

At MLK Park, we encountered several African American men who had once lived in the park vicinity but had moved to other parts of South L.A. or to cities in the San Gabriel or San Fernando Valleys. They now drove or took the bus or metro long distances to return to the park, in much the same way that some African Americans living in suburbs now return to the inner-city churches of their youth. One man, who had been coming to MLK Park for fifteen years, talked about the tug of belonging at the park this way:

> The love you get when you come here. You feel me? You can be nobody anywhere else. You come here, don't nobody judge you. It's all love. We're all equal. Nobody better than the next person. . . . This is like home. This is the foundation.

Emergent Civic Culture

Public parks and community gardens have the potential to develop as sites of civic engagement and political empowerment. Community gardens such as the South Central Farm have been celebrated as sites of resistance and insurgency and in another part of Los Angeles, a small community garden in the MacArthur Park neighborhood hosted a Latina women's empowerment class, political meetings for left-leaning Morena political party, and other activities, such as civic and social celebrations.[43] But in South L.A., at the parks and gardens that we examined, civic engagement was more limited.

This is not to say that there no culture of self-governance at the urban community gardens. In fact, the men do feel a sense of ownership and ongoing privatized relationship to a particular plot of land. They rent

Figure 5.9. At Stanford Avalon Community Garden, each garden plot is behind a locked chain-link gate and is identified by a number.
Photo Credit: Pierrette Hondagneu-Sotelo, USC CSII project team.

their plots and hold meetings to discuss issues such as water use, fees, promoting organic fertilizers, and so on. At GWCG, there are two or three meetings a year and a regular Juneteenth celebration, and the gardeners there seem to enjoy a good deal of autonomy and sovereignty. One man told us he wished they would develop a "Mission Statement," and Jason, who served as president of one section, complained that he was frustrated in his efforts to coax some of the older "stubborn" gardeners from the South to use less water. At GWCG, gardeners paid $30 a month for a single plot and $60 for a double, and at SACG, the fee was $20 a month, although hikes in the water rates always loomed. At both community gardens in the past, graft and corruption had occurred with fee collections, and bitter, smoldering resentments about these injustices still resonated with many people at SACG. Figures 5.9 and 5.10 show plots at SACG.

At SACG the gardeners were required to attend monthly meetings, and when we were active in our research at the gardens, they had recently mobilized against water-rate increases. We also observed them

Figure 5.10. The Stanford Avalon Community Garden plots flank a long dirt alley and span eleven blocks, set below the Department of Water and Power utility towers, just south of the flight path for jets arriving at LAX.
Photo Credit: Pierrette Hondagneu-Sotelo, USC CSII project team.

vote in elections for new representatives. The 209 plots were divided into four sections, each with an elected leader. Recall that SACG began with political demands on the City to replace the bulldozed South Central Farm. At GWCG, the men were a little hazy on the historical origins of the garden, which is understandable since it was founded more than forty years ago. Jason said it was started by a woman, "Miss Lee," who is now deceased. "She had a repertoire of politicians that she knew," he said. "She would be in there with city council in order to maintain this. . . . She was a pretty tough lady."

A few of the Latino immigrant men at SACG had found in the gardens a platform to develop their skills as grassroots leaders. Don Pablo Gutierrez, a tall man who hailed from central-western Mexico had honed many of his leadership skills at South Central Farm, and he was one of the most sought out and respected leaders. Of his informal political work at the gardens, he said, "*Siento que es parte de mi vida. . . .* I feel it's part of my life. . . . Not so much because of what I have done, but because people started coming to me with their problems." Another leader, Carlos Bolon, an illiterate Guatemalan Mayan man had also developed his community-organizing skills at South Central Farm and later in neighborhood councils. He now also took satisfaction in his elected position at the garden and his abilities: "*Siento muy privilegiado. . . .* I feel very privileged to lead a meeting and I feel very happy to serve as the voice of my Latino community."

But not everyone shared these sanguine views. Some of the community garden members expressed criticism of governance structures and voiced allegations of political promises not kept. They did not necessarily respect those who were serving as leaders. When asked about relations with the leaders, José bluntly said, "*No, no hablo con ellos. . . .* No, I don't speak with them, never. I never get into it with them, I just pay them and we see each other around." For him this was a way to avoid problems, and he dismissed the leaders as motivated by graft. "*Es una política. . . .* It's a politics they do just so they can get money out those little plots." And seventy-seven-year-old Ricardo dismissed the political discussions as amateurish, childish squabbles, declaring that "*parece una escuela de niños . . .* it seems like a kindergarten."

At the public parks, there is unrealized potential for civic engagement and community development. Many of the people we interviewed recognize conditions have improved, but they remain far removed from knowing the local leaders and groups that advocated for these infrastructural improvements. They expressed appreciation for whoever had improved the parks, but with the exception of one Recreation Center employee, no one we interviewed on-site at MLK Park mentioned Community Coalition or specific civic leaders who had mobilized for these improvements. This was true at Fred Roberts Park too. One young man there said, "I mean it's a great park and now it's way better than ever. . . . Whoever decided to do this to the park, good for them. They did a lot for the community."

Another man at the same park said, "It looks a lot nicer and kind of makes people want to be like 'Oh, they are making it a little better. I think we should take care of it. Make sure they don't take this away from us." Another man of Panamanian descent, who said he had one used the public parks for "fighting pit bulls, yeah, just trouble basically," reflected on how his life might have been different if the parks had been in better shape when he was growing up. He had served time in prison, but he reflected: "I'm glad they got something to keep the kids entertained [now]. I wish they had when I was younger. I probably wouldn't have went that route. I woulda been all right." In all these instances, they talked amorphously about change-makers as "they." While at the community gardens, the men have created an emergent civic culture of self-governance—however nascent, fragile, and contested it may be— park-goers, both African American and Latino, seem very unplugged and far removed from civic institutions.

Toward an Ethos of Togetherness?

At the parks and gardens in South L.A., Latino and African American men restore and revitalize themselves. As they gather to relax, play, converse and cultivate, they are making what we might call "quiet claims" on public space in the city. In the process they are making a "home away from home" for themselves amid the sprawling fifty square miles of asphalted avenues that is South L.A. Henri Lefebrve used the term "representational space" to refer to places that have been collectively and organically created by daily use.[44] To be sure, the physical infrastructure of public parks and community gardens was established through political struggle, civic projects, and public investment. Now, through their daily activities, these men have reclaimed these places for themselves.

What is produced at these green spaces? Transcendence. A "home away from home." A sense of belonging. These are achievements that should not be discounted. And recognition of what they have created here is not lost on the men here, who express love and pride of these places.

> This is major for us over here. This is where we come and let off steam. We need this park. (Marcus, at MLK Park)

> People come to the park just to relax, to drift away from anything that has to do with just being bothered. You see people happy. You don't find no arguments. . . . I forget about any problems I have. (Carlos, at Fred Roberts Park)

Esta es mi vida. . . . This is my life. I'm entertained, my mind is off things while I take care of a little plant, caress it, take off the little jacket that is bothering it. I'm tired when I leave work. Here is where I rest, where I relax. Here, I feel as though nothing is missing. . . . I feel better here than at my home. (Ricardo, at SACG)

What is perhaps most important to this volume is that they are also creating a new ethos of sharing the commons. While these public green spaces are neither multicultural "cosmopolitan canopies" nor "melting pots," we do see the emergence of a shared narrative of "we are all in this together," (a theme echoed in the construction of place-based civic life that we review in chapter 6). It is true that the men mostly "stay in their own lane" and stick with men of similar racial-ethnic, age, and interest groups. Language and homophily—the tendency of people to bond with those who are similar to them—may help explain this, but these outcomes also have to do with these men striving to create a space for themselves, one where they can enjoy tranquility, companionship, and belonging. But importantly, they have helped to create and they now experience the amelioration of the virulent cross-racial hostility that once characterized South L.A. streets and parks.

This does not necessarily mean ongoing mingling. One African American man said, "Latinos throw their little parties or barbeques and it will be just them. If you got the heart to go up to them, talk to them, to be friends with them, then yeah. But you don't see Black people doing that." And another concurred: "Everyone like sticks to their own. I don't know if you noticed, but look at the basketball court and look at the soccer field, and we create those kinds of segregations." And the community gardens, as we saw, are defined by older men of same racial-ethnic group, who speak the same language. Still, the ethos—the narrative into which the men are fitting their experiences—is one of cross-racial coexistence. At the parks, the men said things such as "Here you got Spanish people out here, Black people out here. They're chillin'. This is dope."

Moreover, some of the men understand the challenges of gentrification and displacement as a shared struggle facing *both* Latinos and African Americans (discussed more in chapters 6 and 7). At MLK Park, we interviewed two young staff members of the Summer Night Lights program, one African American and the other Latino. Speaking of community violence and poverty, Manolo acknowledged the communities face similar problems: "We're still living in shitty areas. We're under-resourced, underprivileged . . . if you go west or north, it's a different story." And DeAndre chimed in and said, "The only time you see tax dollars is when your gentrification starts happening, then they start pouring money in. Y'all see Crenshaw? They stripped the Crenshaw mall down 'cause they know that Crenshaw is coming back. They're going to drive the prices up to make the rent unaffordable to Black and Browns."

A shared home has been created in South L.A., but community members recognize that this shared home may be jeopardized by new developments. This worry about losing what has been gained is a theme that also emerged strongly in our interviews with civic leaders and Black residents, and it is to those issues, as well as to how broader civic life is evolving in response to changing demographics while staying attentive to Black residents, that we now turn.

6

Organizing Community, Building Power

MANUEL PASTOR, ROBERT CHLALA, AND
ALEJANDRO SANCHEZ-LOPEZ

Thus far, we have looked at what we might think of as daily life in South
Los Angeles—how the quotidian accommodations between neighbors
led to the softening of Black–Latino tensions, how the prejudices and
concerns of first arrivers were superseded by the shifting identifications
of a second generation of homegrown Latinos, and how the complexities of segregation and integration play out in the context of parks and
open space. Throughout, we have stressed the prism of homemaking:
how immigrants learned to both navigate and then establish their lives,
their houses, and their community gardens; how Latinos as a whole have
learned to lay claim to, but not dominance over, a new space; and how a
particular pride of place—often built on the sense of resilience it takes to
survive and thrive in South L.A.—has created a new vehicle for bridging
Black and Brown people.

Of course, shifts in social phenomena can occur at very different—
and sometimes discordant—paces. The broad swath of neighborhoods
that compose South L.A. may have swept from being overwhelming
Black to now largely Latino (as described in detail in chapter 2)—but
the political representation has remained almost exclusively African
American. On the other hand, the social service sector and educational
institutions have been forced to adjust more rapidly, often shifting to
engaging with clients and parents in Spanish in ways that have alienated
Black residents who already feel that what once was theirs—after a long
and historical struggle to achieve institutional representation—is now
slipping away. Meanwhile, former pillars of civic life—Black churches
and traditional Black-led organizations—find that the community momentum has shifted in favor of groups that have a more explicit focus on
Black-Brown coalitions and progressive politics.

This chapter explores the changes to civic life in South L.A., particularly how the demographic transition has impacted the work of civic leaders and how the experiences of working through that change are being brought to bear on building coalitions to address today's challenges, particularly the threat of gentrification. We ground our analysis in the history and literature, as well as two waves of interviews with community leaders from public, private, and nonprofit institutions in South L.A., the first conducted over an initial nine-month period in 2015 and a second conducted in 2019. In both waves, we asked respondents about their involvement in South L.A., their perceptions of the social impacts of demographic change, the state of Black–Latino coalition building, and the future of South L.A. In total, we had twenty-eight interviews with civic leaders, including individuals from community-organizing groups, neighborhood councils, law enforcement, elected bodies, and more. The interviewees over the two cohorts were ethnically mixed: nine were Black, thirteen were Latino, three were white, and three were Asian American–Pacific Islanders—and fifteen were women while thirteen were men.

Despite a mix of demography and sectors, we found a shared focus on the need to integrate the new Latino majority *and* the desire to do it in a way that acknowledges, celebrates, and preserves the authentic reality that South L.A. is the heart and home of Black L.A.[1] This takes places in a context of crosscutting pressures: while there is a noticeable gap in Latino leadership of nonprofits and community organizations, there is also a sense of Black loss as neighborhoods, businesses, and institutions see a transition to mainly Latino staff or client orientation or, worse, Black lockout or exclusion as Spanish becomes a prerequisite for a job or apartment or community connection. Black residents can thus feel resentment and tensions even as Latinos feel the constraints of their own limited power. This phenomenon, in which both groups feel like they are coming up short, is not limited to Los Angeles—and while many Black leaders see the positive political calculus from coalition building, ceding power along the way is not easy for politicians or communities alike, particularly those who have had to fight hard for civil rights and political influence.[2]

Of course, one thing that can make power sharing easier is a shared sense of place. But simple appeals to neighborhood pride will not do the trick, particularly in locales such as South L.A., where the devaluation, disinvestment, and distress reflects the ways in which anti-Black racism shaped the flow of public dollars and private loans in the past and continues into the present. Thus, place and race are not counterposed but interwoven in a narrative that builds common ground even as it allows people to see their histories reflected instead of erased.

It is a tricky balancing act, one made more challenging due to the way in which anti-Blackness functions as the fulcrum of white supremacy and so requires that leaders pay asymmetric attention to preserving Black voice.[3] Much of this chapter simply allows the leaders themselves to speak about how they do that balancing. Latinos, for example, often find themselves not only wanting to assert their interests but also needing to demonstrate that this is not an attempt to replace or ignore Black concerns, demonstrating their heightened awareness of their positions within the broader displacement processes.[4] African American leaders know they need to reach out, but when a community has historically had so much taken away, how can you do that without feeding into a profound sense of dislocation?

To better understand that sense of loss—and how it is simultaneously tempered by a sense of quotidian solidarity—we also report on a set of twenty-five interviews with Black residents who describe their own experiences with the demographic transformation of the past decades. One of the main themes that emerged was a sense of competition, particularly around entry-level employment and participation in local school decision-making processes. Part of this is exacerbated by language: while using Spanish is important to encouraging Latino civic voice and welcoming into the mega-neighborhood, the challenge is the way in which it can exclude Black residents who may not have that skill.

Meanwhile, at the time of writing, we found that both Black and Latino leaders face a common and pressing dilemma: Just as new place-based civic identities are being formed—just as there is a new sense of "home"— South L.A. is being threatened by a wave of gentrification. As it turns out, South L.A. is very well positioned for those who seek a respite from Southern California's astronomical housing prices and long, gridlocked commutes. With a new rail line running east–west across the top of South L.A. and another slated to run north–south and to the airport, more people are passing through the area and noticing that the shabbiness of South L.A.'s boulevards—a result of decades of racist disinvestment—stands in stark contrast to many of the well-maintained bungalows housing Black and Latino families.[5] Meanwhile, property flippers seeking to make a quick buck are seeing new possibilities in South L.A. and potential new interest from those who long shied away. One civic leader who was actually a transplant to the neighborhood decades ago commented, "I mean I know when I first moved to South L.A., you never saw white people in South L.A., ever. Like it was 'a thing' if you saw a white person."

Seeing white newcomers is no longer a thing. The last two decades have introduced new people, new business to the area, and a new name to the area we know as South Los Angeles. As noted earlier, the rebranding started in 2003, when residents tired of the negativity associated with "South Central" convinced the Los Angeles city council to change the name to the South Los Angeles term commonly used today.[6] The area's evolving name has introduced new concerns about gentrification and displacement—given that such nicknames have led to an influx of new business and new people in other Los Angeles places like West Hollywood, also known as WeHo.[7] Some younger cohorts (as well as some older residents) see the "South L.A." moniker as washing away a proud history and prefer "South Central." Regardless of what it is called, the changing persona of the area is further fueled by the explosion of charter schools across Los Angeles, a fact that means that higher-income parents can now more easily detach themselves from the struggling schools in the area.

The new interest in South L.A. by those with more means might seem a sort of long-overdue recognition of the strengths of the area, but it also means that the very populations who have demonstrated persistence, endurance, and often grace in getting through tough times are now worried that they will be displaced just as recovery arrives. Having just gone through one big demographic transformation, South L.A. is worried that it will abruptly go through another. The way for the community to exercise more control over the process is through civic power building, and learning how to do that in the multiracial terrain of South L.A. is the focus of this chapter.

Organizing Black and Brown in South L.A.

The concern for and action on multiracial bridge building in Los Angeles is not new: there is actually a long history of intersecting Black and Latino movements in Los Angeles, often in the service of environmental, economic, and social justice. After all, many of formal and informal organizations working for Black self-determination—from World War II–era civil rights activism of the National Association for the Advancement of Colored People (NAACP) to the community empowerment strategies of the Black Panther Party in the 1960s and 1970s to the activism against police violence of today's Black Lives Matter–Los Angeles—have articulated with Latino and other groups, seeking to broaden the alliances necessary to overcome the conditions impacting South Los Angeles in particular and Black communities in general. This sort of Black–Brown framing around social justice was accelerated and intensified in the 1990s as the mega-neighborhood changed demographically *and* sought new ways to recover from the damage left by the economic dislocation and violent policing of the 1980s and the most damaging civil unrest in U.S. history in 1992.

But while Black political and social spaces in South L.A. were, in many ways, always multiethnic, and so today's efforts do not represent a sharp break from but rather an evolution of the past, what is somewhat novel now is that the linkages are now not just between places—say, uniting East L.A. and South L.A. in a common fight—but, rather, within the spaces of South L.A. itself. This is not without problems or concerns: as noted earlier, some have experienced the increasing reach of Black–Brown politics as risking a reduction in Black political power or stifling a legitimate demand for more Latino political representation. We lift up these concerns in what followings, but we also stress the new civic identities that are emerging, particularly for Latinos and particularly around a shared notion of South L.A. as a special place of resilience and resistance.

A few caveats before we begin. First, this is not a full history of Black organizing in Los Angeles, a topic that certainly deserves its own book (although for a good start, see *Black Los Angeles* by Darnell Hunt and Ana-Christina Ramón); the focus here is on the intersections of that organizing with Latinos and demographic change and what that means for contemporary South L.A. leaders. Second, civic life is more than politics: South L.A.'s cultural institutions, such as churches, jazz clubs, and dance spots, are also places of public interactions as are the parks and gardens reviewed in chapter 5. The focus here, however, is more on community organizing, political leadership, and social service institutions. Finally, what happens in South L.A. is not only driven by South L.A.: the region's history is deeply tied to multiple political and civic geographies, including statewide and citywide struggles for higher wages and immigrant rights, as well as to global events, such as the wars in Central America, that prompted the migrations that transformed South L.A.[8] That said, we touch lightly on those factors and focus mainly on organizing within South L.A. itself.

Being Black, Building Coalitions

As South Central L.A. became the center of Black L.A. through the 1930s and 1940s, African Americans developed a range of institutions and organizations designed to meet the challenges of discrimination and exclusion. Fortunately, this did not require a complete reinvention: there was a vibrant institutional base on which to build. For example, the Los Angeles chapter of the NAACP was formed in 1913 and, just fifteen years later, hosted the nineteenth annual convention of the national organization.[9] Just two years before that gathering, the Second Baptist Church—formed in 1885 in what would become the heart of South Central—had christened a new building designed by famous Black architect Paul Williams. Second Baptist became the church that hosted Rev. Martin Luther King, Jr. when he came to Los Angeles to preach.

The thirties and the forties saw both a rapid Black influx from the U.S. South and a flowering of new groupings and institutions. During the Great Depression and World War II, the People's Independent Church established cooperative markets, relief programs, and eventually became an active part of the 1940s Negro Victory Committee, challenging Black exclusion from wartime jobs.[10] One of the committee's main proponents, Charlotta Bass, was the editor and publisher of the *California Eagle*, helped lead civil rights efforts such as the "Don't Buy Where You Can't Work" campaign, and was a key figure in other employment and housing integration struggles.[11]

With some work, these efforts became explicitly multiracial in their orientation. While some have suggested that the mostly middle-class, Black civil rights institutions of the pre–World War II era "formed no alliances" with Mexican, Japanese, or other nonwhite community groups, the historical record suggests otherwise.[12] Charlotta Bass pushed the NAACP to recruit Asian, Mexican, and white members and made the *California Eagle* a vehicle to build multiracial understanding of civil rights.[13] For example, she garnered Black support for the dozens of Mexican youth charged in the Sleepy Lagoon trial of 1943, whom the Los Angeles Police Department (LAPD) blamed for the murder of one young man (likely caused by a car crash) in a racist mass trial.[14] Other, more institutionalized multiracial efforts like the Council for Civic Unity (CCU) also arose during World War II under direct sponsorship of a city government hoping to alleviate racial tensions that could undermine wartime efforts.[15]

The CCU continued in the postwar era, as did a new crop of local civil rights organizations like the Mexican American–run Community Service Organization (CSO), the Jewish American–run Community Relations Committee, and the Japanese American Citizens League, alongside more established groups like local chapters of the Congress of Racial Equality and the NAACP.[16] Such multi-racial efforts fell short of developing into full-fledged, long-term coalitions, but they did impact key issues such as school and housing segregation and provided the base of cooperation that helped propel African American Tom Bradley onto the City Council in 1973 and eventually to the mayor's seat. Because of this intertwining, several historians have stressed that civil rights efforts in Los Angeles were never solely about Black Angelenos.[17]

Indeed, even groups that have sometimes been seen as being solely focused on empowering Black people were impacted by coalitional thinking. For example, the Black Panther Party (BPP) affirmed identity and autonomy, provided self-protection from police and racial violence, and offered and managed social services that could address the economic and social oppression of African Americans. But the BPP worked alongside groups like El Centro de Accíon Social y Autónomo/Center for Autonomous Social Action, East Wind, and other "Third World Left" organizations.[18] The BPP would host organizations like the American Indian Movement, which was active statewide, while also participating in broader citywide actions, like anti-war actions or International Women's Day. In short, the rose of Black–Brown collaboration that eventually bloomed in the concrete of South Los Angeles was seeded by a long history of multicultural and multiracial movement building, even when groups were self-organized by race or ethnicity to advance their community's interest.

Finding a Place in Labor

Another vehicle for interethnic organizing was through labor—a nuanced tale given the historic and ongoing undercurrent of anti-Blackness in unions. While Los Angeles in the early twentieth century has largely been portrayed as an "open shop" city that avoided the Midwest models of union dominance in industrial work, South Central was the site of multiracial worker organizing efforts in Los Angeles, including the efforts in the 1930s of the Council of Industrial Organizations (CIO) and the Communist Party.[19] The leadership of Black radicals like Phillip "Slim" Connelly helped shift the CIO into a force for civil rights and labor organizing.[20] The Communist Party, meanwhile, worked against the mass deportations of immigrants, mostly Asian and Mexican workers, and the police brutality faced by Black residents in the 1920s and early 1930s.[21] It also took on what might have been the unifying issue of high unemployment, but the party's potential to make a difference was undermined by police repression and the fact that many working-class whites chose to affiliate themselves with unions directly.[22]

A bigger shift in the alignment of labor and the Black community came in the 1930s and 1940s as Black and Brown workers pushed against their exclusion. Spurred in part by efforts like the Negro Victory Committee, Black workers organized to pressure steel and other key wartime industries linked to South L.A. toward integration. Guatemalan-born labor activist Luisa Moreno (eventually the first female and first Latino member of the CIO) led successful actions in the agricultural and food-processing industries in Los Angeles in the late 1930s and 1940s (and her daughter attended Manual Arts High School in South L.A.) while, in the same period, recognized Mexican American leaders like Bert Corona organized warehouse workers under the auspices of a local of the International Longshoremen's and Warehousemen's Union.[23]

While white union leaders utilized the end of the war to resegregate the ports, Black workers continued to organize the auto plants (and their suppliers) along the Alameda Corridor, on which many South L.A. workers depended. Those postwar labor unions also provided a new way for Black and Mexican residents to affect not just workplace conditions but neighborhood-level concerns like social welfare and community development. For example, when civil rights organizations tried to shape a city-run Economic and Youth Opportunities Agency slated to receive War on Poverty funds in 1965, the administration of Mayor Sam Yorty—a onetime liberal turned archconservative—attempted to restrict community input, leading the federal government to refuse to fund the program.[24] With some arguing that that was one trigger for the 1965 Watts Rebellion, local community organizations decided to take matters into their own coalitional hands. Teaming up with labor—centered on a more racially integrated and progressive United Auto Workers—they formed the Watts Labor Community Action Committee (WLCAC) to build a new locally controlled organization to generate economic security.[25]

Moving beyond service provision alone, WLCAC built numerous community-owned institutions, including cooperative grocery stores, credit unions, and a building and supply store.[26] Labeled "a national model for community-action agencies," the organization also created what would be the first Community Conservation Corps—a youth skills and employment program that focused on local needs and public works and birthed a model that would last until the present.[27] Institutionalized as a nonprofit service organization, WLCAC did grow an expansive membership base that was among the first South Central organizations to explicitly bring together Latino and Black leadership. This was partly because the Catholic Church, which had a role as a social provider in mostly Latino (and some Black) communities as early as the 1960s, also helped anchor the WLCAC.[28] It was, however, Black-led—by the iconic Ted Watkins, Sr.— and certainly Black-identified, partly because of who was most active in the political and civic life of Watts.

As deindustrialization impacted South L.A. in the 1980s—hitting that part of Southern California almost a decade before impacting other areas in the region—the base for worker organizing and community empowerment was weakened.[29] Reflecting the ongoing shift to lower-paid employment, many groups began to emphasize working poverty and the erosion of general labor standards. For example, the South Central Organizing Committee (SCOC) and East L.A.'s United Neighborhood Organization teamed up with another affiliate of the Industrial Areas Foundation (a national organizing federation that was largely based in faith institutions) to launch a campaign for a "moral minimum wage."[30] In a 1987 campaign, this Black–Brown coalition targeted large retailers and state agency meetings and, with the support of the Catholic Church, unions, and the state Democratic Party, succeeded in achieving an agreement to raise the minimum wage well above the federal level (from $3.35 to $4.25). Implemented in 1988, the move immediately transferred about a billion dollars to the lowest-paid workers in the state and suggested the power of interethnic organizing together for economic justice.

The overall union movement saw the beginning of a revitalization in the late 1980s and early 1990s as labor shifted its attention from the industries in decline to the service jobs on the rise; it is in this era that campaigns to organize janitors, hospitality workers, and others begin to gain their footing and set the stage for a sort of labor resurgence in L.A.[31] While all to the good for progressive politics and for the income of those at the bottom of the wage distribution, the embrace of immigrant workers was sometimes perceived as a shift away from or neglect of Black organizing. While labor would later try to make it up with a mid-2000s effort to secure a strong contract for a largely African American (and South L.A.–based) security guard workforce, the sense that both jobs and union attention were being diverted to Latinos was a real worry, one based on a long-standing (and often well-founded) suspicion of anti-Black racism in unions. [32]

Making Home Together

Another place for multiracial coalition-building came in the realm of community quality of life. One of the most emblematic of these efforts occurred in the mid-1980s when the City of Los Angeles proposed to locate a trash incinerator in South Central, triggering a wave of protest that was led by a newly formed group called Concerned Citizens of South Central.[33] Founded by two Black women, Concerned Citizens was able to create coalitions with other environmental organizations and eventually force the city to abandon its plans in 1987. In about the same period, the state of California was proposing a toxic-waste incinerator in the City of Vernon, an industrial district wedged between South and East L.A. The struggle against that environmental challenge was led by a group called Mothers of East Los Angeles, a group that had previously fought plans to locate a prison in their neighborhood.

Concerned Citizens provided assistance and support—and eventually, those incinerator plans were abandoned as well.[34]

The idea of Black and Brown residents—particularly women leaders—working together to protect and improve neighborhood health took a fuller form with the formation in 1990 of the Community Coalition for Substance Abuse, Prevention and Treatment (now known as Community Coalition, or CoCo). Founded in 1990 under the leadership of (now Congresswoman) Karen Bass and Sylvia Castillo, CoCo's debut focus was on the "crack crisis," informed, in part, by Bass's own role as a physician assistant "[witnessing] the devastating effects of addiction" at L.A. County–University of Southern California (USC) Medical Center.[35] However, CoCo's most visible campaigning—led by Black and Latina women—was focused on shutting down liquor stores, often viewed by communities as a nuisance that attracted addicts, dealers, and other forms of crime.

This was not the first campaign against liquor stores; in the early 1980s, the SCOC (the group responsible for the minimum-wage campaign) launched a similar effort. But that work faltered and even CoCo's efforts initially looked like they were not gaining much traction. However, the Los Angeles Uprising of 1992 provided a unique opportunity: with approximately 224 of the 723 liquor stores in South L.A. destroyed by looting and arsons, CoCo attempted to stop the reopening of the stores.[36] This reinflamed decades-long racial tensions that had come to a head during the uprising: many of the stores that were burned and looted were owned by Korean Americans who saw both the looting and the subsequent effort to permanently shut the shuttered stores as an attack on their livelihoods even as Black residents expressed their own resentments over the lack of ownership of assets in their own communities. These tensions were particularly acute given the murder of fifteen-year-old Latasha Harlins by a Korean-born store owner in the runup to the civil unrest. Bass and CoCo were able to find progressive allies in the Korean American community who worked to raise funds (and secure fast-track workarounds) to help liquor stores reopen as laundries or other businesses. Still, for our purposes here, one of the most interesting elements of the liquor store organizing was that it was not two separate geographic communities collaborating—as with the relationship between Concerned Citizens and Mothers of East Los Angeles—but rather two sets of proximate neighbors involved in multiracial collaboration from the onset.

CoCo's youth group—eventually named South Central Youth Empowered thru Action (SCYEA)—modeled this even more strongly as it gained strength in the early 2000s. By the end of the 1990s, SCYEA youth had grown to five of eight local high schools, creating high school organizing committees that were base-building and strategic hubs for youth activists.[37] After a successful campaign regarding fast-tracking school construction monies to underfunded areas, SCYEA's leadership engaged in a survey of more than a thousand peers.[38] College prep emerged as a key need; students had identified how their school curriculum failed to provide the key courses needed to qualify for the University of California system and instead tracked students toward low-wage jobs.

The campaign expanded beyond a focus on South L.A. to a citywide coalition, with its most prominent partner being East Los Angeles' InnerCity Struggle.[39] Together, under the banner of Communities for Education Equity, the groups won a mandate for Los Angeles Unified School District (LAUSD) to provide the university-prep courses in all schools in adequate numbers. While the citywide alliance of disparate groups was key, within SCYEA itself, Black and Brown youth were building affinities and coalitions, reflecting the more Black-identified and place-rooted Latino second generation we discussed in chapter 4. Rather than an oddity, a one-off, or an imagined historical golden age of collaboration, Black and Brown organizing—and coalition building both within South L.A. and across the city—was increasingly seen as a given.

Of course, there were exceptions, but they were just that: exceptions. In 1990, for example, Watts Century Latino Organization (WCLO) also formed what remains as the sole Latino-focused, power-building organization in South L.A., to our knowledge. Under the leadership of Arturo Ybarra, the WCLO was born out of an effort to turn Latinos out to meetings to fight the Community Redevelopment Agency plans to take land by eminent domain and create an industrial park in Watts. But while this was a Latino-focused group, even it had a Black–Brown cast to its strategy. The WCLO, for example, immediately began work to build bridges with Black residents of Watts, from the Annual Watts Latino/African American Cinco de Mayo celebration starting in 1991 to the cultural exchanges as part of the Watts Community Bridges program started in 1994. As one point, Ybarra was elected the vice president of the 95 percent African American Watts Economic Development Advisory Council.[40]

One of the reasons why Latino-led or -focused organizations did not take off was the relative neglect of the area by citywide and countywide Latino groups. This was most sharply illustrated by a press conference held by Latino political leaders on the third day of the 1992 civil unrest in which they congratulated their constituencies for maintaining peace, mostly because there was little violence or looting in East Los Angeles. Yet as it turns out, roughly half the arrests during the unrest were of Latinos, and by this time, South L.A. was nearly half Latino.[41] This was evidence of profound political disconnection—which many Latino civic leaders in South L.A. complain of to this day. In that context, it is little wonder that many South L.A. Latinos have seen their political salvation less in Latino-based groups and more in local multiracial coalitions that can build power and take on some of the broad regional dynamics affecting life in South L.A.

Scaling for Change

Indeed, through the 1990s and 2000s, South L.A. also became ground zero for a fundamental shift toward what interviewee Isela Gracian of the East Los Angeles Community Corporation refers to as the "science of power-building."[42] This was particularly clear in the work of Action for Grassroots Empowerment and Neighborhood Development Alternatives (AGENDA)—what would later become Strategic Concepts in Organizing and Policy Education (SCOPE). Founder Anthony Thigpenn was shaped by the layers of political movements in South L.A., coming from the BPP and anti–police violence campaigns, and then later moving to grassroots electoral efforts to shift military spending toward community purposes.[43] With AGENDA, Thigpenn set forward a wider vision for social and economic justice, all wrapped up in a belief that "[i]f you want to help South L.A., you can't talk about South L.A. apart from the region."[44]

As part of its regional vision, AGENDA developed strong coalitions with the kinds of groups that shared its values. Some of these organizations, like the union-supported Los Angeles Alliance for A New Economy, were in many ways the institutional embodiment of the emerging "social movement unionism" that was redefining L.A.—and much of AGENDA's initial efforts were focused on getting South L.A. residents a better toehold in the regional economy. One important campaign targeted the development of the DreamWorks campus not far from LAX—and from the western edge of South L.A.—and sought to leverage massive investments into a workforce development pipeline via the community college system. A subsequent Healthcare Career Ladder Training Program pushed for by AGENDA offered a vision for addressing the loss of high-quality employment in automotive and defense industries and providing an alternative pathway in the health system for residents to attain living wages, union representation, and upward mobility.

Of course, one blockage to improving economic outcomes was a lack of political power—and the new constellation of organizations emerging in South L.A. played a key role in shifting politics. AGENDA, for example, was rebranded as SCOPE and continued its work on job development and job quality. But founder Anthony Thigpenn also took time away from his nonprofit duties to run political campaigns, including running the field operation for the 2005 victory of Antonio Villaraigosa, the first Latino mayor elected in the modern history of Los Angeles.[45] Thigpenn then played a hand in the creation of a statewide alliance that eventually morphed into California Calls, a voter mobilization effort that played a key role in a series of California ballot initiatives that instituted a "millionaire's tax" in 2012 and de-felonized drug use in 2014 (and so led to a reduction in the prison population and record cleansing for some formerly incarcerated individuals).

CoCo became another key locus of political power. The founding director, Karen Bass, ran for and won a State Assembly seat, serving in Sacramento between 2004 and 2010; for the last two years of her tenure, she was Speaker of the State Assembly, the first African American female to hold such a position in U.S. history. Forced to leave by term limits, she ran for Congress and won and quickly moved up in leadership; in 2019, she became head of the Congressional Black Caucus. Meanwhile, her successor as president of CoCo, Marqueece Harris-Dawson, ran for and won a city council seat in 2015. Strikingly, Harris-Dawson now represents the council district with the highest share of Black residents and Black voters—but his path to political savvy came through working in and eventually leading an organization explicitly focused on building bridges between Black and Brown residents.

The point here is that South L.A. has become a base for change on a broader geographic scale—and behind that has been an energy that is emerging more from the Black–Brown alliance building than Black civil rights and church institutions that had been strongholds of power in the early and mid-twentieth century. Longtime county supervisor Mark Ridley-Thomas, for example, actually won his seat in 2008 by overpowering a mainstream Black city councilman and former police chief Bernard Parks, who received endorsements from major Black politicians and was popular with many older voters; Ridley-Thomas's secret was a combination of Latino and labor support and a targeting of new and occasional voters.[46] For Ridley-Thomas, this broader reach was not new: a co-founder of the New Majority Task Force, a coalition of Black, Latino, and Asian American leaders that existed in the early 1990s, he was also one of a few influential Black leaders to endorse Villaraigosa in his first unsuccessful run for mayor in 2001 (with the others including Karen Bass and Anthony Thigpenn).[47]

Meanwhile, many of the traditional Black bases of political and civic power—civil rights organizations and churches—have been on the relative decline. The local branch of the Southern Christian Leadership Conference—once headed by Ridley-Thomas—has a much lighter footprint than in the past, a fate shared by the local NAACP. The Urban League—once headed until his retirement in 2005 by the influential and highly respected late John Mack—has seen its budget and staffing dramatically shrink in recent years (although there has been some recuperation in influence with the appointment of a new leader, Michael Lawson, in 2018). There are exceptions to the pattern; for example, the Brotherhood Crusade, a group founded in 1968, remains quite vibrant, and Los Angeles boasts one of the most active and influential chapters (and the first founded) of Black Lives Matter in the nation. Moreover, a range of Black-led groups came together in April 2020 to produce a collective set of demands for improving COVID-19 testing and treatment in Black communities, supporting Black workers and businesses through the crisis, and providing more housing, health care, and community safety, all this suggesting a revitalized and welcome dynamism in Black organizing in Los Angeles.[48]

However, the churches that were once key anchors of Black civic life have been transformed or have waned in their significance in the political life of Black L.A. For example, Second Baptist is now a commuter church surrounded by almost entirely Latino neighbors. First African Methodist Episcopalian—which was the first Black church founded in Los Angeles, was the go-to location for Black Angelenos during and after the 1992 civil unrest, and was once led by the charismatic Reverend "Chip" Murray—has been weakened by scandals. Holman United Methodist—headed between 1974 and 1999 by civil rights icon James Lawson—remains a center for community gathering but its impact is more limited than in an earlier era, even as it continues to work in coalition at a local level.[49]

The political or movement baton has been slowly passing—sometimes just from the passage of time and the changing demography but also, sometimes, with intentionality—but navigating the shores of change is not always easy. What happens when a formerly Black-led organization becomes headed by a Latino—as was the case for both CoCo, which saw Alberto Retana succeed Marqueece Harris-Dawson, and Community Development Technologies (CD Tech), a community development and leadership organization founded by Denise Fairchild in the wake of the L.A. civil unrest that came to be headed by Benjamin Torres? How does that feed into an ongoing sense of "Black loss" informed by a deep history of racial disenfranchisement? How can Latinos—who lack a single elected co-ethnic from the region—gain more voice while affirming the presence, contributions, and voice of Black residents? How does their political empowerment, in an area where they have only recently started to flex their civic muscles, articulate with a larger Latino political movement that may not see building immediate alliances with African Americans as central?[50] And how does the role of place identity help to either help or hinder the ability to work through these tensions and tightropes?

Staying Local, Celebrating Place

We explore all these issues in our next section by exploring the ways that our civic leader interviewees spoke about the challenges they face as leaders. Before we do, it is important to highlight one important element of commonality and continuity that can both help ease *and* exacerbate conflicts: the focus of many organizations on the quality of daily life. This was, of course, the emphasis not only of WLCAC but also of an array of community development corporations, often church-affiliated, that built and maintained housing and came together under the banner of the Coalition of Neighborhood Developers in the wake of the 1992 civil unrest.[51] And it was certainly embodied in the work of Concerned Citizens to resist a trash incinerator and form alliances with other affected communities in East L.A.

The last few decades have seen a particular flowering of place-based efforts, often with unique ties to the broader movement-building groups delineated earlier. For example, Strategic Action for a Just Economy (SAJE) is geographically based in the northern part of South Los Angeles (basically abutting downtown) and initially grew out of earlier efforts to combat redlining and to protect tenants. Formally launched in 1996, its banner moment came only five years later when it was the lead community partner to finalize a community benefits agreement (CBA) with a major developer seeking to expand the downtown sports and entertainment facility that hosted the Lakers. That CBA, which included guarantees of jobs, living wages, affordable housing, and park space set a standard that became mimicked by community organizations and labor allies across the region and eventually the nation.[52]

SAJE later teamed up with Esperanza Community Housing Corporation—itself formed in 1989 out of a tenant's rights struggle and now both a housing developer and the owner of a business incubator called Mercado La Paloma—as well as CD Tech, the St. John's Well Child and Family Center, T.R.U.S.T. South LA (a community developer), and a range of other organizations to negotiate a CBA with USC.[53] This opportunity came when USC sought to expand its own footprint in the neighborhood by converting an aging shopping center into student housing and higher-end shops and restaurants.[54] Confident of its political sway, USC overplayed its own hand—and was eventually forced to set aside a much larger set of funds for building affordable housing than had even been requested by the neighborhood coalition (called UNIDAD for United Neighborhoods in Defense Against Displacement).

Meanwhile, another place-based effort that had less success—both in outcomes and in coalition building—was the battle to preserve South

Central Farm (mentioned briefly in chapter 5). Located on the site where Concerned Citizens had successfully resisted a city incinerator in the late 1980s, the farm was a fourteen-acre community garden feeding more than 350 families.[55] Part of what made that possible was that the land was in legal limbo: the city had acquired it through eminent domain and when it was not used for an incinerator, the former owner went through a laborious legal process to buy it back. He acquired control in 2003, sought to evict the farmers in 2004, and was finally able to do so after a highly publicized set of conflicts and clashes in 2006.[56] But what complicated the struggle—and it has its inflections with the early place-based struggles covered in this section—was the racial undertones of the dilemma confronting these urban farmers.

The farmers at South Central Farm were essentially a group of Latino, often immigrant and frequently undocumented, cultivators who, as detailed in the previous chapter about gardens and daily life, were seeking to grow food for their families and establish a sense of home. But as was noted by one of our interviewees who visited before the struggle took full form, "I remember going and definitely feeling a very—like sensing a very anti-African American vibe." Moreover, the councilperson in charge of the area was a centrist Black official, Jan Perry, who saw South Central Farm as an impediment to potential job creation on the site. While several Black activists became engaged with the struggle and helped change some of the imagery of the farm's fight as entirely Latino, racial tensions over the site and its future were clearly present.[57]

That was also the case because many of the other place-based efforts detailed here—with some exceptions—were seen as more oriented to the needs of Latino residents. This is partly because SAJE, Esperanza, and St. John's—all of which have grown in prominence and influence—work in the far more Latino northeast side of South L.A. This has caused some residents to sense that community development momentum has shifted to prioritize Latino residents, feeding into a Black resentment that previous Black struggles for political influence have set a stage for benefits they may not fully receive. Not helping matters is that some of these groups were headed by white leaders. Because of the swirling feelings and the contemporary political realities, those building civic infrastructure that can serve residents in South L.A. find that they need to be constantly aware if they are adding to tensions or contributing to emerging and sustainable Black-Latino coalitions—and important to the latter, particularly given the history, is the need to actively challenge anti-Black racism.

Of course, one place where one might expect tensions to be resolved is in the faith community. After all, Black churches played a key role in South L.A. during the civil rights movement and politicians still show up on at least the Sundays closest to elections. But as one interviewee explained, while the more Latino Catholic Church has been actively involved in immigrant rights at a county level, there is a subset of Latino churches that "believe that politics and religion should never commingle." According to interviewee Dr. Juan F. Martínez of Fuller Theological Seminary, there are several factors that have kept such churches from engaging. First, Latino Protestant churches have been very small and on the margins of the social structures of the United States, so they often saw no route for influencing decisions. Second, Protestant churches in Latin America had no official role in society because Catholicism was the state religion, and so these sorts of civic muscles were not developed in home countries. Third, Pentecostal theology—which influences many churches in South L.A.—has focused on bringing personal change in people, assuming that if people change, that will have an impact on society. Finally, Latino churches have sometimes been assumed to be allies by others who have not taken the time to understand them—one reason why Dr. Martínez lifted up the work that the Coalition for Humane Immigrant Rights of Los Angeles (CHIRLA) has done to understand Latino churches and bring them into the work from a place of an authentic, reciprocal relationship.

Of course, there are inspiring stories of faith institutions acting as a bridge between communities. For example, on the eighteenth anniversary of the 1992 Los Angeles uprising—April 29, 2010—African American and Latino church leaders along Crenshaw Boulevard led their congregants in a joint worship service that placed their faith as their primary common ground.[58] The product of at least two years of intentional collaboration, including regular breakfast meetings between pastors facilitated by Clergy and Laity United for Economic Justice, 1,500 Latino and African American church members began their service at Iglesias de Restauración (now Restauración Los Ángeles), processed four blocks down Crenshaw Boulevard, and completed their service at West Angeles Church of God.

Yet as moving as the event was, it is important to note the background: the large churches have been neighbors for over two decades—and yet this was the first major meeting of the congregations. Bring together communities is imperative but not easy. As we see in the interviews in the next section, organizers and officials need to be aware of both what is said and what can go unsaid in the name of unity but not unfelt in the real world of community emotion. Other tensions abound: it is clear that leaders need to increase Latino participation in civic life but to do so in a way that does not threaten or diminish African American voices. They have to understand their own positionality—with some suggesting that being neither Black nor Latino (nor white) can occasionally be an advantage. They have to balance the immediate place-based needs of residents with the broader political strategies and possibilities that South L.A. is now incubating, particularly since that can help leverage resources for South L.A. itself. And they have to do all this in a time in which the threat to that better future that residents have hoped for and deserve may soon be lost to them because of gentrification and displacement.

Leading in South L.A.

So how does one lead in this complex and changing terrain? There are challenges for both Black and Latino leaders and officials. For example, while Latino leaders generally recognize the need to call out anti-Black racism—partly out of principle and partly out of a political calculation that this is helpful for establishing bona fides in what has historically been Black space—they are also confronted with a reality more compelling to many residents on the ground: the gap between the share of residents that are Latino in South L.A. and the share of political representatives, nonprofit executive directors, and other leadership positions that are occupied by Latinos. They see remedying that as important, but they also worry that calls for enhancing Latino civic power can devolve into a rhetoric of ethnic succession, whereby Latinos develop a "nationalistic, Latino nativist kind of mentality" that justifies itself by "saying it's about the numbers." While striving to enhance Latino political power, they worry that, without proper acknowledgment of Black organizing and its legacy in South L.A., in addition to political education amongst Latino communities, elevating Latino power could perpetuate anti-Blackness.

African American civic leaders are right to worry about being swept away in this power shift given some past experiences. For example, "[i]n the next-door city of Lynwood, Hispanics were largely kept out of power until they became a majority. After seizing control of the City Council in 1997 they demolished the black political machine."[59] Again, operating out of a mix of principle and calculation, some Black leaders have determined that it is the best interest of African American political power to push for Latino inclusion—if only to prevent a Lynwood tipping point from occurring and sharply diminishing Black political power in an area that many Black residents hold near to their hearts and histories. Adding to this is a recognition that the strongest and most dynamic groups in South L.A.—for example, CoCo and SCOPE—work from a Black–Brown frame that seems to be gaining ground, particularly among younger activists who have grown up with Black and Brown neighbors and friends.

But persuading Black constituents to put out the welcome mat of solidarity when so little economic and political power is held by Black people in the first place can be a tough sell. This is particularly so in an atmosphere where the character of the community is already being changed by business signs in Spanish, school meetings where English is not the first language spoken, and a perceptible sense that employers favor Latino workers (and that the use of the networks of those workers to recruit more workers then effectively keep jobs out of the reach of unemployed African Americans). Black leaders then can sometimes seem either one step ahead—or one step out of touch—with local residents.

On the other hand, for all the residents of South L.A., a series of quotidian challenges to economic security, educational equity, and local quality of life are paramount and can provide a basis for coming together. Among the most important of these challenges: growing pressures of gentrification which threaten to force out both Black and Latino working-class families. But even this is not without racial politics: there is a sense by some that the Latino influx of the last several decades was a sort of first wave of change that has made whites feel safer about moving in. True or not, that is the context in which leaders must thread the unity needle, and in this section, we explore the themes of Latino civic engagement and leadership, the phenomenon of Black loss and Black longing, and the contemporary struggles over gentrification and displacement. While we provide background details to contextualize the challenges faced by civic leaders in South L.A., we try as much as possible to draw on the words of the leaders themselves.

Encouraging Latino Civic Engagement

Although there are many ways of being involved in local decision-making—attending meetings, showing up at marches, lobbying public officials—voting is one of the most traditional means and measures of civic engagement. Figure 6.1 shows a sort of "funneling" of Latino political power—from population to voters—for both Los Angeles County and South L.A. We use as our benchmark the 2014 general election both because it is the middle of the five-year pool for the population data but also because it was a non-presidential-year election, and showing up (or not) to vote then is a clearer indication of resident voter interest and engagement.

Looking at the data in figure 6.1, one immediate headline emerges: Latinos are about two-thirds of the population in South L.A. but wind up being less than 30 percent of the voters. This pattern emerges for several reasons: (1) the Latino population is younger and so the share of those who are of voting age is lower, (2) the Latino population has a sizable number of noncitizen immigrant adults who are ineligible to register and vote, and (3) Latino rates of registration and actual voting are lower than for other groups. Of significance as well: there is also a funneling (or dilution) of power from population to voters for L.A. County, but the drop-off at nearly all the steps of age, citizenship, registration, and voting is far more dramatic in South L.A.

Because of this, even if political leaders are fully committed to promoting Latino civic engagement, the electoral incentive structure requires that they be most concerned about voters who are generally African American (and usually older). It is therefore unsurprising that there are no Latino representatives from this area on the City Council, the Board of Supervisors, Congress, the State Senate, the State Assembly, or the Board of Education of the Los Angeles Unified School District. And while the landscape has been changing in recent years, interviewees suggested that because of some degree of African American resistance, it is not always been easy to secure seats for Latinos on local neighborhood councils, a set of City-supported institutions through which residents can connect with one another, organize to bring more light to their

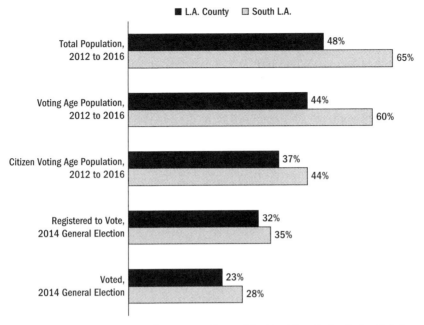

Figure 6.1. Civic Engagement of Latinos as Share of the Total Population in South L.A. and L.A. County

Source: U.S. Census Bureau, UC Berkeley Statewide Database.

Note: Voting age population refers to the population ages eighteen and older. Citizen voting age population refers to the population ages 18 and older who are citizens.

specific needs or causes, and engage with those in power.[60] Another venue for learning to act effectively in the civic realm is the nonprofit sector: there are now more Latinos heading and staffing local nonprofits, a trend that is important because this has historically been one important site where grooming for politics in South L.A. has taken place.

But for Latino leadership to emerge effectively in the nonprofit, community-organization, and eventually political worlds, leaders need to balance a desire to enhance Latino voice with the need to respect what has been built and exists. One such leader eloquently explains the crosscutting pressures:

There's that older African American guard who's like, "Okay, do we really trust you? Do we really know you? Can you really think Black/

Brown?" . . . I feel like a sense that you have to prove yourself all the time . . . every single decision I make from what time we open this building to what time we close the building to like what print will we bring to the program. Who I hire. Who I surround myself with. Who I invite to my house. I mean it's all around this idea that we have to make sure that people see me as an ally and as a bridge builder and someone who is really authentically, intentionally, trying to represent a different vision for what South L.A. can become in the future.

Another leader expressed how he and his base approach promoting a Black and Brown lens to organizing in a historically Black space:

[T]he Black/Brown model, the things that would come out of our mouths when we were in those spaces was not this, "It's our turn," but it was like an analysis of the topic. Because guess what? In addition to organizing the campaigns, we had to read the paper. We had to understand the South L.A. political landscape. We had to have some sense of history and context for what we were doing.

Showing you are "down for the cause" can be a challenge when simultaneously the lack of Latino representation feels palpable at nearly every institutional level. As another leader commented:

[t]here's always that thing, too, that I see in the County level—not to hate or anything, it's just, it is what it is—that you see all the upper management being African American and then the lower management is Latinos. But African Americans fought for those positions for many years and finally got there, but now the whole community changed around them. But now it's . . . do they want to let go of that power? Now, that's political.

It is useful to note the tone of the previous response: it is both pointing to a problem and counseling a bit of understanding and patience as the system works toward change. Of course, some Latino leaders are less patient (as well as more personally and politically ambitious). One leader noted that:

[s]o, what's happened is the African American leadership does, when they get to work, right, and get the programs they need, they give it to the African American leadership. That's power, right. That's the just mechanics of power, to the detriment, I think, of the Latino community.

This same individual noted that "at the neighborhood level, I saw, actually, a lot of collaboration between Latinos and African Americans." But the interviewee also expressed a sort of zero-sum framework, stressing the need for Latinos "to be more aggressive in taking over power at every level." Another leader was noted, "I respect that history, I get it. But what are we going to do in terms of a district that's 93 percent Latino?"

Not everyone thinks along those lines. One Latino leader suggested why they had favored a Black candidate over a co-ethnic for a city council seat on the eastern side of South L.A.:

[H]e had more political clout, he had more influence, especially with the amount of work that we need. We need somebody that's actually going to get things done. It so happens that the Black community has the influence on a larger scale to really put more impact. But it's really up to us to hold him accountable to do the things that we want, not all that he wants.

This clear-eyed analysis of the situation does not alleviate the frustration experienced by some would-be leaders, and it has also created incentives for that elected official, Councilman Curren Price, to pay closer attention than many to Latino issues. Price's staff includes many Latinos and Latinas in leadership positions and, in a highly symbolic move, he was the first council representative from South L.A. to host a "Día de Los Muertos" celebration. More significant, in 2017, he pledged $1 million in his own discretionary funds to immigrant-serving organizations, allowing one group, the highly influential CHIRLA, to open its first satellite office in the immigrant-rich South L.A. area.[61]

The opening of an office to support immigrants was, of course, not simply the result of a political calculus by the councilman; it also reflects a growing recognition on the part of Latino and other leaders that there are large immigrant populations in South L.A. that have gone unnoticed and often unserved by the larger infrastructure. Indeed, strategic planning by CHIRLA in 2013–14 pushed its leaders to the realization that many immigrants from South L.A. (and the southeast cities like Huntington Park and South Bell Gardens that are adjacent) were trekking up to their mid-city offices and could be better served by creating an outpost in their own neighborhood.[62] The organization was looking for an opportunity to expand its footprint while the councilman was looking for a way to establish his credibility—and the convenient marriage of interests has been beneficial to South L.A.'s Latino community.

But while assistance from friendly Black officials is important, some Latinos are also hoping to build an independent base for political power. Complicating that task is a larger Latino political machine in Los Angeles that could help but often fails to understand—or worse, does not care about—the complexities or possibilities of South L.A. One leader reports that

> [i]t's a very hard burden, being a Chicano working in South L.A. for a lot of different reasons. I get shit on all the time from the Eastside people . . . you know? Like why are . . . what do you care about South L.A.? . . . Why are you in South L.A.? You should be on the Eastside, you should be in Northeast L.A. . . . you know?

Those citywide leaders, in short, tend to think that the base of their political power lies elsewhere—including the greater Eastside and increasingly the eastern side of the San Fernando Valley—and see little reason to make the investments in building civic infrastructure in South L.A.

There is some validity in that political calculation: as we noted in chapter 2, while South L.A. has seen its Latino share of the population rise dramatically, only about 11 percent of L.A. County Latinos live in South L.A., well below the 28 percent share of L.A. County African Americans who live in South L.A. For countywide Latino political leaders, South L.A. can be an afterthought, particularly given that area's role as the main platform for African American political power and the sense that funding strong campaigns to forge Latino political power in South L.A. could disrupt Black–Latino coalitions at a city- and countywide level. But that can leave aspiring Latino leaders in South Los Angeles feeling stranded—blocked from upward mobility by an established Black political class, unsupported by broader Latino forces that do not really see them as good bets, and scrambling to find their place and their voice.

As might be expected in that context, much of the Latino engagement in civic life winds up being closer to the ground: health *promotora* programs run by local agencies, community-organizing efforts around jobs and housing, and efforts to secure seats on the local neighborhood councils. One longtime Latino leader put it like this:

> I don't have anything against the African American agencies, I know that they are doing a tremendous work but it's time for us to take some of the load off their backs. . . . That means we have to create our own agencies, our own committee organizations, we have to get organized politically and civically so that our community—no matter if our citizens are legal residents or undocumented—we need to educate them so they can become aware of their civic possibilities and duties and to get them engaged, you know we don't have the luxury to wait any more time for the foundations and corporations and to the elected officials to finally open their eyes . . .

One constraining factor on this sort of "bootstraps" strategy is typical of any Latino or immigrant community: it is simply hard to mobilize constituents who may be working multiple low-wage jobs and are sometimes reluctant to participate because of their legal status. Another constraining factor is more particular to South L.A.: a worry that Latino-specific organizing will be perceived of as anti-Black, particularly if organizers do not build in the political education and community-building necessary to address that. As one leader put it, "[u]nfortunately people are concerned and scared to even begin to align themselves with any Latino leadership pipeline because people are assuming that that's an affront to Black leadership."

Because of these dynamics, some leaders suggested that new Latino-based organizations will need to embrace independence *and* interdependence, advocating strongly for Latinos while being mindful of the need to represent the interests of all South L.A. In particular, they stress the need for a political framework that values and weaves both immigrant rights and Black liberation in a meaningful way, and that understands the ways in which anti-Black racism has structured the racialization of

Latinos in a way that blocks immigrant integration and intergenerational mobility. This is an easier lift for those with the second-generation mindset we noted in chapter 4: they are at ease with being in Black spaces, have friendships and working relationships that go well beyond only Latinos, and often a very specific mentee relationship with a Black leader.

Indeed, one younger civic leader noted the specific role of two older Black leaders in getting started on working on community issues. About his first main mentor, he noted:

> [O]f course, [my mentor] is African American. So when I talk to him, like, hey, this is what I know: I talk to whoever I need to talk to, and it happens to be Black people. It's always been. I remember speaking to him and him saying, "Okay, just get involved." So, to me, getting involved didn't mean Black or Brown. . . . It was just "Get Involved." Whoever is around me is going to get help, I don't care who you are.

Of course, this reliance on Black mentors is partly because, in the words of one leader, "you know that thing about South L.A. is there just isn't a ton of progressive infrastructure for Latinos." There are also worries that putting that infrastructure in place—for example, creating leadership programs that would focus on developing Latino and Latina leaders—might be perceived as a competitive move to feed into a sort of takeover strategy.

Fortunately, a positive relationship between more established Black civic leaders and emerging Latino leaders is not atypical—the leadership of Black-founded and Black-led groups like CoCo, CD Tech, and the Community Health Councils has passed to Latino and Latina hands with both grooming and grace. But all this is against a worrisome sense that a major political break could be coming. In the words of another longtime South L.A. resident but younger Latino leader:

> [W]e're not at the table, we're not driving the conversation because we're not the councilman, the County person. So . . . right now we're tiptoeing. It's like, "Oh, we gotta tiptoe. We gotta tiptoe. We gotta tiptoe . . . because we don't want to offend the establishment." And that establishment happens to be African American. That establishment is also the one that is

funding some of these organizations. But the second that that happens [snaps fingers] it's gonna be a difference, it's gonna change.

Will that "[snaps fingers]" moment be a reprise of a historic pattern of stripping hard-earned political and economic assets from the Black community? Some African Americans in South L.A. worry about this—even as their concerns are often tempered by the same neighborly instincts that moderated the racism of the Latino first generation and fueled the multiracial affections of the second generation. It is to the complexity of the Black experience with Latinos in South L.A. that we now turn.

Understanding Black Loss

In recent decades, once powerful Black-focused organizations and churches in South L.A. have seen members leave and influence be diminished. Particularly since the rise of social movement organizing the wake of the 1992 civil unrest, South L.A. communities have seen the growing effort to create and maintain a Black–Brown movement to improve conditions for all who live in this area today.[63] Despite being able to see an upside in these coalitional efforts, Black residents face a reality in which the attention of civic infrastructure is now diffused across multiple groups even as daily life provides reminders that an earlier heyday of Black Los Angeles seems long gone. There is, in short, an ongoing sense of Black loss that is exacerbated, as we will see, by the growing pressures of gentrification and displacement.

To get a better sense of these issues on a quotidian level, we complemented our civic leader interviews with interviews of twenty-five Black residents across our three focus neighborhoods.[64] The interviews were conducted by a Black (Afro-Latina) researcher who had grown up in the South L.A. area, the logic being that this co-ethnic and co-locational matching of the interviewer with the interviewees was more likely to elicit honest responses to difficult questions. Unlike the Latino interviews—which were also larger in number—these are not as statistically representative of Black residents in South LA. First, this sample size is small—due to both limited resources and our research focus on South L.A. Latino residents; the constraints we faced are explained more in the appendix. Partly because of this, we focused heavily on Watts (fourteen out of twenty-five interviewees); while our logic was that the de-mographic changes in Watts most parallel changes throughout greater South L.A. and such a focus was a reasonable way to allocate scarce in-terview resources, this creates a bias toward the experience in one par-ticular neighborhood.

The sample is also heavily skewed by gender, partly as a result of the snowball technique used by our female interviewer: 84 percent of the re-spondents were women. While this is unbalanced, it is also the case that the gender breakdown of Black women and men in these three South L.A. neighborhoods is also imbalanced—at 58 percent women and 42 percent men. It is interesting to note that interviewees highlighted the influence and impact of women residents in their community as well. There was a trend of interviewees sharing that they considered their local leaders to be the dedicated women who made a name for them-selves by providing necessities to their respective communities or, more aptly, "Black women doing the things they're doing like for the projects."

Finally, and most important, we did not have the resources to inter-view African Americans who moved away to other parts of the county or to the Inland Empire.[65] The experiences of those who have left South L.A. are likely to reveal more irreconcilable issues or tensions as a result of an influx of Latino residents—although as we will see, some of the current residents have contacts with those who moved and express their feelings for them. In that sense, we are missing an important part of the picture, one that we hope will be taken up by other researchers in the future.

For those Black residents who have remained in South L.A., they sometimes feel like they are living in a space that they sometimes see as catering to a newer demographic of people with distinct culture, language, and identity. As a result, Black interviewees shared that they have experienced conflicts both with new neighbors and civic institu-tions that do not seem to serve either population adequately. As Kasi, a woman born and raised in South L.A. put it, "putting people together in the same place does not bring racial reconciliation."

Indeed, while many interviewees expressed positive feelings about their Latino neighbors—a fact we explore more later—others were ei-ther tepid or somewhat negative. Candice, a fifty-four-year-old woman who has lived in South L.A. since her days in middle school, simply said that Black and Latino neighbors rarely "bother" each other, noting that

Latinos are "doing the same thing we doing, a lot of them—trying to make it." She went on:

> I mean, you know, like . . . everybody trying to keep a roof over their head, and I mean, you know, everybody doing about the same thing. We all got kids, and trying to make sure they alright, and doing the right thing out there. . . . [E]verybody's—you know, everybody people.

Other Black interviewees shared that they "know" that their Latino neighbors do not feel warmly towards Black residents and expressed their own wariness and discomfort as well. In the words of Raven, who has lived in Vermont Square for over a decade:

> I'm not against them. I love them. I love everybody . . . but I'm saying some of them could be rude too . . . and I don't understand that because this is not your area to do that, number one. You got to get registered and be legit and then talk to me. You know? This is South Central L.A., not Tijuana.

One recurrent concern was about economic competition as a result of limited job availability—or even that jobs are now only intended for bilingual Latinos. Aiesha, a twenty-five-year-old woman from Watts who has witnessed both positive and negative relationships between Black and Latino residents shared, "It's hard for a Black person to get a job before a Mexican." The perceived reason is discrimination:

> No, I think they get treated better than us. I think they get hired way before us if they don't got no bad background 'cause I know most people check that . . . I seen it happen with my little brother when he trying to get a job . . . they hired nothing but Mexican people.

Another reason was language. One civic leader (and longtime Black resident) said:

> I did hear a lot of "we can't even get jobs at fast-food restaurants anymore, our kids can't get jobs at fast-food restaurants anymore because you have to speak Spanish." . . . And some people said, well, we need to learn Span-

ish, but that—you know, from a lot of people that didn't seem practical and I think there was some—there was a stress about that. Like gosh, now what do we do, we can't even get these jobs. And really I kept hearing that, it was the language. It wasn't like, oh, you know, they're taking our jobs, it was no, you know, to get that job we need to speak Spanish suddenly and we couldn't do it.[66]

Language is another asymmetry in the Black–Latino dynamic. While younger Latinos tend to acquire Spanish in family and English in schools, Black residents may not pick up Spanish—particularly due to the state of public education in South L.A.—unless that is done intentionally. Moreover, after centuries of oppression and decades of labor market discrimination, there is some resentment about needing to know a second language as yet another barrier to economic well-being. Frustration extends beyond the issue of entry-level work requirements. Sierra, a young woman from Watts who grew up in an Afro-Latino household, shared that she mostly experienced South L.A. as a majority Black area until she entered new work spaces. She explained:

So we're in a union meeting and they're speaking Spanish. So it's like, how do you expect anybody to care or anybody to know the things that you're talking about, even though the decisions that you're talking about affects us, if you're speaking a different language?

Respondents also reported a perception of Latino hostility and prejudice. James, also a resident of Watts, pointed to what he saw as Latino rudeness, sharing that "you pump the community full of Latinos who have very few to any real relationship with Black people in America and a lot of them come over here and they have an issue with Black folks almost like we're in their way or we did something to them." Eloise, from Vermont Square, has lived in South L.A. for sixty years, shared her experience of housing discrimination, noting that when she called to inquire about an apartment,

[s]he said it's not available. I said to myself, she probably heard my voice and knowed that I was Black. She didn't want no Black folks. But when it comes to renting, in some places, they don't want nothing but Mexicans.

While, as noted, we did not interview residents who had moved away permanently, some interviewees shared insights on why Black families have left the area. Alongside the other factors that propelled Black flight—a desire for safer spaces and less expensive housing—Eloise, quoted earlier, suggested that many have moved out of Los Angeles to places like San Bernardino and Palmdale because

> they also, like I was saying before, it feel like it's becoming Hispanic territory mostly, and like I said, not everyone gets along with Hispanics, so they'd rather just uproot and go to where they know that there's more African Americans and they feel more at home.

Echoing this in her work actually interviewing Black residents who did move, Deidre Pfeiffer reports on one respondent who suggested that they made the change to find something that South L.A. no longer provided "a feeling of community, of collectivism, of a sense of belonging, of a sense of being insulated from broader societal forces . . . those who were seeking that same kind of level of comfort and sense of belonging moved to where the African Americans were at, which was in San Bernardino and Riverside."[67]

One of our civic leader respondents, a longtime resident of the area, notes that the sense of Black loss is

> very palpable. I mean we would say well, these Latinos, you know, maybe they're poor, they don't have much but they have numbers on their side. Numbers is a kind of capital, right, it's a kind of wealth. We don't have numbers. We don't have money. We don't have political clout. So what do we have? Now, to me, you know, the only capital we have or the consistent capital is community and when that goes what do you have?

This is, of course, consistent with a broader narrative of historic theft of labor and property that characterizes the Black experience in America and so one can see why it resonates. As we note later, this sense of Black erosion has been exacerbated in recent years by the pressures of gentrification, with African Americans feeling like the area is about to improve but that it will do so in a way that drives up rents, steps up policing of their youth, and will eventually force them to join the earlier exodus out of South L.A.

Despite feeling the strain of their home changing around them, many of our interviewees offered their own ways of creating community both amongst themselves and between ethnic groups. One important way to create bonds was through church groups. Avid and longtime South L.A. churchgoer, Gabrielle, prints church flyers in both English and Spanish, "[s]o then the Spanish community knows that they're welcome." Since she was born, Jasmine has attended church in Watts her whole life and has lived in the home her parents built in 1954. She expressed her excitement when her own church created a multicultural space where Latinos would be integrated into their space:

> We had a . . . Catholic Evangelization Center, for example, uh, I've been with them for 20 years. And they, they developed this group called Building Bridges Between Black and Brown and from the moment they started talkin' about it, I said I wanted to be on this committee.

Still, in the words of one respondent, whose family has passed down a historic South Central home for multiple generations: "I would say pastors [are leaders], to a certain extent, but that's kind of fading away. So, the church influence is not as big in this community as it was before, and obviously, that's another part of the shift."

One young woman in Watts expressed that South L.A. community organizations should do a better job at reaching Latino families who may feel uncomfortable in historically Black neighborhoods to look for resources and who maybe be "excluded from the conversation" due to language barriers. Gabrielle looked to community leaders as a resource for bringing Black and Brown business interests together:

> They need somebody who can help bring together Hispanic—business with [Black] business, because to me it seems like Hispanics kind of have their thing going on and Black folks trying to do theirs, but if some kind of way it could be brought together, really both can be built up, then it'd help little mom and pops who wanna go in business, what are those steps to take, and why can't we build together? I mean some kind of way. It seems like we stay separated too much.

Such engagements are already ongoing. For example, the Black owner of a dry cleaner on Central Avenue was elected the first president of a new business association largely composed of Latino entrepreneurs, partly because she had so much experience dealing with City issues. As one Latina owner of a hair and nail salon noted, "[s]he is an honest person, a very hard-working woman and very dedicated to the community. . . . We're all in this together. Among us there are no differences of color."[68]

In addition to opening up their spaces to and forging working relationships with Latino neighbors, many Black residents described how they attempt to spread inclusive attitudes in their daily interactions. One woman shared that she challenges her Black neighbors when she hears complaints about Latinos taking jobs, while Kasi, a thirty-six-year-old woman quoted at the start of this section considers jobs an equally challenging obstacle for Black and Latino residents:

> I think challenge number two, like I said, is jobs, and what other things that we have that are setting up walls so when we do go on those interviews and we're trying to get those jobs that have better career paths, like where you continue to rise and get promoted and a lead if you can get in the door to do that. I feel like it's equally challenging for Blacks and Latinos for maybe different reasons.

And James from Watts also challenged the narrative of "taking jobs":

> And a lot of Black people have issue with [Latinos]; feel like they're taking the jobs, they're taking the opportunities. My God, man, they don't control the job market. They don't control the economics. They don't control anything. They control about as much as you.

Meanwhile, thirty-one-year-old Devon from Watts continued the theme when he said that "[t]he main challenge for everybody is poverty. . . . And that's what connects us basically."

Twenty-six-year-old Desiree from Watts argued that Black and Latino residents face the same issues, elaborating these as

> [t]he gang[s], bull[ies], sometimes finding work. Just because everybody think just because you Hispanic, you can go out and get a job. It's not that

easy either, being Hispanic. You'd be surprised at how many Hispanics that don't actually have jobs or can't get jobs. They in the same predicament we in. Some of them was born and raised here too, so you know, we stereotyping because of the color of they skin. They go through the same thing we go through. They go through struggles and can't eat and homeless and they go through the same thing we go through. They just a different race.

Other Black respondents recognized the particular extra challenges that Latinos might face:

You know I grew up in Watts the majority of my friends were Mexican or Latino. And I've never seen anything as a color issue. . . . [At the same time,] I don't have a barrier of oh, I'm an immigrant so I don't have my papers. I don't feel like I'm going to be deported.

And as one younger Black male respondent put it, things have changed over time:

To be honest, when I was a little kid it was a lot more racial, a lot. Even in middle school we had, like, food fights, Black homies used to be like, "Oh, you hanging out with the Mexicans." . . . Little did they know, I'd go to the Hispanic homie's parties, bro, they feed you, you're drinking, you say, "I need a ride home." They turn you up, the family love you, like especially the ones who grew up with Black folks, like they mama love you, granny love you, abuela, all that. You know. And now it's a little bit more laid back, a little bit more you see like hella like Black and Brown kids hanging out with each other, playing with each other at the park, skateboarding together.

Looking at the overall pattern, one finds a complex mix: simmering tensions coexist with feelings of solidarity and a broader and not always begrudging acceptance of the new reality of a Black–Brown (and now way Browner) South L.A. But even for those who embrace the change, the sense of loss lingers. As one observer noted, this is rooted deeply in the African American experience:

There's a lot of subtleties there and a lot of different history that Black people don't feel comfortable—there's no space to talk about it. . . . [T]hey're always kind of expected to bear the burden or just, you know, get along—just accept and get along and they have, but there's things that they're anxious about that they feel they're losing. That they're actually losing that has, in some ways, nothing to do with Latinos or—it just is this historical sense that we're being marginalized generation after generation after generation . . .[69]

Building Bridges, Centering Blackness

Leading in this stew of emotions—particularly when joblessness, over-incarceration, and under-education remain key issues for African Americans—is a unique challenge for leaders in South L.A. be they Black or Latino (or, as we will see, Asian American or white). The leadership challenge is all the more acute because of the rather dim view Black residents take of the current leadership (as well as because of the relative disengagement of many Latino residents).

One generous perspective was simply that civic leaders were not very present in people's daily lives; as one thirty-six-year-old woman shared: "I don't really know who the leaders are. . . . I feel like I should know more about who our leaders are." This was also the case for first-generation Latino residents who were often unfamiliar with local elected and prominent service providers. Of course, a less positive set of views were also in evidence:

Yeah, they grew up in South L.A., but they probably don't really have the real roots here. . . . I feel like there's a disconnect between the type of problems that we have and the views of the people who are in leadership and how they should be addressed. It's a disconnect.

And it isn't just the elected leadership that provokes some skepticism:

I mean you got people that they consider leadership . . . because they're the ones, who get all the federal and state and private funding, you know what I'm saying? [Naming two groups,] these traditional people that been here for decades who get the subsidies and whatever. And nothing you can say negative about them because I've seen them do wonderful things . . . but like all things, there's an evolution, there's a graduation, there's a new class, there's a new cast.

Much of what feeds this disengagement further is the fact that twenty-five years after the 1992 civil unrest—a moment when civic leaders promised to address the underlying causes of the rebellion with a massive wave of investment—there is a perception that very little has happened to provide employment and positive development. One older resident put it this way:

> My birthday, I'll be eighty-five years old. And I see no difference in what they are doing. They do a little bit to help you out, to keep you, I guess, thinking things have changed, but I'm old enough to know ain't nothing doing nothing.

While these are general background factors, our concern here is about what leaders say it takes to work with communities amid ongoing demographic transformation. Part of it means recognizing the sense of Black loss as well as ongoing worries about political and social displacement that come out of the resident interviews just discussed. One younger Black leader said:

> The reality of African American representation feeling and looking like it's diminishing, I don't want us organizations, our communities to kind of fall into this trap of having people of color fight over crumbs. . . . So, given that we're still disinvested, we still don't have the investments that we need, or the public infrastructure that we need, so we can't get into this day where it's like, "The day for day for Black folks or African Americans have come and gone; now it's time for Latinos."

As a result, organizers and leaders often work to come up with ways to assuage concerns by centering Black needs and the fight against anti-Black racism even as they build Black–Brown organizations. Intentionality—and attention to the emotional landscape—matters. For example, the leader of one group doing organizing of parents of school children notes that

> [l]ike if you don't make it very focused on [Black parents], and you just go knock on doors, and you go stand in front of school, and you do presentations at school . . . you will only have Latino parents. Because you only have Latino parents, Black parents will see it and they actually won't come. So it's kind of a self-fulfilling prophesy. . . . So then you have the fact that Latino parents will becoming empowered, and having all these spaces where they're the only group in the room. And then the notion of empowerment, just like any group, translates into positions and councils, and getting close to the administration in schools, and being connected . . .

Prioritizing Black parent organizing—so that such parents do not become further disenchanted and disengaged—is therefore key. So is pointing to continuing racial differences so that problems most acutely felt by African Americans do not get swallowed up into a generalized whole. For example, referring to the issue of school suspensions, one civic leader pointed out:

> And one of the things that he showed me is how Black kids were moving out of the district at a rate of some exponential number to Latinos, and they were getting expelled more often, and they were given truancy citations, where there's a demand to appear, at a much higher rate.

Erasing such key differences in the interests of an uninformed "solidarity" when there is already a sense of Black erasure in the place itself is not conducive to effective organizing.

Another approach to maintaining Black engagement and Latino awareness has involved lifting up the Black history of South L.A. as a way of grounding all residents in that reality. As one civic leader put it,

> there's been a shift amongst a lot of service providers, including non-profits who've historically done work in the neighborhood, to shift their orientation towards Mexican-Central Americans because of the demographic shift. And I think that was also part of, for a long time, what kind

of was underwriting the kind of increased tensions, because there was this, sort of this like African Americans suddenly were losing everything. We're losing our political base. We're losing anything that was specifically for us. We're losing our homes. We're losing—right? So there was that. And I think that that was a shame, and I think it was something that I remember we discussed at the time and we were very conscious and aware of. And we're like, "That's something we're not going to do." Even though we understand that demographics are shifting, our history is that we're rooted in the African American community. And . . . many of our participants and staff and whatever are Mexican-Central American, but it's been really important to us to keep that sort of rootedness in African American history and not to lose that.

This has certainly been the strategy of CoCo, SCOPE, and a number of other more progressive formations that provide political and historical education to their members and other residents that help to highlight and center the Black experience and the need to combat anti-Black racism.

Of course, just knowing the history doesn't always help when the issues are tough and daily lives are disparate. Consider the case of police–community relations. In the words of one top elected official, that "in a moment of crisis, LAPD has institutional networks related to African Americans, it's not clear that they have the same level of engagement with Latinos." Scholar Aaron Roussell, for example, notes that there are institutional vehicles for community participation in the bureau that polices South L.A. but that the meetings are monolingual rather than bilingual; the Black and Latino participants are generally separated, with the Spanish-language meetings having a downgraded or secondary status and the English-language meeting often dominated by elderly and middle-aged Black residents who often offer complaints about illegal vending and gatherings of day laborers.[70]

But it is also the case the African Americans and Latinos are seen as wanting different things from the police. One high-ranking law enforcement official put it this way:

My experience with the Latino community has been more that they just don't think we come. I mean, I don't really get the complaints about, "You stopped my kid. You're harassing us." We don't get those complaints. We get the complaints that I called the police and you never got here. I called the police and you didn't do anything when you got here . . . Whereas in the Black community it's "You're picking on my kids. We're afraid you're going to shoot us" . . .

This also leads to a different experience of the police. As Roussell argues,[71]

[t]he [police] discourse over Latino in-immigration constructs Latinos as victims of black crime, as deserving and hard workers (regardless of the legality of their work), and as necessary for the maintenance of LA's restructured economy. This leads to negotiations over how to "practice tolerance" toward the new arrivals—that is, how to regulate rather than banish. Latinos in South Division are seen as comprising a distinct group of laborers whose purpose is clear and necessary, if often unruly and sometimes necessitating sharp rebuke and selective deportation. More-over, officers' racial biases regarding divergent Latino and black work ethics and crime propensities translate directly into accommodation or expulsion respectively.

Part of the less antagonistic attitude of Latinos to the police may also stem from the LAPD's commitment—not always honored—to not act as immigration enforcement agents. However, senior leaders in the immigrant rights movement are reporting that the era of Trump has brought new fears about immigration authorities conducting raids in what is, after all, a target-rich South Los Angeles. Moreover, there is an awareness that run-ins with the law, even if they do not immediately lead to a hand-off to immigration authorities, could blemish records in a way that would make legalization more difficult if some sort of comprehensive immigration bill is ever passed by Congress. Because of this, there is more desire by some to link the struggles against detention and deportation with the fights against over-policing and over-incarceration, creating another platform for finding a commonality of Black and Brown community interests.

Recently, CoCo was part of a broader set of groups that sought to pull a specialized police squad out of South L.A. after it was revealed that it was stopping Black motorists at twice their share of the South L.A. population—and because so much of the squad's work was concentrated in South L.A., that meant that African Americans were being pulled over at five times their share of the Los Angeles population.[72] Latinos both in South L.A. and throughout the city have also experienced disproportionate policing and incarceration—although at nowhere near the rates experienced by African Americans—and so there are grounds for common cause.

Despite such potential openings, South L.A. is challenging terrain on which to lead. Some leaders who are neither Black nor Latino find that their racial identity can be an advantage, with neither "side" believing that favoritism is being practiced by the non-Black, non-Latino leader. On the other hand, with some exceptions, there is resentment of the few whites who still lead social agencies or community institutions. So the real task is to develop local talent with a new frame—and many of the more active and effective organizations, such as CoCo, SCOPE, and others, have sought to strike a new balance by stressing Black and Brown unity, with an emphasis on fighting anti-Black racism.

While new Latino allies might be welcome, the need to form these alliances can simply remind residents about what seems to be a steady erosion of Black influence in what was hard-won political territory. Added to the mix is a sort of generational passing of the guard. One resident in her late thirties who has lived in Historical South Central all her life, with the exception of her college years, shared how she has seen the shift in South L.A. leadership:

> So this is kinda hard because I think, for many years, it was the old guard; it was the older people who were really the leaders in our community. And it was Council People—and people really kind of depended upon the system and tried to navigate that system, but I think as we've had more police brutality and just different issues, people getting killed unjustly, now, I think it's more of the millennials are kinda moving in and it's Black Lives Matter groups, it's people working outside of the system.

In a sort of parallel with the generational differences between Latino residents, the newer formations that hope to build Black political power often see cross-ethnic solidarity as necessary to build into their institutional DNA. And one way to build and sustain that framing—and to ensure effective organizing—is to supplement racial identity with spatial identity, that is, to stress the commonality of living in South L.A.

This identification with South L.A. indeed has been the emphasis of some organizers. For example, in 2017, a wide range of organizations came together for the twenty-fifth anniversary of the 1992 civil unrest, noting that in the words of one leader,

> we have now a critical mass of community-based organizations that didn't exist or were in its infancy stage in 1992. So we thought that was a very important piece in terms of building the kind of leadership and civic infrastructure that you need to advance; you know systemic change, right?

With that history of accomplishment in mind, they argued that this is exactly what the city, the state, and the nation need—and so staged a march under the banner "South Los Angeles is the Future." That's an amazing turnaround in self-image from the days in which acrid smoke covered this part of Los Angeles—and it reflects both a spirit of self-confidence and a deep and profound identification with the neighborhood. But if embracing such place identity is one way to bring Black and Brown neighbors together, what happens when the place itself is under increasing pressures that threaten to displace those who stayed, those who arrived, and those who did the hard work of community-building in tough times?

Worrying about Displacement

While conducting the research for this volume, one of the co-authors attended a discussion in 2015 in downtown Los Angeles titled: "Is Gentrification L.A.'s Next Defining Issue?" Sponsored by a major civic organization called Zócalo Public Square, it featured advocates and planners discussing how rising rents and tight housing markets—driven, in part, by a downtown renaissance and growing tech employment on the west side of L.A.—were forcing out artists and residents in neighborhoods throughout the city. The moderator—who perhaps should have prepared just a bit more—noted how this was occurring in Venice, Silverlake, Echo Park, Highland Park, and even

Boyle Heights in East L.A. He then posed a question: What does all this mean for places where there are no such gentrification pressures, such as South L.A.?

The response from an audience steeped in local real estate markets and including a range of activists working in South L.A.: a burst of somewhat derisive laughter followed by shouts of "Yes, it is." And it may be just as surprising to the readership of this volume as it was to that day's moderator—who was properly chagrined, soon educated, and definitely unlikely to make that mistake again—that South L.A. has been under considerable housing pressure. After all, the images that remain in the public's mind are of the civil unrest of 1992, the gang warfare that has too often wracked the area, and excess policing that has given South L.A. the vibe of a war zone. Reinforcing that is that if one drives through South L.A. on the major boulevards, one often sees tattered shops, accumulated trash, hourly hotels, and an abundance of liquor stores operating amid a classic food desert.

But drive off the main thoroughfares and one finds a striking contradiction. As one local bureaucrat (who is also a resident) put it,

> I mean you should go through residential neighborhoods so you can see the stark difference between the neighborhoods and the commercial corridors. Right? People think that South L.A. looks the way it does because people don't take care of their neighborhoods, which is so not true. People take just as good a care of their neighborhoods and they actually go the extra mile because some of these streets are ridiculously manicured and people are cognizant around our property values will decrease, and my equity and my ability to, you know, they take really good care and you'll see . . . for the most part almost every neighborhood in South L.A., very nice. And then you go out on the commercial corridor and you just see the neglect by not people of South L.A. because that's not what they're responsible for. These are mostly outsiders who are responsible for commercial corridors 'cause they are just responsible for the homes.

It is a contrast that led this official to suggest that if the city and larger businesses would simply maintain the boulevards as nicely as residents maintain the neighborhood, community members would rightfully benefit. But the contrast is also a risk since it means that when speculators see the attractive housing stock, they begin to fantasize about the profits could be made by buying and selling to higher-income buyers.

This is not an idle concern. As one leader noted,

> [y]ou know when it [gentrification] was happening around here by USC it's like, "Okay it's part of downtown," but when it starts going and encroaching deeper into areas like West Adams . . . where you have definitely strong, solid, middle-class Black communities that's starting to generate a really strong sense of fear.

Indeed, the West Adams neighborhood—which is in the northernmost part of South L.A.—was rated as among the top ten most competitive neighborhoods in the entire United States in 2016, with competitiveness ranked by how quickly a home sold, how much over asking price it went, annual price increase, and percentage of the offer that came in cash, the latter being a good indicator of "flippers."[73] That result is not so baffling when one realizes that this is the same year the Expo Line—a light rail stretching from downtown L.A. to Culver City and then all the way to Santa Monica—was finally completed, with a series of stops lying just a short distance south of West Adams. Even for those not using the rail, South L.A. is a short drive from the emerging tech industry in Venice and other such neighborhoods on the west side of Los Angeles. As a result, commute-weary employees who actually drive off the main streets—perhaps steered by Waze—see homes that would also give them more time out of their vehicles and with their partners or families.

Of course, those are someone else's homes—and while sometimes they are occupied by older Black residents who may see the value in cashing out and retiring with a nest egg (or Latino homeowners who were delighted that their investments in homemaking had become investments with yield), they may also be held by homeowners who were squeezed by the financial crash of 2007–2008 or renters who can be forced out by price hikes that stretch well past their capacities. The worries about gentrification and displacement are, in short, very real and very deeply felt, particularly by residents resentful that their ability to stick through the hard times will not necessarily extend to the good times. And whatever the new reality is labeled, it is coming: in addition to the rail investments across the top of South L.A., there is a line being completed in the Crenshaw area that will connect to the airport as well as a spate of development around USC and additional spillover pressures from a burst of growth in business and residential activity in downtown L.A.

The downtown pressures are definitely seen by South L.A. residents. As Janice from the Historic South Central/South Park area put it,

> I look at the homeless problem. The reason why we have more homeless in this community is because they started to redevelop downtown Los Angeles. They started to redevelop [the] USC area. So what happens? People get pushed this way . . .

It is also clear to residents that the new improved community enhancements are not necessarily being put there with them in mind. The same resident commented:

> I mean, I think when we get new resources, it's because they're building it around USC. The fact that there's a Trader Joe's coming to USC, that's because they're catering to that community. It's not about increasing access in this particular community. So I'm just keeping it 100—you know, the Expo Line, the Crenshaw Line, all of these assets that are coming, it's not about us.

Even neighborhoods are renamed or rebranded in the way that South L.A. itself has been rebranded. As one observer put it,

> [a]nd it's interesting to me that, all of a sudden, places are being called "downtown" that were never downtown, that were always South L.A. And now, all of a sudden, I hear people referring to them as downtown. I'm like, "Wait. Since when did that become downtown? That's South L.A." You know like around the Mercado and stuff? That never used to be referred to as downtown, and I've recently heard it called that, and I'm just like, "Wow." There's really a real attempt to kind of takeover, like not just in property, but even in language that's used to describe places. So it's kind of interesting.

There's also a demographic shift that is no longer Black to Brown but rather Black and Brown to white. As the same respondent put it,

I've seen a number of homes being purchased by young, white couples, for whom buying a house in South LA has been like the easy route 'cause it's been inexpensive; it's been they can't maybe buy one in a neighborhood they would have bought one in five, ten years ago, but they can in South L.A., particularly after the crash, 'cause a lot of property became available, a lot of people were made—you know, thrown out of their homes. . . . [In the past,] a couple of my crew members were white, and we'd get stopped everywhere. We would get like, "Why are you here in the neighborhood?" 'cause people were just curious at them seeing white people. But now it's not "a thing" to see white folks.

And the new changing demographic has produced a strong reaction along racial lines, particularly in the context of eroding Black space and concerns about diminishing Black political power. The same observer noted, "I think even how Leimert Park has developed as a political entity—not just as a collection of homes or businesses, but as a *political entity*—has also been a response. There's been this very real putting their foot down and being like, 'This is going to stay Black.'"

While concerns about displacement affect everyone, this area of seeming common ground is also riven with some tension.[74] Some Black residents feel that the earlier Latino influx sort of softened the ground for this new white invasion, with their views supported by research suggesting that gentrifiers are less interested in predominantly Black areas and more interested in "diverse neighborhoods that are or have recently been immigrant destinations, drawing in particular Asian and Hispanic populations."[75] As one respondent put it, "[s]o that got me thinking about public housing, public schools, and the nexus where poor public policy drives out a group, and how through an artificial inducement, there's an appearance that all of a sudden the Latino population sort of converged on the community all at once. But why were there all these opportunities to move in?" To many residents, the previous demographic shifts were not simply a reflection of "natural" market dynamics but rather were propelled by racialized public policy decisions, a fact that makes it more difficult to band together now.

But band together they must, and some of the biggest fights in recent South L.A. history have been about preserving affordable housing and securing employment for local residents. There have been successful

Figure 6.2. Protest Signs
Photo Credit: UNIDAD.

campaigns to secure a CBA from private developers building housing and from USC as it sought to expand dorms and shopping for USC students (with protest signs seen in figure 6.2).[76] These two fights were led by an extraordinarily diverse coalition mentioned earlier called UNIDAD, whose acronym ("unity" in English)—speaks volumes about the effort to unite Black and Brown residents in common cause. The working slogan of their People's Plan reflects both a desire for improvement and a keen pride of place: "We want better neighborhoods, with the same neighbors."

Conclusion

Multiracial organizing in South L.A. is not new but the current era has brought a particular set of challenges and opportunities. With the pressures of gentrification on the rise, organizers need to build community power—and that means first building community. That is a complex task, one that cannot be accomplished through facile calls for common ground. After all, both Black and Latino residents may share an interest in educational improvement, but many African American parents believe that Latinos have more access to school administrators and the school-to-prison pipeline is certainly disproportionately stronger for Black children.[77] There may be a shared agenda for economic justice, but it is clear that African Americans are more plagued by issues of joblessness while Latinos, specifically immigrants, are more affected by lower wages.

And while there may be deep conversations about the connection between deportation, over-incarceration, and police brutality, the insecurities and damage each induces are felt in very different ways. Indeed, the racist nature of policing and incarceration is clearly felt more acutely by Black residents, a fact made clear by the murder of George Floyd in May 2020 and the subsequent mobilization of Black Lives Matter and other groups in Los Angeles and around the country. This moment, coming on top of the deaths of Ahmaud Arbery, Breonna Taylor, and others, also propelled a number of important shifts in national politics: a widespread recognition of the embedded white supremacist nature across institutions, industries, and sectors; a broadening and diversified coalition of supporters; and a growing realization that defunding and/or reforming police departments is just the first step to moving on a broader agenda of racial justice.

Leading in this milieu will never be easy. Part of what is needed in South L.A. and other locales where Black and Brown populations are in close proximity is the further development of Latino leaders who recognize how anti-Black racism has not just hurt their neighbors but led to a lack of public investment that impacts all residents. Another part of a successful recipe for enhancing community power will be strengthening existing Black institutions. After all, as one interviewee put it, "[t]here's not a greater community of color than the African American community that sees the critical importance of civic participation and voting." Black-led institutions have served as stewards for justice in areas with limited public services and infrastructure—and improvements attained though Black politics often benefit all people of color. For all these reasons, many Latino leaders in South L.A. understand that Latino political empowerment cannot come at the expense of but rather in coalition with Black influence over policy and politics.

But actually building and sustaining coalitions can be a challenge for everyone involved. Latino leaders can feel a bit stranded when the broader Latino political machine wonders why they are so insistent on alliances with African Americans. Black leaders can feel pressured by residents who feel like yet another piece of South L.A.—its role as a base for Black politics—is slipping away. Yet there is little choice: the future of South L.A. hinges on effectively connecting Black legacy institutions and contemporary African American residents with an emerging Latino majority with its own challenges, grievances, and opportunities. And there is a great reason for hope: a generation of organizers has worked hard at building a new model of Black–Brown civic engagement, one with implications for not just Los Angeles but other areas of the country. It is to these broader implications that we now turn.

7

Summing Up, Looking Elsewhere

MANUEL PASTOR AND PIERRETTE HONDAGNEU-SOTELO

In 2015, a collaboration of community organization and civic institutions submitted an application to the federal government to have part of South L.A. declared a "Promise Zone." An Obama-created effort, the Promise Zone program allowed an area to be prioritized for funding from various federal programs—and the effort to get South L.A. in the mix had already had a complicated history. Los Angeles had received a Promise Zone in 2014 for a mid-city neighborhood, but, to the chagrin of some, South L.A. was not even considered, partly because the initial requirements required participation in an earlier education-based program called Promise Neighborhoods.[1] That outcome, regardless of the rationale, prompted considerable anger from activists and political figures who argued that the need was even higher in South L.A.'s distressed neighborhoods and that L.A. should therefore apply again.[2]

Unfortunately, City officials were told it was unlikely that a single metro area would get two Promise Zones, an admonition that might lead most local organizers to wave a flag of defeat. Not in South L.A.; instead, fifty community-based, public, and private organizations came together to form SLATE-Z (South LA Transit Empowerment Zone) with the stated goal of moving residents into employment and out of poverty. The plan was based on taking advantage of the ongoing investments in new rail lines crisscrossing South L.A., with specific activities aimed at securing both new housing and access to jobs. But organizing around the rail lines had another distinct advantage: the Blue Line (going from downtown to Long Beach) runs through heavily Latino South L.A. while the Expo Line goes through more mixed neighborhoods, and the Crenshaw Line, then in the midst of construction, would run through the current heart of Black (South) L.A. In short, an odd geographic shape configured around rail would benefit both African American and Latino residents; in this case, a sort of gerrymandering was designed to unite rather than divide Black and Brown.

But the application came up short, with the federal agency in charge of the program, the Department of Housing and Urban Development (HUD), indicating that the SLATE-Z area did not exhibit enough housing or employment challenges. That was news to the residents—as indicated in chapter 2, there are deep economic and social challenges facing South L.A. But what organizers soon discovered was that HUD measured housing difficulties as vacant foreclosures and gauged economic difficulties as unemployment. Speaking about housing, the lead on the grant, President Larry Frank of LA Trade Technical College, noted, "That's a Detroit measure, not a South L.A. measure. In South L.A. we have three families fighting for a single apartment and living in a single apartment."[3] The economic measures didn't fit either; as we have stressed throughout this volume, while unemployment is an issue, particularly for the Black community, the more prevalent problem for South L.A., particularly for its now-majority Latino population, is low wages at the jobs residents are able to obtain.

So the civic leaders did something unexpected: they invited then HUD secretary Julián Castro to visit for himself, then wrote a series of memos seeking to change the rules of the competition to better capture the South L.A. reality. The result: in 2016, the rules were changed, and the SLATE-Z proposal was the second-most highly rated application in the country. Of course, the win was bittersweet in one way, partly because it resulted from a competition between marginalized communities nationwide, all of whom were facing the ravages of previous disinvestment. It was also connected to a rail development that may secure jobs but is also creating pressures to displace residents through gentrification. But what is most significant for our purposes here: the win resulted from partnerships that brought together diverse residents and organizations to both challenge the rules of the game and take advantage of new opportunities.

In fact, the SLATE-Z victory symbolizes much about contemporary South L.A. that we have sought to capture in this book. First, the economic and social realities are different and more complex than what many outsiders expect: while the imagination is of a place in permanent distress, ravaged by the 1965 Watts Rebellion, the 1992 Los Angeles Uprising, and the toxic mix of deindustrialization and the crack epidemic, the current reality involves a fear that gentrification will sweep away current residents. In that context, public policy makers and community organizers are actually trying to secure inroads to jobs and housing as quickly as possible. Second, building the political power to influence the distribution of public and private benefits now depends on pulling together Black and Brown residents in new and creative ways: the very geography of the Promise Zone was rearranged to build bridges and ensure that development and jobs would include both African Americans and Latinos. Third, and perhaps most profound, after years of trials and tribulations, South L.A. exhibits a self-confidence, partially based in spatial identity and pride of place, that is so strong that local advocates are willing to simply insist that outsiders have it wrong and that the rules must be altered to accommodate the shared local vision.

What we have tried to suggest in this volume is that often analysts of South L.A. and Black–Brown interactions have it wrong as well. To fully capture the reality on the ground, our traditional concepts around immigrant integration, spatial assimilation, and so much else in our academic theorizing must be altered and adapted. In this chapter, we review what we think can be learned from South L.A. for contemporary sociological theory, consider how the South L.A. experience relates to other areas in which Black–Brown relations may be taking center stage, and then close with considerations of what lies ahead for South L.A. itself. We stress throughout a key concept that has oriented our own research: people have been actively engaged in homemaking and, as we have noted, that involves future-making as well. Having set their roots and made their homes in South L.A., with pride in the resilience and strength they have developed to get through hard times, and deeply concerned about a future that either holds new opportunities or portends heartbreaking loss, both Black and Latino residents are working hard to define and defend a South L.A. they have grown to love.

Learning from South L.A.

In this book, we have charted the course of South L.A.'s dramatic demographic transformation with what we hope is an example of team-based mixed-methods research. We have provided historical and quantitative context, offering a highly detailed quantitative analysis of the ethnic shift from 1980 until the present. While the quantitative work has helped to ground our findings, much of our analysis has relied on the results from an extensive qualitative research project that indicates how people felt and feel about the change. This included audio-recorded interviews with one hundred Latino South L.A. residents, some from the generation of early arrivals and some from a second homegrown generation; twenty-five interviews with African American residents who reported on their experience of the shift, including what has been lost and what has been gained; twenty-eight interviews with a diverse set of South L.A. civic leaders, all discussing the complexity of navigating in the new Black–Brown political terrain; and interviews with and ethnographic observations of a demographically mixed set of public park and community garden users, most of them men, seeking to explore how such green spaces places provide for sanctuary, reflection, and a sense of "home." What we have learned in this empirical process has led us to rethink some theoretical premises and current academic debates.

Complicating Race Relations

The first area for rethinking may simply be in understanding the nature of interethnic tensions and coalitions. In our view, much of the literature either focuses too dramatically on the conflicts between groups or paints too rosy a picture of the natural commonalities between communities of color. The South L.A. experiences suggest that bridge building is forged in daily practice; it occurs over a long time and is far more complex than simple snapshots of one struggle or another can provide. A visit to South Central in the hyped-up days of the 1980s and early 1990s might have offered little reason for hope of lasting alliances—Black and Latino neighbors were more likely to eye each other warily, particularly in the context of a massive influx of immigrants and a worrisome crime rate that caused residents to see others as threats rather than allies. Even then, of course, there were daily accommodations, particularly between neighbors, but they did not always catch the attention of contemporary reporters or analysts. Our research, however, shows how important it is to recognize the temporal quality of these dynamics: even when a neighborhood has experienced deep conflicts and tensions, these do not remain static. Similarly, we can see that even against the backdrop of conflict and tensions, the long-lasting implications of critical moments and relationships that helped guide people through life challenges.

Of course, change does not drop out of the sky. As the hyper-criminalization of South Los Angeles began to lessen, violence slowed, and the era of "shutting in and shutting out"—in which immigrant parents not only shielded their children from the street but also cut themselves off from civic life—began to change. This was helped along by Latino children who became more engaged in life in South L.A. (e.g., through public schools but also through sports, music, and friend-ships) in a way that forced their parents to be as well. This shift is not entirely unique, nor is the fact that it may be more easily discerned by talking to the grassroots rather than the grass tops. As Jennifer Jones in *The Browning of the New South* notes, "conventional wisdom and aca-demic scholarship tell us that black-brown conflict is pervasive; on the ground, the situation looks a lot different."[4] But based on her research on Winston-Salem, North Carolina (as well as reviewing similar dynamics in other parts of the South), she finds that quotidian life plays a role in quelling tension—essentially, contact does make a difference. But she also stresses—as do we—how a shared understanding of racism and a political project of creating "minority shared fate" can overcome job and other competition.[5]

Such a sense of "minority shared fate" was also in the political air of Los Angeles in the late 1980s and early 1990s, although many of these primarily involves leaders of groups rather than on-the-ground mem-bers and residents.[6] Understanding how those political opportunities intersect with the daily practice of identity construction requires under-standing the actual lives of residents and we have endeavored to do that here through extensive interviews. Such an in-depth exploration helped us differentiate between a first generation of Latino immigrants who brought anti-Black attitudes and found those reinforced by U.S. culture, and a second generation of Latinos who grew up in South L.A. and who say they identify with African American culture and politics. Indeed, many people in that first generation seem to span a range between racial ambivalence and categorical anti-Blackness.[7] Yet, at the same time, many of these same individuals also fondly treasure connections they formed with Black neighbors and friends. As these first-generation immigrants struggled mightily to establish new homes for themselves in South L.A., they were often impacted by significant encounters with African Americans who acted as parental mentors or friendly neighbors and so helped them establish a sense of belonging and rootedness.

The second-generation Latinos we interviewed narrated the kind of optimistic, agentic disposition that other researchers have noted among the children of immigrants.[8] But one key difference was their attachment to the place of South L.A. and their deeply felt connection to African American neighbors. They came of age together with Black school mates and friends so when they hear their cousins in East L.A. expressing anti-Black racism, they react with offense. Contact theory, which emphasizes the importance of sustained interracial interactions occurring on common ground, in conjunction with a paradigm of relational racialization helps explain this development.[9] Yet another part of the explanation is that their racial formation occurs in a particular place, and their affinity to Black life resonates with Wendy Cheng's work on place-based racial sedimentation. But a final factor is that their formation of a political identity was shaped by Black struggles in South L.A., including a shared sense of oppression by a larger white power structure.[10]

We should also stress for future researchers one nuance we ourselves discovered: moving away from a conflict-focused view of Black–Brown interaction should not be dependent on finding ongoing instances of calm communication, completely shared space, and instances of kumbaya bliss. Conflict and consensus, like dissonance and solidarity, occur along a continuum. Our study of parks and gardens, for example, documents numerous instances of micro-segregation, with some community gardens populated almost entirely by Latinos and others almost entirely by African Americans. Parks are also often split into use areas that are very different by race, age, and gender.[11] At first, we thought that this was a worrisome sign of distance, particularly since it occurred in public parks, like Martin Luther King (MLK) Park just north of the Vermont Square neighborhood. After all, MLK Park had actually been opened to broader neighborhood use by Black–Brown political organizing, primarily by Community Coalition. Surely, this physical separation meant that the hoped-for moment of interracial understanding had not been fully realized.

Yet self-congregation is to be expected and perhaps it is even healthy. If people are "making home" in public spaces, they may gravitate to others with whom they share language, interests, and other characteristics—indeed, homophily, the tendency of people to bond with those who are similar occurs throughout society. And for Latino and African American men who experience racism and class oppression, self-congregation at the parks and community gardens is also a form of experiencing sovereignty and freedom. We are reminded of the critics who wonder why the Black students may sit together during lunch at a predominantly white institution; perfect integration is an imagined (and often white-centric) ideal, but the reality is that getting refreshed with others with a similar background and perspective can help make the broader project of working together more sustainable. And at the public parks and community gardens that we studied in South L.A., we see the men adopting a new ethos of "we're all in this together," anchoring a shared identification with South L.A., even as they might gather to socialize and spend downtime with men who are similar to them.[12]

The kind of public homemaking and coexistence that African American and Latino men find in the parks and gardens of South L.A. seems to have been less possible just a couple of decades ago. While one could attribute this simply to the passage of time and power of intergroup contact, what we are seeing cannot be separated from the enduring and broader forces of racial segregation that influence Angelenos in South L.A., today. Loïc Wacquant helps tease apart two dynamics: he differentiates imposed segregation from protective segregation—a sword and a shield, respectively.[13] South L.A. has been oppressed by imposed segregation, and for many, the response of South L.A. residents has been protective segregation. This includes the first generation "shutting in and shutting out" during the violence of the 1980s and early 1990s and the self-segregation, self-congregation, and homophily that endure in some contexts in South L.A. (even if, as described in chapter 5, it now has softer edges and is bathed in a popular narrative of everyone "getting along"). This later segregation may be a form of refuge from the broader types of oppression experienced beyond the boundaries of South L.A.; when these men go to work in Downtown or on the Westside, they surely encounter types of racism from which they are free when together at a local community garden in South L.A., enjoying each other's company and the work of their own hands.[14]

Rethinking Immigrant Integration

While we hope that this work, leads to a more complex vision of intergroup relations, another area of rethinking that arises from this project involves the broader topic of immigrant integration. The field has become more complex in its understandings over the years, complete with frames around "liminal legality" and "legal violence" due to uncertain legal status and an awareness that assimilation into white America is no longer necessarily the ideal or the norm.[15] Indeed, our research echoes with the statement of Alarcon, Escala, and Odgers that "there is no single path toward immigrant integration."[16] The traditional approaches that seem to undergird much of the literature have generally assumed that that the comparison group for measuring mobility is the white native-born, that proximity to Blackness socially and otherwise contributes to a segmented assimilation downward, and that spatial progress for a group is synonymous with a move to the suburbs.

The South L.A. case offers several challenges and complexities to that picture. Consider the usually important role of legal status: this is an area which has a much higher share of undocumented residents than other locales, even in L.A. County, and yet deportation and detention did not emerge as a primary concern (indeed, it was barely expressed as a concern at all) among our interviewees. There are unique aspects to Los Angeles which may explain this, including a long-standing commitment by the local police to not enforce immigration laws, the relative openness of the school system to undocumented students and parents, and the highly settled nature of the area's immigrant communities. Additionally, as we have emphasized, there are local and regional differences regarding the immigration advocacy infrastructure, and Los Angeles has been at the forefront of developing strong safeguards. But deportation concerns do surface more dramatically in other parts of the city, and we think at least one contributing factor is that police practices are so thoroughly anti-Black in this area that South L.A. may feel like a safer space (at least in terms of *La Migra*) for older non-Black residents (as we have seen, younger Latinos also expressed concerns about over-policing).

All this suggests that *where* you integrate matters—and not just for relative fears of deportation. Through their daily practices over the years and decades, both first- and second-generation Latinos have come to feel a deep sense of belonging here. Regardless of legal status, as they have created memories, relationships, and attachments to this place—they feel at home in South L.A. This seems particularly true of the second generation in South L.A.; even when they have graduated from college, they do not wish to move out to the suburbs or other neighborhoods. Rather, they see their future in South L.A., which they perceive as a site of familiarity, freedom, and belonging.[17] South L.A. is home and they hope to make it even better.

We realize that the particular networks we used to reach our interviewees might have yielded some degree of bias in the sample, one that reflected our own organizational connections in the neighborhoods that compose South L.A. as well as a familiarity of our graduate student interviewers with those who had garnered some degree of formal and/or political education. So perhaps we have oversampled on those who would stay, a methodological problem shared with our sample of Black residents in which we did not have the resources to interview those who chose to or felt forced to depart the neighborhood. But the truth is that we did not see much evidence of a segmented downfall from growing up in a Black community. Rather, the main outcome we saw was an embrace of a shared worldview—often by individuals who were clear strivers and often informed by a deep political analysis of the way that white supremacy structures individual and community opportunity—that tends to align the Black and Latino experiences in ways that contribute to alliances for social change.

We also saw the embrace of place: Latinos raised in South L.A. see themselves as quite distinct from East L.A. Latinos, largely because of their deep relationship with Black histories and futures. That spatial location matters in understanding immigrant integration is not entirely new. Being Latino is not a monolithic experience, and it clearly varies across geography; indeed, one of the most seminal volumes in Latino studies, George Sanchez's *Becoming Mexican-American*, reminds us of the centrality of place, particularly Boyle Heights, in forming Chicano identity, and Lisa García Bedolla's brilliant intervention, *Fluid Borders*, likewise reminds of how different the Latino experience can be even when contrasting two communities, East L.A. and Montebello, that are less than ten miles apart.[18]

So the fact that Latino life experiences and social formation in South L.A. have been anchored by experiences of relational racialization with African Americans is crucial. It means that their world views are not centered in reaction to whiteness—and indeed not entirely centered on notions of *Latinidad* either.[19] Because they are so deeply shaped by the specific anti-Black racism experienced by one's neighbors, friends, and potential allies, the idea of ethnic succession, in which a new ethnic group takes over territory from an earlier group, is anathema. This can lead to the sort of leadership challenges we covered in chapter 6 in which emerging Latino leaders seek to balance their sense that Latinos are underrepresented in political life with a desire to honor Black elders and preserve Black influence. We witnessed some unease with walking that tightrope, but we also saw a sense of solidarity that overwhelmed a sense of Latino triumphalism; while a sense that "our time has come" quietly expressed by a few, that was a rare sentiment.

Making (and Losing) Home

Our South L.A. study offers novel challenges to traditional views of ethnic conflicts, immigrant integration, and ethnic succession. But it also provides more support for a threading concept to begin to reframe the field: the notion of homemaking. We are not pioneers in this thinking. As we noted in the introductory chapter, we build on scholarship already underway in shifting migration studies to acknowledge how immigrants plant their roots, establish their right to belong, and create the lived reality of a new home.[20] This does not, of course, take away from the fact of the importance of transnational ties and constant exchanges across the border—but in the United States, at least, time in country has been steadily growing. In 1990, for example, about 56 percent of immigrants had been in the United States for more than a decade; in 2017, that figure had risen to 72 percent.[21] Homemaking in this context should become a more prominent feature of immigration studies.

If it does, place will occupy a more central role in our thinking. We have stressed earlier that location matters: becoming (and being) Latino in South L.A. is very different than becoming Latino in East L.A. The latter is defined as a significant Mexican American locale, with a unique civil rights history told through the prism of the Chicano movement and the student walkouts of the 1960s. By contrast, South L.A. is historically a Black space in which learning about the proud histories of the civil rights movement and the Black Panther Party is more likely to be a formative educational experience. More significant, the asymmetry of exposure means that Latinos in South L.A. cannot conceive of their political projects for empowerment apart from their alliance with Black people while those from other parts of the city and county may see this in a far more abstract light. In this context, Black–Brown civic organizing becomes the rule rather than the exception for Latinos with civic ambition, a sort of political habit deeply ingrained into their thinking and their being.

Indeed, in this process of self-discovery and self-definition, place becomes an identity on its own. The pride that we witnessed in South L.A. may strike some observers as curious: with all the challenges and problems, how can residents feel so positively about the places where they live and grew up? Much of it has to do with resilience: to borrow a phrase, if you can make it in South L.A., you can make it anywhere. The informal acronym that one second-generation respondent offered for his beloved neighborhood of Watts—We are All Taught To Survive—is not a sign of desperation but a signal of self-confidence. And it is fed by more than a sense of toughing it out: Latinos in South L.A. have seen steady improvement as crime rates have gone down over the last several decades, homeownership has gone up, and despite struggling schools, many young people have made their way to institutions of higher learning. A key aspect of immigrant homemaking is future-making, and while Latino residents did not always find their fabled golden egg, they see their future in South L.A. For researchers, our takeaway here is that identity—as a Latino or anything else—is deeply grounded in place and creative combinations of frameworks from immigration, urban, racial formation studies, *and* human geography may be helpful in the research ahead.

And that gets us to a final analytical lesson to lift up from this work: the need to recognize the ongoing sense of Black loss as South L.A. shifts from clearly defined Black space to something else altogether. It might be easy to dismiss this sentiment, to frame it in the inevitability of ethnic change, to note how every place in Los Angeles has a sense of the temporary, to move on quickly to how the newest and largest ethnic group in the territory of South L.A. is defining itself, and to highlight the arrival of a new Latino project in what is, of course, a fundamentally Latin American city.[22] But as tempting as that might be and as celebratory as that might sound, it would ignore the realities of Los Angeles and frankly the realities of American demographic transformation at this point in our history.

After all, Latinos eclipsed African Americans as the nation's largest "minority" group as early as 2003, and the difference between the two in terms of numbers and share of the U.S. population will, as we note later, be increasing over time. Certainly, Indigenous Nations have faced genocide, cultural erasure, and so much more. But a defining, persistent, and fundamental feature of the modern American racial structure has been anti-Blackness.[23] We have noted how Latinos need to navigate that reality in South L.A.—to advance the interest of Latino residents, they need to acknowledge and couch their concerns in a Black–Brown framework. As such, some leaders wonder about whether there will or should be a place for an independent Latino political voice. Of course, one could also argue that highlighting the Black experience can actually benefit the emerging Latino majority since it clarifies the racialized xenophobic strands informing today's anti-immigrant hysteria and contributes to a more defined "people of color" identity and politics. But it is also the case that Black–Brown framing can diminish the specificity of anti-Black racism and fail to capture the hearts and minds of Black Angelenos who find themselves a minority group in a territory that was hard-earned and now feels tragically lost.

That sense of loss, of course, is about more than demographic change. As we have noted, the ongoing pressures from gentrification are also contributing to a sense that Black space in Los Angeles—and in many other urban areas—is being slowly erased or obscured. But the immediate communities that are most in contact, in both L.A. and many other cities, are Black and Brown, and needing to build coalitions can feel like one additional burden in a game that is already stacked against Black people who have seen their assets stripped and their claims denied over the broad swath of American history. This can be exacerbated by the asymmetry of exposure outlined in the South L.A. case—in which

Latinos are entering Black space at a rate that far outpaces the entrance of Black Americans into self-defined Latino space—and inflict a high psychic cost on African Americans as they adjust to the new political realities.

The demographic complexity of civic life in South L.A. (and elsewhere as we note later) also impacts Latinos. Against the backdrop of changing demography and persistent economic distress, Latino leaders perceive that the direct political paths are mostly blocked, but they also realize that the best way forward is to form alliances with Black leaders rather than appeal to a nationalist turn. Black residents and leaders have learned to value their Latino neighborhoods and constituents, but there is an undeniable sense that Black Los Angeles has been transformed in ways that are unrecognizable and somewhat foreign to older residents (and can fail to center the concerns about anti-Blackness voiced by younger African American activists). Although the 2020 reaction to the murder of George Floyd gave momentum to organizing by Black Lives Matter activists in Los Angeles and elsewhere, many traditional Black institutions are still struggling to be fully relevant in this changing context. As a result, Black–Brown coalitions are the center of the emerging political gravity and starting to achieve some success. But for all involved, this requires growing new skills—and occasionally facing and overcoming new conflicts.

What Happens in South L.A. . . .

The fascinating thing is that this is a set of challenges not confined just to South Los Angeles. African Americans and Latinos currently compose the largest nonwhite shares of the American populations, at 12.3 percent and 18.1 percent, respectively, and will continue to be the largest nonwhite groups going forward, with current projections showing Black and Latino shares at 12.7 and 24.1 percent, respectively, by 2050.[24] Data on measures of exposure—a segregation measure that captures the likelihood of a person of one racial or ethnic group living in a neighborhood with a member of another group—suggest that both African Americans and Latinos are less likely to live near white people now than in 1990 while they are both more likely to live near each other now than then. So while much past work has focused on the Black–white color line, more future research should decenter whiteness and focus on the relationships between the groups that will, by 2044, compose America's "new majority."

While this is a big question for the nation as a whole, the relationships between and dynamics within Black and Brown communities cannot simply be derived by a consideration of broad categories; as is the case for our study of South L.A., relations reflect specific regional histories and unique constellations of economic, social, and political conditions that are not uniform across the national landscape. In short, the lessons we have pulled from our work in South Central—the need to understand time and context, the importance of home, the complexity of organizing—can cross to new locales but they need to be nuanced and adapted as they make that journey. Some of this is already being done brilliantly by scholars like Jennifer Jones in her study of North Carolina, Frederick Opie in his examination of quotidian coalition building in New York City, or Wilson and Taub in their look at four different neighborhoods in Chicago.[25]

In other work, we have tried to take up the comparative task by examining alliance building across four different sorts of metropolitan areas: (1) "nascent" regions that had a significant Black population but were gaining a quite small but rapidly growing influx of Latino immigrants (e.g., Jackson, Mississippi); (2) "advanced" metro areas that were further along in that process and tended to have a more sizable Latino immigrant population while also having a stable or slightly growing Black population (e.g., Milwaukee); (3) "emerging" regions or areas that have seen a growing Black population even as Latinos have also seen their numbers rise, largely because of job growth or affordable housing (e.g., some of the sprawling suburbs of California); and (4) "legacy" regions that had large Black and Latino populations, with the former having been largely established in prior decades and now shrinking as Latinos grow in terms of numbers if not political influence (e.g., South Los Angeles and, as we note later, Oakland).[26]

Each of these regions presents different incentives for alliance building, and that leads to different coalitional strategies. For example, in the "nascent" case of Jackson, Mississippi, two factors have conspired to produce Black–Brown alliances, even though the Latino population is less than 3 percent of the metro population. First, the significant civil rights legacy of the state means that standing up for the human rights of immigrants is in the civic DNA (at least of the Black leadership; suppressing human rights is, of course, a whole other strand of leadership in that Deep South state). Second, Mississippi is the state with the greatest share of Black residents in the Union, giving local African American political figures a material incentive for demonstrating loyalties with a growing population that could be just as loyal of allies down the political road. As a result, the state's legislative Black caucus, as well as Black civil rights organizations (including the state's branch of the National Association for the Advancement of Colored People), and labor have played leading roles in fighting anti-immigrant bills, including attempts to mandate immigration checks by law enforcement.[27]

In the "advanced" region of Milwaukee, an area marked by stark residential segregation and a scarring history of deindustrialization, alliances have been harder to come by. As in South Los Angeles, African Americans came to the city in the 1940s and were able to obtain middle-class status with working-class jobs in manufacturing. Many of those jobs have since vanished, and the state now has the nation's second-highest incarceration rates for African Americans.[28] The area has a long-established Puerto Rican population but also a newer Latino cohort that works in retail and service. Here, finding common ground is tough: economic aspirations may be similar, but high levels of residential segregation—that is, the absence of shared space—has gotten in the way of everyday interactions that help build identities inflected with mutuality.[29]

The "emerging" region of Orlando, meanwhile, has experienced the rapid economic and population growth typical of Florida in the last few decades. The share of the population that identifies as Black actually increased between 1990 and 2017, with the gain placing Orlando in the top ten in such gains for the one hundred largest metro areas.[30] Moreover, of all the top metros with a Black population that exceeds 10 percent of the total population, the Orlando metro is fifth in the country in terms of the share of those identifying as Black who are also immigrant: 22 percent as of 2017.[31] This suggests a possibility for alliances around immigration issues, but that possibility is not always realized, partly because of the sheer sprawl of Orlando and partly because a highly diverse Latino population, including a large Puerto Rican population who are already citizens, makes it difficult to find commonalities even in that group.[32] This inability to gain traction is also typical of the California suburbs or exurbs we and others have studied.[33] While there are exceptions, such as the exciting progressive work that went on under the leadership of a young Black mayor, Michael Tubbs, in Stockton, these sprawling locales are often areas where people are detached from civic life and hard to organize.[34]

By contrast, Oakland is a "legacy" case: in a stark demographic parallel to South Los Angeles, African Americans were nearly half of the city's population in 1980 and now constitute about 22 percent while Latinos were less than a tenth of the population in 1980 but now constitute 27 percent.[35] Given the shifts, one would have anticipated some tensions—and these have occurred. But it is also the case that legacy matters in a different way: a history of multiracial organizing and Black radicalism, including being the founding location of the Black Panther Party, has created a political tradition whereby Black–Brown coalitions are, to some degree, expected.[36] Similar to South Los Angeles, a big part of the work in such coalitions involves recognizing the fundamental role of anti-Blackness of determining the terrain on which lives get lived (or taken), dreams get realized (or dashed), and alliances get formed (or broken). And, similar to Los Angeles, all this is now taking place against a backdrop of skyrocketing rents and gentrification pressures that contribute to a sense of Black erasure and have made organizing together on a shared place identity absolutely crucial to ensure that both Black and Brown neighbors can stay and thrive.

There are many other areas to study and many other Black–Brown racial dynamics at play across the country. In North Carolina alone, there are several studies by Helen Marrow and Jennifer Jones.[37] Jones finds that Mexicans are structurally and culturally marginalized, in part due to their identification with African Americans and in part due to institutional exclusion. Conversely, Marrow finds distancing from African Americans in her work, something Jones attributes to the different political-economic context at play during an earlier period of data collection. The somewhat simple point here is that context, history, timing, and power are central in understanding and working toward a Black–Brown alliance in any place. Most significant, such alliances get built to last on the ground and in the community—and that is where research should take place as well. Too often, Black and Latino alliances are looked at in terms of political elites rather than everyday people.[38] But there is also a strong body of research that grounds racial dynamics in place and everyday life, and so better sketches out the possibilities for both real tensions and real coalition building.[39] We hope that this volume contributes to that growing body of work and helps researchers further complicate the analysis going forward.

The Future of South L.A.

While the future of research on Black–Brown coalition building, the formation of a new intersectional *Latinidad*, and the importance of place and homemaking to identity formation may be bright—so much to study, so much to learn, so much to share—the future of South L.A. itself seems increasingly under threat. Across the United States, large cities have seen a clustering of well-paid knowledge workers that is driving up rents and driving out residents.[40] Commonly known as "gentrification," it is not a new phenomenon, nor is it a trend limited to the United States.[41] But the current wave of gentrification is powered by new as well as old forces: shifting job composition to knowledge work, sharp increases in income inequality, massive amounts of capital looking for "safe" real estate investments, decreases in crime that alter real estate values, changing preferences towards urban amenities, the growth of charter schools that allow detachment from local public schools, a strategic set of public investments that have helped regenerate once-tired downtown areas and more.[42] And all this is happening within the context of a globalizing world full of new economic pressures and flows of people.

   While much of that sounds like a potential plus for urban America, development has also brought displacement from the very homes that Black and Brown residents have worked so hard to call their own.[43] In their robust volume, Chapple and Loukaitou-Sideris offer one of the most comprehensive literature reviews on the history of gentrification in the United States.[44] They lift up the tension between the need for more compact development and gentrification pressures finding that whether a place gentrifies and displaces residents is highly context-specific. But with a landscape as varied as Los Angeles County and a national history of violence and serial displacement of communities of color, South L.A. is a community that looks warily at a new wave of public investment, wondering whether it is a welcome reversal of decades of neglect or mostly a potential threat to neighborhood continuity.[45]

As we noted in chapter 6, there is reason to worry: a spate of new light rail lines is placing large swaths of South L.A. just a few stops from major job centers, a phenomenon that threatens the racial order of Los Angeles by challenging the now-informal boundaries of segregation.[46] There are also real estate pressures from all sides: Silicon Beach threatens from the west; huge real estate investments in Downtown and Koreatown, as well as the expanding footprint of the University of Southern California provide pressure from the north; and an emerging set of massive entertainment complexes to the southwest in Inglewood complete the pincer movement. For some who are encountering South L.A. for the very first time, either because they are driving or railing through or because they simply forced to shop for housing in less expensive locales, they encounter a secret well known to neighborhood residents: South L.A.'s tattered boulevards sit beside neighborhoods with tidy bungalows and well-kept lawns. All this is creating a tempting target for speculators who see how the combination of new transit stations, well-paid tech and entertainment workers being priced out of L.A.'s Westside, and the attractive housing stock all create incentives for a real estate takeover.

But people live where that takeover is slated to happen: as is typical, one person's neighborhood discovery is another person's longtime home. And home, as we have noted in chapter 2, has been hard-won in South L.A. African Americans were locked out of most of the territory through the pre–World War II period and then became the overwhelming share of residents in the area in the wake of white flight after the Watts Rebellion. Many Black residents felt like a new world of possibilities had opened to them—decent housing coupled with nearby industrial employment created a path to a middle-class living from a working-class job. Discrimination in labor markets remained rampant but a community had been built, replete with its own churches, stores, and institutions. Meanwhile, one of South L.A.'s own, Tom Bradley, rose in the early 1970s to be the mayor of the entire city, demonstrating the sort of multiracial bridge building that could foreshadow a better future.

But home was shattered by the combination of deindustrialization, crack cocaine, militarized gangs, and hyperactive police. Many African American families moved out through the 1980s, and the pace only quickened after the 1992 civil unrest. Latino immigrants moved in, seeking to find their own sense of home as they were pushed from both sending countries and the overstuffed traditional entry neighborhoods in mid-city and the Eastside. Shutting in and shutting out, home became a privatized sphere for many immigrant Latinos, perhaps with a semipublic respite in a nearby garden. Meanwhile, their children found a new home of their own in schools, sports teams, and youth activities where they learned to respect the Black legacy of South L.A., to treasure their Black friends and allies, and to develop a sense of identity based not only on race but also on place. South L.A. Latinos emerged as a distinct breed, embracing different music, different politics, and different attachments.

In this context, Black–Brown organizing emerged as the baseline for building power. Powerful as that might be, it has also presented complexities for both Latino and African American leaders. Latinos are called on to show strong alliances with Black allies even as they experience a sense of frustration with the slow pace of Latino representation in formal politics (see chapter 6). For African Americans, the need for coalitions is clear—after all, that is how Bradley achieved citywide power. But that can also seem like one more thing—in this case, a dominant political voice—is slipping way just like so many community assets have in the past. For both, the sense of inquietude is exacerbated by a sense that the whole project of home is disappearing for everyone: if prices continue to rise, this place that has been home to L.A.'s Black and Brown working class will instead be the playgrounds for a new gentry with little knowledge of just how sacred this ground is to its residents.

It is particularly ironic that the pressures of displacement and displacement are rising just as South L.A. is coming into its own. The SLATE-Z effort with which we began this chapter is emblematic of this new era. Organizations came together across sector, industry, and race/ethnicity to build a coalition that had no single leader but had a singular and effective vision. Place-based, Black–Brown, and working at multiple scales—from house meetings to community gatherings to the White House—South L.A. was able to win at a game in which the rules were originally stacked against it. It reflected many things, but paramount among them was a sense of self-confidence that the neighborhood could not only win a particular grant competition but also change the nature of development and evaluation itself. Basking in the SLATE-Z triumph, it really did feel like the neighborhood was living up to a slogan that was promoted during the twenty-fifth anniversary of the L.A. civil unrest: "South LA is the Future."

But that future is uncertain. While there is much on which to build, including a sophisticated set of social movements and community-based organizations we described in chapter 6, the pressures stacked against South L.A. could easily overwhelm any configuration of power. What the residents will have in their favor is something we discovered along the way in our research: their own sense that this home won is a home worthy of defending.

We get it. As the reader might surmise from the discussion of rethinking theory, we as authors had academic ambitions when we took up this project, including the desire to challenge concepts of ethnic succession, develop notions of place identity and home, and explore what it means to do deeply coalitional organizing for social justice. What we did not fully anticipate when we started this journey—even though we and members of our team had worked in and around South L.A. for years—was that we would find ourselves doing just what earlier Black migrants as well as first- and second-generation Latino interviewees did before us: fall in love with the place.

Indeed, that love was further cemented even as we were completing this final chapter. Stalled on what we thought might be a good closing sentence, we put down the pen (or rather keyboard) and dashed off to join the celebration of a new housing development in South L.A., Rolland Curtis Gardens (see figure 7.1).[47] The project has a fascinating history. After a private developer sought to evict longtime low-income tenants in 2011, the tenants organized, fought back, and persuaded a community-based land trust to acquire the property.[48] The road was long and winding—and one of us helped along the way with advice about policy and funding—but the then 48 units have since been rede-

Figure 7.1. Rolland Curtis Garden Opening Celebration
Photo Credit: Abode Communities.

veloped to 140 affordable units, providing homes to those who worried that they would be forced to leave. One speaker at the celebration noted that the project was "an example of Black–Brown unity" because of the nature of the political struggle to secure tenant protections. The mayor, in attendance along with the local councilman, noted that "[t]his is what history looks like."

It is also what home looks like—or could look like if the residents of South L.A. are able to organize to protect themselves against displacement. We think that there is a chance that they might be able to do just that. After all, in the last few years, knocking around the Twittersphere has been a hashtag we illustrated in chapter 1, #WeAreSouthLA. Meant to evoke a sense of pride in a place of struggle, it is frequently connected to a sense of people fighting for living wages and better schools and against police abuse and racial discrimination. If you peruse the postings associated with the tag, you will notice a myriad of faces, ethnicities, and genders all sharing joy about being from an area others have written off. Famed rapper Tupac Shakur once wrote, "You wouldn't ask why the rose that grew from the concrete had damaged petals. On the contrary, we would all celebrate its tenacity. We would all love its will to reach the sun."[49] The spirit of resilience and strength of which Tupac wrote is in great abundance in South L.A. We hope that have captured it here and that it will continue to allow the residents to define themselves, their home, and their future.

ACKNOWLEDGMENTS

Our first thanks must go to the many South L.A. residents and civic leaders who were generous with their time and wisdom and without whom this book wouldn't have happened. Thank you to the Latino residents who allowed us to tape one hundred interviews (with both Latino immigrants who first moved to South L.A. and the second generation reared there), to the twenty-five Black residents we interviewed, to the additional forty-four park and community garden interviewees, and to the twenty-eight local leaders who also agreed to an interview. To the residents, we are humbled by how you have led lives of pride and integrity and we hope for a nation that can show that same sense of solidarity you have so often shown each other. To the civic leaders, thank you for your ongoing work to free South L.A. from the shackles of oppression so the world can see the beauty of this place so many people call home. Your work and your wisdom inspire us.

We owe a particular debt of gratitude to Benjamin Torres, executive director and chief executive officer of Community Development Technologies (CD Tech) at Los Angeles Trade Tech College, who was among the initial leaders suggesting that we conduct the research we present here. We also want to thank a range of other movement-building leaders who have both led on Black–Brown organizing and consistently influenced our thinking in this space: Anthony Thigpenn (California Calls), Marqueece Harris-Dawson (Los Angeles Council Member for District 8), Alberta Retana (Community Coalition), Joanne Kim (Los Angeles Council District 8), Maisie Chin (CADRE), Lola Smallwood Cuevas (founder of the Los Angeles Black Workers Center), Gloria Walton (Strategic Concepts in Organizing and Policy Education), Tim Watkins (Watts Labor Community Action Committee), Arturo Ybarra (Watts/Century Latino Organization), and Gerald Lenoir (Othering & Belonging Institute).

Thanks also to our funders on this project, including the W. K. Kellogg Foundation, the California Endowment, and the James Irvine Foundation, as well as the Advancing Scholarship in the Humanities and Social Sciences Research program at our home institution, the University of Southern California (USC). Pierrette is grateful for the Weatherhead Fellowship she held at the School for Advanced Research in Santa Fe, New Mexico, during 2017–18, which allowed her the time to carefully read through transcripts and field notes and write several chapters. We would also like to acknowledge the many affiliated professors and graduate students of the USC Center for the Study of Immigrant Integration (CSII), who have shaped our thinking on immigrant integration—especially Jody Agius Vallejo, the current associate director of CSII, but also the amazing research and administrative staff who both worked on this project and kept the center going on a myriad of other efforts. Eunice Velarde Flores and Jamie Flores have helped immensely with administrative duties to support the infrastructure that is needed to conduct projects and write a book. Gladys Malibiran and Lauren Portillo Perez provided important communications assistance and other staff both made the space for us to work on this project and occasionally helped with specific data and other requests.

We already acknowledged in chapter 1 the unconventional attribution of authorship of this volume. Pierrette and Manuel were the principal investigators (PIs) on this project, with Manuel directing the quantitative research and Pierrette directing the qualitative research. They also served as the lead writers, both of them threading everything into a single narrative. But Pierrette and Manuel wanted to acknowledge the co-authors because of their contribution to this project. They were out in the field collecting interviews, at their desks analyzing the quantitative data, typing up field notes, and frequently discussing emergent themes around the seminar table or the coffee room. Their thinking deeply influenced the analysis presented in this book. We also include them as co-authors because we all know many instances where research assistants and staff researchers are rendered invisible in publications, and we wanted to avoid reproducing that scenario. In that light, Pamela Stephens, Veronica Montes, Walter Thompson-Hernández, Alejandro Sanchez-Lopez, Robert Chlala, Jose Miguel Ruiz, Antar Tichavakunda, and Adrián Trinidad played different research roles, but all invested significant time and energy into the research and ideas fueling these chapters. Moreover, each is committed in their own way to the ongoing strengthening of the Black–Brown coalitions in South L.A. and elsewhere.

Many others also contributed in significant ways to this volume. Our gratitude to Kristie Valdez-Guillen (University of California, Los Angeles [UCLA] Musicology) and Jessica Medina (morena strategies), who were part of the ethnographic interviewing research team, and to Caro Vera (at that time, a student at UCLA Luskin) for her work on copyediting the original report that was a basis for this book. Cynthia Moreno (data analyst) joined the team as we were developing the book and helped to do a set of final interviews and bring the book across the finish line. Thanks to Rhonda Ortiz, USC CSII project manager who helped to develop the vision and purpose of this project, wrote many grants to fund it, developed staff, and generally provided institutional support for this project. Thanks also to Vanessa Carter, senior data analyst and writing specialist who ensured day-to-day project management, conducted interviews, wrote (so many) drafts, provided guidance to researchers, and provided continuity between the many phases of this project. Gabriel Watson (formerly data management specialist) also refreshed the data analysis to bring the book as up-to-date as possible. Finally, Janice Burns-Miller—an independent contractor with roots in South L.A. and connections to policy work in the region—helped round out the project by interviewing Black residents in the mega-neighborhood.

We are both grateful to colleagues—some academics, some not—who have had a deep impact on the way we conceptualized immigrant integration as involving both homemaking and Black–Brown alliances, as well as colleagues and allies who also helped us better understand and contextualize South L.A. These include Estela Benisimon, Angela Glover Blackwell, Paolo Boccagni, Maisie Chin, Juan De Lara, Phil Ethington, Niels Frenzen, Ange-Marie Hancock Alfaro, John Iceland, Jack Jedwab, Jennifer Jones, Jane Junn, Josh Kun, Lon Kurashige, Doug Massey, Tatiana Melguizo, Natalia Molina, John Mollenkopf, Aurea Montes-Rodriguez, Dowell Myers, Viet Than Nguyen, Jorge Nuño, Vilma Ortiz, Gary Painter, Alejandro Portes, john powell, Laura Pulido, Karthik Ramakrishnan, Vanesa Ribas, Victor Rios, Emily Ryo, Leland Saito, George Sanchez, the late Mark Sawyer, Josh Sides, Roberto Suro,

Edward Telles, Veronica Terriquez, Abel Valenzeula, Jody Agius Vallejo, Pete White, and Jamie Winders.

Thank you to the reviewers, editors, and staff at NYU Press. You have improved the quality of this work by leaps and bounds, and we thank you for your thoughtful feedback. Special thanks to our editor, Ilene Kalish, for believing in this project and encouraging us to see it through to publication.

Finally, thanks to our spouses for supporting us and to our children for inspiring us. The world you will inherit has been scarred by racism and exclusion, but in key places like South L.A., people are coming together to imagine and create another world. We have already seen you in South L.A. and elsewhere, joining local efforts for justice and healing. May that continue to be your path and our path going forward.

APPENDIX

Research Process, Methods, and Data

THE OVERALL RESEARCH PROCESS

This appendix reviews the research process, methods, main data sources, and the fit between our interview sample and the data universe in South L.A. We start with the process since reviewers expressed a degree of curiosity about the complexities involved in managing a large research team of faculty, staff, and students in a complex terrain like South L.A.—complicated at times, as we note later, because of certain security issues but also because of the racial politics implicit in a project looking at massive demographic shifts in what was the beating heart of Black Los Angeles. Partly because one of our favorite chapters in Robert Sampson's landmark volume, *Great American City*, is his discussion of the research journey and partly because it was such a significant experience for us, we were happy to oblige.[1]

The first thing to stress is that this project was born out of existing relationships and expertise. Manuel Pastor has been working in South L.A. and with South L.A. community organizations since the late 1980s and early 1990s, especially with multiracial and Black-led power-building organizations like Strategic Concepts in Organizing and Policy Education, Community Coalition, Community Development Technologies (CD Tech), and others. One of the primary instigators of this particular project was the president and chief executive officer of CD Tech, Benjamin Torres, one of the first Latinos to take the helm of what had been a Black-led organization in South L.A. He was hoping that someone could write an asset-based story of the evolution of Latino civic identity in South L.A. and do it in a way that would not fall into what he perceived as a trap of Latino triumphalism about rising numbers. The task, from his view, was to understand the development in the nuanced context of Black–Brown relationships.

The University of Southern California (USC) Center for the Study of Immigrant Integration (CSII) was the institutional home for the work. Rechristened in 2020 as the Equity Research Institute (ERI), CSII was, at the time we began our initial research in 2014, co-directed by Manuel Pastor and Pierrette Hondagneu-Sotelo; more significantly, it had already done such a study looking at African Americans and immigrants and had a legacy of working with both Black-led and immigrant organizations, and so the fit seemed natural on all fronts.[2] The project also drew the support of other community-based groups who were eager for the phenomenon of Black–Brown organizing to be highlighted and shared with a broader philanthropic and civic audience. Hondagneu-Sotelo's expertise in ethnographic research, role as associate director of CSII, deep familiarity with immigrant Los Angeles, and connections with many graduate students who might be interested in working on this project brought special strengths to the partnership. And so we began . . .

Like many research projects, one of the first steps was to find funding. Despite having been a well-funded center for nearly a decade, we struggled to find any foundation that was willing to invest in a project on Black–Brown relations and Latino civic identity in South Los Angeles. We eventually found support from the W. K. Kellogg Foundation, the California Endowment, and the James Irvine Foundation, but we initially carried the project's costs based on the center's reserves. This led us to underinvest in some parts of the work that would have been fruitful. For example, since the Latino story of South L.A. had not really been told before, we started our work there. That meant that our study of African American reactions to the Latinization of South L.A. was initially confined to Black civic leaders rather than residents and when we were finally able to subsequently expand that sample to local residents, the scale was smaller, and we were unable to include some who might have moved away. While we think the research remains of great use and that the early bet of our own funds was merited, we are struck by the challenges we faced in attracting philanthropic support, including from key local funders in Southern California, for a community-engaged project on Black–Brown identity formation.

In assembling the team of researchers, we sought to include people who had connections with the mega neighborhood in one way or another. One exception was Veronica Montes—now at Byrn Mawr College—who was a CSII postdoctoral fellow; what she brought to the project aside from her ethnographic skills was her own experience as an undocumented Mexican immigrant in Los Angeles in the 1980s, a life experience that helped build trust with first-generation interviewees. We were able to recruit USC graduate students Kristie Valdez-Guillen (then a PhD student at USC American Studies and Ethnicity) and Jessica Medina (then a graduate student at USC Sol Price School of Public Policy), along with Walter Thompson-Hernández (who had just finished his graduate work at Stanford), all of whom had grown up in or around South L.A.; they, along with Veronica and Pierrette, composed the ethnographic interviewing team. Pamela Stephens and Alejandro Sanchez-Lopez were the primary data analysts from USC CSII staff, Vanessa Carter was responsible for ensuring the project moved forward day to day, and Rhonda Ortiz managed the project.

A word about the team. At USC CSII, we have generally built research teams slowly and sequentially to allow for people to get to know each other and to build trust as they go deep with the materials. For this project, we felt that telling the asset-based story of Latinos in South L.A. was urgent, particularly given the conflict-driven story that was generally dominating media and the academy but did not reflect our experience on the ground. The strength of this team was its broad perspective but one of its weaknesses was our failure to engage in more trust building—something especially important for a research project that had a large in-depth, qualitative interviewing portion and that was trying to understand nuanced meanings about race in a highly charged context. The biggest challenge on a theoretical and practical level was how to highlight *both* the unique Latino story in South L.A. *and* the legacy and presence of anti-Black racism and Black political struggle that determined the terrain.

The team met regularly in the beginning to shape the project. We chose historic South Central, Vermont-Slauson/Vermont Square, and Watts as our neighborhoods, even before the team was fully formed—and asked the qualitative team to begin interviewing in those places. Jessica Medina had grown up in Watts and so was tasked to conduct interviews there. Walter Thompson-Hernández was dispatched to Vermont-Slauson, due east of his childhood home in Huntington Park, and Kristie Valdez-Guillen took Historic South Central. Veronica Montes and Pierrette primarily interviewed the older first-generation immigrants, and all those interviews occurred in Spanish.

Pierrette and Veronica designed the interview guide, as well as a template that we used for typing up post-interview field notes, and together they conducted training in qualitative interviewing. Kristie Valdez-Guillen prepared the institutional review board (IRB) human subjects forms, and we followed that protocol with all the interviewees. While we sought respondents from our three neighborhoods, we relied on snowball sampling to reach out to interviewees, making sure we diversified our contacts. We interviewed in people's kitchens, backyards, and garages; in corners of cafes; and a few times at our campus offices: and we asked the same set of open-ended questions for the immigrant interviewees and a slightly different series of questions for the second generation, which allowed us to tap into their varied upbringings and social formations. The interviews asked about people's life experiences in South L.A., the transformations they had witnessed and relations with African Americans.

In all interview encounters, we strived for conversational rapport. Afterward, we rushed to type up post-interview field notes, where we recorded unspoken tensions, silences, and emotions, as well as emergent themes and questions. Most of the interviews lasted about one hour, and all were audio-recorded, transcribed verbatim by a professional service, and coded, although the initial coding later required backtracking and rethinking as more trends emerged. Coding and analyzing narrative interviews require a different pace than quantitative analysis. For their participation, interviewees received a gift card and at the conclusion, we asked if they knew someone else who might be interested in being interviewed. The qualitative interview team met regularly to share emergent themes and issues.

At the same time, Pamela Stephens took the lead on a detailed demographic analysis of the mega-neighborhood and the three small case study areas. Meanwhile, Pamela, Alejandro, Manuel, Vanessa, and Pierrette (along with some of the graduate students) developed an interview template for civic leaders and began interviews with that group; a subsequent set of interviews with civic leaders as we were finalizing the book in 2019 was conducted by Manuel, Vanessa, and Cynthia Moreno.

In the earlier period, we ran all tracks of research at the same time so that they could influence each other. We met regularly as a research team to discuss findings and help each other think through findings and methodologies.

Accessing the ethnographic interviews with residents was easier in some places than others. Historic South Central was particularly challenging because of our relative lack of connections there. It was helpful that Kristie, Jessica, and Walter were all in the USC CSII office at least once a week so that they could trade stories, strategies, and support. While they came to the office to attend to logistics—downloading transcripts, filling out face sheets, filling in interviewee logs, and so on—another key reason was to attend regularly scheduled team meetings. Those meetings raised difficult issues, for example, the risk of this project feeding into an existing attitude of anti-Blackness given the focus on Latinos. At the same time, we did not want to sweep under the rug evidence of Latino anti-Black racism; while it was difficult to write about this, we sought to faithfully represent the veracity of what our interviewees told us. Moreover, while our own intention was to consistently note the need to center the struggle against anti-Black racism, this was sometimes easier voiced than practiced and ran up against the fact there was real frustration expressed by some Latino interviewees about their lack of political influence.

Adding to the tension was our internal organization. Basically, we, too, are part of society, so we were not separable from a set of issues raised in interviews with civic leaders regarding the role of white organizational leadership in a distinctly nonwhite space like South L.A. How that played out in our own team was complicated. Only two members of our core team—Pamela Stephens and Walter Thompson-Hernández—were Black-identifying, with Walter being Afro-Latino. And while this project was headed by two Latino PIs, two white women, Rhonda and Vanessa, had prominent roles in the daily housekeeping management of the research. In those roles, they were in charge of monitoring the tasks assigned to the research assistants and other staff, and sometimes this created friction. These various dynamics—which also reflected positional power since Rhonda Ortiz was our managing director—went partly under-recognized by the two PIs because one of the two, Vanessa, was the only member of the professional research team living at that time (and still living to this day) in South L.A. In retrospect, that was a fact that created a certain familiarity with the neighborhood but, of course, did not erase racial dynamics.

That racial tension was exacerbated by the fact that Vanessa was not just managing the project on a day-to-day basis but was responsible, because of her long writing relationship with Manuel, for coordinating the writing process and achieving a unified voice across the chapters of the report on which this book is based. Vanessa's positionality, as well as her white conditioning, showed up in her editing—both in content and process—and that caused tensions on the team. Of course, the task of building a unified voice would be hard under any circumstances, and we likely did not lay a strong enough foundation around expectations in writing. Black–Brown coalitions take years to build—so to throw together a multiracial team with many racial and power dynamics at play and expect it to easily come to consensus in an era in which every aspect of race relations was being challenged was aspirational, at best.

Another dimension of the tension had to with timing of phases of the project. As mentioned, this was a project that took longer than anticipated to attract sufficient external support. Not wanting to wait, we launched into the field as soon as we could using our own reserves. This meant that we had to phase the work and we prioritized the Latino resident and civic leader interviews. We did a wave of interviews of Black residents roughly a year later, appropriately led by an Afro-Latino researcher who grew up in the South L.A. area and was generally received by residents as African American (she was actually attracted to the project after seeing an interim presentation at Charles Drew University in Watts, one part of our community engagement strategy that clearly worked!). But this meant that our interviews with Latino residents were not fully informed by ground-level (rather than civic leader) perceptions of what the demographics changes had meant for Black residents. In retrospect, both waves should have occurred simultaneously so as not to create a sort of informational asymmetry that could lead Black concerns to receive lesser attention.

These various tensions wound up having an important impact on the long-term trajectory of our research center, including a deeper examination of how racial equity and inequity played out in our workplace;

that process continues to this day and has resulted in significant shifts in how we do our work and who we lift up and engage as leaders. Our own fraught process did lead to organizational growth and the eventual report was well received by both Black and Latino community members who weighed in on an early version at a presentation at USC, were part of the formal presentation of the full report at LA Trade Tech, the local community college, and many of whom used subsequently used it as a vehicle for both staff training and the attraction of philanthropic support for their organizing efforts in South L.A.

RESEARCHING PARKS AND GARDENS

While internal racial and power dynamics were at play within our overall team, a different set of racial, gender, and social issues unfolded in the parks and garden research that composes chapter 5. First of all, walking up to people relaxing in public parks and community gardens and asking to interview them with an audio recorder is not an easy proposition. But even before getting to that stage, there were other key decisions: which sites to select, how to establish trust, rapport and respect, and what questions to ask. Pierrette Hondagneu-Sotelo began the research process with research assistant Kristie Valdez, scouting parks and community garden sites in South Los Angeles in the fall of 2014. By the spring of 2015, Pierrette organized a diverse group of undergraduate students, graduate students, and postdoctoral scholars to assist in visiting several parks and gardens in South L.A. at different times of day, recording typed field notes into a template, separating observations and analysis. The ethnography team of spring 2015 included three Latinx undergraduate USC students raised in the neighborhoods of South L.A.; two postdoctoral fellows in sociology from, respectively, the Ukraine and Mexico; and one Latina and one African American graduate student, as well as Pierrette.

The group met regularly to discuss observations and experiences. It quickly became apparent that sending young Latina female students out to the parks subjected them to catcalls and low-grade sexual harassment, so they subsequently only went out in pairs. Ultimately, Pierrette selected sites in the neighborhoods where we were already interviewing Latina/o residents, places that local residents frequented, and where the student research assistants felt comfortable. At this point, the focus was discerning who was at the parks and gardens at different times of day, what they were doing, and observing the texture of interactions between Latinos and African Americans. We eliminated as study sites several smaller community gardens devoid of much activity and public parks that were either underutilized or which seemed unsafe.

For example, we excluded South Park, a large park from the turn of the last century, still characterized by "city beautiful"–era majestic palm trees and semitropical plants. Adult soccer and baseball players held games there, and sometimes, their friends and family members came to watch and buy food items from street vendors, but there was also a liquor store on the corner and a daily gathering of homeless men, drinking, and catcalling at young women. This seemed to keep many residents away too, as we saw parents with children and toddlers in strollers walking nearby, deliberately skirting past the park. South Park had once been the pride and joy of South L.A., with a spectacular bandshell where jazz legends had performed in the 1940s, but now it reflected the spotty abandonment of post-deindustrialization. And although we spent a lot of time observing at Ted Watkins Park in Watts, formerly known as Will Rogers Park, where Loukaitous-Sideris had conducted an important observational study with her UCLA student research assistants, we ultimately decided to omit that park because it was too big and because we were already focusing on the community gardens in Watts.[3] Other parks and gardens were excluded because we just could not be everywhere.

During the summer of 2015, a small grant allowed Pierrette to hire two male USC students (Antar Tichavakunda and Adrián Trinidad) and to purchase $30 gift cards from Home Depot and Target for interview participants; in the fall of 2015, another student, Jose Miguel Ruiz, joined us. The team conducted interviews with people at the Greater Watts Community Garden and Stanford Avalon Community Garden in Watts and at Martin Luther King Park and Fred Roberts Park, located, respectively, near Vermont Square and historical South Central neighborhoods. We primarily interviewed African American and Latino men, but also a handful of women and in addition, Pierrette interviewed four civic leaders whose work focuses on gardens or parks (and whose words are captured in chapter 6 as well as chapter 5).

All the interviews were conducted with IRB human subjects approval, audio-recorded and transcribed verbatim, and later coded twice. After an interview, each interviewer typed out detailed field notes and reflections as well as a face sheet with basic demographic info (place of birth, residence, age, etc.). In total, we interviewed fifty-three people (of the fifty-three, nine were double interviewees, meaning that they were also included in first-generation Latino sample and so were administered two instruments). This included sixteen people at Stanford Avalon Community Garden, seven at the Greater Watts Community Garden, eighteen at Martin Luther King Park, and twelve at Fred Roberts Park. It should be noted that some of the interviewees at Stanford Avalon Community Garden also served as respondents for chapter three, as first-generation Latino immigrant residents of South L.A. All the interviews were transcribed verbatim and coded first by Adrián and later by Pierrette.

These were open-ended interviews that asked questions about experiences with parks and gardens while growing up, current relationships and daily practices in parks and gardens, and opinions about community needs and governance. Reflecting the demographics, all the Stanford Avalon Community Garden interviews were conducted in Spanish, and all the Greater Watts Community Garden interviews were conducted in English. At the parks, we used both languages. For this project, we promised confidentiality and anonymity to the individuals we met at the parks and gardens, and we keep our promise by concealing their names, but all the interviewees were informed that we would use the real names of the parks and gardens.

At the Stanford Avalon Community Garden and the Greater Watts Community Garden, we usually approached prospective interviewees by commenting on their garden and what they were growing, and we introduced ourselves as researchers from USC interested in how the neighborhood has changed and what is now happening here. We approached people respectfully, aware that we were in their space. At some point, often after several visits, we asked if we could interview them, and if they said yes, we set up a future interview appointment and returned to sit for a one-hour-long conversation, usually held under a shade structure in privacy between the interviewer and interviewee.

The community gardeners were older, mostly men over age fifty-five, who regularly visited their plots several times a week or even daily. Not everyone wanted to participate, but those who did obliged by returning at a later date. Pierrette conducted most of the interviews at the gardens, assisted by the other team members. At the Greater Watts Community Garden, the African American gardeners were protective of their privacy, and we obliged, conducting fewer interviews there. Jose Miguel Ruiz, who is steeped in community food cultivation and gardening traditions, made a big splash at the Greater Watts Community Garden when he gifted the gardeners with sacks of goat manure, which he had gathered at a family member's Central Valley farm. For these men, this was a much more meaningful gesture than the gift cards. When Jose Miguel and Pierrette were able to discuss and share photos of their own gardens, this helped establish their legitimacy as gardeners with mutual interests. At the community gardens, the research offered more ethnographic possibilities for building relationships over time, as the same people were at the same sites on a regular basis. This allowed us to join in community events, meetings and often many casual conversations before even asking someone to participate in an interview.

At the public parks, we had to be nimble and flexible. Park goers were playing sports, pushing kids on swings, hanging out, drumming at the drum circle, or resting with friends. Sometimes they said they would return in two or three days to sit for an interview, but often they would not show. The itinerant nature of park-going became evident. We interviewed a range of people, including not only those who had been coming to the same park over the years but also newcomers and re-entrants. One woman who had grown up in foster care said she had never gone to any park as a child. One man in his early thirties, visiting Martin Luther King Park with his partner and toddler, said, "This is actually my first time back in the park, in like what? Thirteen or 14 years?" He had served time in federal prison, and although he had been released a year and half before, it was his first time returning to the park.

Conducting open-ended, audio-recorded interviews with mobile populations circulating through the park meant interviewing respondents then and there. The best interview recruitment strategy was to walk around the park, observe, and gather the courage to approach someone for an interview. Having young men of color as interviewers opened up many opportunities here. Antar Tichavakunda did the majority or interviews at Martin Luther King Park, and Jose Miguel Ruiz and Adrián Trinidad focused on Fred Roberts Park. Adrián Trinidad had grown up near that park, and he sometimes started a conversation that might lead to an interview while playing pickup basketball. Antar Tichavakunda, who is African American, was often met with respondents who congratulated him for being a USC student and saying something like "happy to help a brother," but he also received advice to look out for himself. The park interviews were shorter, often thirty to forty-five minutes long, and sometimes two people participated at once (e.g., two friends or a couple). The "two in one" interview may have sacrificed reflexive depth but opened up more dialogic, casual, and spontaneous responses.

The interview process often brought the interviewers close to the violence that can be part of daily life in South L.A. After his third interview at Martin Luther King Park, Antar Tichavakunda recorded the following excerpt in his post-interview notes:

> As I concluded the interview I felt the unsettling, tense energy that precedes a fight. One woman hanging out with the gang members by the bathroom was yelling. . . . Around my last question I heard the sound of fist hitting skin, excited voice and profanity. The two women in the gang members groups were fighting. I tried to act nonchalant and said, "Why they fighting, man?" Frederick was truly nonchalant and waved if off, barely looking in their direction, saying, "Nothing surprising there, man," and went back to answering the question that I had asked. This shook me.

Antar finished that interview and went home. He returned to conduct many more interviews but stopped on his last day when he realized that while he was talking with an interviewee, the man was simultaneously directing a young man to go assault another youth. Such are the realities of fieldwork in the complex terrain of South L.A.

Were the complexities and challenges we described earlier worth it? We will let the reader be the judge of that for the book, but we do know one thing: they were unavoidable. If one really wants to do engaged research which seeks to respond to community concerns, keep honest to the academic enterprise, and interrogate racial and other inequalities in the very construction of knowledge, blunders, and injuries will characterize the learning process. While we grew weary in the process, we also grew wiser and encourage other scholars to proactively work through some of the issues examined here.

QUANTITATIVE DATA SOURCES AND METHODS

We now turn to what some (not us!) might consider a less fascinating aspect of the research process: the methodological issues involved in constructing the quantitative data used primarily in chapter 2 but often in other parts of the text as well. We specifically want to highlight the relationship between the summary and microdata that we employed.

For 1970, 1980, 1990, and 2000 summary data, we relied on various files available from Geolytics in which tract-level summary data has been fit into 2010 census tract shapes, making the series compatible with the 2012–2016 American Community Survey (ACS) and hence our tract tagging for the area called South L.A. There are, however, a few issues about the decadal data worth highlighting. First, the 1970 data includes whites, Blacks, and Hispanics—but neither the white nor the Black data net out Latinos (or Hispanics) in those racial categories. This is not a significant problem for the Black series since there were very few Latino Blacks in Los Angeles County in that era (likely less than one percent of all Latinos according to calculations from data available from the National Historical Geographic Information System). It is, however, a problem for whites given the tendency of Hispanics to identify as white or other (and more frequently as white in earlier census tabulations).[4]

For this reason, we almost always start our other tables which require the complete demographics with 1980, but we do provide a map of South L.A. in 1970 since we are convinced that the Black share is reliable and the Hispanic share is indicative. We say "indicative" because it is also the case that Hispanics are not well defined in the 1970 Census since the question was not asked of the full sample until 1980; rather, this is Geolytics best guess for 1970 using some approximation based on national origin, language, and other factors. Hence, we are more secure with demographic breaks from 1980. Moreover, many of our other time-series tables begin at 1990 because that is when a question of concern or breakdown by nativity or some other factor was first asked or created. When we show contemporary summary data, they are from the 2012–2016 ACS.

The microdata are also useful because these are individual answers that can be tabulated in unique ways. The problem is geographic: the main area measure in the microdata is the public use microdata areas (PUMAs), and these do not line up perfectly with the tract-level definition we use for South L.A. Fortunately, there are five PUMAs that are relatively good stand-ins for the South L.A. boundaries, and so we combine them. However, because they are not perfect in terms of boundaries, that leads to the following nuance. Because we use tract-based summary data for many basic tabulations but microdata for more complex calculations involving nativity, years in country, English abilities of Latino immigrants, and other such matters, there is sometime a very slight mismatch (e.g., the share of Latinos in South L.A. according to a tract analysis does not perfectly line up with what we get from the analysis based on microdata and PUMA boundaries). We are willing to sacrifice the exactness of the match for the precision provided by the individualized answers in the microdata.

The geographic scale at which the U.S. Census Bureau provides microdata—PUMAs—are much larger than the census tracts we used in the summary data and even larger than the smaller neighborhoods that compose South L.A. As noted, we were able to select a series of five PUMAs that roughly fit the South L.A. boundaries but using PUMA-level data without any modifications could lead to larger mismatches when we move down to the neighborhood level. For example, if we simply pull from the PUMA that includes Watts, we would have also included Florence, Broadway-Manchester, and Green Meadows—areas that are also part of South L.A. that have slightly different populations. So we fit the microdata to the neighborhoods by using an *iterative proportional fitting* procedure, a process that essentially involves reweighting individual observations until we better match the age-gender-race profile of the neighborhood on which we are focusing. Fortunately, each of our neighborhoods was drawn from a single PUMA; while we have done this drawing from multiple

PUMAs in other work, this is a more complex procedure also involving geographic weighting, which we were able to avoid here.

COMPARING THE LATINO INTERVIEW SAMPLE TO THE NEIGHBORHOODS

The care we took in matching the microdata to the neighborhood data also allowed us to do a careful check on the correspondence between our interview sample and the universe characteristics. Recall that the Latino respondents whose stories and qualitative responses make up the bulk of chapters 3 and 4 come from the three different South L.A. neighborhoods discussed in chapter 2. The sample was drawn through a snowball set of techniques, and it is therefore reasonable to ask how representative the sample might be of the underlying Latino population in those three neighborhoods. To get at that, table A.1 offers a profile of the Latino population in the three focus neighborhoods with all data drawn from the 2012–16 ACS. Table A.2 shows the characteristics of the one hundred individuals we interviewed. In that table, there are instances where fields were left blank due to nonresponse; the number of "blanks" are listed for the reader, but they were not used in the calculations for percentages.

So how does the sample compare to the likely universe? Note that by design, we were drawing even samples from the three neighborhoods (Vermont Square, Watts, and Central Avenue) so we could better capture each area's experience while, in reality, they have different population totals. For example, the Central Avenue neighborhood is home to almost 60 percent of Latinos from these three neighborhoods, and that means that we oversampled on the other neighborhoods where there is more Black–Latino contact in the current period. Also, we were deliberating trying to get at first- and second-generation residents, that is, to oversample on those who moved in the 1980s and 1990s and their children (or at least their children's generational cohorts).

That said, one can see that our sample has a gender balance close to that of the actual South Los Angeles neighborhoods, with a larger share of women (55 percent) in the sample compared to that of Latina women in these South L.A. neighborhoods (49 percent). The employment rate of those interviewed—including both full- and part-time—is representative of Latinos in South L.A., with both showing about 62 percent of Latino residents currently holding jobs. Those who say they are unemployed are

TABLE A.1. Census-based Demographics in Focus Neighborhoods
ACS-based Profile of Latinos (aged 18 and over) in the Three Focus Neighborhoods

	#	%					
Total				Age			
Population	125,409		Highest Level of Education*	18–24	25–44	45–64	65+
Vermont Square	35,928	29%	<High School Grad	26%	54%	74%	87%
Watts	17,776	14%	High School Grad	33%	26%	16%	7%
Central Avenue	71,705	57%	College**	41%	20%	9%	∧
			Graduate Schooling	∧***	∧	∧	∧
Gender							
Female	61,276	49%		US-Born	Foreign-Born		
Male	64,133	51%	<High School Grad	24%	68%		
			High School Grad	31%	21%		
Age			College**	44%	11%		
18–24	25,696	20%	Graduate Schooling	1%	0.5%		
25–29	16,703	13%					
30–34	16,451	13%	Employment****	#	%		
35–39	14,410	11%	Employed (– PT)	71,052	57%		
40–49	24,614	20%	Part-Time	6,399	5%		
50–59	16,233	13%	Unemployed	7,652	6%		
60+	11,300	9%	Not in the Labor Force	40,223	32%		

* People not in group quarters, 25 years old or more.
** "College" means attended some level of college (some college, AA, BA).
*** The "∧" symbol indicates that numbers are not available.
**** Ages 18 and older to match interview sample, not in group quarters, not military.
Source: U.S. Census.

overrepresented in our sample—at 19 percent in comparison compared to 6 percent in the ACS—but that is likely because the Census or ACS definition of unemployment requires that one be actively seeking work and the more colloquial definition of unemployment (which would have been the respondent understanding) includes discouraged workers who are no longer looking.

The ages of our interviewees are very nearly representative of the underlying Latino population in the three neighborhoods, with a lower

TABLE A.2. Interview Sample Demographics

Profile of Latino Interviewees*

	#	% (among non-blank)
Total		
Interviews	97	
Interviewees	100	
Neighborhoods		
Vermont Square	30	30%
Watts	35	35%
Central Avenue	32	32%
General South L.A.	3	3%
Gender		
Female	55	55%
Male	45	45%

Highest Level of Education	18–24	25–44	45–64	65+
<High School Grad	7%	16%	68%	67%
High School Grad	43%	16%	21%	33%
College**	43%	53%	11%	0%
Graduate Schooling	7%	16%	0%	0%
Blank	3	8	5	3

	U.S.-Born	Foreign-Born
<High School Grad	6%	50%
High School Grad	24%	23%
College**	48%	27%
Graduate Schooling	21%	0%

Age	#	
18–24	17	18%
25–29	25	26%
30–34	10	10%
35–39	9	9%
40–49	12	13%
50–59	9	9%
60+	14	15%
Blank	4	
Generation		
1st	39	39%
1.5	16	16%
2nd	44	44%
Blank	1	

Employment	#	% (among non-blank)
Employed (– PT)	55	60%
Unemployed	17	19%
Part-time	2	2%
Retired	5	5%
Student	7	8%
Homemaker	5	5%
Blank	9	

Years in South L.A.***	#	% (among non-blank)
<10	2	2%
10–19	25	29%
20–29	42	49%
30+	17	20%
Other/Blank	14	

*In the cases where we have "blank" counts, we did not include those counts for percentages.

**"College" means attended some level of college (some college, AA, BA).

***"Other/Blank" category means interviewees listed something like "25+" or "31 years except college" or did not provide that information.

Source: CSII South L.A. interview sample.

sampling of those ages 40 to 49 (13 percent in the sample vs. 20 percent in the underlying population). Additionally, the interviews show overrepresentation of those between 25 and 29 years old and 60 years and older. Our oversampling of these specific age groups, however, was by design as we were trying to investigate the experience of first- and second-generation Latino arrivals. That also led to an oversample on the U.S.-born: while only about 28 percent of Latino adults in the three South L.A. neighborhoods are U.S.-born, our sample is 44 percent U.S.-born.

Where our sample most diverges from the underlying population, however, is in education levels. For example, our foreign-born interviewees are more likely to have been to and/or graduated from college, with 27 percent in our sample compared to just over 11 percent the ACS population. There is also an underrepresentation of both U.S.-born and foreign-born Latinos who have not graduated from high school in our sample. Of those that are U.S.-born, we do have close representation of those who have been to and/or graduated college, with 48 percent in the sample and 44 percent in the three South L.A. neighborhood population. There is, however, an overrepresentation of U.S.-born Latinos with some degree of graduate-level education in our sample at 21 percent; this was likely due to our sampling method using graduate student interviewers who have grown up in South L.A. Their experience with the community yielded important advantages in terms of both reach and trust with interviewees, but it did have an impact of somewhat skewing the sample in terms of education levels.

Finally, the table on the actual interviewees offers some data that cannot be collected from the Census: the share of Latinos who are part of a "1.5 generation" (i.e., were born abroad but grew up in the United States) and the length of time that respondents had lived in South L.A. (the ACS only has information on how many years one had lived in the United States or in the same house, with the latter not necessarily relevant to time in South L.A. and the latter equally irrelevant because of the tendency of low-income households to move). As can be seen, our sample includes very few recent arrivals and has more emphasis on those with more time in South L.A. Again, this was by design, and overall, we are pleased with the ways in which the sample likely represents the population we were trying to profile quantitatively and qualitatively.

All research is partial and incomplete, and this book is no exception. Along the way, we recognized critical arenas of inquiry that we wished we had the resources to examine, such as Black and Brown dynamics in real estate transactions, schools, and commercial enterprises, to name a few. It is our hope that this book will serve an invitation to subsequent researchers and funders to support further work on understanding and supporting South L.A.

NOTES

CHAPTER 1. MAKING SENSE, MAKING HOME

1 Vaca, *The Presumed Alliance*.

2 On the Black taco truck phenomenon, see First We Feast, "South L.A.'s African-American Taco Movement | Food Grails," May 10, 2017, YouTube video, 13:25, https://www.youtube.com/watch?v=tMsQsAvHpqU.

3 For an extensive discussion of the pathways Mexican Americans do take to move into the middle class, see Jody Agius Vallejo's *Barrios to Burbs*.

4 Department of Economic and Social Affairs, Population Division, "The International Migration Report 2017 (Highlights)" (United Nations, 2017), https://www.un.org.

5 A burgeoning body of scholarship looks at African American migration, reconsidering the Great Migration of the twentieth century as a process of dislocation, homemaking, and subject transformation. As the sociologist Karida Brown notes in her book *Gone Home*, migration and the search for home became, for African Americans, "a taken-for-granted way of life. However, through their collective experience with dislocation, displacement, and homelessness, they reveal much about the practice of homemaking, communal memory, and reinscribing oneself back into place"; see Brown, *Gone Home*, 6. And in *The Warmth of Other Suns*, based on oral histories with African Americans who made the trek from the South to the Northern and Western cities, Isabel Wilkerson writes that "[a] central argument of this book has been that the Great Migration was an unrecognized immigration within this country. The participants bore the marks of immigrant behavior. They plotted a course to places in the North and West that had some connection to their homes of origin. They created colonies of the villages they came from, imported the food and folkways of the Old Country, and built their lives around the people and churches they knew from back home. They took work the people already there considered beneath them"; see Wilkerson, *The Warmth of Other Suns*, 537. See also the classic historical monograph that examines Black, Polish, and Italian migrant work and community lives in Pittsburgh by Bodnar, Simon, and Weber, *Lives of Their Own*.

6 Wilkerson, *The Warmth of Other Suns*, 536.

7 Some of the interviewees in the parks and garden work were also first-generation immigrants interviewed as part of the Latino residents group, and so quotes from them are included in our discussion of that generation in the text. Specifically,

nine of the fifty-three were double interviewees; details are provided in the appendix.

8 In an ambitious comparative study of immigrant integration, Okomoto and colleagues focus on the personal and interactional processes experienced by Mexican and Indian immigrants in Philadelphia and Atlanta. They find that when immigrants feel welcomed, they are more likely to participate in civic institutions and organizations. In their study, Mexican immigrants reported feeling far less welcomed than did higher-status Indian immigrants. Significantly, and relevant for our study, the researchers report that Mexican immigrants were especially made to feel unwelcomed in white suburban neighborhoods. Okomoto et al., "Welcoming, Trust, and Civic Engagement: Immigrant Integration in Metropolitan America," 68.

9 Data calculated using the 1970, 1980, and 1990 Census figures from the IPUMS SDA tool; Ruggles et al., *Integrated Public Use Microdata Series: Version 7.0* [data set].

10 Hamilton and Chinchilla, *Seeking Community in a Global City*; Romo, *East Los Angeles*; Sanchez, *Becoming Mexican American*.

11 Abigail Rosas described interactions between Black and Latino patrons at Broadway Federal Bank in South L.A. this way: "They stand in line to cash checks and open savings and checking accounts without really speaking to one another."; see Rosas, "Banking on the Community: Mexican Immigrants' Experiences in a Historically African American Bank in South Central Los Angeles, 1970–2007," 79. She concluded that "this seems to be a function of the limited English-speaking skills of Latino patrons." The Black-owned bank hired bilingual employees to handle interactions with monolingual clients, but Rosas points out that the head of the bank still conceived of it as a Black institution. Interestingly, she also notes that when its history of struggle to develop and strive was exposed to Latino patrons, they were both impressed and more likely to want to continue to patronize the institution.

12 As will become clearer in our subsequent methodological discussion, all names of nonpublic figures are pseudonyms, in keeping with usual academic practice.

13 While college is often regarded as a vehicle for social mobility, Leah Schmalzbauer and Alelí Andrés found that even when working-class Latino youth are recruited to elite universities and colleges, they still face worries and responsibilities for their mixed-status family members, and these burdens generally remain invisible to their faculty and peers. Concerns about their parents' deportability and financial precarity may impede their academic journeys. See Schmalzbauer and Andrés, "Stratified Lives."

14 Molotch, "Granite and Green: Thinking beyond Surface in Place Studies," 155.

15 Boccagni, *Migration and the Search for Home*.

16 HoSang and Molina, "Introduction: Toward a Relational Consciousness of Race," 84.

17 Rosas, *South Central Is Home.*

18 Jones, *The Browning of the New South.*

19 For example, in their book *Inheriting the City: The Children of Immigrants Come of Age*, Kasinitz, et al., offer a very nuanced examination of social mobility and integration outcomes for the second-generation young adults of five immigrant groups in New York City. Based on an extensive telephone survey, over three hundred in-depth interviews conducted by sixteen graduate students, and ethnographies conducted from the late 1990s to the early 2000s, the authors conclude that there is a "second generation advantage" benefiting the children of immigrants, one that accrues from both the immigrant parents and also from the influence of native-born peers. Another very robust finding from this exhaustive study points to the high achievements of the Russian, Jewish, and Chinese second generation and the disadvantages facing the Black and Latino second generation. Of note is that the sample did not include Mexican-origin respondents or persons with undocumented status (and nearly all the parents of their second-generation respondents had legal status too); that is definitely not true of the immigrant population in South L.A. In any case, as noted, we are less focused on outcomes than on processes of identity formation. See Kasinitz et al., *Inheriting the City.*

20 See Iceland and Nelson, "Hispanic Segregation in Metropolitan America"; Massey, "Dimensions of the New Immigration to the United States and the Prospects for Assimilation"; Massey and Denton, "Spatial Assimilation as a Socioeconomic Outcome." Assimilation theory has animated a good deal of research focused on empirically distinguishing and measuring metrics of education and income among generations. In Robert Park and Earnest Burgess's influential formulation of assimilation, Southern and Eastern European immigrants in Chicago in the early twentieth century would pass through stages of contact, conflict, and accommodation that lead to eventual assimilation; see Park and Burgess, *The City.* In the mid-twentieth century, during a period of low immigration, Milton Gordon extended these ideas about assimilation by adding three more other stages and optimistically predicting that African Americans and other nonwhite groups would be absorbed into the mainstream because of favorable civil rights policies. See Gordon, *Assimilation in American Life.*

21 Gans, "Comment: Ethnic Invention and Acculturation: A Bumpy-Line Approach"; Portes and Rumbaut, *Legacies*; Portes and Zhou, "The New Second Generation."

22 Alba and Nee, *Remaking the American Mainstream.*

23 In his latest book, *The Great Demographic Illusion*, Richard Alba continues his interrogation of assimilation by addressing the "majority-minority" narrative, the idea that white residents will become a minority by 2044 (give or take a year, depending on the demographic estimates used). Using demographic data, he shows a redrawing of racial/ethnic boundaries, with intermarriage of Asian Americans and Latinos with whites helping to create new routes of assimilation and mobility. As Alba sees it, the current "phenomenon of mixed minority-majority back-

grounds is a sign of growing integration into the mainstream by substantial portions of the new immigrant groups, especially individuals with Asian or Hispanic origins." Alba, *The Great Demographic Illusion*, 7.

24 Jiménez, *The Other Side of Assimilation*.

25 Jiménez, *The Other Side of Assimilation*; Myers, *Immigrants and Boomers*; Portes and Rumbaut, *Legacies*; Vasquez, "The Whitening Hypothesis Challenged: Biculturalism in Latino and Non-Hispanic White Intermarriage."

26 Vallejo, *Barrios to Burbs*.

27 Ramírez, *Assimilation: An Alternative History*, 143.

28 See Portes, Guarnizo, and Landolt, "The Study of Transnationalism"; Portes, Guarnizo, and Landolt, "Commentary on the Study of Transnationalism." In the more recent piece, they argue that transnationalism in migration studies is a "mid-range concept" and not a theoretical paradigm because of a less than coherent "set of core assumptions, explanatory concepts, typologies and theories"; Portes, Guarnizo, and Landolt, "Commentary on the Study of Transnationalism," 1488. For an alternative view, emphasizing the importance of analytically distinguishing between transnational processes, institutions, relationships, and outcomes, see works by sociologist Peggy Levitt and Dehesa, "Rethinking 'Transnational Migration and the Re-Definition of the State' or What to Do About (Semi-) Permanent Impermanence"; Levitt and Schiller, "Conceptualizing Simultaneity." For our purposes, the vast amount of migration scholarship animated by concerns to study transnationalism from both "below" and "above," and involving both private and public institutions that engage in cross-border activities constitutes an undeniably important theoretical tradition but not the most useful one for our purposes in this project.

29 Basch, Schiller, and Blanc, *Nations Unbound*; Portes, Guarnizo, and Landolt, "The Study of Transnationalism"; FitzGerald, *A Nation of Emigrants*; Hagan, *Migration Miracle*; Levitt, *The Transnational Villagers*; Levitt, *God Needs No Passport*; Rouse, "Mexican Migration and the Social Space of Postmodernism"; Smith, *Mexican New York*.

30 Aranda, Hughes, and Sabogal, *Making a Life in Multiethnic Miami*; Levitt and Schiller, "Conceptualizing Simultaneity"; Mazzucato, "The Double Engagement."

31 FitzGerald, *A Nation of Emigrants*; Orozco and Lapointe, "Mexican Hometown Associations and Development Opportunities"; Smith and Guarnizo, *Transnationalism from Below*; Zabin and Escala, "From Civic Association to Political Participation: Mexican Hometown Associations and Mexican Immigrant Political Empowerment in Los Angeles."

32 Waldinger and Duquette-Rury, "Emigrant Politics, Immigrant Engagement."

33 We explain in the appendix how we calculate the undocumented population in the American Community Survey to arrive at these figures.

34 Alarcon, Escala, and Odgers, *Making Los Angeles Home*.

35 Abrego, *Sacrificing Families*; Boehm, *Returned*; Coutin, *Legalizing Moves*; De Genova, "Migrant 'Illegality' and Deportability in Everyday Life"; De Leon,

The Land of Open Graves; Eschbach et al., "Death at the Border"; Golash-Boza, *Deported*; Gonzales, *Lives in Limbo*; Menjívar, "Liminal Legality"; Ngai, *Impossible Subjects*; ibid.; Ryo, "Less Enforcement, More Compliance: Rethinking Unauthorized Migration"; Telles and Ortiz, *Generations of Exclusion*.

36 Armenta, *Protect, Serve, and Deport*; Macías-Rojas, *From Deportation to Prison*; Stumpf, "The Crimmigration Crisis."

37 See Abrego and Schmalzbauer, "Illegality, Motherhood, and Place"; Andrews, *Undocumented Politics*. The targets have also been more likely to be Latino men than Latina women; see Golash-Boza and Hondagneu-Sotelo, "Latino Immigrant Men and the Deportation Crisis."

38 Mollenkopf and Pastor, *Unsettled Americans*.

39 Andrews, *Undocumented Politics*; Hondagneu-Sotelo, *God's Heart Has No Borders*; Nicholls, "Forging a 'New' Organizational Infrastructure for Los Angeles' Progressive Community"; Pastor, *State of Resistance*; Pastor, Ortiz, and de Graauw, "Opening Minds, Opening Doors, Opening Communities: Cities Leading for Immigrant Integration"; Uitermark and Nicholls, "From Politicization to Policing"; Lopez, *"The Development of Innovative Integration Models in Los Angeles."*

40 Boccagni, *Migration and the Search for Home*.

41 Blunt and Dowling, *Home*; Cancellieri, "Towards a Progressive Home-Making"; Duyvendak, *The Politics of Home—Belonging and Nostalgia in Europe and the United States*; Kusenbach and Paulsen, *Home*; Morley, "Belongings"; Castañeda, *A Place to Call Home*.

42 Boccagni, *Migration and the Search for Home*.

43 Levitt et al., "Rethinking 'Transnational Migration and the Re-Definition of the State' or What to Do about (Semi-) Permanent Impermance."

44 Aranda, Hughes, and Sabogal, *Making a Life in Multiethnic Miami*.

45 Aranda, Hughes, and Sabogal, *Making a Life in Multiethnic Miami*, 8.

46 Cancellieri, "Towards a Progressive Home-Making."

47 Alarcon, Escala, and Odgers, *Making Los Angeles Home*.

48 Rojas, "The Enacted Environment of East Los Angeles."

49 Lauster and Zhao, "Labor Migration and the Missing Work of Homemaking."

50 Allport, *The Nature of Prejudice*.

51 Pettigrew, "Intergroup Contact Theory"; Pettigrew and Tropp, "A Meta-Analytic Test of Intergroup Contact Theory"; Pettigrew and Tropp, "How Does Intergroup Contact Reduce Prejudice?"; Pettigrew and Tropp, *When Groups Meet*.

52 Schwirian, "Models of Neighborhood Change."

53 Vargas, *Catching Hell in the City of Angels*.

54 Martinez, *The Neighborhood Has Its Own Rules*.

55 Martinez, *The Neighborhood Has Its Own Rules*, 73.

56 Martinez, *The Neighborhood Has Its Own Rules*.

57 Kim, *Imperial Citizens*; Zamora, "Racial Remittances."

58 See "Reported Crimes by City Los Angeles County, 2018," Los Angeles Almanac, http://www.laalmanac.com/.

59 See Vin Villa, "Charcoal Alley," in Equity Research Institute USC, "Roots|Racíes: Latino Engagement, Place Identities, and Shared Futures in South Los Angeles," July 12, 2016, YouTube video, 1:30, https://www.youtube.com/watch?v=OS02K S99cDQ.

60 Marquez, *Black-Brown Solidarity*.

61 Jones, *The Browning of the New South*.

62 See Edna Lizabeth Chavez, "'I Learned to Duck Bullets Before I Learned to Read': Edna Chávez at March for Our Lives Rally," Democracy Now!, https://www.democracynow.org.

63 Johnson, *Spaces of Conflict, Sounds of Solidarity*.

64 Johnson, *Spaces of Conflict, Sounds of Solidarity*, 1.

65 Kun and Pulido, *Black and Brown in Los Angeles*.

66 As noted earlier, we maintain anonymity for most of our respondents unless they are clearly identified public actors. When we provide names and descriptions later for community interviews, both Black and Latino, the names are pseudonyms but the general details of age, gender, and profession are accurate. Because our civic leaders are more easily identifiable—and they often spoke with us quite frankly—we provide less detail when we are not directly attaching their name to a comment.

67 Hunt and Ramón, *Black Los Angeles*; Sides, *Post-Ghetto*; Stephens and Pastor, "What's Going On? Black Experiences of Latinization and Loss in South Los Angeles"; Vargas, *Catching Hell in the City of Angels*.

68 Cheng, *The Changs Next Door to the Díazes*.

69 Omi and Winant, *Racial Formation in the United States*; Pulido, *Black, Brown, Yellow, and Left*; Saito, *Race and Politics*.

70 Cheng, *The Changs Next Door to the Díazes*, 11. In her book *Caste*, Isabella Wilkerson makes a similar metaphor about the United States. She suggests that the election of Trump in 2016, rather than a sudden aberration in U.S. racial politics, represents something more like long-brewing, subterranean "silent earthquakes." She writes that "[t]hey are as potent as those we can see and feel but they have long gone undetected because they work in silence, unrecognized until a major quake announces itself on the surface." She suggests that we cannot understand the nation without understanding the deep foundational racial hierarchies rooted in the institution of slavery and the dehumanization and subordination of African Americans. Wilkerson, *Caste*, 11.

71 Cheng, *The Changs Next Door to the Díazes* , 19.

72 Lee and Bean, "America's Changing Color Lines: Immigration, Race/Ethnicity, and Multiracial Identification."

73 Kim, *Imperial Citizens*; Levitt, "Social Remittances"; Roth, *Race Migrations*; Zamora, "Racial Remittances."

74 Kim, *Imperial Citizens*; Roth, *Race Migrations*; Zamora, "Racial Remittances."

75 Zamora, "Racial Remittances," 477.

76 Zamora also writes in a later article "Mexican Illegality, Black Citizenship, and White Power" that Latino immigrants, especially those who are undocumented, view African Americans as privileged with respect to U.S. citizenship, reinforcing the foreign-citizen boundaries.

77 Zamora, "Racial Remittances," 477.

78 Romo, "Between Black and Brown."

79 Zamora, "Racial Remittances," 477.

80 Tran, "Coming of Age in Multi-Ethnic America."

81 Molina, HoSang, and Gutiérrez, *Relational Formations of Race*.

82 Molina, "Examining Chicana/o History through a Relational Lens," 47.

83 See Ribas, *On the Line*, 8. Ribas takes up immigrant integration in a meat-processing factory in North Carolina, noting Latinos social distancing from Black workers and neighbors within a system dominated by whiteness. Also in North Carolina, but contrary to Ribas's findings, Helen Marrow reports animosity from African Americans toward Latinos; see Marrow, *New Destination Dreaming*.

84 Dávila, *Latinos, Inc*; Fox, *Hispanic Nation*.

85 Be sure to read his book, Thompson-Hernández, *The Compton Cowboys*.

86 The research process itself was complicated and at times messy, raising up issues of race, safety, and accountability both in our team and in our relationship with community partners. We discuss this in more detail in the appendix.

87 It's definitely worth a look (see Equity Research Institute USC, "Roots|Raíces"). The lyrics of the song—which pretty much capture the whole logic of the study in less than two minutes—are featured as the extended epigraph (or "opener") to this book.

CHAPTER 2. ALWAYS CHANGING, ALWAYS CONTESTED

1 See Ong et al., "The State of South LA." and Leavitt and Heskin, "South-Central Los Angeles: Anatomy of an Urban Crisis."

2 Madley, "It's Time to Acknowledge the Genocide of California's Indians."

3 Robinson, "Race, Space, and the Evolution of Black Los Angeles."

4 Hondagneu-Sotelo, *Paradise Transplanted*, 39.

5 Zappia, "Reclaiming the Soil: Gardening and Sustainable Development in South Los Angeles," 57.

6 Surls and Gerber, *From Cows to Concrete*.

7 McWilliams, *California*.

8 Fogelson, *The Fragmented Metropolis*, 78.

9 Robinson, "Race, Space, and the Evolution of Black Los Angeles."

10 As cited by Hunt and Ramón, *Black Los Angeles*, 12.

11 For how these migration shifts played out in Venice, California, see Andrew Deener's *Venice: A Contested Bohemia in Los Angeles Venice*. His second chapter tracks a similar period as what we cover in this chapter and many similar trends including how Black exclusion from other neighborhoods created vibrant community and institutions, the 1980s' criminalization of Black bodies and tensions

with the newer Latino community, and the struggle for civic voice—although differently experienced—by both Latinos and African Americans in a neighborhood now gentrified by mostly white residents with higher incomes.

12 Sides, *L.A. City Limits*, 16.

13 Robinson, "Race, Space, and the Evolution of Black Los Angeles," 35; Grant, Oliver, and James, "African Americans: Social and Economic Bifurcation."

14 See Kun and Pulido, *Black and Brown in Los Angeles*, 10. Asian immigrants were the targets of the Alien Land Law (1913), California legislation that prohibited Asian immigrants from owning land. During the Great Depression, the federally implemented mass deportation programs, euphemistically called "repatriation," removed not only foreign-born Mexican residents but also thousands of U.S. citizens of Mexican origin.

15 Grant, Oliver, and James, "African Americans: Social and Economic Bifurcation."

16 Flamming, *Bound for Freedom*, 261.

17 For more, see Hudson and Williams, *Paul R. Williams, Architect*.

18 Smith, *The Great Black Way*, 209–10.

19 See Nicolaides, *My Blue Heaven*. As Josh Sides notes, "[a]s late as 1948, even as waves of African American migrants flooded Los Angeles, Compton's segregationists held the day: of a population of forty-five thousand, fewer than fifty were African Americans"; see Sides, "Straight into Compton," 585.

20 Avila, *Popular Culture in the Age of White Flight*, 26.

21 Grant, Oliver, and James, "African Americans: Social and Economic Bifurcation"; Robinson, "Race, Space, and the Evolution of Black Los Angeles"; Sides, *L.A. City Limits*.

22 The United Packinghouse Workers were the exception to the union practice of excluding Black workers. See Grant, Oliver, and James, "African Americans: Social and Economic Bifurcation," 381.

23 Grant, Oliver, and James, "African Americans: Social and Economic Bifurcation."

24 Sides, *Post-Ghetto*, 35.

25 Sides, *L.A. City Limits*, 98.

26 Sitton, *Los Angeles Transformed*, 180.

27 Robinson, "Race, Space, and the Evolution of Black Los Angeles."

28 Robinson, "Race, Space, and the Evolution of Black Los Angeles."

29 Sides, *L.A. City Limits*, 114.

30 Robinson, "Race, Space, and the Evolution of Black Los Angeles."

31 Robinson, "Race, Space, and the Evolution of Black Los Angeles."

32 Sides, *L.A. City Limits*.

33 Robinson, "Race, Space, and the Evolution of Black Los Angeles."

34 See Chapple, "From Central Avenue to Leimert Park: The Shifting Center of Black Los Angeles"; Robinson, "Race, Space, and the Evolution of Black Los Angeles." As we note later, Leimert Park is now being threatened by gentrification that is displacing longtime Black residents and businesses.

35 Robinson, "Race, Space, and the Evolution of Black Los Angeles."

36 Robinson argues that Bradley was the second Black mayor of Los Angeles; Francisco Reyes was the first, with his term starting in 1793, when the city was Spanish and race/ethnicity lines were much more fluid.

37 Robinson, "Race, Space, and the Evolution of Black Los Angeles."

38 Sides, *L.A. City Limits*, 180.

39 Banks, "The Crack Epidemic's Toxic Legacy."

40 For further discussion, see Hipp et al., "Ethnically Transforming Neighborhoods and Violent Crime Among and Between African-Americans and Latinos: A Study of South Los Angeles." In addition, in the 1970s, in the city of Los Angeles overall, Black people were 5.6 times more likely than white non-Hispanics to become homicide victims. See Centers for Disease Control and Prevention, "Homicide—Los Angeles, 1970–1979," https://www.cdc.gov.

41 Robinson, "Race, Space, and the Evolution of Black Los Angeles," 50.

42 Mitchell, "The Raid That Still Haunts L.A."; also see Davis, *City of Quartz* for more on the raid.

43 Robinson, "Race, Space, and the Evolution of Black Los Angeles."

44 Pfeiffer, "Moving to Opportunity," 55.

45 Sides, *Post-Ghetto*, 3.

46 Pastor, De Lara, and Scoggins, "All Together Now," 12.

47 Grant, Oliver, and James, "African Americans: Social and Economic Bifurcation."

48 Robinson, "Race, Space, and the Evolution of Black Los Angeles."

49 Camarillo, "Black and Brown in Compton: Demographic Change, Suburban Decline, and Intergroup Relations in a South Central Los Angeles Community, 1950–2000"; Camarillo, "Cities of Color."

50 Gutierrez, "An Historic Overview of Latino Immigration and the Demographic Transformation of the United States"; Hondagneu-Sotelo, *Gendered Transitions*.

51 Zappia, "Reclaiming the Soil: Gardening and Sustainable Development in South Los Angeles," 58.

52 Hamilton and Chinchilla, *Seeking Community in a Global City*.

53 Pastor, *Latinos and the Los Angeles Uprising*, 32.

54 Pastor, "Economic Inequality, Latino Poverty, and the Civil Unrest in Los Angeles," 207.

55 Sloane, "Alcohol Nuisances and Food Deserts: Combating Social Hazards in the South Los Angeles Environment."

56 Pastor and Prichard, "LA Rising: The 1992 Civil Unrest, the Arc of Social Justice Organizing, and the Lessons for Today's Movement Building."

57 Sides, *L.A. City Limits*, 6.

58 Pastor and Walton, "Looking Forward, Not Back."

59 Sims, "In Los Angeles, It's South-Central No More."

60 For that project, see "Mapping L.A. Neighborhoods," *Los Angeles Times*, http://maps.latimes.com/.

61 The data sources for this figure are from the American Community Survey (ACS) summary files for 2016, with earlier years from Geolytics. See the appendix for details on methods.

62 Terriquez and Carter, "Celebrating the Legacy, Embracing the Future: How Research Can Help Build Ties between Historically African American Churches and Their Latino Immigrant Neighbours."

63 Ruggles et al., *Integrated Public Use Microdata Series: Version 7.0* [data set].

64 Among other things, the appendix at the end of this volume discusses the data sources and methods in more detail. Note that the vintage for both summary and micro-data is 2012 to 2016. We actually did the vast majority of the fieldwork in 2015 so when we equipped the ethnographic part of the team with data profiles for their areas, we utilized the 2009–2013 pooled ACS as this was the most recent vintage available at the time. However, for this book, we have updated the data picture with the 2012–16 pooled ACS since this offers a better data view of the area during the time we were actually conducting interviews and observations.

65 See Le et al., "Paths to Citizenship: Using Data to Understand and Promote Naturalization", for a description of the methods used in estimating the undocumented population.

66 To avoid repetitive citation, please note that the data generally come from either the ACS Summary or microdata files as detailed in note 64; when the data is from another source (such as education statistics), we offer a citation.

67 Again, unless otherwise noted, data calculations are from the sources listed earlier and noted in the appendix.

68 Ochoa and Ochoa, *Latino Los Angeles*.

69 Ethington, Frey, and Myers, "The Racial Resegregation of Los Angeles County, 1940–2000."

70 For the general stabilization of the foreign-born population in Los Angeles, see Myers, Pitkin, and Ramirez, "The New Homegrown Majority in California: Recognizing the New Reality of Growing Commitment to The Golden State."

71 Schnyder, "Criminals, Planters, and Corporate Capitalists: The Case of Public Education in Los Angeles."

72 Ong et al., "The State of South LA," 3.

73 This is a good instance where there is a slight mismatch between the summary and microdata as discussed in the appendix. According to the summary data, the Latino homeownership rate is 32 percent; according to the microdata, Latino immigrants in South L.A. own homes at rates similar to their U.S.-born counterparts—30 percent and 29 percent, respectively. The value added from using the microdata is the ability to partition the Latino subgroup by nativity—something the Census does not do in its summary data—but there are issues with direct comparisons of the data for these subcounty or substate levels.

74 See Bledsoe and Wright, "The Anti-Blackness of Global Capital." Scholars are now recognizing diverse patterns of racialization processes in urban gentrification. For example, sociologist Alfredo Huante examines a differently racialized pattern of

gentrification occurring in historically Mexican American East L.A.; see Huante, "A Lighter Shade of Brown? Racial Formation and Gentrification in Latino Los Angeles."

75 Leonard and Flynn, "Effects of the Foreclosure Crisis on California's Minority Homeowners."

76 Rugh, "Why Black and Latino Home Ownership Matter to the Color Line and Multiracial Democracy."

77 Taylor, *Race for Profit*.

78 By more than one generation, we mean grandparents and/or children present in the household.

79 The data on the undocumented come from estimates created by USC CSII, with a description of the methodology available in Le et al., "Paths to Citizenship: Using Data to Understand and Promote Naturalization." Because of the undercount of the undocumented, we used a different set of weights compared to throughout most of the earlier analysis (which relies on the standard population weights of the Census).

80 See Asad and Hwang, "Indigenous Places and the Making of Undocumented Status in Mexico-US Migration." These authors find that as the eighties and nineties gave way to a limitation of the pathways to legal entry, the share of Mexicans from indigenous locales migrating increased, leading them to conclude that if a Mexican migrant originated from an indigenous place, they are more likely to cross the border without documentation.

81 Menjivar and Abrego, "Legal Violence: Immigration Law and the Lives of Central American Immigrants"; Ryo, "Less Enforcement, More Compliance: Rethinking Unauthorized Migration."

82 On the deportation figures, see "Table 39. Aliens Removed or Returned: Fiscal Years 1892 to 2017," Department of Homeland Security, https://www.dhs.gov.

83 Smith, "How LAPD's Law-and-Order Chief Revolutionized the Way Cops Treated Illegal Immigration."

84 For example, a recent analysis showed that an elite LAPD unit was stopping Black drivers at a rate five times their share in the city population. Chang and Poston, "'Stop-and-Frisk in a Car."

85 The labor force participation rate is defined as the share of people either employed or actively looking for work out of the total population sixteen years and older.

86 Jiménez, *The Other Side of Assimilation*, 131.

CHAPTER 3. *ECHANDO RAICES*, SETTLING IN

1 García and Schmalzbauer, "Placing Assimilation Theory," 65.

2 HoSang and Molina, "Introduction: Toward a Relational Consciousness of Race."

3 Ahmed, "Home and Away"; Lauster and Zhao, "Labor Migration and the Missing Work of Homemaking."

4 Blunt and Dowling, *Home*; Blunt and Sheringham, "Home-City Geographies," Boccagni, "Burden, Blessing or Both?"; Cancellieri, "Towards a Progressive

Home-Making"; Duyvendak, *The Politics of Home—Belonging and Nostalgia in Europe and the United States*; Hondagneu-Sotelo and Ruiz, "'Illegality' and Spaces of Sanctuary: Belonging and Homeland-Making in Urban Community Gardens"; Kusenbach and Paulsen, *Home*.

5 Kim, *Imperial Citizens*; Roth, *Race Migrations*; Zamora, "Racial Remittances."

6 In a different context, in a southern city, sociologist Jennifer A. Jones also uses the term "African American embrace" to refer to instances where Latino immigrants were warmly received when they turned to their African American neighbors for support. Jones *The Browning of the New South*, 128, reports that "Blacks largely accepted the challenge, embracing Latinos as neighbors, coworkers, friends and allies." See her chapter 5, "Making Minorities: The African American Embrace and Minority Linked Fate," in her book, *The Browning of the New South*, 126–66.

7 There is some overlap among these categories: Security/Familiarity/Control/Future-making. These categories allow us to feature subject-centered analysis of Latino immigrant integration. And we see that the process is not monolithic, as even among people who are demographically similar in age, gender, nation of origin, social class, and time of arrival, we see a variety of experiences. But by organizing into these four arenas of homemaking practices, we can see patterns.

8 Sociologist Eduardo Bonilla-Silva introduced the term "color-blind racism" to denote liberal white narrative strategies for denying the existence of racism. Among first-generation Latino immigrant interviews, the language of color-blind racism was strikingly absent. See Bonilla-Silva, *Racism without Racists*.

9 Boccagni, *Migration and the Search for Home*, 7.

10 Rojas, "The Enacted Environment of East Los Angeles," 48.

11 Rojas, "The Enacted Environment of East Los Angeles," 50.

12 Arreola, *Hispanic Spaces, Latino Places*; Arreola, "Placemaking and Latino Urbanism in a Phoenix Mexican Immigrant Community"; Rojas, "The Enacted Environment of East Los Angeles."

13 "Magnified moments" is a concept inspired by Arlie Hochschild's narrative analysis. According to her, these are "episodes of heightened importance, either epiphanies, moments of intense glee or unusual insight, or moments in which things go intensely but meaningfully wrong. In either case, the moment stands out"; Hochschild, "The Commercial Spirit of Intimate Life and the Abduction of Feminism: Signs from Women's Advice Books," 4.

14 For a statistical analysis of how "older adults dwelling in struggling cities experience an uptick in disorderly household conditions" see Schafer, Settels, and Upenieks, "As Goes the City? Older Americans' Home Upkeep in the Aftermath of the Great Recession."

15 Space constraints and the scope of this project do not allow for an extensive discussion of Latino dynamics of homeownership. On that topic, see McConnell and Marcelli, "Buying into the American Dream?"; Rugh, "Why Black and Latino Home Ownership Matter to the Color Line and Multiracial Democracy"; Salgado and Ortiz, "Mexican Americans and Wealth."

16 See "Reported Crimes by City Los Angeles County, 2018," Los Angeles Almanac, http://www.laalmanac.com/.

17 As we suggest throughout this manuscript, our sense is that police attention is directed at Black males, particularly younger African Americans, and, to some extent, at younger Latinos. This leaves older immigrants feeling less targeted. It is also possible that Latino immigrants have learned some of the "legal passing" tactics and strategies that Angela S. Garcia has examined in San Diego County. See Garcia, *Legal Passing*.

18 While there is evidence elsewhere of the significance of migrant communities relying on "transnational social protection" resources, evidence of this pattern did not appear among our interviewees. See Aranda, Hughes, and Sabogal, *Making a Life in Multiethnic Miami*; Levitt et al., "Transnational Social Protection."

19 Tuan, "Rootedness Versus Sense of Place," 4.

20 Kusenbach and Paulsen, *Home*, 11.

21 Kusenbach and Paulsen, *Home*.

22 Boccagni, *Migration and the Search for Home*, 7.

23 Duyvendak, *The Politics of Home*.

24 Aranda, Hughes, and Sabogal, *Making a Life in Multiethnic Miami*.

25 Mares, "Tracing Immigrant Identity through the Plate and the Palate."

26 Kusenbach, "Salvaging Decency"; Mallett, "Understanding Home"; Marcuse, "Housing in Early City Planning."

27 Homeownership is a critical indicator of economic achievement and class mobility. As sociologist Mary Pattillo observes, housing may be viewed as both a right and as a commodity, and "[u]nlike most other commodities, which are quickly consumed and exhausted, housing retains value during consumption, increases and decreases in value over time, can have several owners/consumers, and can persist across decades, if not centuries"; see Pattillo, "Housing: Commodity versus Right," 515. While homeownership is the main source of household wealth for Mexican Americans, many African Americans have lost housing wealth; see Rugh, "Why Black and Latino Home Ownership Matter to the Color Line and Multiracial Democracy"; Taylor, *Race for Profit*. Jody Agius Vallejo and Lisa Keister argue that wealth and net worth is an important aspect of immigrant integration; see Vallejo and Keister, "Immigrants and Wealth Attainment."

28 Nicolaides, *My Blue Heaven*.

29 Arreola, *Hispanic Spaces, Latino Places*; Cancellieri, "Towards a Progressive Home-Making"; Chang, *The Global Silicon Valley Home*; Lopez, *The Remittance Landscape*; Rojas, "The Enacted Environment of East Los Angeles."

30 Rapoport, "A Critical Look at the Concept 'Home,'" 29.

31 See Ahmed et al., *Uprootings/Regroundings*, 9. The first author thanks anthropologist Hector Beltran for pointing out the importance of future-making and hope-making in the migrant–home nexus.

32 Smith, *Mexican New York*.
33 Waters, *Black Identities*.

CHAPTER 4. BEING BROWN, KNOWING BLACK

1 Portes and Rumbaut, *Immigrant America*; Portes and Zhou, "The New Second Generation."
2 Smith, "Black Mexicans, Conjunctural Ethnicity, and Operating Identities: Long-Term Ethnographic Analysis."
3 Based on interviews with ninety-seven Latino-origin millennials in Chicago, sociologist Nilda Flores-Gonzalez elaborates on the term "racial middle," suggesting that some Latino millennials tilt toward whiteness, some towards Blackness and others to a "solid" racial middle; see Flores-González, *Citizens but Not Americans*. Much has been written about Latino racial-ethnic identities. On variations of Latino racial identities, the importance of place and segregated neighborhoods in shaping Latino racial identities is also affirmed in Pulido and Pastor, "Where in the World Is Juan—and What Color Is He?" Place matters: Ballinas and Bachmeier find that Mexican Americans are more likely to identify as white in Texas than in California because of differences in social values; Ballinas and Bachmeier, "'Whiteness; in Context." For an analysis of Mexican American racial-ethnic identity formation that focuses on generational differences, see Vasquez, "Blurred Borders for Some but Not 'Others'"; Vasquez, *Mexican Americans across Generations*.
4 Rendón, "The Urban Question and Identity Formation: The Case of Second-Generation Mexican Males in Los Angeles," 178.
5 Marquez notes that while "foundational Blackness" can inform Latinos, as well as Native American, Arab Americans, and Asian American views with "a method and language through which the antiracist critiques from those same groups are developed and politicized," he finds that in Houston, African Americans and Latinos are joined by a "similar expendability" that "helps fuse black and Latina/o politics into a hybrid subjectivity"; see Marquez, *Black-Brown Solidarity*, 52. Among our second-generation Latino subjects, none of them expressed a view of themselves as expendable. Rather, as we explain in this chapter, they more often conveyed the immigrant optimism of their parents, but they brought a specific race- and place-based sensibility to this.
6 See Cheng, *The Changs Next Door to the Díazes*, 11. As she also notes, "outside of schools, interethnic and interracial interactions may happen only unevenly, (but) in the public schools, sustained interethnic and interracial interactions happen every day between students, staff and administrators."; see Cheng, *The Changs Next Door to the Díazes*, 65. While the scope of our study did not allow us to conduct ethnographies or interviews in the public schools of South L.A., important studies point to the critical role of South L.A. schools in transforming racial-ethnic relations. See historian Abigail Rosas's study of Head Start in "Chapter 5: Teaching Together: Interracial Community Organizing," in *South Central Is*

Home. and sociologist Glenda M. Flores' study of Compton elementary school classroom dynamics in "Chapter 4: Co-ethnic Cultural Guardianship: Space, Race, and Region," in Flores, *Latina Teachers*.

7 Estrada, *Kids at Work*.

8 Sánchez-Jankowski, *Burning Dislike*.

9 Sánchez-Jankowski, *Burning Dislike*, 191.

10 There is significant scholarship on both Latino and Black youth in gangs, but the scope of our project does not extend into this arena. However, it is important to note that most recently the scholarly literature has challenged the notions of gang life as static. Research by Victor M. Rios emphasizes the ways in which institutions and authority figures criminalize Latino and Black youth, and research by Edward O. Flores examines how faith-based projects provide pathways out of gang life and also assistance for formerly incarcerated men. See Rios, *Punished*; Flores, *God's Gangs*.

11 Lopez, *Hopeful Girls, Troubled Boys*; Smith, "Black Mexicans, Conjunctural Ethnicity, and Operating Identities: Long-Term Ethnographic Analysis."

12 Bickham Mendez and Schmalzbauer, "Latino Youth and Struggles for Inclusion in the 21st Century," 169, 165.

13 Louie, *Keeping the Immigrant Bargain*; Smith, "Black Mexicans, Conjunctural Ethnicity, and Operating Identities: Long-Term Ethnographic Analysis."

14 Blume, "The Huge L.A. School Construction Project Is Done, so What Does It Add up To?"

15 Cooley, *Human Nature and the Social Order*.

16 Rendón, "The Urban Question and Identity Formation," 165.

17 Vallejo, *Barrios to Burbs*; Vallejo and Lee, "Brown Picket Fences."

18 Flores, *Latina Teachers*.

19 As noted in chapter 1, the term Latinx was not in very common use at the time we were doing our interviews and indeed is not widely used in working-class immigrant settings despite its relatively rapid take-up in the academy.

20 HoSang and Molina, "Introduction: Toward a Relational Consciousness of Race," 1; Marquez, *Black-Brown Solidarity*, 52.

21 Allport, *The Nature of Prejudice*; HoSang and Molina, "Introduction: Toward a Relational Consciousness of Race"; Pettigrew, "Intergroup Contact Theory."

22 Flores-González, *Citizens but Not Americans*; Marquez, *Black-Brown Solidarity*.

23 Rendón, "'There's Nothing Holding Us Back.'"

24 Smith, *Mexican New York*; Vallejo, *Barrios to Burbs*. For research on the civic engagement of young adult children of Latino immigrants, see Terriquez, "Legal Status, Civic Organizations, and Political Participation among Latino Young Adults"; Terriquez and Lin "Yesterday They Marched, Today They Mobilized the Vote."

25 Davison et al., "Technology Leapfrogging in Developing Countries—An Inevitable Luxury"; Sandoval-Strausz, "Latino Landscapes."

CHAPTER 5. SHARING GROUND, CARVING SPACE

1 Blunt and Sheringham, "Home-City Geographies," 827.

2 Boccagni and Duyvendak, "On the 'Scaling Up' of Home in Majority-Minority Relations: A Conceptual Inquiry and a Research Agenda."

3 García and Schmalzbauer, "Placing Assimilation Theory," 65.

4 For another look at the role of experiencing nature and healing, in this case through caring for and riding horses in nearby Compton, see Thompson-Hernández, *The Compton Cowboys*.

5 As noted in the appendix, nine of the fifty-three were double interviewees who were also administered the interview instrument for first-generation Latinos and so were counted in that interview sample as well.

6 Of the ten largest cities in the United States, Los Angeles ranks seventh in terms of the share of residents within a ten-minute walk of a park (data from the 2018 ParkScore available at "ParkServe® Data Downloads," The Trust for Public Land, https://www.tpl.org/). Moreover, there are significant disparities by race and neighborhood in terms of this access.

7 Byrne, "When Green Is White."

8 Byrne and Wolch, "Nature, Race, and Parks"; García, Gee, and Jones, "A Critical Theory Analysis of Public Park Features in Latino Immigrant Neighborhoods"; Loukaitou-Sideris, "Urban Form and Social Context"; Trouille, "Fencing a Field"; Wolch, Wilson, and Fehrenbach, "Parks and Park Funding in Los Angeles"; Byrne, "When Green Is White."

9 According to the Trust for Public Land, there are currently 632 public parks in the City of Los Angeles ("Los Angeles, CA," The Trust for Public Land, https://www.tpl.org/). There are approximately 125 urban community gardens. As already noted, these remain inequitably distributed across the city. In 2017, Los Angeles City Council voted to continue a stalled project of demolishing old warehouses in South L.A. and redeveloping them into affordable houses with a four-acre park; see Chiland, "Affordable Housing and Public Park Set to Replace Old Industrial Buildings in South LA." And in 2018, the Los Angeles City Council approved a Adopt-a-Lot pilot project, which will transform vacant lots into parks, community markets and community gardens; see Barragan, "New Program Helps Residents Turn Empty Lots into Community Gathering Spaces." The latest iteration of plans is summarized in "Park Proud LA: Strategic Plan 2018–2022," published by LA Department of Recreation and Parks, (accessed August 31, 2019, https://www.laparks.org/). While new policies and projects are underway, and things seem to be improving, these new changes must remedy decades of neglect and divestment, so it remains to be seen if these efforts will undo long-standing intra-metropolitan disparities of open green spaces in the Los Angeles region; see Joassart-Marcelli, "Leveling the Playing Field?"

10 The Summer Night Lights program, is a public/private effort organized by the Gang Reduction and Youth Development Foundation in conjunction with the L.A. Mayor's Office of Public Safety. It has recently expanded to include Fall Fri-

day nights and year-round support and services to the youth who are hired to run the programs. See "The GRYD Foundation," accessed September 22, 2019, https://grydfoundation.org/.

11 See Ron Finley's essay, "They Tried to Arrest Me for Planting Carrots," at Zocalo Public Square, accessed August 30, 2019, https://www.zocalopublicsquare.org/. See Ron Finley's TED Talk; TED, "A Guerilla Gardener in South Central L.A. | Ron Finley," March 6, 2013, YouTube video, 10:45, accessed September 21, 2019, https://www.youtube.com/watch?v=EzZzZ_qpZ4w.

12 In part because of property rights, urban community gardens are ephemeral, but one reliable estimate of the number of community gardens throughout Los Angeles County is 125. The Los Angeles Community Garden Council has provided advice to 125 local gardens (see "Message from the Executive Director, LACGC," accessed August 31, 2019, http://lagardencouncil.org/). University of California, Los Angeles master's students in the Urban and Regional Planning Capstone Research project conducted a thorough survey of agricultural sites in L.A. County that culminated in the report, "Cultivate Los Angeles: Assessing the State of Urban Agriculture in Los Angeles County," accessed August 31, 2019, https://cultivatelosangeles.org/. The survey was broad and encompassed locating where school gardens as well as agricultural activities such as beekeeping and chicken coops are located in the eighty-eight cities that make up Los Angeles County, and the study also highlighted the hodgepodge of city codes that regulate horticultural activities. While there are over a thousand urban agricultural sites in L.A. County, the latest 2017 count enumerates 158 urban community gardens in LA County, a region that spans 4,751 square miles. Sixteen of these are in South L.A.

13 Journalist Sahra Sulaiman chronicled South L.A. resident's surprise and joy at the new mini-park installed on Vermont Avenue in South L.A. in 2014. See "They Never Do Things Like This in My Neighborhood!: New Park Along Vermont Ave. Surprises, Delights Residents," January 16, 2014, accessed September 22, 2019, https://la.streetsblog.org/. See also her reporting on the lack of tree canopy in South L.A., in "Desperately Seeking Shade: How South L.A. Bus Riders Weather the Elements," July 12, 2012, last accessed September 22, 2019, https://la.streetsblog.org/.

14 National park rankings show that Los Angeles has improved public park access yet remains in the bottom half of all cities in the U.S. Trust for the Public Land, a national organization, each year ranks park accessibility among the one hundred largest U.S. cities. According to their Park Score metric, Los Angeles fell from sixty-fifth to seventy-fourth place on the list in 2017. In 2018, L.A. regained sixty-sixth place and in 2019 moved up to fifty-fifth place. See Trust for the Public Land report, "Los Angeles, CA," last accessed September 22, 2019, https://www.tpl.org/.

15 McDowell, "Towards an Understanding of the Gender Division of Urban Space," 59.

16 Cranz, "Women in Urban Parks," S95.

17 We still find social restrictions on women's presence in public streets and parks in the early years of the twenty-first century, even in a global city such as Los Angeles. But that does not mean we do not see acts of defiance, transgression, and resistance against these norms. One significant sign of collective resistance can be found in streets at night, through the efforts of the nighttime bicycle brigades organized by Clitoral Mass and Ovarian Psycos. These are women of color bicycle brigades organized on the Eastside of Los Angeles. As sociologist Jennifer Candipan notes, "[t]he idea of cycling as a means of taking over a space in protest becomes a way by which members begin to think about how to engage in subversive acts of resistance on a daily basis"; see Candipan, "Clitoral Mass: A Women-of-Color Ride Through Los Angeles," 8; "'Change Agents' on Two-Wheels: Claiming Community and Contesting Spatial Inequalities through Cycling in Los Angeles."

18 The children and youth of South Central L.A. do not embrace their local parks and neighborhood streets as safe, desirable play areas. An innovative photovoice study of Black and Latino middle schoolers in South Central conducted by sociologist Elaine Bell Kaplan reveals widespread ambivalence and avoidance of these public areas. One boy reported, "I didn't really play in my neighborhood because it wasn't safe"; see Kaplan, *We Live in the Shadow,* 114. As we saw in chapter 4, our second-generation respondents who grew up here also recalled childhood years avoiding certain streets, parks, and alleyways.

19 Our research, like this entire book, is a deliberate departure from a long tradition in urban sociology and ethnography, where volumes of research highlight poor African American and Latino men engaged in crime and violence; see Goffman, *On the Run*; Venkatesh, *Gang Leader for a Day*. Instead, we focus on non-sensationalized, quotidian interactions and activities. In this regard, our efforts are in line with Hunter et al., "offering a corrective to existing accounts that depict urban blacks as bounded, plagued by violence, victims and perpetrators"; see Hunter et al., "Black Placemaking," 31. This is also an alternative to ethnographies that narrowly focus on immigrant men only "in contexts of work, family and behavior deemed to be deviant (e.g., alcoholism, violence and drugs)"; see Hondagneu-Sotelo, "Place, Nature and Masculinity in Immigrant Integration," 113. See also Choi and Peng, *Masculine Compromise.*

20 For a corrective and critique of this view, see Aptekar, "Visions of Public Space."

21 Mares and Peña, "Urban Agriculture in the Making of Insurgent Spaces in Los Angeles and Seattle."

22 Loukaitou-Sideris, "Urban Form and Social Context," 90.

23 Google Reviews shows park-goers' posted reviews of recreation centers at public parks. When we consulted this website on August 18, 2019, we found a wide range of opinions among the ninety-two reviews. On the positive side, reviewers said "Great place for kids," "fun park," "has everything you need for a proper workout," and "a diamond in the rough." Critiques included declarations such as "The junkies must go!" and "an inebriated woman was about to attack me and my children," as well as a plea, "I am homeless, just sleep on the floor at MLK park."

One critic alleged, "No security, no police, seriously ridiculous. . . . This is NOT a park for kids or family . . . hoodlums, bums, crack-heads, drug heads, winos, gang-bangers, etc.," last accessed September 22, 2019, https://www.google.com/.

24 The Fred Roberts Park was established in 1957 and is named for the first Black man elected to the California State Assembly, Frederick Madison Roberts. For fifty-two years, the city made no renovations on this park until a city council vote in the early 2000s brought about new construction and improvements between 2009 and 2012. The park reopened in 2012 with new recreational facilities and landscaping; see Alice Wen, "Renovation of the Fred Roberts Recreation Center," 2012, accessed August 31, 2019, https://prezi.com/).

25 Wattstax has been glibly referred to as the "Black Woodstock," but that moniker does not do it justice. This was a benefit concert organized by Stax Records that was held in the summer of 1972 at the LA Coliseum, featuring leading soul, gospel, funk, and rhythm-and-blues performers. The concert drew over one hundred thousand Black residents, and the name of the concert fore-fronted Watts as both a place *and* as an ideal of Black pride, resistance, and artistic expression.

26 The struggle to save the South Central Farm may be viewed in the Oscar-winning documentary *The Garden*, directed by Scott Hamilton Kennedy. The South Central Farm began in the 1990s and grew to include over three hundred substantial-sized parcels, each averaging 1,500 square feet. Until it was bulldozed in 2006, the South Central Farm was reportedly the largest urban community garden ever documented in the United States.

27 Blunt and Sheringham, "Home-City Geographies."

28 Contreras, "There's No Sunshine," 657.

29 Another form of sanctuary for a younger cohort is skateboarding which has acquired popularity in South L.A. Research from a national survey confirms the important role of skateboarding in fostering mental well-being. The 5,717 skaters surveyed by Corwin et al. report that the top reasons respondents say they skateboard are "to have fun" and "get away from stress."; see Corwin et al., "Beyond the Board: Findings from the Field." Early on in our ethnographic research at the parks, we saw vibrant and racially diverse skateboard culture at Ted Watkins Memorial Park in Watts and at Gilbert Linsdey Park near historic South Central Avenue. These were intriguing subcommunities, but we simply did not have the resources to include an investigation of these sites and this set of activities in our study.

30 On the tradition of African American agricultural self-determination, resistance, and collective food sovereignty, see White, *Freedom Farmers*.

31 Flores, *God's Gangs*.

32 These narratives are consistent with research that shows poor unwed fathers want to be involved fathers, but find it difficult to do in the context of structural poverty and fragile families; see Edin and Nelson, *Doing the Best I Can*.

33 McKeever, "Park 'Rats' to Park 'Daddies': Community Heads Creating Future Mentors."

34 "Old heads" is a term elaborated by the sociologist Elijah Anderson; see Anderson, *Streetwise*; Anderson, *Code of the Street*. The term refers to older African American men who served as caring mentors to African American male youth, advising them on cultural norms and at times intervening in their life decisions. He argued that in the context of de-industrialization and the erosion of employment, old heads struggled to maintain advice on "respectable" job paths, and switched to advising younger men on streetwise survival strategies in violent neighborhoods and in the drug trade.

35 Schmalzbauer, *The Last Best Place?*

36 Selling food on the streets and sidewalks of Los Angeles was an illegal practice until very recently. In 2018, then California governor Jerry Brown decriminalized street vending in the state, and the L.A. City Council later voted to legalize this practice in Los Angeles. This follows over a decade of mobilization by the Los Angeles Street Vendors Campaign; see Tim Arango, "L.A. Street Sellers Outlawed No More."

37 African American men are six times more likely to be incarcerated than white men, and Latino immigrant men, mostly those from Mexico and Central America, make up 90 percent of deportees. On racial disparities in incarceration rates, see reports by the Sentencing Project ("Criminal Justice Facts," https://www.sentencingproject.org/); Open Invest (Who's in Prison in America?, https://www.openinvest.co/); and the NAACP Criminal Justice Fact Sheet ("Criminal Justice Fact Sheet," https://www.naacp.org/, accessed September 22, 2019). On gendered and racial deportation patterns, see Golash-Boza and Hondagneu-Sotelo "Latino Immigrant Men and the Deportation Crisis."

38 Austin, "'Not Just for the Fun of It!' Governmental Restraints on Black Leisure, Social Inequality, and the Privatization of Public Space."

39 Trouille, "Fencing a Field."

40 Hamilton, "3 Men Are Charged with Hate Crimes in an Attack on Latinos at an L.A. County Park."

41 This video can be viewed at Jubilee Shine, "39TH & WESTERN DRUM CIRCLE MLK PARK," August 16, 2010, YouTube video, 2:50, last accessed on August 26, 2019, https://www.youtube.com/watch?v=wRG6-wZCLhs.

42 Ramírez, "'It's Not How It Was.'"

43 Hondagneu-Sotelo and Ruiz, "'Illegality' and Spaces of Sanctuary: Belonging and Homeland-Making in Urban Community Gardens"; Mares and Peña, "Urban Agriculture in the Making of Insurgent Spaces in Los Angeles and Seattle."

44 Lefebvre, *The Production of Space.*

CHAPTER 6. ORGANIZING COMMUNITY, BUILDING POWER

1 Brown-Saracino, "Explicating Divided Approaches to Gentrification and Growing Income Inequality."

2 There is a significant literature highlighting Black-Latino solidarity efforts across the U.S. from organizers and academics; see Black Alliance for Just Immigra-

tion, "Crossing Boundaries, Connecting Communities: Alliance Building for Immigrants Rights and Racial Justice"; Dzidzienyo, *Neither Enemies nor Friends*; Grant-Thomas, Sarfati, and Staats, "African American-Immigrant Alliance Building"; Jaret and Alvarado, "Building Black-Brown Coalitions in the Southeast: Four African American-Latino Collaborations"; Kun and Pulido, *Black and Brown in Los Angeles*; Marquez, *Black-Brown Solidarity*; Mindiola, Niemann, and Rodriguez, *Black-Brown Relations and Stereotypes*; Ribas, *On the Line*; Telles, Sawyer, and Rivera-Salgado, *Just Neighbors*; Winders, *Nashville in the New Millennium*.

3 Nakagawa, "Blackness Is the Fulcrum."

4 Brown-Saracino, "Explicating Divided Approaches to Gentrification and Growing Income Inequality."

5 Joanne Kim, chief operating officer of Community Coalition at the time of this interview, noted that it is business owners from outside of South L.A. who generally own the land along the main arteries in South L.A. and let them fall below the standards of how South L.A. residents keep their homes. As of the publication of this book, Kim was the senior advisor to City of L.A. councilmember Marqueece Harris-Dawson.

6 Gold and Braxton, "Considering South-Central by Another Name."

7 Jennings, "Can South L.A. Re-Brand Again? How Does 'SOLA' Sound?—Los Angeles Times."

8 Pastor, *State of Resistance*.

9 See Bauman, "The Black Power and Chicano Movements in the Poverty Wars in Los Angeles," 279; Pool, "Delegates Travel to L.A.'s Past." A branch of the National Urban League, another prominent national civil rights group, was established in 1921; see Sides, "You Understand My Condition," 236.

10 Sides, *L.A. City Limits*.

11 Gottlieb et al., *The Next Los Angeles*.

12 Flamming, *Bound for Freedom*.

13 Kurashige, "Between 'White Spot' and 'World City': Racial Integration and the Roots of Multiculturalism"; Freer, "L.A. Race Woman"; Kurashige, "The Many Facets of Brown."

14 Gottlieb et al., *The Next Los Angeles*.

15 See Bernstein, *Bridges of Reform*. There was also an anarchist strand of organizing that was explicit about multiracial organizing; these more radical groups had some presence in South L.A. but were less institutionally powerful than the groups discussed in the main text; see Struthers, *The World in a City*. Nonetheless, they contributed to a legacy on which subsequent left-leaning efforts could build.

16 Bernstein, *Bridges of Reform*.

17 Bernstein, *Bridges of Reform*.

18 Pulido, *Black, Brown, Yellow, and Left*.

19 Sides, *L.A. City Limits*.

20 Laslett, *Sunshine Was Never Enough*.

21 Laslett, *Sunshine Was Never Enough*, 112.

22 Laslett, *Sunshine Was Never Enough*.

23 Laslett, *Sunshine Was Never Enough*; Ruiz, "Una Mujer Sin Fronteras"; Sanchez, *Becoming Mexican American*, 242; Stull, "Luisa Moreno."

24 Bauman, "The Black Power and Chicano Movements in the Poverty Wars in Los Angeles."

25 Bauman, "The Black Power and Chicano Movements in the Poverty Wars in Los Angeles"; Laslett, *Sunshine Was Never Enough*.

26 Bauman, "The Black Power and Chicano Movements in the Poverty Wars in Los Angeles," 285.

27 See Bauman, *Race and the War on Poverty*, 74. WLCAC was also instrumental in creating a county hospital nearby Watts that would prove to be among the significant employer of local residents—and that would later fall into such dysfunction that it was shut in 2007 before being reborn and rechristened in 2015; see Bauman, "The Black Power and Chicano Movements in the Poverty Wars in Los Angeles," 285; Colliver, "How 'Killer King' Became the Hospital of the Future."

28 Bauman, "The Black Power and Chicano Movements in the Poverty Wars in Los Angeles."

29 Laslett, *Sunshine Was Never Enough*.

30 Johnson, *Spaces of Conflict, Sounds of Solidarity*, 153; Morales and Pastor Jr, "Can't We All Just Get along? Interethnic Organization and Economic Development."

31 Milkman, *L.A. Story*.

32 One notable effort was made by Clergy and Laity United for Economic Justice (CLUE), connected with the community-labor alliance: the Los Angeles Alliance for a New Economy. Under the guidance of Rev. Alexia Salvatierra and in partnership with Civil Rights giants like Rev. James Lawson, CLUE organizers worked to build a coalition of Black and Brown pastors that eventually led to an historic joint worship service mentioned later in this chapter. Pastor, De Lara, and Scoggins, "All Together Now?"

33 Bullard, "Race and Environmental Justice in the United States," 330.

34 Pardo, *Mexican America Women Activists*.

35 Murch, "Crack in Los Angeles," 171.

36 Park, "Confronting the Liquor Industry in Los Angeles," 116.

37 Rogers et al., "Building Power, Learning Democracy: Youth Organizing as a Site of Civic Development"; Shah, Mediratta, and McAlister, "Securing a College Prep Curriculum for All Students."

38 Shah, Mediratta, and McAlister, "Securing a College Prep Curriculum for All Students."

39 Warren, Mira, and Nikundiwe, "Youth Organizing."

40 See Ciria-Cruz, "To Live and Let Live in South Los Angeles." For more on the history of Watts/Century Latino Organization, see www.wattscenturylatino.org /history.

41 Pastor Jr., "Latinos and the Los Angeles Uprising."

42 As noted earlier, public figures such as Ms. Gracian are often referred to by their real names as opposed to pseudonyms, a practice that was made clear in the interview process.

43 Pastor, Benner, and Matsuoka, *This Could Be the Start of Something Big.*

44 See Pastor, Jr., "Common Ground at Ground Zero?," 277. For an overview of the intensification of movement-building infrastructure in the 1990s, see Nicholls "Forging a 'New' Organizational Infrastructure for Los Angeles' Progressive Community." South L.A. benefited from and contributed to the L.A. region's developing ecosystem of power building at this time, of which Black–Brown coalition building is a subset.

45 Buntin, "Rainbow Strategist."

46 Barkan, "Taking a Closer Look at How Ridley-Thomas Came from 20 Points Behind to Win Going Away."

47 Regalado, "Community Coalition-Building."

48 See https://www.blmla.org/newsfeed/2020/4/16/black-los-angeles-demands-in-light-of-covid-19-and-rates-of-black-death.

49 This phenomenon of Black churches having a commuter base after demographic shifts is not limited to Los Angeles. See McRoberts *Streets of Glory.*

50 And might require some in the immigrant rights movement to face the anti-Blackness that has shown up in that movement (e.g., the de-prioritization of Black immigrants, messaging that villainizes felons, etc.).

51 Pastor and Prichard, "LA Rising: The 1992 Civil Unrest, the Arc of Social Justice Organizing, and the Lessons for Today's Movement Building."

52 Saito and Truong, "The L.A. Live Community Benefits Agreement."

53 TRUST South LA was started as a result of the downtown CBA; its initial plans to construct housing in the downtown area fell apart as the Great Recession shook Southern California real estate but a new opportunity emerged later near USC to convert and expand an apartment building that was soon to lose its affordability covenants.

54 Pastor et al., "Planning, Power, and Possibilities: How UNIDAD Is Shaping Equitable Development in South Central L.A."

55 Barraclough, "South Central Farmers and Shadow Hills Homeowners."

56 Irazábal and Punja, "Cultivating Just Planning and Legal Institutions."

57 And such tensions remained to the end. When the city council finally approved a project for warehouses and offices on the site in 2019, a Latino farmer showed up to appeal for more time when the executive director of Concerned Citizens—the group that had united with Latina mothers to resist an incinerator—argued that "[f]ourteen acres of gardening is not going to generate the kind of wages that we need. Where's the upward mobility from that? Where's the growth opportunity? Where can I go from being a farmer?" See Reyes, "Latest Battle over South Central Farm Ends—This Time Not with Arrests, but a Vote."

58 Watanabe, "South Los Angeles Latinos and Blacks Find Unity in Worship."

59 *The Economist*, "Where Black and Brown Collide."

60 To look at the current demographics of the neighborhood councils, we gathered the names of every person currently sitting in a South L.A. neighborhood council seat (via https://empowerla.org/) that included the following councils: Central Alameda, Community and Neighbors for 9th District, Empowerment Congress Central Area NDC, Empowerment Congress Southeast Area, Empowerment Congress Southwest Area, Empowerment Congress West Area Neighborhood Development Council, North Area Neighborhood Development Council, Park Mesa Heights Community Council, South Area (UNNC), South Central, Voices of 90037, Watts NC, West Adams, and Zapata-King. We then embarked on designating a race or ethnicity to each member. We looked to various public outlets to determine this: council websites, LinkedIn profiles, newspaper articles with group pictures, and more. The obvious limitations in this method are that we could not find a picture of everyone and even this measure involved some assumptions. With those caveats in mind, we found that in overall South LA, neighborhood council demographics were 54 percent Black, 31 percent Latino, and 14 percent white. For our three neighborhoods of interest, we found that neighborhood councils in Central Avenue are 19 percent Black, 74 percent Latino, and 7 percent white; in Vermont Square are 50 percent Black, 36 percent Latino, and 4 percent white; and in Watts are 67 percent Black and 33 percent Latino. This difference between Watts and Vermont Square is particularly interesting and likely speaks to the culture and state of Black–Brown organizing in each locale. Observers report that the neighborhood councils do seem to be shifting to include more Latino residents in some Latino-dense areas; however, as can be discerned, the shares are short of the Latino presence in each area.

61 Chou, "LA Councilman Pledges $1 Million in Grants for Immigrants' Legal Services"; Martinez, "CHIRLA Opens Satellite Office in South L.A. to Provide Legal Services to Immigrants."

62 The history of CHIRLA's strategic planning and its desires to create a South L.A. office were relayed to us in an interview with CHIRLA's executive director, Angelica Salas, on July 3, 2019.

63 Pastor and Prichard, "LA Rising: The 1992 Civil Unrest, the Arc of Social Justice Organizing, and the Lessons for Today's Movement Building."

64 In the discussion that follows, we also sometimes include quotations from civic leaders who themselves grew up in South L.A., thus supplementing the resident interview base analysis with more experiences.

65 Pfeiffer, "African Americans' Search for 'More for Less' and 'Peace of Mind' on the Exurban Frontier."

66 A similar theme of losing jobs in fast food, particularly for teens, is heard in the resident interviews in Roussell "Policing the Anticommunity," 829–30.

67 Pfeiffer, "African Americans' Search for 'More for Less' and 'Peace of Mind' on the Exurban Frontier," 79.

68 Tobar, "Cooperation on Central Ave."

69 Related to this observation is the literature on Afro-Pessimism, which is a critical analysis of race and anti-Blackness that explains how the Black and non-Black divide (as opposed to the white and Black binary) creates the experience of Black people in the West and around the world. It posits, among other things, that the use of "people of color" blinds masses to the unique experiences and continued oppression of Black people due to the continued impacts of slavery. See Sexton "People-of-Color-Blindness: Notes on the Afterlife of Slavery."

70 Roussell, "Policing the Anticommunity."

71 Roussell, "Policing the Anticommunity," 839.

72 Chang and Poston, "'Stop-and-Frisk in a Car."

73 Bean, "Redfin Names the Most Competitive Neighborhoods of 2016."

74 Hwang and Lin, "What Have We Learned about the Causes of Recent Gentrification?"

75 Brown-Saracino, "Explicating Divided Approaches to Gentrification and Growing Income Inequality," 524.

76 Pastor et al., "Planning, Power, and Possibilities: How UNIDAD Is Shaping Equitable Development in South Central L.A."

77 The Million Dollar Hoods team out of UCLA found that the Los Angeles School Police Department (operating in schools within the Los Angeles Unified School District [LAUSD]) had arrested, cited, or diverted Black youth at a highly disproportionate rate between 2014 and 2017—out of all arrests, citations, and diversions made, Black youth composed 25 percent despite being about only 8 percent of the total LAUSD population. For more on this, see milliondollarhoods.org/.

CHAPTER 7. SUMMING UP, LOOKING ELSEWHERE

1 Wyler, "How Much Difference Can Obama Really Make on the Economy?"

2 Another complicating factor behind the resentment, according to our informants, was the sometimes tense relationship between Mayor Eric Garcetti and South Los Angeles, a place that had gone strongly for his opponent in the 2013 contest; see Finnegan and Welsh, "The Road to Eric Garcetti's Election Romp." Some wondered why Garcetti had not promoted South L.A. rather than the mid-city organization that submitted the successful program; again, a main reason was the need to have had a Promise Neighborhoods effort in place first, but the context made that story less persuasive, particularly since mid-city had been a stronger base of support for Garcetti's electoral campaign.

3 See Jennings, "After Failed Attempt, South L.A. Wins Promise Zone Designation, Which Could Bring in Money." Interestingly, in keeping with our observation in chapter 6 that it can be helpful to be neither Black nor Brown in South L.A., SLATE-Z was fronted by a white community college president with a long history of political organizing in the area, including service as deputy mayor to L.A.'s first Latino mayor in modern history, Antonio Villaraigosa, and get-out-the-vote organizing with famed African American political strategist Anthony Thigpenn.

4 Jones, *The Browning of the New South*, 7.

5 See also Marquez, *Black-Brown Solidarity*; Rosas, *South Central Is Home*.

6 See Pastor, Jr., "Common Ground at Ground Zero?"; Pastor and Prichard, "LA Rising: The 1992 Civil Unrest, the Arc of Social Justice Organizing, and the Lessons for Today's Movement Building"; Regalado, "Community Coalition-Building." Ribas rightly points out that Black–Latino and Black–immigrant relationships operate within a white power structure, naming this dynamic "prismatic engagement"; see Ribas, *On the Line*. We, admittedly, focus heavily on how race is constructed between nonwhite groups, with a lens that is more akin to that of HoSang and Molina, "Introduction: Toward a Relational Consciousness of Race."

7 There can also be a sense that African Americans may have it better by virtue of their position as citizens, a topic explored in Zamora "Mexican Illegality, Black Citizenship, and White Power."

8 Rendón, *Stagnant Dreamers*.

9 See Allport, *The Nature of Prejudice*; Pettigrew, "Intergroup Contact Theory"; HoSang and Molina, "Introduction: Toward a Relational Consciousness of Race." The ways in which timing matters is also explored in Marrow's exploration of Latino second-generation downward mobility trends in new immigrant destination places in the South in light of post-2005 increases in immigration enforcement and state-level exclusionary policies; see Marrow, "Hope Turned Sour."

10 See Cheng, *The Changs Next Door to the Díazes*. This theme of how a broader white power structure can impact the identity of minoritized groups who may have limited contact with white people *per se* is explored in Ribas, *On the Line*; Alba and Duyvendak, "What about the Mainstream?"

11 Loukaitou-Sideris, "Urban Form and Social Context."

12 In an ideal world, women and girls would also have the leisure time and freedom to gather for conviviality away from domestic chores and fears of threat, but, as stressed in chapter 5, that is not yet happening.

13 Loïc Wacquant, "A Janus-Faced Institution of Ethnoracial Closure: A Sociological Specification of the Ghetto."

14 Building on Wacquant's conceptualization of self-segregation as protective, see Hunter et al., "Black Placemaking." They find that celebration, play, poetry, and more are privileged by Black residents as a means of building of endurance, belonging, and resistance—at the same time that their neighborhoods are racially oppressed by larger forces.

15 Menjivar, "Liminal Legality"; Menjivar and Abrego, "Legal Violence: Immigration Law and the Lives of Central American Immigrants."

16 Alarcon, Escala, and Odgers, *Making Los Angeles Home*, 208.

17 Similar themes are echoed in Kasinitz et al.'s analysis of the second generation in New York where the authors suggest that the second generation are at an advantage to contribute to their home neighborhoods; see Kasinitz et al., *Inheriting the City*.

18 Sanchez, *Becoming Mexican American*; Garcia Bedolla, *Fluid Borders*.

19 See HoSang and Molina, "Introduction." John. D. Marquez labels approaches that only look at a minority group vis-à-vis whites as "ethnic comparimentalization" Marquez, *Black-Brown Solidarity*, 20.

20 Blunt and Dowling, *Home*; Boccagni, *Migration and the Search for Home*; Cancellieri, "Towards a Progressive Home-Making"; Kusenbach and Paulsen, *Home*; Morley, "Belongings."

21 Calculated from Census Microdata as available from Ruggles et al., *Integrated Public Use Microdata Series: Version 7.0* [data set].

22 On the constantly shifting nature of Los Angeles, see Bobo, *Prismatic Metropolis*; Revoyr, *Southland*; Waldinger and Bozorgmehr, *Ethnic Los Angeles*.

23 Blackwell et al., *Uncommon Common Ground*; Vargas, *The Denial of Antiblackness*.

24 Current percentages are taken from the 2017 American Community Survey from and the 2050 projections from the National Equity Atlas.

25 Jones, *The Browning of the New South*; Opie, *Upsetting the Apple Cart*; Wilson and Taub, *There Goes the Neighborhood*.

26 Pastor et al., "Bridges | Puentes: Building Black-Brown Solidarities Across the U.S."

27 Bacon, "How Mississippi's Black/Brown Strategy Beat the South's Anti-Immigrant Wave"; Campbell, "Will a Black-Latino Alliance in Mississippi Change Politics in the Deep South?"; Eaton, "Black-Latino Coalitions Block Anti-Immigrant Laws in Mississippi."

28 Nellis, "The Color of Justice: Racial and Ethnic Disparity in State Prisons"; Pawasarat and Quinn, "Wisconsin's Mass Incarceration of African American Males: Workforce Challenges for 2013."

29 An additional complicated factor has been the antiunion campaign of former Republican governor Scott Walker (2011–2019); labor has been fighting a rearguard battle against this attack and had less time to play the unifying role that it has played in the Los Angeles context.

30 Calculated by the authors using the underlying data in the National Equity Atlas.

31 Calculated by the authors using the 2017 American Community Survey as available from Ruggles et al., *Integrated Public Use Microdata Series: Version 7.0* [data set].

32 Here, we view Afro-Latinos as those with Latin American roots, a broader category than simply those who identify as Black and also speak Spanish.

33 Pastor, De Lara, and Scoggins, "All Together Now"; De Lara, *Inland Shift*.

34 Kaufmann, "A Young Mayor Makes the Case for a Guaranteed Income."

35 Calculated by the authors using the 1980 Census and the 2017 American Community Survey as available from Ruggles et al., *Integrated Public Use Microdata Series: Version 7.0* [data set].

36 Self, *American Babylon*.

37 Marrow, "Hispanic Immigration, Black Population Size, and Intergroup Relations in the Rural and Small-Town South"; Marrow, *New Destination Dreaming*; Jones,

"Blacks May Be Second Class, but They Can't Make Them Leave"; Jones, *The Browning of the New South.*

38 Vaca, *The Presumed Alliance.*

39 Betancur and Gillis, *The Collaborative City*; Bobo, *Prismatic Metropolis*; Jones, *The Browning of the New South*; Rosas, *South Central Is Home*; Zamora, "Mexican Illegality, Black Citizenship, and White Power."

40 Florida, *The New Urban Crisis.*

41 Chapple and Loukaitou-Sideris, *Transit-Oriented Displacement or Community Dividends?*; Freeman, *There Goes the Hood*; Fullilove, *Root Shock*; Janoschka and Sequera, "Gentrification in Latin America"; Newman and Wyly, "The Right to Stay Put, Revisited."

42 Chapple and Loukaitou-Sideris, *Transit-Oriented Displacement or Community Dividends?*; Hwang and Lin, "What Have We Learned about the Causes of Recent Gentrification?"

43 For more on how Black communities across the United States are experience displacement pressures, see the Movement for Black Lives' economic justice plank of its policy platform at "Economic Justice," Movement for Black Lives, policy.m4bl.org/.

44 Chapple and Loukaitou-Sideris, *Transit-Oriented Displacement or Community Dividends?*

45 For a national view, see Fullilove and Wallace, "Serial Forced Displacement in American Cities, 1916–2010." Also see Saito, *The Politics of Exclusion*, for more on racialized public policy decision making in Los Angeles and other U.S. metros.

46 Gordon, "Daily Mobility in the Black-White Segregated City."

47 City News Service, "City Celebrates Opening of Affordable Apartment Complex in South L.A."

48 "A Neighborhood Champion," News from the Frontlines, Liberty Hill, 6 Sept 2013, www.libertyhill.org/.

49 Shakur, "Mama's Just a Little Girl."

APPENDIX

1 Sampson, *Great American City.*

2 Pastor, De Lara, and Scoggins, "All Together Now."

3 Loukaitou-Sideris, "Urban Form and Social Context."

4 See Pulido and Pastor, "Where in the World Is Juan—and What Color Is He?"

BIBLIOGRAPHY

Abrego, Leisy. *Sacrificing Families: Navigating Laws, Labor, and Love Across Borders*. Palo Alto, CA: Stanford University Press, 2014.

Abrego, Leisy J., and Leah Schmalzbauer. "Illegality, Motherhood, and Place: Undocumented Latinas Making Meaning and Negotiating Daily Life." *Women's Studies International Forum* 67 (March 1, 2018): 10–17.

Ahmed, Sara. "Home and Away: Narratives of Migration and Estrangement." *International Journal of Cultural Studies* 2, no. 3 (December 1, 1999): 329–47.

Ahmed, Sara, Claudia Castada, Anne-Marie Fortier, and Mimi Sheller, eds. *Uprootings/Regroundings: Questions of Home and Migration*. Oxford, UK: Berg Publishers, 2003.

Alarcon, Rafael, Luis Escala, and Olga Odgers. *Making Los Angeles Home: The Integration of Mexican Immigrants in the United States*. Oakland: University of California Press, 2016.

Alba, Richard. *The Great Demographic Illusion: Majority, Minority, and the Expanding American Mainstream*. Princeton, NJ: Princeton University Press, 2020.

Alba, Richard, and Jan Willem Duyvendak. "What about the Mainstream? Assimilation in Super-Diverse Times." *Ethnic and Racial Studies* 42, no. 1 (2017): 105–24.

Alba, Richard, and Victor Nee. *Remaking the American Mainstream: Assimilation and Contemporary Immigration*. Cambridge, MA: Harvard University Press, 2003.

Allport, Gordon W. *The Nature of Prejudice*. Reading, MA: Addison-Wesley, 1979.

Anderson, Elijah. *Streetwise: Race, Class, and Change in an Urban Community*. Chicago: University of Chicago Press, 1990.

———. *Code of the Street: Decency, Violence, and the Moral Life of the Inner City*. New York: W. W. Norton, 1999.

Andrews, Abigail Leslie. *Undocumented Politics: Place, Gender and the Pathways of Mexican Migrants*. Oakland: University of California Press, 2018.

Aptekar, Sofya. "Visions of Public Space: Reproducing and Resisting Social Hierarchies in a Community Garden." *Sociological Forum* 30, no. 1 (March 2015): 209–27.

Aranda, Elizabeth M., Sallie Hughes, and Elena Sabogal. *Making a Life in Multiethnic Miami: Immigration and the Rise of a Global City*. Boulder, CO: Lynne Rienner Publishers, 2014.

Arango, Tim. "L.A. Street Sellers Outlawed No More." *New York Times*, January 11, 2019, sec. Multimedia/Photos. https://www.nytimes.com/.

Armenta, Amada. *Protect, Serve, and Deport: The Rise of Policing as Immigration Enforcement*. Berkeley and Los Angeles: University of California Press, 2017.

Arreola, Daniel D. *Hispanic Spaces, Latino Places: Community and Cultural Diversity in Contemporary America*. Austin: University of Texas Press, 2004.

———. "Placemaking and Latino Urbanism in a Phoenix Mexican Immigrant Community." *Journal of Urbanism* 5, no. 2–3 (November 2012): 157–70.

Asad, Asad L., and Jackelyn Hwang. "Indigenous Places and the Making of Undocumented Status in Mexico-US Migration." *International Migration Review* 53, no. 4 (December 2019): 1032–77.

Austin, Regina. "'Not Just for the Fun of It!' Governmental Restraints on Black Leisure, Social Inequality, and the Privatization of Public Space." *Southern California Law Review* 71, no. 4 (May 1998): 667–714.

Avila, Eric. *Popular Culture in the Age of White Flight: Fear and Fantasy in Suburban Los Angeles*. Berkeley: University of California Press, 2004.

Bacon, David. "How Mississippi's Black/Brown Strategy Beat the South's Anti-Immigrant Wave." *Nation*, April 20, 2012. https://www.thenation.com.

Ballinas, Jorge, and James D. Bachmeier. "'Whiteness' In Context: Racial Identification among Mexican-Origin Adults in California and Texas." *Du Bois Review: Social Science Research on Race* (November 2020): 1–26. doi:10.1017/S1742058X20000223.

Banks, Sandy. "The Crack Epidemic's Toxic Legacy." *Los Angeles Times*, August 7, 2010. http://articles.latimes.com/.

Barkan, Steve. "Taking a Closer Look at How Ridley-Thomas Came from 20 Points Behind to Win Going Away." *The Front Page Online* (blog), November 24, 2008. www.thefrontpageonline.com.

Barraclough, Laura R. "South Central Farmers and Shadow Hills Homeowners: Land Use Policy and Relational Racialization in Los Angeles." *The Professional Geographer* 61, no. 2 (April 14, 2009): 164–86.

Barragan, Bianca. "New Program Helps Residents Turn Empty Lots into Community Gathering Spaces." *Curbed LA*, December 14, 2018. https://la.curbed.com/.

Basch, Linda, Nina Glick Schiller, and Christina Szanton Blanc. *Nations Unbound: Transnational Projects, Postcolonial Predicaments, and Deterritorialized Nation-States*. New York: Routledge, 1993.

Bauman, Robert. "The Black Power and Chicano Movements in the Poverty Wars in Los Angeles." *Journal of Urban History* 33, no. 2 (January 1, 2007): 277–95.

———. *Race and the War on Poverty: From Watts to East L.A.* Norman: University of Oklahoma Press, 2014.

Bean, Keena. "Redfin Names the Most Competitive Neighborhoods of 2016." Redfin Real-Time, December 29, 2016. https://www.redfin.com.

Bernstein, Shana. *Bridges of Reform: Interracial Civil Rights Activism in Twentieth-Century Los Angeles*. New York: Oxford University Press USA—OSO, 2010. http://ebookcentral.proquest.com/.

Betancur, John Jairo, and Douglas Gillis, eds. *The Collaborative City: Opportunities and Struggles for Blacks and Latinos in U.S. Cities*. New York: Garland Publishing, 2000.

Bickham Mendez, Jennifer, and Lisa Schmalzbauer. "Latino Youth and Struggles for Inclusion in the 21st Century." *Ethnicities* 18, no. 2 (2018): 165–77.

Black Alliance for Just Immigration. "Crossing Boundaries, Connecting Communities: Alliance Building for Immigrants Rights and Racial Justice." Oakland, CA: Black Alliance for Just Immigration, 2010.

Blackwell, Angela Glover, Stewart Kwoh, Manuel Pastor, and American Assembly. *Uncommon Common Ground: Race and America's Future.* New York: W. W. Norton & Co., 2010.

Bledsoe, Adam, and Willie Jamaal Wright. "The Anti-Blackness of Global Capital." *Environment and Planning D: Society and Space* 37, no. 1 (2019): 8–26.

Blume, Howard. "The Huge L.A. School Construction Project Is Done, so What Does It Add up To?" *Los Angeles Times,* August 21, 2017, sec. California. https://www.latimes.com.

Blunt, Alison, and Robyn Dowling. *Home.* London: Taylor & Francis, 2006.

Blunt, Alison, and Olivia Sheringham. "Home-City Geographies: Urban Dwelling and Mobility." *Progress in Human Geography,* July 9, 2018, https://doi.org/10.1177/0309132518786590.

———. "Home-City Geographies: Urban Dwelling and Mobility." *Progress in Human Geography* 43, no. 5 (October 2019): 815–34.

Bobo, Lawrence, ed. *Prismatic Metropolis: Inequality in Los Angeles.* The Multi City Study of Urban Inequality. New York: Russell Sage Foundation, 2000.

Boccagni, Paolo. "Burden, Blessing or Both? On the Mixed Role of Transnational Ties in Migrant Informal Social Support." *International Sociology* 30, no. 3 (May 1, 2015): 250–68.

———. *Migration and the Search for Home: Mapping Domestic Space in Migrants' Everyday Lives.* New York: Palgrave Macmillan, 2017.

Boccagni, Paolo, and Jan Willem Duyvendak. "On the 'Scaling Up' of Home in Majority-Minority Relations: A Conceptual Inquiry and a Research Agenda." HOMinG: Working Paper 6, 2019.

Bodnar, John E., Roger D. Simon, and Michael P. Weber. *Lives of Their Own: Blacks, Italians, and Poles in Pittsburgh, 1900–1960.* Illini books ed. The Working Class in American History. Urbana: University of Illinois Press, 1983.

Boehm, Deborah. *Returned: Going and Coming in an Age of Deportation.* Oakland: University of California Press, 2016.

Bonilla-Silva, Eduardo. *Racism without Racists: Color-Blind Racism and the Persistence of Racial Inequality in America.* 4th ed. Lanham, MD: Rowman & Littlefield Publishers, 2003.

Brown, Karida L. *Gone Home: Race and Roots through Appalachia.* Chapel Hill: The University of North Carolina Press, 2018.

Brown-Saracino, Japonica. "Explicating Divided Approaches to Gentrification and Growing Income Inequality." *Annual Review of Sociology* 43, no. 1 (July 31, 2017): 515–39.

Bullard, Robert D. "Race and Environmental Justice in the United States." *Yale Journal of International Law* 18, no. 1 (1993): 319–35.

Buntin, John. "Rainbow Strategist." *Governing*, July 2005. http://www.governing.com.

Byrne, Jason. "When Green Is White: The Cultural Politics of Race, Nature and Social Exclusion in a Los Angeles Urban National Park." *Geoforum* 43, no. 3 (May 2012): 595–611.

———, and Jennifer Wolch. "Nature, Race, and Parks: Past Research and Future Directions for Geographic Research." *Progress in Human Geography* 33, no. 6 (December 2009): 743–65.

Camarillo, Albert M. "Black and Brown in Compton: Demographic Change, Suburban Decline, and Intergroup Relations in a South Central Los Angeles Community, 1950–2000." In *Not Just Black and White: Historical and Contemporary Perspectives on Immigration, Race, and Ethnicity in the United States*, edited by Nancy Foner and George M. Fredrickson, 358–76. New York: Russell Sage Foundation, 2004.

———. "Cities of Color: The New Racial Frontier in California's Minority-Majority Cities." *Pacific Historical Review* 76, no. 1 (February 2007): 1–28.

Campbell, Alexia Fernández. "Will a Black-Latino Alliance in Mississippi Change Politics in the Deep South?" *The Atlantic*, January 26, 2015. https://www.theatlantic .com.

Cancellieri, Adriano. "Towards a Progressive Home-Making: The Ambivalence of Migrants' Experience in a Multicultural Condominium." *Journal of Housing and the Built Environment* 32, no. 1 (March 1, 2017): 49–61.

Candipan, Jennifer. "Clitoral Mass: A Women-of-Color Ride Through Los Angeles." *Metropolitics*. June 2, 2015. https://www.metropolitiques.eu.

———. "'Change Agents' on Two-Wheels: Claiming Community and Contesting Spatial Inequalities through Cycling in Los Angeles." *City and Community* 18, no. 3 (2019): 965–82.

Castañeda, Ernesto. *A Place to Call Home: Immigrant Exclusion and Urban Belonging in New York, Paris and Barcelona*. Stanford, CA: Stanford University Press, 2018.

Centers for Disease Control and Prevention. "Homicide—Los Angeles, 1970–1979," 1986. https://www.cdc.gov.

Chang, Cindy, and Ben Poston. "'Stop-and-Frisk in a Car': Elite LAPD Unit Disproportionately Stopped Black Drivers, Data Show." *Los Angeles Times*, January 24, 2019. https://www.latimes.com.

Chang, Shenglin. *The Global Silicon Valley Home: Lives and Landscapes Within Taiwanese American Trans-Pacific Culture*. Stanford, CA: Stanford University Press, 2006.

Chapple, Karen, and Anastasia Loukaitou-Sideris. *Transit-Oriented Displacement or Community Dividends? Understanding the Effects of Smarter Growth on Communities*. Urban and Industrial Environments. Cambridge, MA: The MIT Press, 2019.

Chapple, Reginald. "From Central Avenue to Leimert Park: The Shifting Center of Black Los Angeles." In *Black Los Angeles: American Dreams and Racial Realities*, edited by Darnell M. Hunt and Ana-Christina Ramón, 60–80. New York: NYU Press, 2010.

Cheng, Wendy. *The Changs Next Door to the Díazes.* Minneapolis: University of Minnesota Press, 2013.

Chiland, Elijah. "Affordable Housing and Public Park Set to Replace Old Industrial Buildings in South LA." *Curbed LA*, February 21, 2017. https://la.curbed.com.

Choi, Susanne Y. P., and Yinni Peng. *Masculine Compromise: Migration, Family, and Gender in China.* Oakland: University of California Press, 2016.

Chou, Elizabeth. "LA Councilman Pledges $1 Million in Grants for Immigrants' Legal Services." *Daily News* (blog), February 24, 2017. http://www.dailynews.com.

Ciria-Cruz, Rene P. "To Live and Let Live in South Los Angeles." *NACLA Report on the Americas* 40, no. 3 (2007): 37–41.

City News Service. "City Celebrates Opening of Affordable Apartment Complex in South L.A." KFI AM 640. November 7, 2019, sec. Local News. https://kfiam640.iheart.com.

Colliver, Victoria. "How 'Killer King' Became the Hospital of the Future." The Agenda, November 8, 2017. http://politi.co.

Contreras, Randol. "There's No Sunshine: Spatial Anguish, Deflections, and Intersectionality in Compton and South Central." *Environment and Planning D: Society and Space* 35, no. 4 (August 2017): 656–73.

Cooley, Charles Horton. *Human Nature and the Social Order.* New York: Charles Scribner's Sons, 1902.

Corwin, Zoe B., Tattiya Maruco, Neftalie Williams, Robert Reichardt, and Maria Romero-Morales. "Beyond the Board: Findings from the Field." Los Angeles: USC Pullias Center for Higher Education, 2019. https://pullias.usc.edu.

Coutin, Susan Bibler. *Legalizing Moves: Salvadoran Immigrants' Struggle for U.S. Residency.* Ann Arbor: University of Michigan Press, 2003.

Cranz, Galen. "Women in Urban Parks." *Signs: Journal of Women in Culture and Society* 5, no. S3 (April 1980): S79–S95.

Dávila, Arlene M. *Latinos, Inc.: The Marketing and Making of a People.* Berkeley: University of California Press, 2001.

Davis, Mike. *City of Quartz: Excavating the Future in Los Angeles.* New York: Verso, 1990.

Davison, Robert, Doug Vogel, Roger Harris, and Noel Jones. "Technology Leapfrogging in Developing Countries—An Inevitable Luxury." *Electronic Journal on Information Systems in Development Countries* 1, no. 5 (2000): 1–10.

De Genova, Nicholas P. "Migrant 'Illegality' and Deportability in Everyday Life." *Annual Review of Anthropology* 31, no. 1 (October 1, 2002): 419–47.

De Lara, Juan. *Inland Shift: Race, Space, and Capital in Southern California.* Berkeley: University of California Press, 2018.

De Leon, Jason. *The Land of Open Graves.* Oakland: University of California Press, 2015.

Deener, Andrew. *Venice: A Contested Bohemia in Los Angeles.* Chicago: University of Chicago Press, 2012.

Department of Economic and Social Affairs, Population Division. "The International Migration Report 2017 (Highlights)." United Nations, 2017. https://www.un.org.

Duyvendak, Jan Willem. *The Politics of Home—Belonging and Nostalgia in Europe and the United States.* London: Palgrave Macmillan, 2011.

Dzidzienyo, Anani. *Neither Enemies nor Friends: Latinos, Blacks, Afro-Latinos.* New York: Palgrave Macmillan, 2005.

Eaton, Susan. "Black-Latino Coalitions Block Anti-Immigrant Laws in Mississippi." *Race, Poverty & the Environment* 18, no. 2 (2011). http://www.reimaginerpe.org.

The Economist. "Where Black and Brown Collide." August 2, 2007. http://www.economist.com.

Edin, Kathryn, and Timothy J. Nelson. *Doing the Best I Can: Fatherhood in the Inner City.* Berkeley: University of California Press, 2014.

Eschbach, Karl, Jacqueline Hagan, Nestor Rodriguez, Rubén Hernández-León, and Stanley Bailey. "Death at the Border." *International Migration Review* 33, no. 2 (June 1, 1999): 430–54.

Estrada, Emir. *Kids at Work: Latinx Families Selling Food on the Streets of Los Angeles.* New York: New York University Press, 2019.

Ethington, Philip J., William H. Frey, and Dowell Myers. "The Racial Resegregation of Los Angeles County, 1940–2000." Public Research Report, no. 2001–04, a University of Southern California and University of Michigan Collaborative Project, 2001. https://cpb-us-e1.wpmucdn.com.

Finnegan, Michael, and Ben Welsh. "The Road to Eric Garcetti's Election Romp." *Los Angeles Times*, May 23, 2013. https://www.latimes.com.

FitzGerald, David. *A Nation of Emigrants: How Mexico Manages Its Migration.* Berkeley: University of California Press, 2008.

Flamming, Douglas. *Bound for Freedom: Black Los Angeles in Jim Crow America.* Berkeley: University of California Press, 2005.

Flores, Edward Orozco. *God's Gangs: Barrio Ministry, Masculinity, and Gang Recovery.* New York: NYU Press, 2014.

Flores, Glenda M. *Latina Teachers: Creating Careers and Guarding Culture.* New York: New York University Press, 2017.

Flores-González, Nilda. *Citizens but Not Americans.* New York: New York University Press, 2017.

Florida, Richard. *The New Urban Crisis: How Our Cities Are Increasing Inequality, Deepening Segregation, and Failing the Middle Class—and What We Can Do About It.* New York: Basic Books, 2017.

Fogelson, Robert M. *The Fragmented Metropolis: Los Angeles, 1850–1930.* Berkeley: University of California Press, 1993.

Fox, Geoffrey E. *Hispanic Nation: Culture, Politics, and the Constructing of Identity.* Tucson: University of Arizona Press, 1997.

Freeman, Lance. *There Goes the Hood: Views of Gentrification from the Ground Up.* Philadelphia, PA: Temple University Press, 2011.

Freer, Regina. "L.A. Race Woman: Charlotta Bass and the Complexities of Black Political Development in Los Angeles." *American Quarterly* 56, no. 3 (2004): 607–32.

Fullilove, Mindy Thompson. *Root Shock: How Tearing Up City Neighborhoods Hurts America, and What We Can Do About It.* New York: New Village Press, 2016.

———, and Rodrick Wallace. "Serial Forced Displacement in American Cities, 1916–2010." *Journal of Urban Health* 88, no. 3 (June 2011): 381–89.

Gans, Herbert J. "Comment: Ethnic Invention and Acculturation: A Bumpy-Line Approach." *Journal of American Ethnic History* 11, no. 1 (1992): 42–52.

Garcia, Angela S. *Legal Passing: Navigating Undocumented Life and Local Immigration Law.* Oakland: University of California Press, 2019.

García, Angela S., and Leah Schmalzbauer. "Placing Assimilation Theory: Mexican Immigrants in Urban and Rural America." *The Annals of the American Academy of Political and Social Science* 672, no. 1 (July 1, 2017): 64–82.

García, Jennifer J., Gilbert C. Gee, and Malia Jones. "A Critical Theory Analysis of Public Park Features in Latino Immigrant Neighborhoods." *Du Bois Review: Social Science Research on Race* 13, no. 2 (2016): 397–411.

Garcia Bedolla, Lisa. *Fluid Borders: Latino Power, Identity, and Politics in Los Angeles.* Berkeley: University of California Press, 2005.

Goffman, Alice. *On the Run: Fugitive Life in an American City.* First Picador ed. Fieldwork Encounters and Discoveries. Chicago: University of Chicago Press, 2015.

Golash-Boza, Tanya Maria. *Deported: Immigrant Policing, Disposable Labor and Global Capitalism.* New York and London: NYU Press, 2015.

———, and Pierrette Hondagneu-Sotelo. "Latino Immigrant Men and the Deportation Crisis: A Gendered Racial Removal Program." *Latino Studies* 11, no. 3 (September 1, 2013): 271–92.

Gold, Matea, and Greg Braxton. "Considering South-Central by Another Name." *Los Angeles Times.* April 10, 2003. https://www.latimes.com.

Gonzales, Roberto G. *Lives in Limbo: Undocumented and Coming of Age in America.* Oakland: University of California Press, 2015. https://www.ucpress.edu.

Gordon, Daanika. "Daily Mobility in the Black-White Segregated City: Linking Material Realities and Repertoires of Meaning." *Sociological Perspectives* 61, no. 4 (2018): 661–80.

Gordon, Milton Myron. *Assimilation in American Life: The Role of Race, Religion, and National Origins.* New York: Oxford University Press, 1964.

Gottlieb, Robert, Regina Freer, Mark Vallianatos, and Peter Dreier. *The Next Los Angeles: The Struggle for a Liveable City: Updated with a New Preface.* Berkeley: University of California Press, 2006.

Grant, David M., Melvin L. Oliver, and Angela D. James. "African Americans: Social and Economic Bifurcation." In *Ethnic Los Angeles*, edited by Roger David Waldinger and Mehdi Bozorgmehr, 379–413. New York: Russell Sage Foundation, 1996.

Grant-Thomas, Andrew, Yusef Sarfati, and Cheryl Staats. "African American-Immigrant Alliance Building." Columbus, OH: The Kirwan Institute for the Study of Race and Ethnicity, May 2009.

Gutiérrez, David. "An Historic Overview of Latino Immigration and the Demographic Transformation of the United States." In *American Latinos and the Making of the United States: A Theme Study.* Washington, DC: National Park System Advisory Board, National Park Service, 2013. https://www.nps.gov.

Hagan, Jacqueline Maria. *Migration Miracle: Faith, Hope, and Meaning on the Undocumented Journey.* Cambridge, MA: Harvard University Press, 2008.

Hamilton, Matt. "3 Men Are Charged with Hate Crimes in an Attack on Latinos at an L.A. County Park." *Los Angeles Times,* March 3, 2016.

Hamilton, Nora, and Norma Stoltz Chinchilla. *Seeking Community in a Global City: Guatemalans and Salvadorans in Los Angeles.* Philadelphia, PA: Temple University Press, 2001.

Hipp, John R., George E. Tita, Luis Daniel Gascon, and Aaron Roussell. "Ethnically Transforming Neighborhoods and Violent Crime Among and Between African-Americans and Latinos: A Study of South Los Angeles." John and Dora Haynes Foundation of Los Angeles, 2010. https://faculty.sites.uci.edu.

Hochschild, Arlie. "The Commercial Spirit of Intimate Life and the Abduction of Feminism: Signs from Women's Advice Books." *Theory, Culture & Society* 11, no. 2 (1994): 1–24.

Hondagneu-Sotelo, Pierrette. *Gendered Transitions: Mexican Experiences of Immigration.* Berkeley: University of California Press, 1994.

———. *God's Heart Has No Borders: How Religious Activists Are Working for Immigrant Rights.* Berkeley: University of California Press, 2008.

———. *Paradise Transplanted: Migration and the Making of California Gardens.* Berkeley: University of California Press, 2014.

———. "Place, Nature and Masculinity in Immigrant Integration: Latino Immigrant Men in Inner-City Parks and Community Gardens." *NORMA* 12, no. 2 (April 3, 2017): 112–26.

———, and Jose Miguel Ruiz. "'Illegality' and Spaces of Sanctuary: Belonging and Homeland-Making in Urban Community Gardens." In *Constructing Immigrant "Illegality": Critiques, Experiences, and Responses,* edited by Cecilia Menjívar and Daniel Kanstroom, 246–71. Cambridge: Cambridge University Press, 2013.

HoSang, Daniel, and Natalia Molina. "Introduction: Toward a Relational Consciousness of Race." In *Relational Formations of Race: Theory, Method, and Practice,* edited by Natalia Molina, Daniel Martinez HoSang, and Ramón A. Gutiérrez, 1–21. Oakland: University of California Press, 2019.

Huante, Alfredo. "A Lighter Shade of Brown? Racial Formation and Gentrification in Latino Los Angeles." *Social Problems,* no. spz047 (November 27, 2019). https://academic.oup.com

Hudson, Karen E., and Paul R. Williams. *Paul R. Williams, Architect: A Legacy of Style.* New York: Rizzoli, 2000.

Hunt, Darnell M., and Ana-Christina Ramón, eds. *Black Los Angeles: American Dreams and Racial Realities.* New York: NYU Press, 2010.

Hunter, Marcus Anthony, Mary Pattillo, Zandria F. Robinson, and Keeanga-Yamahtta Taylor. "Black Placemaking: Celebration, Play, and Poetry." *Theory, Culture & Society* 33, no. 7–8 (December 2016): 31–56.

Hwang, Jackelyn, and Jeffrey Lin. "What Have We Learned about the Causes of Recent Gentrification?" *Cityscape: A Journal of Policy Development and Research* 18, no. 3 (2016): 9–26. https://www.www.huduser.gov

Iceland, John, and Kyle Anne Nelson. "Hispanic Segregation in Metropolitan America: Exploring the Multiple Forms of Spatial Assimilation." *American Sociological Review* 73, no. 5 (October 1, 2008): 741–65.

Irazábal, Clara, and Anita Punja. "Cultivating Just Planning and Legal Institutions: A Critical Assessment of the South Central Farm Struggle in Los Angeles." *Journal of Urban Affairs* 31, no. 1 (February 1, 2009): 1–23.

Janoschka, Michael, and Jorge Sequera. "Gentrification in Latin America: Addressing the Politics and Geographies of Displacement." *Urban Geography* 37, no. 8 (November 16, 2016): 1175–94.

Jaret, Charles, and Joel Alvarado. "Building Black-Brown Coalitions in the Southeast: Four African American-Latino Collaborations." Atlanta: Georgia State University and Southern Regional Council, 2009.

Jennings, Angel. "Can South L.A. Re-Brand Again? How Does 'SOLA' Sound?—Los Angeles Times." *Los Angeles Times*, April 21, 2015. https://www.latimes.com.

———. "After Failed Attempt, South L.A. Wins Promise Zone Designation, Which Could Bring in Money." *Los Angeles Times*, June 6, 2016. https://www.latimes.com.

Jiménez, Tomás. *The Other Side of Assimilation: How Immigrants Are Changing American Life*. Oakland: University of California Press, 2017.

Joassart-Marcelli, Pascale. "Leveling the Playing Field? Urban Disparities in Funding for Local Parks and Recreation in the Los Angeles Region." *Environment and Planning A: Economy and Space* 42, no. 5 (May 2010): 1174–92.

Johnson, Gaye Theresa. *Spaces of Conflict, Sounds of Solidarity: Music, Race, and Spatial Entitlement in Los Angeles by Johnson*. Berkeley: University of California Press, 2013.

Jones, Jennifer A. "Blacks May Be Second Class, but They Can't Make Them Leave: Mexican Racial Formation and Immigrant Status in Winston-Salem." *Latino Studies* 10, no. 1–2 (2012): 60–80.

———. *The Browning of the New South*. Chicago: The University of Chicago Press, 2019.

Kaplan, Elaine Bell. *"We Live in the Shadow": Inner-City Kids Tell Their Stories through Photographs*. Philadelphia, PA: Temple University Press, 2013.

Kasinitz, Philip, John H. Mollenkopf, Mary C. Waters, and Jennifer Holdaway. *Inheriting the City: The Children of Immigrants Come of Age*. Cambridge, MA: Harvard University Press, 2008.

Kaufmann, Greg. "A Young Mayor Makes the Case for a Guaranteed Income." *Nation*, August 16, 2019. https://www.thenation.com.

Kim, Nadia Y. *Imperial Citizens: Koreans and Race from Seoul to LA*. Stanford, CA: Stanford University Press, 2008.

Kun, Josh, and Laura Pulido, eds. *Black and Brown in Los Angeles: Beyond Conflict and Coalition*. Oakland: University of California Press, 2014.

Kurashige, Scott. "The Many Facets of Brown: Integration in a Multiracial Society." *Journal of American History* 91, no. 1 (June 1, 2004): 56–68.

———. "Between 'White Spot' and 'World City': Racial Integration and the Roots of Multiculturalism." In *A Companion to Los Angeles*, edited by William Deverell and Greg Hise, 56–71. New York: John Wiley & Sons, 2014.

Kusenbach, Margarethe. "Salvaging Decency: Mobile Home Residents' Strategies of Managing the Stigma of 'Trailer' Living." *Qualitative Sociology* 32, no. 4 (December 1, 2009): 399–428.

———, and Krista E. Paulsen, eds. *Home: International Perspectives on Culture, Identity, and Belonging*. Bern, Switzerland: Peter Lang, 2013.

Laslett, John H. M. *Sunshine Was Never Enough: Los Angeles Workers, 1880–2010*. Oakland: University of California Press, 2012.

Lauster, Nathanael, and Jing Zhao. "Labor Migration and the Missing Work of Homemaking: Three Forms of Settling for Chinese-Canadian Migrants." *Social Problems* 64, no. 4 (November 1, 2017): 497–512.

Le, Thai V., Manuel Pastor, Justin Scoggins, Dalia Gonzalez, and Blanca Ramirez. "Paths to Citizenship: Using Data to Understand and Promote Naturalization." Los Angeles: USC Center for the Study of Immigrant Integration, January 2019. https://dornsife.usc.edu/csii.

Leavitt, Jacqueline, and Allan D. Heskin. "South-Central Los Angeles: Anatomy of an Urban Crisis." Los Angeles: Lewis Center for Regional Policy Studies, June 1993.

Lee, Jennifer, and Frank Bean. "America's Changing Color Lines: Immigration, Race/Ethnicity, and Multiracial Identification." *Annual Review of Sociology* 30 (2004): 221–42.

Lefebvre, Henri. *The Production of Space*. Reprint. Malden, MA: Blackwell, 2011.

Leonard, Paul, and Lara Flynn. "Effects of the Foreclosure Crisis on California's Minority Homeowners." Policy Brief. Center for Responsible Lending, June 20, 2012. http://www.responsiblelending.org.

Levitt, Peggy. "Social Remittances: Migration Driven Local-Level Forms of Cultural Diffusion." *The International Migration Review* 32, no. 4 (1998): 926–48.

———. *The Transnational Villagers*. Oakland: University of California Press, 2001.

———. *God Needs No Passport: Immigrants and the Changing American Religious Landscape*. New York: New Press, 2007.

———, and Rafael de la Dehesa. "Rethinking 'Transnational Migration and the Re-Definition of the State' or What to Do About (Semi-) Permanent Impermanence." *Ethnic and Racial Studies* 40, no. 9 (July 15, 2017): 1520–26.

———, and Nina Glick Schiller. "Conceptualizing Simultaneity: A Transnational Social Field Perspective on Society." *The International Migration Review* 38, no. 3 (2004): 1002–39.

———, Jocelyn Viterna, Armin Mueller, and Charlotte Lloyd. "Rethinking 'Transnational Migration and the Re-Definition of the State' or What to Do about (Semi-) Permanent Impermanence." *Oxford Development Studies* 45, no. 1 (2017): 2–19.

———, Jocelyn Viterna, Armin Mueller, and Charlotte Lloyd. "Transnational Social Protection: Setting the Agenda." *Oxford Development Studies* 45, no. 1 (January 2, 2017): 2–19.

Lopez, Linda. "The Development of Innovative Integration Models in Los Angeles." *The Annals of The American Academy of Political and Social Sciences* 690, no. 1 (July 2020): 184–191.

Lopez, Nancy. *Hopeful Girls, Troubled Boys: Race and Gender Disparity in Urban Education*. New York: Routledge, 2003.

Lopez, Sarah Lynn. *The Remittance Landscape: Spaces of Migration in Rural Mexico and Urban USA*. Chicago: University of Chicago Press, 2015.

Louie, Vivian. *Keeping the Immigrant Bargain: The Costs and Rewards of Success in America*. New York: Russell Sage Foundation, 2012.

Loukaitou-Sideris, Anastasia. "Urban Form and Social Context: Cultural Differentiation in the Uses of Urban Parks." *Journal of Planning Education and Research* 14, no. 2 (1995): 89–102.

Macías-Rojas, Patrisia. *From Deportation to Prison: The Politics of Immigration Enforcement in Post-Civil Rights America*. New York: NYU Press, 2016.

Madley, Benjamin. "It's Time to Acknowledge the Genocide of California's Indians." *Los Angeles Times*. May 22, 2016. http://www.latimes.com.

Mallett, Shelley. "Understanding Home: A Critical Review of the Literature." *The Sociological Review* 52, no. 1 (2004): 62–89.

Marcuse, Peter. "Housing in Early City Planning." *Journal of Urban History* 6, no. 2 (February 1, 1980): 153–76.

Mares, Teresa M. "Tracing Immigrant Identity through the Plate and the Palate." *Latino Studies* 10, no. 3 (2012): 334–54.

———, and Devon G Peña. "Urban Agriculture in the Making of Insurgent Spaces in Los Angeles and Seattle." In *Insurgent Public Space: Guerrilla Urbanism and the Remaking of Contemporary Cities*, edited by Jeffrey Hou, 253–67. New York: Routledge, 2010.

Marquez, John D. *Black-Brown Solidarity: Racial Politics in the New Gulf South*. Austin: University of Texas Press, 2013.

Marrow, Helen. "Hispanic Immigration, Black Population Size, and Intergroup Relations in the Rural and Small-Town South." In *New Faces in New Places: The Changing Geography of American Immigration*, edited by Douglas S. Massey, 211–49. New York: Russell Sage Foundation Publications, 2008.

———. *New Destination Dreaming: Immigration, Race, and Legal Status in the Rural American South*. Stanford, CA: Stanford University Press, 2011.

Marrow, Helen B. "Hope Turned Sour: Second-Generation Incorporation and Mobility in U.S. New Immigrant Destinations." *Ethnic and Racial Studies* 43, no. 1 (January 2, 2020): 99–118.

Martinez, Alex. "CHIRLA Opens Satellite Office in South L.A. to Provide Legal Services to Immigrants." LAist, August 19, 2017. https://laist.com.

Martinez, Cid. *The Neighborhood Has Its Own Rules: Latinos and African Americans in South Los Angeles*. New York: NYU Press, 2016.

Massey, Douglas S. "Dimensions of the New Immigration to the United States and the Prospects for Assimilation." *Annual Review of Sociology* 7 (January 1, 1981): 57–85.

———, and Nancy A. Denton. "Spatial Assimilation as a Socioeconomic Outcome." *American Sociological Review* 50 (1985): 94–106.

Mazzucato, Valentina. "The Double Engagement: Transnationalism and Integration. Ghanaian Migrants' Lives Between Ghana and The Netherlands." *Journal of Ethnic and Migration Studies* 34, no. 2 (March 1, 2008): 199–216.

McConnell, Eileen Diaz, and Enrico A. Marcelli. "Buying into the American Dream? Mexican Immigrants, Legal Status, and Homeownership in Los Angeles County." *Social Science Quarterly* 88, no. 1 (March 2007): 199–221.

McDowell, L. "Towards an Understanding of the Gender Division of Urban Space." *Environment and Planning D: Society and Space* 1, no. 1 (1983): 59–72.

McKeever, A. James. "Park 'Rats' to Park 'Daddies': Community Heads Creating Future Mentors." In *Child's Play: Sport in Kids' Worlds*, edited by Michael A. Messner and Michela Musto, 221–36. Critical Issues in Sport and Society. New Brunswick, NJ: Rutgers University Press, 2016.

McRoberts, Omar M. *Streets of Glory: Church and Community in a Black Urban Neighborhood*. Chicago: University of Chicago Press, 2003.

McWilliams, Carey. *California: The Great Exception*. Berkeley: University of California Press, 1949.

Menjívar, Cecilia. "Liminal Legality: Salvadoran and Guatemalan Immigrants' Lives in the United States." *American Journal of Sociology* 111, no. 4 (February 2006): 999–1037.

———, and Leisy Abrego. "Legal Violence: Immigration Law and the Lives of Central American Immigrants." *American Journal of Sociology* 117, no. 5 (March 2012): 1380–1421.

Milkman, Ruth. *L.A. Story: Immigrant Workers and the Future of the U.S. Labor Movement*. New York: Russell Sage Foundation, 2006.

Mindiola, Tatcho Jr., Yolanda Flores Niemann, and Nestor Rodriguez. *Black-Brown Relations and Stereotypes*. Austin: University of Texas Press, 2009.

Mitchell, John L. "The Raid That Still Haunts L.A." *Los Angeles Times*. March 14, 2001. http://articles.latimes.com.

Molina, Natalia. "Examining Chicana/o History through a Relational Lens." In *Relational Formations of Race: Theory, Method, and Practice*, edited by Natalia Molina, Daniel HoSang, and Ramón A. Gutiérrez, 43–59. Oakland: University of California Press, 2019.

———, Daniel HoSang, and Ramón A. Gutiérrez, eds. *Relational Formations of Race: Theory, Method, and Practice*. Oakland: University of California Press, 2019.

Mollenkopf, John, and Manuel Pastor, eds. *Unsettled Americans: Metropolitan Context and Civic Leadership for Immigrant Integration*. Ithaca, NY: Cornell University Press, 2016.

Molotch, Harvey. "Granite and Green: Thinking beyond Surface in Place Studies." *Theory and Society* 40, no. 2 (March 2011): 155–59.

Morales, Rebecca, and Manuel Pastor Jr. "Can't We All Just Get along? Interethnic Organization and Economic Development." In *The Collaborative City: Opportunities and Struggles for Blacks and Latinos in U.S. Cities*, edited by John J. Betancur and Douglas C. Gills, 157–76. New York: Garland Publishing, 2000.

Morley, David. "Belongings: Place, Space and Identity in a Mediated World." *European Journal of Cultural Studies* 4, no. 4 (November 1, 2001): 425–48.

Murch, D. "Crack in Los Angeles: Crisis, Militarization, and Black Response to the Late Twentieth-Century War on Drugs." *Journal of American History* 102, no. 1 (June 1, 2015): 162–73.

Myers, Dowell. *Immigrants and Boomers: Forging a New Social Contract for the Future of America*. New York: Russell Sage Foundation, 2008.

———, John Pitkin, and Ricardo Ramirez. "The New Homegrown Majority in California: Recognizing the New Reality of Growing Commitment to The Golden State." Los Angeles: University of Southern California, School of Policy, Planning and Development, 2009. http://www.usc.edu.

Nakagawa, Scot. "Blackness Is the Fulcrum." *Race Files: A Project of CHANGELAB* (blog), May 4, 2012. http://www.racefiles.com.

Nellis, Ashley. "The Color of Justice: Racial and Ethnic Disparity in State Prisons." Washington, DC: The Sentencing Project, 2016. https://www.sentencingproject.org.

Newman, Kathe, and Elvin K. Wyly. "The Right to Stay Put, Revisited: Gentrification and Resistance to Displacement in New York City." *Urban Studies* 43, no. 1 (January 2006): 23–57.

Ngai, Mae M. *Impossible Subjects: Illegal Aliens and the Making of Modern America*. Politics and Society in Twentieth-Century America. Princeton, NJ: Princeton University Press, 2004.

Nicholls, Walter Julio. "Forging a 'New' Organizational Infrastructure for Los Angeles' Progressive Community." *International Journal of Urban and Regional Research* 27, no. 4 (December 1, 2003): 881–96.

Nicolaides, Becky M. *My Blue Heaven: Life and Politics in the Working-Class Suburbs of Los Angeles, 1920–1965*. Chicago: University of Chicago Press, 2002.

Ochoa, Enrique, and Gilda L. Ochoa. *Latino Los Angeles: Transformations, Communities, and Activism*. Tucson: University of Arizona Press, 2005.

Okamoto, Dina G., Linda R. Tropp, Helen B. Marrow, and Michael Jones-Correa. "Welcoming, Trust, and Civic Engagement: Immigrant Integration in Metropolitan America." *The Annals of The American Academy of Political and Social Sciences* 690, no. 1 (July 2020), 61–81.

Omi, Michael, and Howard Winant. *Racial Formation in the United States: From the 1960s to the 1980s*. New York: Routledge, 1986.

Ong, Paul, Theresa Firestine, Deirdre Pfeiffer, Oiyan Poon, and Linda Tran. "The State of South LA." Los Angeles: UCLA School of Public Affairs, August 2008.

Opie, Frederick. *Upsetting the Apple Cart: Black-Latino Coalitions in New York City from Protest to Public Office.* New York: Columbia University Press, 2014.

Orozco, Manuel, and Michelle Lapointe. "Mexican Hometown Associations and Development Opportunities." *Journal of International Affairs* 57, no. 2 (2004): 31–51.

Pardo, Mary. *Mexican America Women Activists: Identity and Resistance in Two Los Angeles Communities.* Philadelphia, PA: Temple University Press, 1998.

Park, Kyeyoung. "Confronting the Liquor Industry in Los Angeles." *The International Journal of Sociology and Social Policy* 24, no. 7/8 (2004): 103–36.

Park, Robert E., and Ernest W. Burgess. *The City.* Chicago: The University of Chicago Press, 1925.

Pastor, Jr., Manuel. "Common Ground at Ground Zero? The New Economy and the New Organizing in Los Angeles." *Antipode* 33, no. 2 (March 1, 2001): 260–89.

———. "Latinos and the Los Angeles Uprising: The Economic Context." Los Angeles: Tomás Rivera Center, 1993. https://socialinnovation.usc.edu.

Pastor, Manuel. *Latinos and the Los Angeles Uprising: The Economic Context.* Claremont, CA: The Tomas Rivera Center, 1993.

———. "Economic Inequality, Latino Poverty, and the Civil Unrest in Los Angeles." *Economic Development Quarterly* 9, no. 3 (1995): 238–58.

———. *State of Resistance: What California's Dizzying Descent and Remarkable Resurgence Mean for America's Future.* New York: New Press, 2018.

———, Chris Benner, and Martha Matsuoka. *This Could Be the Start of Something Big: How Social Movements for Regional Equity Are Reshaping Metropolitan America.* Ithaca, NY: Cornell University Press, 2009.

———, Vanessa Carter, Alejandro Sanchez-Lopez, and Robert Chlala. "Planning, Power, and Possibilities: How UNIDAD Is Shaping Equitable Development in South Central L.A." Los Angeles: USC Program for Environmental and Regional Equity, September 2015. http://dornsife.usc.edu/pere.

———, Juan De Lara, and Justin Scoggins. "All Together Now? African Americans, Immigrants and the Future of California." Los Angeles: USC Center for the Study of Immigrant Integration, September 2011. http://dornsife.usc.edu/csii

———, Rhonda Ortiz, and Els de Graauw. "Opening Minds, Opening Doors, Opening Communities: Cities Leading for Immigrant Integration." New York: USC Center for the Study of Immigrant Integration, America Society/Council of the Americas, Welcoming America, December 15, 2015. http://dornsife.usc.edu/csii.

———, and Michele Prichard. "LA Rising: The 1992 Civil Unrest, the Arc of Social Justice Organizing, and the Lessons for Today's Movement Building." Los Angeles, CA: USC Program for Environmental and Regional Equity, April 2012. http://dornsife.usc.edu/pere.

———, Ashley K. Thomas, Preston Mills, Rachel Rosner, and Vanessa Carter. "Bridges | Puentes: Building Black-Brown Solidarities Across the U.S." Los Angeles: USC Equity Research Institute, 2020.

———, and Gloria Walton. "Looking Forward, Not Back: How South Los Angeles Is the Future." KCET, April 28, 2017. https://www.kcet.org.

Pattillo, Mary. "Housing: Commodity versus Right." *Annual Review of Sociology* 39 (2013): 509–31.

Pawasarat, John, and Lois M. Quinn. "Wisconsin's Mass Incarceration of African American Males: Workforce Challenges for 2013." Milwaukee: University of Wisconsin-Milwaukee Employment and Training Institute, 2013. https://www4.uwm.edu.

Pettigrew, Thomas F. "Intergroup Contact Theory." *Annual Review of Psychology* 49, no. 1 (1998): 65–85.

Pettigrew, Thomas F., and Linda R. Tropp. "A Meta-Analytic Test of Intergroup Contact Theory." *Journal of Personality and Social Psychology* 90, no. 5 (2006): 751–83.

———. "How Does Intergroup Contact Reduce Prejudice? Meta-Analytic Tests of Three Mediators." *European Journal of Social Psychology* 38, no. 6 (2008): 922–34.

———. *When Groups Meet: The Dynamics of Intergroup Contact.* When Groups Meet: The Dynamics of Intergroup Contact. New York: Psychology Press, 2011.

Pfeiffer, Deirdre. "African Americans' Search for 'More for Less' and 'Peace of Mind' on the Exurban Frontier." *Urban Geography* 33, no. 1 (January 2012): 64–90.

———. "Moving to Opportunity: African Americans' Safety Outcomes in the Los Angeles Exurbs." *Journal of Planning Education and Research* 33, no. 1 (2012): 49–65.

Pool, Bob. "Delegates Travel to L.A.'s Past: Black History: NAACP Conventioneers Help Rededicate the Historic Dunbar Hotel. It Was Once a Cultural Hub." *Los Angeles Times*, July 11, 1990. https://www.latimes.com.

Portes, Alejandro, Luis E. Guarnizo, and Patricia Landolt. "The Study of Transnationalism: Pitfalls and Promise of an Emergent Research Field." *Ethnic and Racial Studies* 22, no. 2 (January 1, 1999): 217–37.

———. "Commentary on the Study of Transnationalism: Pitfalls and Promise of an Emergent Research Field." *Ethnic and Racial Studies* 40, no. 9 (July 15, 2017): 1486–91.

Portes, Alejandro, and Rubén G. Rumbaut. *Legacies: The Story of the Immigrant Second Generation.* Berkeley: University of California Press, 2001.

———. *Immigrant America: A Portrait.* Berkeley: University of California Press, 2014.

Portes, Alejandro, and Min Zhou. "The New Second Generation: Segmented Assimilation and Its Variants." *The Annals of the American Academy of Political and Social Science* 530, no. 1 (1993): 74–96.

Pulido, Laura. *Black, Brown, Yellow, and Left: Radical Activism in Los Angeles.* Berkeley: University of California Press, 2006.

———, and Manuel Pastor. "Where in the World Is Juan—and What Color Is He?: The Geography of Latina/o Racial Identity in Southern California." *American Quarterly* 65, no. 2 (2013): 309–41.

Ramírez, Catherine S. *Assimilation: An Alternative History.* Berkeley: University of California Press, 2020.

Ramírez, Carolina. "'It's Not How It Was': The Chilean Diaspora's Changing Landscape of Belonging." *Ethnic and Racial Studies* 37, no. 4 (March 21, 2014): 668–84.

Rapoport, Amos. "A Critical Look at the Concept 'Home.'" In *The Home: Words, Interpretations, Meanings and Environments*, edited by David N. Benjamin, David Seta, Eje Aren, and David Saile, 25–52. Aldershot, UK: Avebury, 1995.

Regalado, Jaime. "Community Coalition-Building." In *The Los Angeles Riots: Lessons for the Urban Future*, edited by Mark Baldassare, 205–35. Boulder, CO: Westview Press, 1994.

Rendón, María G. "The Urban Question and Identity Formation: The Case of Second-Generation Mexican Males in Los Angeles." *Ethnicities* 15, no. 2 (2015): 165–89.

———. *Stagnant Dreamers: How the Inner City Shapes the Integration of Second-Generation Latinos*. New York: Russell Sage Foundation, 2019.

———. "'There's Nothing Holding Us Back': The Enduring and Shifting Cultural Outlooks of Inner City Second-Generation Latinos." *City & Community* 18, no. 1 (2019): 151–72.

Revoyr, Nina. *Southland*. New York: Akashic Books, 2003.

Reyes, Emily Alpert. "Latest Battle over South Central Farm Ends—This Time Not with Arrests, but a Vote." *Los Angeles Times*, July 2, 2019. https://www.latimes.com.

Ribas, Vanesa. *On the Line: Slaughterhouse Lives and the Making of the New South*. Oakland: University of California Press, 2016.

Rios, Victor M. *Punished: Policing the Lives of Black and Latino Boys*. New York: NYU Press, 2011.

Robinson, Paul. "Race, Space, and the Evolution of Black Los Angeles." In *Black Los Angeles: American Dreams and Realities*, edited by Darnell Hunt and Ana-Christiana Ramón, 21–59. New York: NYU Press, 2010.

Rogers, John, Kavitha Mediratta, Seema Shah, Joseph Kahne, and Veronica Terriquez. "Building Power, Learning Democracy: Youth Organizing as a Site of Civic Development." *Review of Research in Education* 36 (2012): 43–66.

Rojas, James. "The Enacted Environment of East Los Angeles." *Places Journal* 8, no. 3 (April 1, 1993). https://placesjournal.org.

Romo, Rebecca. "Between Black and Brown: Blaxican (Black-Mexican) Multiracial Identity in California." *Journal of Black Studies* 42, no. 3 (2011): 402–26.

Romo, Ricardo. *East Los Angeles: History of a Barrio*. Austin: University of Texas Press, 1983.

Rosas, Abigail. "Banking on the Community: Mexican Immigrants' Experiences in a Historically African American Bank in South Central Los Angeles, 1970–2007." In *Black and Brown in Los Angeles: Beyond Conflict and Coalition*, edited by Josh Kun and Laura Pulido, 67–89. Oakland: University of California Press, 2014.

———. *South Central Is Home: Race and the Power of Community Investment in Los Angeles*. Palo Alto, CA: Stanford University Press, 2019.

Roth, Wendy. *Race Migrations: Latinos and the Cultural Transformation of Race*. Stanford, CA: Stanford University Press, 2012.

Rouse, Roger. "Mexican Migration and the Social Space of Postmodernism." *Diaspora: A Journal of Transnational Studies* 1, no. 1 (1991): 8–23.

Roussell, Aaron. "Policing the Anticommunity: Race, Deterritorialization, and Labor Market Reorganization in South Los Angeles: Policing the Anticommunity." *Law & Society Review* 49, no. 4 (December 2015): 813–45.

Ruggles, Steven J., Katie Genadek, Ronald Goeken, Josiah Grover, and Matthew Sobek. *Integrated Public Use Microdata Series: Version 7.0* [data set]. Minneapolis: University of Minnesota, 2017. https://doi.org/10.18128/D010.V7.0.

Rugh, Jacob S. "Why Black and Latino Home Ownership Matter to the Color Line and Multiracial Democracy." *Race and Social Problems* 12, no. 1 (March 1, 2020): 57–76.

Ruiz, V. "Una Mujer Sin Fronteras." *Pacific Historical Review* 73, no. 1 (February 2004): 1–20.

Ryo, Emily. "Less Enforcement, More Compliance: Rethinking Unauthorized Migration." *UCLA Law Review* 62 (2015): 622–70.

Saito, Leland, and Jonathan Truong. "The L.A. Live Community Benefits Agreement: Evaluating the Agreement Results and Shifting Political Power in the City." *Urban Affairs Review* 51, no. 2 (March 2015): 263–89.

Saito, Leland. *The Politics of Exclusion: The Failure of Race-Neutral Policies in Urban America*. Stanford, CA: Stanford University Press, 2009.

Saito, Leland T. *Race and Politics: Asian Americans, Latinos, and Whites in a Los Angeles Suburb*. Urbana: University of Illinois Press, 1998.

Salgado, Casandra D., and Vilma Ortiz. "Mexican Americans and Wealth: Economic Status, Family and Place." *Journal of Ethnic and Migration Studies* 46, no. 18 (May 3, 2019): 3855–73.

Sampson, Robert J. *Great American City: Chicago and the Enduring Neighborhood Effect*. Chicago: University of Chicago Press, 2012.

Sanchez, George J. *Becoming Mexican American: Ethnicity, Culture, and Identity in Chicano Los Angeles, 1900–1945*. Reprint. New York: Oxford University Press, 1995.

Sánchez-Jankowski, Martín. *Burning Dislike: Ethnic Violence in High Schools*. Oakland: University of California Press, 2016. https://www.jstor.org.

Sandoval-Strausz, A. K. "Latino Landscapes: Postwar Cities and the Transnational Origins of a New Urban America." *Journal of American History* 101, no. 3 (2014): 804–31.

Schafer, Markus H., Jason Settels, and Laura Upenieks. "As Goes the City? Older Americans' Home Upkeep in the Aftermath of the Great Recession." *Social Problems* 67, no. 2 (July 25, 2019): 379–97.

Schmalzbauer, Leah. *The Last Best Place? Gender, Family, and Migration in the New West*. Stanford, CA: Stanford University Press, 2014.

———, and Alelí Andrés. "Stratified Lives: Family, Illegality, and the Rise of a New Educational Elite." *Harvard Educational Review* 89, no. 4 (December 2019): 635–60.

Schnyder, Damien M. "Criminals, Planters, and Corporate Capitalists: The Case of Public Education in Los Angeles." In *Black California Dreamin': The Crises of California's African-American Communities*, edited by Ingrid Banks, Gaye Johnson,

George Lipsitz, Ula Taylor, Daniel Widener, and Clyde Woods, 107–26. Santa Barbara, CA: UCSB Center for Black Studies Research, 2012.

Schwirian, Kent P. "Models of Neighborhood Change." *Annual Review of Sociology* 9, no. 1 (1983): 83–102.

Self, Robert O. *American Babylon: Race and the Struggle for Postwar Oakland*. Princeton, NJ: Princeton University Press, 2003.

Sexton, Jared. "People-of-Color-Blindness: Notes on the Afterlife of Slavery." *Social Text* 28, no. 2 (2010): 31–56.

Shah, Seema, Kavitha Mediratta, and Sara McAlister. "Securing a College Prep Curriculum for All Students." Providence, RI: Brown University, Annenberg Institute for School Reform, 2009. https://www.issuelab.org.

Shakur, Tupac, featuring Kimmy Hill. "Mama's Just a Little Girl." Track 7 of disc 1 on *Better Dayz*. Los Angeles: Interscope Records, 2002.

Sides, Josh. "'You Understand My Condition': The Civil Rights Congress in the Los Angeles African-American Community, 1946–1952." *Pacific Historical Review* 67, no. 2 (May 1998): 233–57.

———. "Straight into Compton: American Dreams, Urban Nightmares, and the Metamorphosis of a Black Suburb." *American Quarterly* 56, no. 3 (2004): 583–605.

———. *L.A. City Limits: African American Los Angeles from the Great Depression to the Present*. Berkeley: University of California Press, 2006. http://site.ebrary.com.

———. *Post-Ghetto: Reimagining South Los Angeles*. Berkeley: University of California Press, 2012.

Sims, Calvin. "In Los Angeles, It's South-Central No More." *New York Times*, April 10, 2003, sec. U.S. https://www.nytimes.com.

Sitton, Tom. *Los Angeles Transformed: Fletcher Bowron's Urban Reform Revival, 1938–1953*. Albuquerque: University of New Mexico Press, 2005.

Sloane, David C. "Alcohol Nuisances and Food Deserts: Combating Social Hazards in the South Los Angeles Environment." In *Post-Ghetto: Reimagining South Los Angeles*, edited by Josh Sides, 93–108. Berkeley: University of California Press, 2012.

Smith, Doug. "How LAPD's Law-and-Order Chief Revolutionized the Way Cops Treated Illegal Immigration." *Los Angeles Times*, February 5, 2017. https://www.latimes.com.

Smith, Michael P., and Luis Guarnizo, eds. *Transnationalism from Below*. Vol. 6. Comparative Urban and Community Research. New Brunswick, NJ: Transaction Publishers, 1998.

Smith, R. J. *The Great Black Way: L.A. in the 1940s and the Last African American Renaissance*. New York: PublicAffairs, 2007.

Smith, Robert. *Mexican New York: Transnational Lives of New Immigrants*. Berkeley and Los Angeles: University of California Press, 2005.

Smith, Robert Courtney. "Black Mexicans, Conjunctural Ethnicity, and Operating Identities: Long-Term Ethnographic Analysis." *American Sociological Review* 79, no. 3 (June 1, 2014): 517–48.

Stephens, Pamela, and Manuel Pastor. "What's Going On? Black Experiences of Latini-zation and Loss in South Los Angeles." *Du Bois Review: Social Science Research on Race*, First View, September 21, 2020, 1–32.

Struthers, David M. *The World in a City: Multiethnic Radicalism in Early Twentieth-Century Los Angeles*. Urbana: University of Illinois Press, 2019.

Stull, Carolyn. "Luisa Moreno." In *Encyclopedia Britannica*. Encyclopaedia Britannica, Inc., August 26, 2019. www.britannica.com.

Stumpf, Juliet. "The Crimmigration Crisis: Immigrants, Crime, and Sovereign Power." *American University Law Review* 56, no. 2 (January 1, 2006). https://digitalcommons.wcl.american.edu.

Surls, Rachel, and Judith B. Gerber. *From Cows to Concrete: The Rise and Fall of Farming in Los Angeles*. Santa Monica, CA: Angel City Press, 2016.

Taylor, Keeanga-Yamahtta. *Race for Profit: How Banks and the Real Estate Industry Undermined Black Homeownership*. Chapel Hill: University of North Carolina Press, 2019.

Telles, Edward E., and Vilma Ortiz. *Generations of Exclusion: Mexican Americans, Assimilation, and Race*. New York: Russell Sage Foundation, 2008.

Telles, Edward, Mark Sawyer, and Gaspar Rivera-Salgado. *Just Neighbors: Research on African American and Latino Relations in the United States*. New York: Russell Sage Foundation, 2011.

Terriquez, Veronica. "Legal Status, Civic Organizations, and Political Participation among Latino Young Adults." *The Sociological Quarterly* 58, no.2 (2017): 315-336.

——— and Vanessa Carter. "Celebrating the Legacy, Embracing the Future: How Research Can Help Build Ties between Historically African American Churches and Their Latino Immigrant Neighbours." *Community Development* 43, no. 3 (2013): 1–15.

——— and May Lin. "Yesterday They Marched, Today They Mobilized the Vote: A Developmental Model for Civic Leadership among the Children of Immigrants." *Journal of Ethnic and Migration Studies* 46, no. 4 (2020): 747–69.

Thompson-Hernández, Walter. *The Compton Cowboys: The New Generation of Cowboys in America's Urban Heartland*. New York: HarperCollins Publishers, 2020.

Tobar, Héctor. "Cooperation on Central Ave." *Los Angeles Times*. February 11, 2011, sec. Main News; Part A; Metro Desk.

Tran, Van C. "Coming of Age in Multi-Ethnic America: Young Adults' Experiences with Diversity." *Ethnic and Racial Studies* 42, no. 1: Special Issue: Super-diversity in Everyday Life (January 2, 2019): 35–52.

Trouille, David. "Fencing a Field: Imagined Others in the Unfolding of a Neighborhood Park Conflict." *City & Community* 13, no. 1 (March 2014): 69–87.

Tuan, Yi Fu. "Rootedness Versus Sense of Place." *Landscape* 24, no. 1 (1980): 3–8.

Uitermark, Justus, and Walter Nicholls. "From Politicization to Policing: The Rise and Decline of New Social Movements in Amsterdam and Paris." *Antipode* 46, no. 4 (2013): 970–91.

Vaca, Nicolas C. *The Presumed Alliance: The Unspoken Conflict Between Latinos and Blacks and What It Means for America*. New York: Rayo, 2004.

Vallejo, Jody Agius. *Barrios to Burbs: The Making of the Mexican American Middle Class*. Stanford, CA: Stanford University Press, 2012.

———, and Lisa Keister. "Immigrants and Wealth Attainment: Migration, Inequality and Integration." *Journal of Ethnic and Migration Studies* 46, no. 18 (2020): 3745–61.

———, and Jennifer Lee. "Brown Picket Fences: The Immigrant Narrative and 'Giving Back' among the Mexican-Origin Middle Class." *Ethnicities* 9, no. 1 (2009): 5–31.

Vargas, João Costa. *Catching Hell in the City of Angels: Life and Meanings of Blackness in South Central Los Angeles*. Minneapolis: University of Minnesota Press, 2006.

Vargas, João Helion Costa. *The Denial of Antiblackness: Multiracial Redemption and Black Suffering*. Minneapolis: University of Minnesota Press, 2018.

Vasquez, Jessica M. "Blurred Borders for Some but Not 'Others': Racialization, 'Flexible Ethnicity,' Gender, and Third-Generation Mexican American Identity." *Sociological Perspectives* 53, no. 1 (March 2010): 45–71.

———. *Mexican Americans across Generations: Immigrant Families, Racial Realities*. New York: New York University Press, 2011.

———. "The Whitening Hypothesis Challenged: Biculturalism in Latino and Non-Hispanic White Intermarriage." *Sociological Forum* 29, no. 2 (June 2, 2014): 386–407.

Venkatesh, Sudhir. *Gang Leader for a Day: A Rogue Sociologist Takes to the Streets*. New York: Penguin Books, 2009.

Wacquant, Loïc. "A Janus-Faced Institution of Ethnoracial Closure: A Sociological Specification of the Ghetto." In *The Ghetto: Contemporary Global Issues and Controversies*, edited by Ray Hutchison and Bruce Haynes, 1–31. Boulder, CO: Westview Press, 2012.

Waldinger, Roger David, and Mehdi Bozorgmehr. *Ethnic Los Angeles*. New York: Russell Sage Foundation, 1996.

Waldinger, Roger, and Lauren Duquette-Rury. "Emigrant Politics, Immigrant Engagement: Homeland Ties and Immigrant Political Identity in the United States." *RSF: The Russell Sage Foundation Journal of the Social Sciences* 2, no. 3 (June 1, 2016): 42–59.

Warren, Mark R., Meredith Mira, and Thomas Nikundiwe. "Youth Organizing: From Youth Development to School Reform." *New Directions for Youth Development* 2008, no. 117 (March 1, 2008): 27–42.

Watanabe, Teresa. "South Los Angeles Latinos and Blacks Find Unity in Worship." *Los Angeles Times*. May 1, 2010. http://articles.latimes.com.

Waters, Mary C. *Black Identities: West Indian Immigrant Dreams and American Realities*. Cambridge, MA: Harvard University Press, 2001.

White, Monica M. *Freedom Farmers: Agricultural Resistance and the Black Freedom Movement*. Justice, Power, and Politics. Chapel Hill: University of North Carolina Press, 2019.

Wilkerson, Isabel. *The Warmth of Other Suns: The Epic Story of America's Great Migration*. Reprint ed. New York: Vintage, 2011.

———. *Caste: The Origins of Our Discontents*. New York: Random House, 2020.

Wilson, William Julius, and Richard P. Taub. *There Goes the Neighborhood: Racial, Ethnic, and Class Tensions in Four Chicago Neighborhoods and Their Meaning for America*. New York: Knopf Doubleday Publishing Group, 2011.

Winders, Jamie. *Nashville in the New Millennium: Immigrant Settlement, Urban Transformation, and Social Belonging*. New York: Russell Sage Foundation, 2013.

Wolch, Jennifer, John Wilson, and Jed Fehrenbach. "Parks and Park Funding in Los Angeles: An Equity-Mapping Analysis." *Urban Geography* 26, no. 1 (February 1, 2005): 4–35.

Wyler, Grace. "How Much Difference Can Obama Really Make on the Economy?" *Atlantic*, January 29, 2014. https://www.theatlantic.com.

Zabin, Carol, and Luis Escala. "From Civic Association to Political Participation: Mexican Hometown Associations and Mexican Immigrant Political Empowerment in Los Angeles." *Frontera Norte* 14, no. 27 (2002): 7–41.

Zamora, Sylvia. "Racial Remittances: The Effect of Migration on Racial Ideologies in Mexico and the United States." *Sociology of Race and Ethnicity* 2, no. 4 (October 1, 2016): 466–81.

———. "Mexican Illegality, Black Citizenship, and White Power: Immigrant Perceptions of the U.S. Socioracial Hierarchy." *Journal of Ethnic and Migration Studies* 44, no. 11 (August 18, 2018): 1897–1914.

Zappia, Natale. "Reclaiming the Soil: Gardening and Sustainable Development in South Los Angeles." In *Post-Ghetto: Reimagining South Los Angeles*, edited by Josh Sides, 55–71. Berkeley: University of California Press, 2012.

ABOUT THE AUTHORS

PIERRETTE HONDAGNEU-SOTELO is the Florence Everline Professor of Sociology in the Department of Sociology at the University of Southern California. Her research uses interviews and ethnography to show the texture of Latino immigrant struggles in workplaces, homes, and neighborhoods. She has previously published nine books, including *Doméstica* (2001/2007) and *Paradise Transplanted* (2014).

MANUEL PASTOR is Distinguished Professor of Sociology and American Studies & Ethnicity at the University of Southern California (USC), where he directs the Equity Research Institute and is the USC Turpanjian Chair in Civil Society and Social Change. His research focuses on the economic, environmental, and social conditions facing low-income urban communities—and the social movements seeking to change those realities. His most recent book is *State of Resistance* (2018).

ROBERT CHLALA received his PhD from the University of Southern California's Department of Sociology, and his community-engaged research explores how U.S. grassroots movements are shaping the future of work in ways that attend to race, gender, and ideals of abolition.

ALEJANDRO SANCHEZ-LOPEZ received his MA in Urban Planning from the University of Southern California's Sol Price School of Public Policy and is currently a planner for the City of Long Beach working on autonomy for Black and Brown communities.

VERONICA MONTES received her PhD in Sociology at University of California, Santa Barbara, held a postdoctoral fellowship at USC, and is now Assistant Professor of Sociology and Co-Director of Latin American, Iberian and Latina/o Studies at Bryn Mawr College, where her research focuses on gender and belonging among Mexican and Central American immigrants.

JOSE MIGUEL RUIZ received his MSW from the University of Southern California, and he is the founder and chief executive officer of CultivaLA, a nonprofit organization transforming urban agriculture through people, social enterprise, and environmental justice in Downtown Los Angeles.

PAMELA STEPHENS is a PhD candidate in Urban Planning at the University of California, Los Angeles, where her work centers on the ways that urban planning practices produce Black spaces in Los Angeles, further examining how Black communities build power within and across them.

WALTER THOMPSON-HERNÁNDEZ is a multimedia journalist, former New York Times reporter, and author of *The Compton Cowboys* (2019).

ANTAR A. TICHAVAKUNDA received his PhD in Urban Education Policy at the University of Southern California, and is Assistant Professor of Education Leadership at the University of Cincinnati, where he uses qualitative methods to study the sociology of race and higher education.

ADRIÁN TRINIDAD is a PhD Candidate in Urban Education Policy at the University of Southern California's Rossier School of Education. Raised in South Los Angeles, Adrián studies racialization, equity, and organizational change in community colleges.

INDEX

Page numbers in *italics* indicate figures, photos, and tables